D0492727

The Oratory School
* 0 0 0 1 1 5 6 3 *

THE WEST HIGHLAND RAILWAY

Arisaig, the most westerly station on BR, in 1959. K1 2–6–0 No. 62011 is on the train for Mallaig crossing an up service including an observation car converted from former LNER streamlined stock

THE WEST HIGHLAND RAILWAY

The History of the Railways of the Scottish Highlands—Vol 1

by

John Thomas

extra material by

Alan J. S. Paterson

DAVID ST JOHN THOMAS
DAVID & CHARLES

British Library Cataloguing in Publication Data

Thomas, John, *1914–*
The West Highland Railway.—3rd ed.
1. British Rail. *Scottish Region*—History
2. Railroads— Scotland—Highlands—History
I. Title II. Paterson, Alan J. S.
385′.09411′5 HE3039.H5

ISBN 0–946537–14–3

First published 1965
Second impression 1966
Second edition with new introduction 1976
Third edition with new material 1984

Printed by Redwood Burn Ltd, Trowbridge
Published by David St John Thomas and distributed by David & Charles, Brunel House, Newton Abbot, Devon

Distributed in the United States of America by David & Charles Inc
North Pomfret, Vermont, 05053, USA

CONTRASTS AT CRIANLARICH

The top photograph shows another double-headed train with two Glens, No. 9221 Glen Orchy and No. 9100 Glen Dochart, on an up express in 1926. Many passengers would be taking refreshment in the famous tea room that is still open while the locomotives' tanks are replenished. In the 1971 photograph by Derek Cross (below) No. D5369 heads an Oban–Glasgow train which has just joined the West Highland line from the truncated Callander & Oban while No. D5355, which has just arrived from the Scottish Pulp works at Corpach, waits to reverse down the spur to the Callander & Oban to enable the wagons to be reloaded with logs

Contents

CHAPTER 1

From a Carriage Window

There are many ways of seeing landscape, and none more vivid, in spite of canting dilettanti, than from a railway train.
—Robert Louis Stevenson.

BY MOUNTAIN MOOR AND LOCH

Queen Street station, the North British terminus in Glasgow, had seen nothing like it since the day the station was opened in 1842. The date was Saturday, 11 August 1894, the time 8 o'clock in the morning. The polished carriages of the Glasgow gentry arriving in a steady stream were depositing their occupants in the station forecourt, and railway staff were at hand to conduct the distinguished guests to a train of brand-new claret-coloured carriages waiting at the main departure platform.

The visitors were gathering to celebrate an event unique in British railway history. That day there was to be opened ceremonially a main line through one hundred miles of mountain and moorland with not a branch line nor scarcely a village worthy of the name in all its length. For the first time a massive tract of hitherto rail-less country (except for a straggling cross-country line) was being opened up for traffic. At long last the West Highland Railway was ready for service. 'It throws open to the public,' said the *Railway Herald*, 'wide and interesting tracts of country which have been almost as much unknown to the ordinary tourist hitherto as Central Africa was ten years ago to the geographer.' And a guide book in a popular railway series had this to say of the country traversed by the new railway: 'Like England it is situated in the temperate zone, but nearer to the frigid polar regions and hence its climate is relatively cold, dense and moist.'

The passengers who took their seats in the coaches specially built by the North British at Cowlairs Works for the West Highland Railway did not need long to find that a map of the railway was printed on the inside of each window blind. The route was inspected with interest and enthusiasm. The line could be seen leaving the North British Glasgow—Helensburgh line at Craigendoran on the Clyde coast and climbing up beside the Gareloch through Row (later Rhu) and Shandon to Garelochhead. The passengers traced it, still climbing, across to the east side of Loch Long, then followed it all the way up the loch, with one brief deviation inland to Arrochar. A short valley took the railway across to Loch Lomond; then it forced its way up Glen Falloch past Crianlarich and on through Strathfillan to Tyndrum and Bridge of Orchy.

There it started on its long climb to the bleak 400 square miles of the Moor of Rannoch, crossed the very roof of Scotland and then made a swift descent down Loch Treigside and through the gorges of the Spean to a sea-level terminus at Fort William, in the shadow of Ben Nevis. Never before in Britain had such a length of line been opened in one day. Never before had opening-day guests been taken on so spectacular and exciting a trip. Here was a railway fascinating beyond words, every foot of it with a place in the past, a story in every mile.

The West Highland was a railway within a railway. It had its own board of directors and its own capital (later it was to have its own very special atmosphere), but the North British had undertaken to staff and work the line with its own men, engines, and rolling stock. For the privilege of thus extending its influence into the Western Highlands the North British had been willing to guarantee a dividend of 3½ per cent to the West Highland Railway shareholders. By 1894 attempts to build railways into the West Highlands had been going on for fifty years. All the attempts had failed, most of them because of opposition from the firmly established Highland Railway and its natural ally, the Caledonian. The Highland Railway, not without reason, considered that any railway pushed into the West Highlands would harm its own hard-won, precarious line from Stanley Junction up over the Grampians into Inverness. The Caledonian, on the other hand, feared a possible threat to its subordinate the Callander & Oban Railway.

It must have been a source of satisfaction to the North British directors on that opening day to know that it was their bronze-green engines and claret coaches that would enter Fort William and not the blue engines of the Caledonian. The Caledonian had regarded the West of Scotland as its special preserve; thirty years before it had fought tooth and nail to prevent the North British from absorbing the Edinburgh & Glasgow Railway and so gaining access to the west. But the Edinburgh & Glasgow had fallen to the enemy and the North British had become firmly entrenched on the north bank of the Clyde.

Long before that, when the ink on the Caledonian's original Act of 1845 was barely dry, the railway was concerned in bills to promote lines into the West Highlands. And now the North British had triumphed again, albeit through the agency of its foster-child the West Highland Railway, and had penetrated deep into the heart of Caledonian territory. And the fight was far from over. A year earlier, the West Highland had made a bid to take its line on to Inverness, and it was to make another attack on the Highland capital in a matter of weeks. For all that, among the guests on the ceremonial train were representatives of the Caledonian and Highland companies. They were on the way to sup at the enemy's table in Fort William in the moment of his triumph.

Guests of honour on the train were the Marquess and Marchioness of Tweeddale. Behind-the-scenes moves had been made to have Queen Victoria herself honour the great occasion. But it was 1894, people no longer got excited over the opening of a railway, and royalty had long ceased to patronize such events. The West Highland had to make do with the chairman's wife.

THE THREE LOCHS

At 8.15 the ceremonial train, headed by two of the smart 4—4—0s specially built for the line, started on its journey. It had been preceded 40 minutes earlier by the regular passenger train, for the railway had been open for public services since the previous Tuesday—7 August. One of the press men on board thought it odd that he should have received an invitation to an opening when the line had already been opened. 'But,' he subsequently wrote, 'the guests were not perturbed by the fact that other people had gone before them. It gave them an assurance of safety and they enjoyed the scenery all the better.'

The first stage of the journey—the 1½-mile climb up Cowlairs Incline on the end of the steel cable—took the train to the high ground on the northern fringe of Glasgow.* As soon as the cable was slipped the two 4—4—0s whisked their train round the western suburbs and headed down the valley that carries the Clyde to the sea. On they rattled through suburban stations. Heads turned as passengers waiting for the morning trains to the city watched the unusual spectacle of two flag-decked locomotives with an important-

* See the author's *The Springburn Story*. David & Charles, Dawlish, 1964.

looking train on their tail sail by. At Bowling the railway picked up the broadening river and ran with it through Dumbarton and Cardross to Craigendoran where the river opened out into the firth. And it was at Craigendoran that the West Highland Railway began. From the large windows of their coaches the guests could see the railway diverging to the right from the Helensburgh line of the North British and begin at once to climb sharply into the hills. A curtain of mountain peaks hung on the horizon barely 10 miles away. It was hardly conceivable that in half an hour the train would be deep among those very mountains.

First there was a halt at Craigendoran station to have a hot axle-box given attention. Then the special was off on the curving climb up the hillside, the engines' exhausts crackling, cinders pattering down on the carriage roofs. Within seconds the passengers were looking down on the roofs of Craigendoran pier buildings with the

CRAIGENDORAN PIER.

pretty North British paddle boats clustered round them like celluloid ducks in a bath. Within minutes the whole panorama of the Firth of Clyde with Port Glasgow, Greenock and Gourock strung out along the opposite shore, opened out below the railway. Two miles of stiff climbing brought the train to Helensburgh Upper station, then followed a relaxed 6 miles as the engines followed the undulating track round the hillside above the Gareloch. Through the gaps in the trees the guests could see the ever-changing views of the loch and the rolling wooded hills that enclosed it. Row and Shandon stations, sparkling in their fresh green paint, slipped behind. Discerning passengers could feel the dip and sway of the coaches as the gradients beneath the wheels changed abruptly. Once on Garelochside the train swung into a great left hand bend and the engines were clearly visible from carriages even in the middle of the train.

A stop for water at Garelochhead, then the train swung out on the hillside, crossing the head of the loch and giving the passengers a fine panoramic view all the way down to Greenock. Suddenly, a high wall of rock blotted out the view, but less than a minute later the train emerged from the cutting and presented the passengers with an entirely different view. The Gareloch with its trim villages and pleasant wooded hills had given place in the blinking of an eye to the lonely, rugged grandeur of Loch Long. The speed of the transition was bewildering. One minute the train was in the Lowlands, the next it was in the Highlands. The passengers might well have entered another country. Far below was Loch Long, thrusting a fiord-like finger far into the mountains of Argyll. The precipitous slopes plunged straight down the rugged peaks into the dark water.

The train wound along the mountain face steadily climbing higher and higher above the water. A mile or two of this and it slipped into Glen Mallin and continued its journey with a range of bare mountains between the railway and the loch. At the top of the Glen was Glen Douglas passing place, the first of several outposts established in lonely places to break the long empty sections—a short platform, a signal box and a simple cottage to house the railway family. Glen Douglas was the first summit of the line—560 ft above sea level. The train slowed briefly as the fireman of the second engine exchanged tablets with the signalman, then it slewed abruptly to the left, burrowed down through a rock cutting on a reverse curve and came out once again on the mountainside high above Loch Long. It wound along on a ledge stepped out of the mountain and just wide enough to hold the railway. A wall of freshly cut rock rose up outside the right-hand carriage windows; on the left side a precipice dropped more than 500 ft to the water's edge. The guests were thrilled at one place to find themselves looking down the face of a perpendicular wall. Through the large windows of their saloons they could see the engines nosing cautiously in and out of the crevices as they negotiated a continuous series of reverse curves. Often the engines were out of sight of spectators in the middle of the train. At one point, perched on a buttress overhanging the loch was a cottage built to house the surfaceman whose job it was to patrol this spectacular length of railway.

Where Loch Long ended against a barrier of mountain peaks the railway turned to the right into a short valley—an ancient portage connecting salt-water Loch Long with fresh-water Loch Lomond. No sooner was Loch Long lost to view at the left-hand windows than the right-hand windows presented the delighted passengers with the beauties of Loch Lomond; few of them had seen the famous waterway to such advantage. The little-used coach road hugged the shore, but the railway ran high up on the face of the hill giving wide views over the loch. In the years to come many patrons were to glory in this view of Loch Lomond. Writing about it and other West Highland high-level views the Scottish author J. J. Bell said: 'We have, indeed, several stretches of line which in scenic outlook are immeasurably richer than the roads leading to the same destinations, and one of them is the West Highland Railway.'

After a brief stop at Arrochar and Tarbet station, the train steamed off through a birchwood and for the next 8 miles meandered round the hillside, sometimes edging out close to the water, at others swinging back into the recesses of the hillface. Ben Lomond across the loch dominated the scene at first. Then came Inversnaid village with its waterfall plummeting down a

A WEST HIGHLAND STATION (ARROCHAR AND TARBET).

wooded ravine. It was a dullish morning with cloud caps on the highest mountain tops, but for all that the rich colourings of the Loch Lomond scene captivated the guests. The heather patches on the mountains were beginning to assume their autumn purple, and the thick bracken rolled green down to the water's edge, while here and there were rowan trees hanging with scarlet berries.

UP THE VALE OF AWFUL SOUND

At the head of Loch Lomond came another dramatic change of scene. Direct from the end of the platform at Ardlui the train plunged into the craggy entrance to Glen Falloch, and started on a gruelling climb that was to last for 15 miles and take it over 1,000 ft above sea level. The railway climbed higher and higher up the west

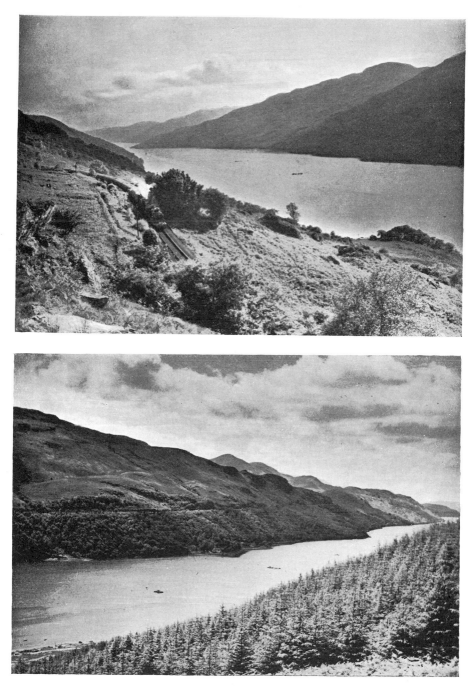

THE WEST HIGHLAND SCENE—1

(1) *Excursion train hauled by B12 Class 4—6—0 and* LNER *No. 9695 above Loch Long*

(2) *Loch Long, showing the railway on the mountainside*

THE WEST HIGHLAND SCENE—2

(3) *Loch Lomond. The* G & NW *would have followed the far shore of the loch*

(4) *Glens doublehead a Glasgow—Fort William train on Glen Falloch viaduct in* LNE *days*

wall of the glen, twisting constantly left and right in an effort to gain altitude. Glen Falloch became narrower and wilder with each milepost. The steep slopes pitched down to the bottom of the valley along which the Falloch river ran its noisy course, down to Loch Lomond. Waterfalls large and small cascaded into the glen from the surrounding mountains. The passengers had a wonderful view for many minutes of the great Ben-y-Glas Fall, foaming over a precipice and plunging 120 ft to the rocks below with a force that sent a curtain of vapour to the tree tops. The rush and roar of water was the characteristic sound of Glen Falloch. William Wordsworth called it 'the vale of awful sound'. Even Wordsworth the railway hater would have been impressed by the new sound that invaded Glen Falloch that day—the bark and crackle of Matthew Holmes's little West Highland bogies as they struggled to lift their ten coaches up the glen.

Another highlight of the journey was reached when the engines curved, still climbing, on to the Glen Falloch viaduct carrying the line over the gorge of the Black Water—the Dubh Eas—at a height only 7 ft less than that of the recently-completed Forth Bridge. Passengers who looked forward as the engines leaned to the right with the curvature of the bridge could see the flash of their pounding coupling rods. Up they climbed through the remnants of the ancient Caledonian Forest and under the curious triangular hill, Cruach Ardran. After 7 stiff miles the glen opened out, and the

CRIANLARICH.

steady beat of the exhausts quietened as the train breasted a minor summit—to become known to generations of West Highland footplatemen as 'the fireman's rest'—and drifted down into Crianlarich.

The huts and equipment used by the contractor were still to be seen alongside the station. The railway company had established Crianlarich as the halfway posting establishment between Glasgow and Fort William. The engines were groomed and watered for the task that lay immediately ahead and the passengers were given refreshments. Crianlarich hamlet stood in the bottom of a natural bowl set among great mountains, penetrated by three deep passes. The West Highland came up from the south through Glen Falloch, the Callander & Oban Railway came in from the east through Glen Dochart, and both railways shared Strathfillan to continue their way north.

The ceremonial train pulled out of Crianlarich station, crossed the Oban line at right angles on a viaduct, swung through a 90° curve and began the ascent of the eastern side of Strathfillan. The Oban line, keeping to the floor of the valley on the western side, ran on a parallel course with the West Highland for 5 or 6 miles. The train climbed steadily up the strath, rising all the time above

VIADUCT OF WEST HIGHLAND RAILWAY AT CRIANLARICH.

the Oban line. Beyond Tyndrum, the hamlet at the head of the valley, two glens opened out from the main valley like the arms of a Y. The Oban line disappeared through the western pass to run by Dalmally and Loch Awe and Loch Etive to the coast at Oban. The

West Highland line entered a deep V-cut penetrating the mountains to the north. Five minutes more steaming took the train to the county march of Perth and Argyll and at the same time to a summit 1,024·75 ft above sea level.

By consulting their programmes of the day's events and the maps on the window blinds the passengers would have discovered that they were approaching one of the most eagerly-awaited features of the line—the Horse Shoe Curve. Directly ahead of the engines was Ben Doran, by far the most striking of all the West Highland mountains. There was nothing very remarkable about its 3,523 ft of height; it was the symmetry of the beautifully-moulded cone visible at a glance from the base to the summit that made Ben Doran as distinctive and distinguished as the Fuji Yama of the tapestries and lacquered trays.

A broad valley separated the train from Ben Doran, but instead of cutting straight across the valley on a viaduct or embankment the line suddenly swerved to the right round the shoulder of Ben Odhar, until it was heading almost due east. Then it turned north again,

BRIDGE OF DOCHART.

and then struck westward along the side of Ben Doran. The passengers could look across the valley and see the line they had just traversed: above the railway, marking its course round the mountainsides, hung a U-shaped pall of smoke.

Bridge of Orchy proved to be a typical West Highland 'bridge' settlement—a bridge over a river, a few stone cottages, an inn. That day the inn exhibited a flag in honour of the coming of the railway. On the climb northwards away from Bridge of Orchy the sense of adventure aboard heightened. The narrow coach-road that had kept company with the railway from Loch Lomondside diverged to the left and disappeared over the rim of the Black Mount. The line struck north into barren roadless country that only a handful of intrepid travellers had ever seen before. Between Bridge of Orchy and Inverlair lay 30 miles of the most desolate and forbidding country in Europe, and in the middle of it was the Moor of Rannoch.

THE MOOR OF RANNOCH

Passengers who knew their Robert Louis Stevenson remembered how in *Kidnapped* David Balfour and Alan Breck had caught their first glimpse of the Moor.

> The mist rose and died away and showed us that country lying as waste as the sea; only the moorfowl and the peewits crying over it and far over to the east a herd of deer moving like dots. Much of it was red with heather; much of the rest broken up with bogs and hags and peaty pools; some had been burned black in a heath fire; and in another place there was quite a forest of dead firs standing like skeletons. A wearier looking desert man never saw.

Climbing again on the 21 mile drag that would take it to the summit of the line the train roared up the valley of the Tulla water. Below and to the west lay Loch Tulla and beyond it the Black Mount and the jagged peaks of Glen Etive and Glencoe. The scenery changed perceptibly with every mile that passed. Trees vanished. Vegetation other than scrub and heather became scarcer and scarcer. The bare, stony framework of the mountains protruded in patches through the thin outer covering of turf. Traces of civilization melted away.

After an 8-mile steady climb came Gortan (later Gorton), a West Highland outpost on the edge of the Moor. There was a signal box and a house to shelter the family who had relinquished their former life in a more hospitable region of the North British system to attend to the safety of the trains in their passage over the Moor. The train rolled out into the wilderness. Never before had the passengers witnessed such a scene of desolation. For mile after mile a dun-coloured sea flecked with grey granite stretched from either side of the line to the horizon. The dreary surface of the Moor was blotched with mud-filled ditches and pools of dark water. Black bog lapped at the railway line: in the worst places it was floated over the bog on a raft of brushwood and heather. The Caledonian Forest long ago had covered all of the Moor. Not a tree now remained, but the black roots, pickled for ages in the bog, were everywhere to be seen.

The train wound among the peat hags at never more than 25 m.p.h. It crossed the Gauer Water, a dark stream coursing sluggishly through the bog, and presently the appearance of a distant signal heralded the approach of civilization. Ahead lay Rannoch station, an oasis wrested from the Moor by the railway engineers to house and shelter the men who would pass the trains and service this lonely section of the line. The visitors marvelled at the isolation of the settlement. 'How will they get food supplies? How will their children get to school? What will it be like in the depths of winter?' Such bustling questions must have occupied their minds. The shareholders among them might well have been asking themselves where on earth the traffic was to come from to make the railway pay.

From a re-start at Rannoch the train struggled upwards towards the highest part of the Moor. Through a cutting in the Cruach Rock it went, and soon it was swinging gently on a series of shallow reverse curves as the track sought out the best route through the peat bogs. It was now crossing the great tableland of Scotland. Mountain ranges and peaks ringed the horizon; rain clouds hung on the tops, and intermittent drizzle swept the highest parts of the Moor. One eye-witness at least was unperturbed by the indifferent weather. 'Nobody could have wished a better day,' he was to write, 'except those who were anxious to see every clearly-cut peak outlined against the sky—and then they would have paid the penalty of sweltering in the sunshine. The clouds swathed the mountaintops, but they did not dissolve into more than a few drops of rain.' The red train with its two bronze-green engines made a brave sight as it mounted towards the high north-west corner of the Moor. Then at last it reached Corrour, the third of the railway settlements on the Moor and the summit of the line.

More than three hours had passed since the run at sea level beside the Firth of Clyde at Craigendoran. In that time 72 miles had been covered and 1,347 ft had been climbed above sea level. Now the passengers were faced with an exciting, headlong plunge back to sea level at Fort William in a distance of only 28 miles.

THROUGH THE GORGES OF THE SPEAN

The carriage wheels drummed faster and faster over the rail joints as the train gathered speed down the valley that led the railway away from the inhospitable Moor. At once the scenery began to change, trees beginning to appear again. At the end of the valley the brakes hissed and the two engines curved slowly out on to the face of yet another mountain. Loch Treig filled a great hollow in the mountains 450 ft below, and across the water rose the massif of which Ben Nevis was the apex. Loch Treig, a hitherto seldom-seen loch, had no roads by its shores. The railway began high above at the western end, and for 5 miles dropped down and down the mountainside until it reached the water's edge. No fewer than 150 bridges were provided to carry it over the innumerable watercourses that poured down the slopes.

At the end of the loch the River Treig leapt and tumbled down a wooded glen, the railway running beside it. Then a mile down the glen the train swung through 90°, passed through Inverlair station, and entered the gorges of the Spean. The coach-road from Kingussie on the Highland Railway came in from the east and ran parallel to the railway. No road had been seen since Bridge of Orchy.

After the long, bleak trip across the Moor of Rannoch and down Loch Treigside, the richly-wooded Glen Spean with its occasional cultivated strips by the river seemed bright and friendly. The railway kept close company with the Spean as it roared through the rocky channels it had cut for itself in the floor of the valley through the ages. The passengers watched the river shoot in a smother of foam through black-walled chasms and froth down to lower levels in a series of cascades. They saw it roar round obstructing boulders and then suddenly broaden out to flow between lush meadows. But never for long. The gorge closed in again and the constricted river surged along in a flurry of amber and white rapids.

At one point a sharp brake application brought down speed to 10 m.p.h., and the engines felt their way through the perfect crescent of the Monessie Gorge. There was just room for railway and river to squeeze through the narrow defile. The line ran on a ledge halfway up the right-hand wall of the gorge and the passengers could look directly down on to the brown water churning over a jumbled mass of granite boulders. There were to be times, and they were not far off, when the floodwaters of the Spean would climb 15 ft up the walls of the Monessie Gorge in an hour.

Once clear of the Spean gorges the train sped steadily westwards through Lochaber. Tablets were exchanged at Roy Bridge and at Spean Bridge, the last station before Fort William. As the last miles dropped behind, the passengers made themselves ready for the ceremonial welcome that awaited them. Many of them admired the mass of Ben Nevis rising close by the railway to the left of the train.

LOCHABER WELCOME

The first houses of the first town in 100 miles drifted past the carriage windows. Then came the mingled sound of bagpipes and muffled cheering. The train slowed and stopped at a temporary wooden platform on the outskirts of the town. Directly ahead, an ornamental arch flanked by battlemented towers spanned the railway, and closed double gates barred the progress of the train. The whole edifice looked solid and imposing, although it was only a flimsy framework of timber clothed with the green and purple of fern and heather, and adorned with flags and heraldic devices.

Cameron of Lochiel, a director of the West Highland, Provost Young of Fort William, and the Chief Constable of Inverness-shire were among the important local people who greeted the train from the south. Lady Tweeddale stepped from the train—it was her first visit to the West Highlands by any means—and was conducted to the closed archway. She was handed a golden key hung from a gold shield engraved 'W.H.R.' in diamonds. She turned the key in a gold padlock ostensibly securing the gate of the archway, and that was the signal for members of the railway staff hidden among the foliage to pull the gates slowly open. The moment that Fort William had awaited for half a century had come at last. The train steamed into the town as pipers played a merry march on the battlements above.

Some 400 guests repaired to a large marquee near the station. Its interior was decorated with a thousand blooms brought up from Glasgow the previous day. Mr Rupprecht of the North British Hotel in Glasgow presided over a meal worthy of the occasion. There were the usual speeches. The seating arrangements were such that Cameron of Lochiel was sandwiched between a director of the Highland Railway and the vice-chairman of the Caledonian Railway, gentlemen who had done their damnedest to keep the West Highland out of Fort William and who were to fight relentlessly to prevent the expansion of the West Highland into their territories. But Lochiel was in benevolent mood. 'I will let bygones be bygones and never say a word about the past,' he told the company. To which he might well have added under his breath, 'For today only'. A succession of speakers prophesied a bright future for the new railway. The reporter from the *Glasgow Evening News* had his doubts. In the next issue of his newspaper he wrote:

It would be difficult to parallel it (the railway) for sparseness of population. For mile upon mile of its length not a single vestige of human life or habitation is to be seen. Its very stations between Crianlarich and Fort William are at present simply names—oases in the barren moorland. A paying traffic must be a matter of slow growth, and it will test the management severely to make ends meet long years after the present time. All who have the interest of our Highland population at heart will join in hoping that a brighter day has dawned for them, and that with the breaking down of the natural barriers which have so long confined them, there will follow an era of prosperity of which parallels can be found wherever the railway has found an entrance.

CHAPTER 2

West Highland Pre-History

THE MANIA YEAR

The Great National Direct Independent Land's End to John o' Groats Atmospheric Railway.

That was one of the headings that caught the eye of the avid reader who scanned the announcements of new railways that filled the newspaper columns in the Mania Year, 1845. 'It will cross Loch Ness on a magnificent viaduct not less than 5,500 feet long,' went on the announcement, 'and a tunnel will pierce through the centre of Ben Nevis. Travellers will thus be enabled in the transit to see two of the finest objects in the North Highlands of Scotland.' It was not until the reader was assured that the proposed railway would proceed from terminus to terminus by the most indirect route and scrupulously avoid all cities and centres of industry that he realized that he was having his leg pulled. Yet the unknown satirist's fake prospectus was hardly less outrageous than some of the genuine prospectuses that appeared alongside it. Promoters were greedy for ground on which to lay their paper railways. No place was too ridiculous to merit their interest.

Of all the wildcat schemes of the Mania Year none were more maniacal than those that envisaged the penetration of the Western Highlands of Scotland. Here was country that was a great mass of mountain peaks cut and cross-cut with deep V-shaped valleys, many of them filled with ribbon lochs. It was raw, barren country without industry, and with hundreds of square miles completely depopulated. It presented a mighty challenge to the railway engineer, yet there was little for a railway to do once it was built.

For all that, in 1845 West Highland schemes with grand-sounding names were legion. There was the Scottish Western Railway and the Scottish North Western Railway, the Caledonian & Grand Northern Railway, the Caledonian Northern Direct, and the Scottish Grand Junction Railway. The language of the prospectuses of some of the projected companies was scarcely less extravagant than that of the mythical Land's End and John o' Groats. The Scottish Grand Junction 'connecting the whole of the Western and Northern counties of Scotland with the Scottish Central and Caledonian Railways' thus described its route through the rugged heart of the Highlands.

> The country to be traversed by the proposed lines has been surveyed and is found to present every facility. For the most part it is a dead level and the surface is so regular that the cost of construction will be much below the average of Railway undertakings. The works are generally light—there are no tunnels—and the bridges will be few in number and of inconsiderable magnitude.

In spite of this farrago of falsehood, the Scottish Grand Junction and its rivals received wide public acclaim and financial support. And it was not by accident that names appeared among the committee members of the West Highland schemes that were already familiar to students of the official literature of the Caledonian Railway. The Caledonian had gained its Act in July 1845. It was one of the most ambitious railways promoted up to that time; it was backed by London financiers, and engineered by men of the highest repute. The Caledonian was destined to be a great railway. Already, with the first sod scarcely turned, the board-room had visions of creating a great national line. There were two northern citadels to be conquered—Aberdeen and Inverness. The Caledonian had an eye on a series of satellite railways that, end on end, were to provide through communication with Aberdeen within fifteen years. With one long tentacle stretching through the rich valleys of eastern Scotland to the Dee, it was natural that the Caledonian should give thought to establishing a complementary line running through the rugged west to a terminus on the Ness. Hence the Caledonian finger in the various West Highland pies.

In the autumn of 1845 Locke and Errington, who had surveyed trunk lines from Birmingham to Castlecary in the Forth-Clyde valley, were in Stirling surveying a route for the Scottish Central Railway, the first of the lines that was to take the Caledonian influence on towards Aberdeen. Fresh from their successes with the Grand Junction and the Caledonian, Locke and Errington were highly esteemed as railway engineers; their names on a prospectus provided the hallmark of respectability. Investors raised their eyebrows when the prospectus of the Caledonian & Grand Northern Railway seemed to indicate that Locke and Errington had transferred their interest from the gentle east to the wild west, and had engineered a major railway from Glasgow through the West

Highlands and the Great Glen to Inverness. But in the same newspaper column that exhibited the C & GN prospectus there appeared this letter.

Stirling 6 Sept. 1845

Sir,

I observe that Parties promoting the above Line of Railway have done Mr. Locke and myself the honour to nominate us Engineers of the Scheme. It is usual to have the sanction of a professional man for placing his name before the public in connection with any project, for the propriety of which he may, to a certain extent, be held accountable. I have received no applications from either of the interim secretaries, or from the Solicitors named in the advertisement, and have no connection whatever with the above line.

I am, Sir,
Your servant,
J. E. Errington.

That was the end of the Caledonian & Grand Northern Railway.

In September 1845 the Scottish Western Railway entered the field. Like most of the West Highland projects of the period, the SWR aimed at providing communication between the western seaboard and the industrial Lowlands. The Scottish Western was to start at Oban and thread its way along lochsides and through glens (by the route taken three decades later by the Callander & Oban Railway) to join at Callander a proposed railway in the Caledonian sphere of influence. From Crianlarich, a branch was to strike south down Glen Falloch and Loch Lomond to make connection at Balloch with another proposed Caledonian-sponsored line, the Caledonian & Dumbartonshire. The Scottish Western therefore had a choice of two routes to Glasgow from Oban, both dominated by the Caledonian. The promoters pointed out that if hostile landowners barred their passage down Glen Falloch, they would take the line east through the Trossachs to the Blane Valley, and link up with the Campsie branch of the Edinburgh & Glasgow Railway.

The Scottish Western committee was well sprinkled with names of reputable Scots—landowners, lairds, merchants, and MPs. The scheme had the confidence of the public, and within a few days of the appearance of the prospectus the railway office announced that they 'found it impossible to comply with the requests of many respectable applicants' who indicated their intention to take up the £700,000 in SWR shares.

One, John Lammond, criticized the Scottish Western on the grounds that it was too expensive. He could see no point in building a railway down Loch Lomondside. He had a plan to make a line from Oban to the head of Loch Lomond, and to link this northern line 'by means of strong and powerful steamers' to the Caledonian & Dumbartonshire at Balloch. The estimated cost of Lammond's line was a mere £300,000. His announcement said, 'A full prospectus of the West Highland Railway will appear in a few days.' It never did appear, but the episode is interesting because it introduced the title West Highland Railway for the first time.

The Scottish Western was followed within a few weeks by the Caledonian Northern Direct and the Scottish Grand Junction Railway. The proposed route of the Scottish Grand Junction was almost identical with that of the Scottish Western: Oban to Callander and a branch down Glen Falloch, thence through the Trossachs to a junction with the Caledonian & Dumbartonshire at Milngavie. The Grand Junction also planned a second main line, starting at Tyndrum and passing eastward through Glen Ericht to join up with the proposed Perth & Inverness Railway (later the Highland Railway main line) at Dalwhinnie. The end result would have been a Y-shaped system with Glasgow at the base of the stem, and Oban and Dalwhinnie (later it was hoped Inverness) at the tips of the arms. The Grand Junction was headed by Sir Alexander Campbell and the Scottish Western by Sir James Campbell. The Campbells did the right thing: they got together in Glasgow on 30 October 1845, and as a result the Scottish Western agreed to withdraw, leaving the field clear for the Scottish Grand Junction.

The Caledonian Northern Direct was more or less a repetition of the southern half of the Scottish Grand Junction. Apparently it was promoted to ensure a Caledonian-controlled line of communication should the Scottish Grand Junction get permission for the Callander—Oban, Tyndrum—Dalwhinnie section and be refused the extension. The prospectus said in part:

> It is therefore proposed to form a Company to make a Railway from a point on the Caledonian and Dumbartonshire Junction Line near Milngavie through Strathblane and Strathendrick into the Valley of the Forth, between Gartmore and Buchlyvie, thence by Aberfoyle, Lochard, Lochchon and Loch Katrine, by Glengyle through Glen Falloch and Glen Dochart to a point near Tyndrum, there to form a Junction with the proposed lines from Oban to Callander and from Tyndrum to Dalwhinnie and Inverness.

After informing investors that it would 'be difficult to over-estimate the earning capacity of the line', the prospectus gave the usual assurance that the West Highlands presented no difficulties to the engineers: 'The line will be for the most part along valleys and margins of lakes, the gradients are good and there are no engineering difficulties.' A ruling gradient of 1 in 100 was promised and a tunnel three-quarters of a mile long was to pierce the mountain barrier between the Trossachs and Glen Falloch. By contrast George Marton, engineer of the rival Scottish Grand Junction, proposed to take his line from the Trossachs over the tops of the mountains on gradients of 1 in 40, which he planned to surmount 'by application of the atmospheric principle'.

The Caledonian Northern Direct's proposed capital was £600,000 to be issued in shares of £25 each. The Duke of Montrose was provisional chairman, and his committee was studded with well-known names: John James Hope Johnston, chairman of the Caledonian (significantly); John Orr Ewing, merchant of Glasgow; Peter Denny, the famous shipbuilder and Provost of Dumbarton; Henry Dann, director of the Shrewsbury, Oswestry & Chester Railway; George Whitmore, deputy chairman of the North Kent Railway; and many more. By 28 October 1845 the Caledonian Northern Direct announced that it had allocated all its stock 'from a multiplicity of applications'. *The Glasgow Argus*, which strongly criticized certain railway proposals in England, said of the Scottish projects: 'These lines are all together of a *bona fide* character and as wide apart from what are appropriately termed bubble lines as truth is from falsehood.' But bubble lines they were, and very soon the bubbles burst. The end of the Mania saw the Scottish schemes swept away and forty years were to pass before the idea of a trunk line through the Western Highlands was resurrected.

LIMITED SUCCESS

In the twenty years that followed 1845 the Scottish railways concentrated on extending and consolidating their lines. By 1865 the Highland Railway had a trunk route to Inverness by Blair Atholl, Aviemore and Forres, and associated companies took the line north of Inverness as far as Bonar Bridge. The Caledonian main line stretched from Carlisle to Perth, and in the following year the absorption of the Scottish North Eastern was to give the Caledonian the long-sought-after through route from Carlisle to Aberdeen. The Highland Railway ran up through the centre of Scotland like a spinal column. The country to the east of the line was well served by railways, but the country to the west was still rail-less.

With their main lines secure, both the Caledonian and the Highland turned their attention to possible conquests in the West Highlands. This time there was no talk of a trunk line from north to south. Instead the respective companies backed schemes which would take what were virtually long branch lines from the parent trunk lines through the glens and over the mountain passes to two points on the western seaboard. The Callander & Oban was authorized to build a line between the two towns of the title by the route favoured by the 1845 promoters, and the Dingwall & Skye Railway was authorized to construct a line from Dingwall across Wester Ross to the coast at Kyle of Lochalsh. The object of both schemes was to tap the trade of the west coast and islands—mainly fish—and route it to the parent lines. The Callander & Oban was to be worked by the Caledonian, the Dingwall & Skye by the Highland. But most of the money for the Dingwall & Skye had come out of the Caledonian's coffers; plainly the Caledonian had not weakened over the years in its determination to control the West Highlands.

Five years of trials and difficulties taught the sponsors of those lines what it meant to take railways into those inhospitable regions. By 1870 the Skye line reached as far as Strome Ferry on Loch Carron, and the plan to take it on to the projected terminus at Kyle of Lochalsh was abandoned. The Callander & Oban had fared much worse. By 1870 the promoters had been able to build only 17 miles of track. Overwhelming engineering difficulties had drained away the company's capital, and the line stuck in Glen Ogle for lack of finance. Enough money was found to take it on another 15 miles to Tyndrum and there, after an Act had been obtained abandoning the route westward to Oban, the Callander & Oban established a rail-head. The line as it stood ended in the middle of nowhere. It had failed entirely in its purpose to link the western seas with the Lowlands. Four years passed before a fresh injection of capital gave the Callander & Oban heart to seek a new Act for the extension of the line to Oban, which point was reached in 1880. The Highland did not get to the Kyle of Lochalsh until 1897.

THE GLASGOW & NORTH WESTERN RAILWAY

By 1880 the public conscience was becoming troubled about the plight of the people of North West Scotland. At long last Westminster wakened to the fact that the population of the West Highlands and Islands were in dire straits. The deliberate and ruthless depopulation of the area during the Highland Clearances, massive governmental indifference and neglect and primitive or non-existent transport had combined to make the area one of the most backward in Europe. The bulk of the people lived on the poverty line. The pride of family that had characterized the clan system had to a large measure been lost and some of the clan chiefs had become grasping landlords, sometimes absentees whose indolent lives in the fleshpots of England had to be supported by rents wrested from their Highland estates. Then came the Crofters' War, when the fisherfolk and crofters rebelled against their oppressors and staged rent strikes. The result was the setting up of the Crofters' Commission, whose members were dispatched to the trouble-spots on a painstaking fact-finding mission, with a mandate to report on the causes of the West Highland malaise and suggest methods of improving the lot of the West Highlanders. It was against this background that the promotion of the Glasgow & North Western Railway was announced.

The Glasgow & North Western was the grandest railway ever to be promoted in the British Isles. It was to stretch for 167 miles from Glasgow to Inverness, taking in vast tracts of new country embracing Loch Lomond, the Moor of Rannoch, Glen Coe, part of the Argyllshire coast, Fort William, Fort Augustus and Loch Ness. Unlike the Highland Railway and the extensions into the West Highlands, the G & NW was not locally financed. London money was behind it, and it was engineered in Westminster by Thomas Walron Smith who had twenty years of experience building railways in Sweden, Wales, and Ireland.

The enterprise was backed, not by the Caledonian, but by the North British who hoped to work it. That was enough to spark off a full-scale railway war in Scotland. The Caledonian and North British were bitter rivals. The North British with its base in Edinburgh had developed the east side of the country, the Caledonian based in Glasgow regarded the west side as its preserve. The Caledonian had suffered a serious setback when in 1865 the North British had absorbed the Edinburgh & Glasgow Railway and gained access to Glasgow and the west. Now the North British was threatening to extend its influence into country long regarded by the Caledonian and its partner, the Highland, as their territory. It was a prospect that neither company could contemplate with equanimity.

The bold new railway was planned to leave the North British Helensburgh branch at Maryhill on the northern fringe of Glasgow and stretch north-west across 20 miles of pleasant, undulating country to the southern shore of Loch Lomond. There were plans to develop this initial length of line—which was double—as a prosperous outer suburban section. It passed just to the west of Milngavie, the terminus of the North British branch from Glasgow, soon to be linked with the stations on the Glasgow District Railway then in course of construction. The G & NW hoped to make a junction with the Milngavie line and send some trains into the new Queen Street Low Level station, serving the GDR suburban stations west of Glasgow on the way.

From Milngavie the line crossed some high ground to the west side of Craigallion Loch, climbed into the hills flanking the Blane Valley (through which passed the North British Aberfoyle branch) and then struck across moorland and hill pasture towards Loch Lomond, crossing a mile west of Drymen another North British possession, the Forth & Clyde Junction Railway. There the Glasgow & North Western proposed a double junction enabling its traffic to reach Balloch and Dumbarton on one hand and Stirling and Alloa on the other. The approach to Loch Lomond was by the Pass of Balmaha. The double line was to end at a railway-owned pier from which boats would ply to various destinations on the loch.

Beyond Balmaha the character of the line changed abruptly. Pastureland and moors gave place to mountains rising in some places sheer out of the loch. The single line continued for some 20 miles up the eastern shore of the loch partly in cuttings but mainly on embankments varying in height from 7 to 35 ft above the water. The line wound round the contours, skirted the base of Ben Lomond, and crossed the garden in front of Inversnaid Hotel, eventually to reach the head of the loch and enter Glen Falloch. Still forging north, it climbed up the eastern side of the glen 200 ft above the existing coach road, and passed so close to the great waterfall Ben-y-Glas that the spray was expected to fall on the rails. At the end of an 8-mile climb the line emerged from the glen to cross the Callander & Oban line at Crianlarich where a 'spacious staircase' was envisaged linking the two railways.

The next stage took the line up Strathfillan through Tyndrum, and on past Glen Orchy and round the shores of Loch Tulla to a summit of 1,077 ft on the Black Mount. Then came a gentle fall over moorland, followed at once by a spectacular 4½-mile plunge down Glen Coe on gradients of 1 in 50 and 1 in 53 to sea level at Ballachulish. Now that the line had won its way over the difficult terrain of the interior, the way to Inverness lay open to it in an almost straight line 76½ miles long. The railway continued across Loch Leven at the Dog Ferry, passed along the shore of Loch Linnhe to Fort William, and went on to cross the Spean at Mucomir Bridge and reach the shores of Loch Oich and Loch Ness. A 19-mile length of dead-level line, partly on a causeway built out into the water, was planned for Loch Ness side.

THE WEST HIGHLAND SCENE—3

(5) *'Loch Arkaig' on a Glasgow—Crianlarich train*

(6) *Crianlarich period piece,* 1938

THE WEST HIGHLAND SCENE—4

(7) *Ben Doran, 3,523 ft. The railway near the Horse Shoe Curve*

The Glasgow & North Western was to reach its own station in South Inverness and take a final sweep round the town to a junction with the Highland Railway, and so gain access to the Highland station. A branch planned to run down to Inverness Harbour was intended to secure for the Glasgow & North Western a share of the east coast as well as the west coast fish trade. The railway was to have twenty-eight stations, seven tunnels totalling 1,336 yd, and five viaducts totalling 498 yd; the whole enterprise was to cost £1,526,116.

THE BATTLE IN PARLIAMENT

The Glasgow & North Western Railway bill was presented in Parliament in November 1882, and its consideration in committee extended throughout April and May 1883. It was a memorable episode in railway Parliamentary history, and it shed an interesting light on social conditions in the West Highlands. For weeks each side collected potential evidence against the other. Witnesses were interviewed, briefed and brought to London at considerable expense to their sponsors.

Opposition to the Glasgow & North Western was massive: rail interests, steamer interests and private individuals combined to thwart the scheme. The Highland Railway had more cause than most to fear the newcomer. The Highland or its constituent companies had created their railway using local money and talents at a time when their territory offered no attraction to southern speculators. The new venture, which could prosper only at the expense of the Highland, would, they insisted, be unfair. The Caledonian, with an eye to developing the West Highlands through its subsidiary the Callander & Oban, and with more than a passing thought for its capital invested in the Skye line, gave the Highland wholehearted support. The Caledonian Canal Commissioners and the steamboat operators on Loch Lomond abhorred the idea of a railway line running parallel with their steamer routes, and they prepared to fight the bill. David MacBrayne, who had a near-monopoly of West Highland steamer services, likewise protested against the railway. And there were landowners, dedicated to the idea of preserving the West Highlands for deer and sheep, who dipped into their pockets to finance the anti-railway factions.

Nevertheless, there was optimism in the Glasgow & North Western camp. Every day the newspapers reported the proceedings of the Crofters' Commission as it made its slow progress through the West Highlands. and it was plain from the reports that the crying need of the area was *transport*. Despite the opposition, there never had been a time more propitious for the promotion of a railway in the West Highlands.

At the outset the Glasgow & North Western Railway had taken pains to placate possible hostile landowners through whose estates the line was to pass. They were issued with prospectuses and maps to show how the promoters had gone out of their way to avoid what the reports called 'gentlemen's seats'. At Rowardenan the line was diverted from the side of Loch Lomond and screened by a curtain of rocks and trees from an important shooting lodge. In places where the line had no alternative but to cross estates, the owners were promised that it would be decently shrouded in trees and carried over estate roads on pretty ornamental bridges.

The Duke of Montrose was assured that although the line would pass half a mile to the west of the ducal seat, Buchanan Castle, it would not be visible from the castle grounds. But the duke insisted that it *would* be visible from the castle towers and he sent his map back to the G & NW with an acceptable diversion pencilled in—a diversion that entailed an impossible rise to a 1,200 ft summit and an equally impossible fall. Special care had to be taken to avoid Lord Lovat's house: not only was Lord Lovat a hostile landowner, but he was also a director of the Highland Railway.

In order to avoid giving possible offence to the residents of Fort Augustus, the railway was kept a third of a mile away from the town, and Fort William was similarly avoided. But so overjoyed were the people of Fort William at the prospect of getting a railway that they would hear nothing of the proposed detour round the town. The local council invited the G & NW to bring the line straight up the coast and take it across the end of the pier and along the side of Loch Linnhe between the town and the water. That decision was to cause bitter recrimination in the years to come! The disused military fort had been purchased about 1867 by Mr Campbell of Monzie, and his will stipulated that the fort had to be given for the site of a station in the event of a railway reaching Fort William. When the Glasgow & North Western made its survey, it found the old barrack blocks occupied as dwelling houses, but considered that the station could be established without unduly disturbing the occupants.

Not all Highland landowners were hostile to the railway. One George Grant McKay of Glengloy commented: 'At present there is great destitution in some parts of the West Highlands, but there is none near where there is a railway. Destitution flies away from within a considerable distance of a railway.' McKay was in a position to know. He had made a practice of buying estates where railways were due to pass, and selling them after the railway had been established. In this way he bought an estate at Lairg for £50,000 and sold it for £100,000 when the railway came—on his own admission. The fact that the Glasgow & North Western was to cross his land near Loch Lochy troubled him not at all.

'THE DEER WILL NOT LIKE IT'

The contestants paraded witnesses ranging literally from peers to ploughmen before the Parliamentary committee, and day after day the glib London lawyers put the Highlanders through their paces. Discussions on fish, sheep and tourists—in that order—occupied many sessions. The G & NW barrister, Mr Littler, made much of the point that while Scotland's 425-mile eastern seaboard from Berwick to Thurso had 44 points from which fish could be carried by rail, the west coast, with 1,200 miles of seaboard from the Mull of Kintyre to Cape Wrath, had only two points. The west coast fishing industry was being stifled for lack of communication with the markets of the south. Fish landed at the small villages in the north-west coast was being carted over the rough mountain roads and down the glens that entered the Great Glen from the north to be distributed in Fort Augustus and Fort William. Such fish, claimed George Grant McKay of Glengloy, could be sent on the railway to Glasgow and the south. Mr Pope, counsel opposing the G & NW on behalf of the Highland, was sceptical.

'What! Would you cart herrings for 30 miles along a mountain road?' he asked McKay. 'Yes,' replied McKay. 'It is done every day. Hundreds of carts pass my door on their way to Fort Augustus.' 'They drive them 30 miles?' persisted the barrister. 'Yes. You seem to think it impossible.' 'Oh, no,' smirked Pope, 'I only laugh at the idea.' 'But you would not laugh if you knew more about it,' countered McKay.

Pope then changed his tactics in an effort to discredit the witness. 'You are going to be a railway director?' 'No, I am not,' said McKay. 'But you said so.' 'I never said anything of the kind.' 'You did not say you were going to be a director?' insisted Pope. 'No, I said if I were asked, but I have not been asked. I am only speaking the truth.' 'But I want to know how far it is based on intelligence. I see no disgrace in it,' continued the lawyer. 'You seem to think it is a good joke,' complained McKay. 'You don't like to be joked at?' 'Not when I am speaking in earnest on important matters.' 'Surely you cannot be in earnest about the herrings?' taunted Pope. 'Yes, I am. There will be no difficulty whatever in getting down the glens.'

'What about Fort Augustus?' inquired Pope, changing his tactics again. 'Is that a large place?' 'Yes.' 'Is there a monastery there?' 'Yes.' 'Is that the place where the gigantic Highlander used to be?' 'Yes. Gordon Cumming.' 'And it was he who used to charge half a crown for seeing his museum as the boat passed?' 'Yes, but if you think Fort Augustus is only a monastery and a museum you are mistaken.'

'Well,' conceded Pope, 'I agree with you in your description of the country—it is very pretty, but I don't think it is as pretty as Perth.'

'Were you ever in it?' asked McKay with exasperation.

'Oh, yes, I have shot all over it,' replied Pope airily.

The evidence continued at this level for hours on end. The opposition plan was to poke fun at the West Highlands and any West Highlanders who were naive enough to support the railway. Pope questioned McKay at length about some of the places the railway was to pass through. Talking about Dores he asked, 'Is that simply a public house?' 'It is a small village.' 'Take Tyndrum, which is marked on the railway map in bigger letters than Edinburgh——'

The committee room dissolved in laughter. When the merriment had subsided Pope went on: 'Is there only a public house there?' 'Yes,' admitted McKay. 'Then King's House, is that the place where the man murdered his wife, and was not found for a week because there was nobody about?' 'Yes. It is as wild a place as you could imagine,' confessed McKay. 'And that is the *valuable land* which Lord Breadalbane objects to the railway going through,' he added as a parting shot.

Fishermen were called to testify that west coast fish were very inferior to east coast fish. The implication was that money spent on a railway built to transport west coast fish would be money wasted. Mr Holmes, a fish dealer of Berwick on Tweed, was brought to Westminster to extoll the virtues of east coast fish. But in cross-examination Mr Littler drew from him the admission that much of the fish landed from east coast boats had been caught in western fishing grounds.

'What brought you here to give evidence against this Bill?' asked the railway lawyer. 'I don't know,' admitted Holmes. 'I was asked to give evidence.' 'You wanted a nice trip to London, perhaps?' 'It has been a nice trip.' 'I hope you will go back none the worse for it,' commented Littler.

There was endless talk about sheep. The Clearances had converted the country north of the Caledonian Canal into a series of sheep farms, and every year there was a mass movement of sheep from Sutherland and Ross and Cromarty down to the southern markets. Until recent times the sheep had been driven down a well-defined system of drove roads all the way to Glasgow, Edinburgh, Falkirk, Stirling and other towns in the south. With the coming of the railways, collecting-points had been established at Dalwhinnie on the Highland line and Tyndrum on the Callander & Oban, from whence the journey south was made by train. The G & NW planned to establish sheep stations in the Great Glen and so greatly shorten the distance covered by the drovers. The North Western's prospectus gave the sheep population north of the Great Glen as 470,000, but the Highland, which gave the impression of having been round counting the beasts, said there were 214,759 sheep precisely. Whatever the figure, the transport of sheep was a vital factor in the economy of any railway, existing or projected, and the Highland and Callander & Oban were determined not to lose the traffic to a rival.

Throughout the hearing much solicitude was shown for the animals of the West Highlands. A landowner in the Glencoe area who could not get to London in person sent this message to a friend who was a witness:

> I am quite in favour of the Glasgow and North Western Railway. The station at King's House would save our sheep the long walk to Tyndrum and place our glen in direct land communication with Glasgow which would greatly increase the value of my property. I shall be glad if you would say anything on my behalf before the Committee.

The impact of the railway on the deer population of the area was discussed in detail. When the Glasgow & North Western told the Parliamentary committee of its plans to erect special deer fencing where the line passed through the deer forests, an opposition spokesman objected, 'The deer will not like it.' Lord Abinger, who was generally favourable towards the railway and whose territory straddled the proposed line in Lochaber, suggested that the line should be unfenced in the deer forests. But Walron Smith said that he could provide a fence that the deer would get over with ease. Lord Abinger confessed: 'I have had a rare rough time of it with Lady Abinger and some others about the railway.' For some reason the ladies of the West Highlands, like the deer, did not like the railway.

When the fish and the sheep had been disposed of, talk in the committee room turned to tourists. Ever since Queen Victoria had made her famous tour of the Highlands in 1848, tourism had brought welcome revenue to the area. The all-water 'Royal Route' took its patrons in stages from Glasgow to Inverness by way of the Firth of Clyde, the Crinan Canal, the Firth of Lorne, Loch Linnhe and the Caledonian Canal. For those who could spare the time and expense involved it was a magnificent trip, but the Royal Route had its limitations. The Highland Railway had opened Inverness to a new class of tourist, and the North Western proposed to do the same for the West Highlands. The Caledonian Canal Commissioners feared that once a railway was built alongside the canal the revenue they derived from Royal Route steamers would dwindle.

The lawyer appearing for the canal was at pains to point out that the railway would serve the communities on the south side of Loch Ness only and that should the steamers be driven out of business the people on the north side of Loch Ness would lose their transport. The railway countered this accusation by presenting its plan to connect the stations on Loch Ness side with the communities across the loch by means of ferries. The canal spokesman was of the opinion that 'it would be impossible to have a ferry across the loch to the railway stations because Loch Ness is very stormy. The steamers go up and down the loch easily, but going across they would meet a very stormy sea.'

As the spring days of 1883 passed, the long-drawn-out arguments for and against the railway unfolded. In the effort to defeat it, the Highland went to the trouble and expense of employing D. M. Crouch, C.E., of Crouch & Hogg, Glasgow, to re-survey the whole of the North Western's route and submit plans to it. The Highland then came to the committee with the accusation that the North Western had underestimated the difficulties and costs of construction. Crouch put the overall cost of the line at £2,118,000, which was £645,000 more than Walron Smith's estimate.

It had been the hope of the Glasgow & North Western promoters that in the course of the hearing they would be able to announce a North British—North Western agreement over the financing and working of the line; meetings with North British officers were taking place in the background. But then came a shock. The North British looked askance at the North Western's plan to urbanize and develop the territory within 30 miles of Glasgow—with the consequent threat to existing or planned North British residential branches—and withdrew support from the North Western. But the North British had no sooner withdrawn than the Glasgow & South Western Railway offered the G & NW running powers over the City of Glasgow Union Railway into St Enoch, the G & SW terminus in Glasgow, in return for certain running powers over the North Western. In its letter to the North Western, the South Western described St Enoch as 'the best possible home that could be provided'.

The two-month Parliamentary hearing ended on 31 May, and the committee room was cleared to allow the members to debate the case and reach a conclusion. Not ten minutes later someone came rushing to Littler, who was relaxing in a lounge in the House of Commons, with the news that the railway case was lost. Dumbfounded, the barrister hurried back to the committee room to find the members preparing to leave. They had taken only five minutes to decide that there wasn't enough traffic to warrant another railway in the Highlands. The Highland Railway's plea had been upheld.

Then followed a dramatic scene when Littler pleaded to be allowed to speak. The committee, impatient after listening for weeks on end to dissertations on herrings and sheep, urged the lawyer to say what he had to say and be gone. But Littler insisted that his argument was of the highest importance, and he asked time to prepare a speech for presentation the following day, a Saturday. Reluctantly, the committee agreed to meet then.

But Littler was only playing for time. On the Saturday morning he made a last desperate bid to retrieve something from the wreck. He pointed out that Fort William was eager for a railway, and that the G & NW would be willing to content itself with a line from Fort William down through Tyndrum to Ardlui and was prepared to abandon the rest of the scheme. 'That would give Fort William and the district their communication with the outer world,' explained Littler,

> and would form a connection with the Callander and Oban Railway to which in these circumstances it would form a feeder rather than a system which would detract from the traffic of that railway. We should, if the Committee were willing, be content to accept that part of the scheme, and I may say it is a part which in no way affects the Highland company, on whose opposition the scheme has failed.

The committee was unsympathetic. 'I think,' said the chairman, 'it would be very much more regular if such a line was applied for in another session of Parliament.'

'Very good, Sir, and I say no more,' replied Littler.

Thus ended the story of the Glasgow & North Western. It would have been a magnificent railway. Its winding course up Loch Lomond would have presented superb views, the descent of Glencoe would have been something without parallel on Britain's railways, and the high-speed sweep along the water-level causeway on Loch Ness side would have made a thrilling approach to Inverness. The station names would have looked exciting on a timetable: Rowardenan, Inversnaid, Inveroran, King's House, Pap of Glencoe, Glencoe Bridge, Onich, Falls of Foyers. What would have happened if the G & SW and not the North British had worked and perhaps eventually absorbed the North Western makes fascinating speculation. The Glasgow & South Western would have stretched all the way from Stranraer to Inverness skirting miles of glorious coastline both north and south of the Clyde. What would have been the name of that grand railway? Scottish Great Western?

Such dreams evaporated on that Saturday morning in June when the doors of the committee room finally closed and the contestants strolled out into the London streets. Victor and vanquished alike went back to Scotland a lot lighter in the pocket. But the London lawyers made a fat killing.

EARLY DAYS

(8) *Lord Abinger cutting the first sod*

(9) *The ceremonial arrival of the first train at Fort William*

(10) *Fort William station, interior*

WEST HIGHLAND STATIONS

(11) *Whistlefield*
(12) *Ardlui*

WEST HIGHLAND BRIDGES

(13) *Glen Falloch viaduct with Ben More, 3,843 ft, in distance*

(14) *Craigenarden viaduct, Loch Lomond*

IN GLEN FALLOCH

(15) *A Class 5 heads a Glasgow—Mallaig train at the entrance to Glen Falloch*

Chapter 3

Plans Win Through

'ANOTHER WEST HIGHLAND SCHEME!'

In its issue of 19 January 1889 *The Railway Times* printed a trenchant editorial under the above heading:

> As a field for the extension of railway enterprise we fail to understand the special fascination which the Western Highland districts seem to possess for the promoter. That portion of Scotland is certainly not well supplied with railway communication, and the fact that there are people living 50 miles from a railway might well be regarded as evidence of necessity, but the check to development which has allowed this condition of things to prevail—the small prospect of securing sufficient traffic to pay—exists with as much force now as heretofore, and the introduction of renewed efforts in that direction might well give rise to a suspicion that other influences than the power of the country to furnish remunerative traffic have operated on the minds of those who have promoted the Bill.

In other words the North British was making another attempt to establish itself in the West Highlands. In spite of the fears and strictures of *The Railway Times* the latest West Highland scheme was the one that succeeded.

Four years separated the failure of the Glasgow & North Western Railway and the launching of the West Highland Railway, and in those four years the social and political climate had changed. The publicity given to the findings of the Crofters' Commission had smoothed the way for the promoters of the West Highland. The members of the Commission were unequivocal in their insistence that lack of transport was at the root of the West Highland troubles. Parliament, and even some of the hostile landowners, realized that something *must* be done.

The West Highland Railway was conceived in a mail coach rumbling along the rough road from Fort William to Kingussie one morning in the mid-80s. In those days the people of Lochaber had to travel 50 miles to Kingussie on the Highland Railway to reach a railhead. The mail coach left Fort William every weekday at 6 a.m. and did not reach Kingussie until 12.20 p.m. The fares were 13s 6d second class and 16s 6d first class, plus 1s driver's fee in each class. A Mr Boyd of Fort William was a passenger in the coach that morning. Boyd had been very disappointed over the recent failure of the G & NW and as the Kingussie coach made its slow way eastward he reflected on the handicaps of life in rail-less Lochaber.

'It was at Kingussie,' he afterwards said,

> that I first thought of doing all that lay in my power to get a railway to Fort William. I had been on a journey to Banffshire and was the only passenger by coach that morning. On going to the hotel at Kingussie I was surprised to find *The Scotsman* for that day already there. For a moment I thought of Fort William and Lochaber and said to myself, 'Well, it may be 5 o'clock, it may be 8 o'clock before the letters and papers reach Fort William, and if it is stormy they may not arrive until the following day.' In soliloquising thus I thought of the backwardness of Lochaber, how far behind Kingussie, Inverness and Oban it was, and I might tell you frankly that when I thought of these things I wept.

On his return to Lochaber, Boyd got in touch with George Malcolm, the factor of Invergloy, and propounded his scheme. This time there was to be no attempt to reach Inverness; the new railway was to link Lochaber with the south and give an outlet to the western sea. Malcolm shared Boyd's enthusiasm, and the two men obtained the moral and financial support of local landowners. According to Boyd the Caledonian was invited to build the railway, but would have nothing to do with it. The North British, when sounded, showed a lively interest. *The Scotsman* said of the venture:

> We have here an endeavour to mark an era in the development of the Highlands. Access to markets has heretofore been deemed the one thing needful to raise into activity our island populations who live near seas teeming with fish. The people of these districts—whether the lairds, the tenants or the crofters—are too poor to provide capital for such works, and the return in dividend is so doubtful (though perhaps not hopeless) that the subscription lists might be viewed askance on the Stock Exchanges.

The West Highland Railway, like its predecessor, was backed by the North British who proposed to operate it, but in many other ways it differed from the Glasgow & North Western. The West Highland was to leave the existing North British coastal line to Helensburgh at Craigendoran, and pass by the Gareloch and Loch Long and Loch Lomond to Ardlui—a route not hitherto considered by the railway promoters. At Ardlui the line was to join the proposed route of the G & NW, but the West Highland was to keep to the west side of Glen Falloch whereas the North Western had been planned to climb up the east wall of the glen.

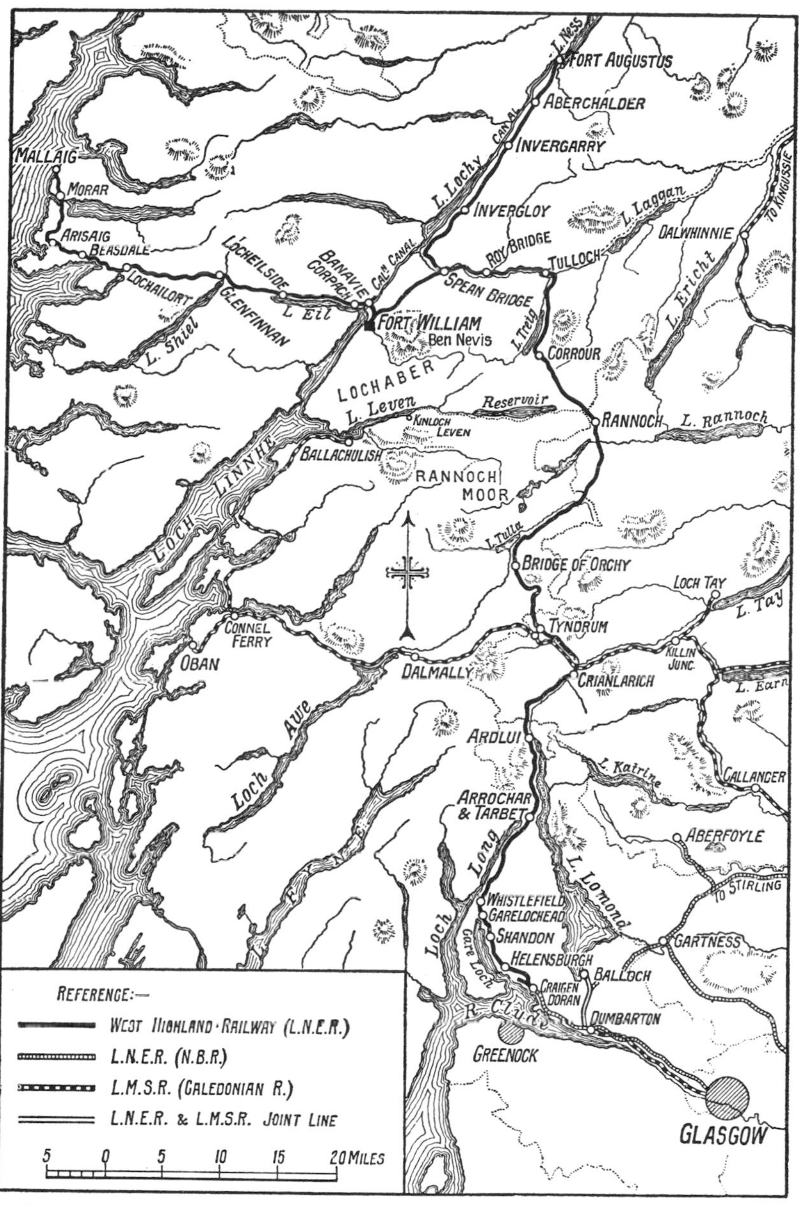
L. Ness
FORT AUGUSTUS
ABERCHALDER
INVERGARRY
CANAL
L. Lochy
INVERGLOY
L. Laggan
DALWHINNIE
TO KINGUSSIE
MALLAIG
MORAR
ARISAIG
BEASDALE
LOCHAILORT
LOCHEILSIDE
GLENFINNAN
BANAVIE
CORPACH
CALn CANAL
ROY BRIDGE
TULLOCH
SPEAN BRIDGE
L. Eil
L. Shiel
FORT WILLIAM
Ben Nevis
L. Treig
L. Ericht
CORROUR
LOCHABER
L. Leven
Reservoir
KINLOCH LEVEN
RANNOCH
L. Rannoch
BALLACHULISH
RANNOCH MOOR
LOCH LINNHE
L. Tulla
BRIDGE OF ORCHY
LOCH TAY
L. Tay
CONNEL FERRY
OBAN
TYNDRUM
KILLIN JUNC.
DALMALLY
CRIANLARICH
L. Earn
Loch Awe
ARDLUI
L. Katrine
CALLANDER
ARROCHAR & TARBET
Loch Long
ABERFOYLE
L. Lomond
TO STIRLING
WHISTLEFIELD
GARELOCHEAD
Gare Loch
SHANDON
GARTNESS
HELENSBURGH
BALLOCH
CRAIGENDORAN
R. Clyde
DUMBARTON
GREENOCK
GLASGOW
REFERENCE:—
WEST HIGHLAND·RAILWAY (L.N.E.R.)
L.N.E.R. (N.B.R.)
L.M.S.R. (CALEDONIAN R.)
L.N.E.R. & L.M.S.R. JOINT LINE
5 0 5 10 15 20 MILES

From Crianlarich the West Highland was to follow the route of the North Western up Strathfillan to Bridge of Orchy, but instead of continuing westwards over the Black Mount and down Glencoe to the coast, the West Highland was to strike north through 30 miles of elevated, depopulated country which included the Moor of Rannoch, and drop down Loch Treigside into the heart of Lochaber. It was then to thread its way through the gorges of the Spean and enter Fort William from the east. The last stage of the route was round the end of Loch Eil and on to Roshven on the coast where a terminal and pier were to be built to service the island steamers and the fishing fleets. There was no mention of a foray in the direction of Inverness.

In the 100 miles of route between the Firth of Clyde and Fort William there were only five main proprietors—the Colquhoun Trustees, the Marquess of Breadalbane, Sir Robert Menzies, Sir John Stirling Maxwell and William Frederick Scarlett, Baron Abinger. All of them, if not actually connected with the railway, at least assented to its passage. Lord Abinger became the first chairman, and several clan chiefs joined him on the board, among them Cameron of Lochiel, Mackintosh of Mackintosh and Colquhoun of Luss.

It was a different story north and west of Fort William. Feudal landowners, still dedicated to the idea of keeping people out of their domains, opposed the scheme with such tenacity that the West Highland Railway was forced to abandon the extension to Roshven, and with it the hope of terminating at a vital fishing port. In fairness to the Highlanders, some Lowlanders were the bitterest opponents of the railway. Professor Blackburn, Emeritus Professor of Mathematics at the University of Glasgow, owned 60,000 acres at Roshven and the new harbour was to take shape under the windows of his mansion house. 'The whole thing is abominable,' he said. He was supported in his protest by his eminent colleague at Glasgow University, Sir William Thomson, Professor of Natural Philosophy, who told of the difficulty he had of getting into Roshven in his yacht. The committee considering the bill seemed to place more faith in Sir William's words than in the Admiralty sailing charts which described Roshven as the best harbour on the west coast of Scotland.

LOST ON RANNOCH MOOR

On the evening of 29 January 1889 seven gentlemen gathered in the hotel at Spean Bridge. On the following day they were to set

(A) *BR Class 5 4-6-0 No 73077 and K2/2 2-6-0 No 61792 head a Fort William to Glasgow train around the horseshoe curve at Tyndrum in March 1956*

67474

out on a walk that was to take them across the Moor of Rannoch to Inveroran nearly 40 miles to the south. It was a walk that was to become a West Highland legend.

The party consisted of three men from the Glasgow firm of civil engineers, Formans & McCall—Charles Forman himself, James Bulloch his chief engineer and a young assistant engineer, J. E. Harrison—with Robert (later Sir Robert) McAlpine, head of the contracting firm of Robert McAlpine & Sons, John Bett, the 60-year-old factor of the Breadalbane Estates, Major Martin of Kilmartin, factor of the Poltalloch Estates, and N. B. McKenzie, solicitor, of Fort William, the local agent for the West Highland Railway bill. Of the seven, only James Bulloch had been across Rannoch Moor before. The purpose of the expedition was to obtain additional information about the route across the Moor and in particular to meet Sir Robert Menzies of Rannoch Lodge to discuss some minor deviations where the line passed through his land. It was an intrepid, not to say foolhardy, journey for such an odd assortment of men in the depths of winter.

At daybreak on 30 January the party left Spean Bridge by coach. It was a grey, cold morning with lowering clouds and a threat of sleet. By mid-morning they reached Inverlair Lodge where—after having their last substantial meal for two days—they set off on foot on a track that led 2½ miles to the north end of Loch Treig. The shores of Loch Treig were trackless and Lord Abinger had arranged that a boatman would meet the party and row them 6 miles up the loch to its southern end where they would be given food and shelter for the night at his shooting lodge, Craig-uaine-ach. On the following day they were to cross the Moor of Rannoch.

The expedition must have presented an incongruous sight as its members walked in single file along the mountain-girt track in the gathering darkness of the January afternoon. Old John Bett wore his high-sided felt hat and carried his umbrella. McKenzie, tall, polished and dignified as became a gentleman of his profession, also carried his umbrella. Forman, who was not too robust—he was to die later of consumption—must have had qualms about the venture, but McAlpine, who was described as 'stout, full-blooded and loquacious', was in high spirits.

From the outset things went wrong. A guide whom Lord Abinger had sent to conduct the party along the track to Loch Treig failed to turn up. When the men reached the loch they were well behind schedule and there was no sign of either boat or boatman. Eventually they found a decrepit boathouse which they proceeded to

(B) *Former North British Railway Class C15 4-4-2T No 67474 leaves the siding at Arrochar & Tarbet to back into the platform with the stock for the local service to Craigendoran. Taken in May 1959, the service was withdrawn in 1964*

break down. The noise of their activities brought an irate Highlander on the scene, but when they explained who they were the Highlander revealed that he was the boatman and that the boat was hidden in bushes by the lochside. An ancient tarred craft was duly launched and all eight men squeezed into it and set sail up the now dark and stormy loch. Very soon night enveloped the party and squalls of sleet assaulted them. One can picture that strangest of railway ménages sailing up the loch in the darkness, the younger members helping with the rowing, others using their boots to bail out the water that constantly seeped into the vessel, and the solicitor and the aged land agent sheltering as best they could under their umbrellas.

The boat was kept close into the eastern shore. Once when they went to investigate a light they grounded on a patch of gravel. There was a great deal of shouting and arguing and the commotion aroused two lochside gamekeepers who came out in their own boat, rescued the railway party, and conducted them to Lord Abinger's shooting lodge, which they reached about midnight, hungry, wet and cold. Another disappointment awaited them. A messenger who had been dispatched by a mountain track to warn the lodge-keeper of the party's approach had not appeared, and neither food nor beds were ready. However, the keeper provided a meal of sorts and produced blankets under which the travellers huddled, listening to the beat of the rain and hail on the roof.

By the morning a strong wind was driving the rain and sleet across the loch. In these conditions the seven men set off to climb a track that was to ascend in 3 miles to a height of 1,300 ft and was to take them to the northern edge of the Moor of Rannoch. Ahead of them stretched 23 miles of utterly desolate, trackless, stormswept waste. The keeper took them to the end of the track and pointed out the direction they had to take. Then he went back, no doubt thankfully, to the shelter of the lodge.

For hour after hour the seven men squelched through the morass, jumping from tuft to tuft to escape the worst of the bog. Rain alternated with sleet squalls. It was slow, exhausting work. The incredible thing was that they were heading for a business meeting due to be held in the middle of the wilderness about noon. Sir Robert Menzies had arranged to come out from Rannoch Lodge, some 4 miles to the east of the line of the proposed railway, and meet them on the north bank of the River Gauer. Guided by James Bulloch, the party came within sight of the Gauer after four hours of trudging across the Moor, and the figure of a man could be seen

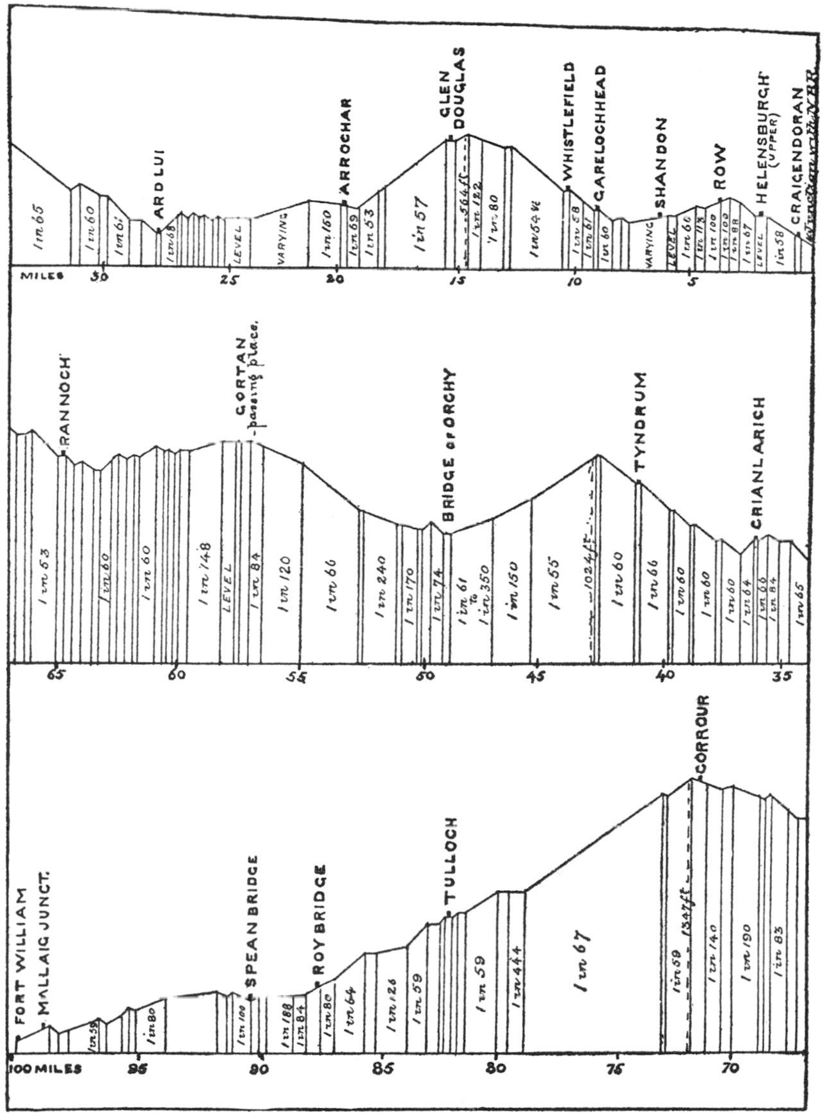
ARDLUI
ARROCHAR
GLEN DOUGLAS
WHISTLEFIELD
GARELOCHHEAD
SHANDON
ROW
HELENSBURGH (UPPER)
CRAIGENDORAN
RANNOCH
GORTAN -passing place.
BRIDGE of ORCHY
TYNDRUM
CRIANLARICH
FORT WILLIAM
MALLAIG JUNCT.
SPEAN BRIDGE
ROY BRIDGE
TULLOCH
CORROUR
MILES
100 MILES

standing by the river. But when they reached the spot they found that he was Menzies' head keeper, who invited them to go with him to Rannoch Lodge for the night. About three hours of daylight remained; the nearest cottage was 8 miles away and their ultimate destination was still 14 miles distant. They decided to carry on.

It did not take them long to realize that they had made a mistake, but it was too late to turn back. They had passed the point of no return. As the going became rougher the men straggled across the Moor in ones and twos seeking the best footholds. When dusk fell in the early afternoon they could no longer distinguish the relatively dry spots and they plunged and floundered in the bog, sometimes falling full length. Bett and McKenzie became tired and dispirited, and the younger men helped them by carrying their kit. At length Bett collapsed, protesting that he could go no further. Major Martin and young Harrison stayed with him and did what they could to comfort him, improvising a tent using his umbrella. Forman and McKenzie stumbled on, but very soon they had to admit exhaustion and sought shelter behind a large boulder. McAlpine, although he did not know the Moor and had little sense of direction, decided to carry on alone in the hope of reaching Inveroran, where he could get help for the others. Bulloch set off independently, trusting that his limited knowledge of the Moor would enable him to locate the cottage at Gorton where he had called when making a survey of the line.

Bulloch had been wandering through the darkness for several hours when he tripped over a fence and fell so heavily that he lay stunned on the ground for four hours. When he regained consciousness he realized that fences were scarce on Rannoch Moor and that this one must lead somewhere. He groped his way along it until he found himself on a track. He followed the track, and out of the darkness loomed the Gorton cottage.

Meanwhile, far out on the Moor, Bett had lapsed into unconsciousness. Martin and the young engineer tried to keep warm by running round in circles, and once during the process they lost Bett. When they found him again they tied a handkerchief to his protecting umbrella so that it would be easily recognizable in the dark.

From time to time Martin and Harrison lit matches to see the time on their watches. Then, about 2.30 in the morning, they saw lights bobbing on the Moor and heard the distant bark of dogs. Matches were lit, this time as flares. Eventually two men appeared and explained that they were shepherds from Gorton cottage. They had been roused by Bulloch and told of the plight of the party.

CRIANLARICH IN THE THIRTIES

(16) *A Glen taking water on a wintry March day in 1930*

(17) *Morning break in the mid-thirties. The train is composed entirely of North British stock*

(18) *Crianlarich station in 1937. The station buildings were burned down on 30 March 1962*

GORTON

(19) *Trains crossing in* LNE *days. Note the railway carriage school*
(20) *January* 1963

Shouts in the distance revealed the whereabouts of Forman and McKenzie, and soon the shepherds had gathered the remaining five members of the party together and guided them towards safety. John Bett, still semi-conscious, had to be half carried, half dragged. The rescuers knew of a small hut 2 miles away, and not without difficulty they found it. Inside was a rusty stove, with a heap of wet peats. Some dry peats were extracted from the centre of the heap and the shepherds soon had a fire roaring with such purpose that the entire stove and chimney glowed red-hot. Steam from the clinging wet clothes of the refugees mingling with the acrid fumes of peat reek filled the hut.

Once they had made their guests comfortable the shepherds returned to their cottage where they had left the sleeping Bulloch. By daybreak they were back at the hut with supplies of hot food and drink. By 10.30 the railway party had revived sufficiently to make the journey to Gorton, which they reached about mid-day. They were glad to find Bulloch safe and well, but they were anxious about McAlpine about whom nothing had been heard. Almost at once news was received that he was safe in a cottage three miles down the valley of the Tulla Water. He had reached the place early in the morning, hatless, soaking wet and covered in mud after having spent 14 hours alone on the Moor.

John Bett was put on a cart and the party set off to cover the remaining 8 or 9 miles to Inveroran. They picked up McAlpine on the way, and that evening all were made welcome by the host of Inveroran Inn. As they slept, a blizzard broke over the West Highlands and next morning as they made their way down to Tyndrum station on the Callander & Oban Railway they had to climb over deep snowdrifts. If the blizzard had come 24 hours earlier the outcome of the expedition might have been tragically different.

OPPOSITION

The usual opposition to the West Highland bill came from the now traditional quarters. The Highland Railway fearing (rightly) that the West Highland would at some future date be used as a jumping-off point for a renewed assault on Inverness fought determinedly. But its case had no substance. As described in the bill, the West Highland's nearest approach to the Highland was at Inverlair and that was 32 miles away from Highland metals. There was no mention (on paper) of any intention of taking the line on to Inverness.

The Caledonian Railway for its part considered that it had a potentially better route from Glasgow to Fort William and, moreover, it was already two-thirds built. The Callander & Oban reached the west coast at Connel Ferry. The Caledonian proposed to build a line up the coast through Ballachulish to Fort William, entering the town from the south as the G & NW would have done. The Caledonian's case was that it could complete the Glasgow—Fort William link at a third of the cost and in a third of the time needed for the West Highland. It undertook, too, to build the line the moment the West Highland bill was thrown out of Parliament. It further argued, with justification, that the Appin coast was well populated (by West Highland standards) whereas the Moor of Rannoch was desolate and barren. The Caledonian made much of the wisdom (or lack of it) of attempting to cross Rannoch Moor by rail. The story of the lost survey party got around, the counsel for the Caledonian questioning Forman pointedly about it. Forman, telling a diplomatic lie, denied that the episode had taken place. But his young assistant, Harrison, afterwards wrote that the story was 'guaranteed and free from varnish'.

There was no doubt that the West Highland offered the most direct route to Lochaber. Moreover, it was the one that the people of Lochaber wanted. In April 1889 the preamble to the bill was proved. G. B. Weiland, the secretary of the North British, was also secretary of the West Highland, but the North British took immediate steps to strengthen its position by replacing Lord Abinger as West Highland chairman with its own chairman, the Marquess of Tweeddale. It also undertook to contribute £150,000 towards the cost of construction of the line and to guarantee 3½ per cent to the holders of the £800,000 of West Highland stock. It further agreed to staff and work the line when it was ready. 'This is really a North British scheme propounded as an attack on Caledonian territory,' said *The Railway Times* when these terms were announced. The journal was full of foreboding for the future of the enterprise, and described it as

> owing more to misdirected ambition than to its own merits. We do not say, if the shareholders of the North British through their directors express their willingness to throw away their money into a scheme from which they are likely to derive little if any benefit, that they should be prevented from so doing; but we doubt much whether they have not like many others before them, been deceived by over-coloured pictures.

JUBILATION

A very different atmosphere prevailed in Fort William. When news of the passing of the preamble reached the town the population was jubilant. There were processions and music in the streets, and after nightfall bonfires were lit on the heights commanding the town. Each successive phase of the bill's passage through Parliament was greeted with enthusiasm.

When the bill passed its third reading in the Commons on 3 July 1889 the news reached the town shortly after 5 o'clock, and the town crier was sent round the streets to announce the glad tidings. Fort William decided on a night of rejoicing. The centrepiece of the festivities was to be a torchlight procession through the town, but in those northern latitudes there was still a trace of daylight left at 11 p.m. It was, therefore, decided to delay the start of the procession until 10.30. Meanwhile, hotels and villas were decorated and lit up, and the townsfolk gathered together all the fireworks they could find. By 10 o'clock the crowds were gathering at the prescribed collecting point. What happened after that was described in the local paper.

> Punctually at 10.30 p.m. a torchlight procession started from Captain Peter Cameron's monument in Fassifern Road and marching to the strains of the bagpipes by Bank Street it proceeded along the High Street to the West End of the town. Everywhere along the route the people lined the streets and the windows and vigorously cheered the processionists whose numbers rapidly increased as they moved along. The effect was extremely picturesque. The night was calm, the light was ''tween the gloamin' and the mirk' and Loch Linnhe lay placid as an inland lake. Coloured Roman lights shot up at intervals from among the torches and rockets flashed brilliantly across the sky. The distant report of the ships' guns on the Corpach side of the loch heightened the effect of a display which was really very fine.

The people gathered on the foreshore near the pier. There were speeches galore. 'This is a profound night for Lochaber and Fort William,' declared one speaker, and he was roundly cheered. More rockets were fired off and the merry evening ended with a 'liberal distribution of refreshments'. The railway was coming to Lochaber.

The Caledonian intruded with a parting shot. Its protégé the Callander & Oban promoted a branch line down Glen Falloch from Crianlarich to Ardlui 'to obviate the present coach journey'. The C & O line was to take the eastern side of the glen on what was substantially the route of the G & NW, and the cost was estimated at £50,000.

There was more to this move than met the eye. The hitherto privately-owned Loch Lomond steamers had just passed into North British control. The North British not only had the steamers, but had rail access to the south end of Loch Lomond at Balloch, and the new West Highland Railway would give it access to the northern reaches of the loch. The Caledonian saw itself being excluded from one of Scotland's most lucrative tourist assets by its keenest rival. Already the Caledonian was bidding for a stake in the Loch Lomond traffic by seeking rail access and a pier of its own at the south end of the loch, and the Crianlarich—Ardlui branch was intended to give it a railway-served pier at the north end. The preamble to the bill was not proved, and the absurdity of having two railways serving the same depopulated valley was avoided.

CHAPTER 4

Construction of the Line

THE CONTRACTORS

The engineers of the West Highland were Formans & McCall of Glasgow, a firm founded in 1828 which had been responsible for some of the earliest Scottish railways. The title was adopted when Charles Forman, son of the Scots-Canadian founder, became a partner. The contractors were Lucas & Aird, a famous Westminster firm with strong Scottish connections. The dominant figure was John Aird, a Member of Parliament, whose crofter father had emigrated from the Highlands to London early in the 19th century to found and develop a contracting business with international ramifications. John Aird and Charles Forman were the key figures in the construction of the West Highland Railway.

Charles de Neuville Forman deserves to be better remembered as a railway engineer. He was born on 10 August 1852 and died on 2 February 1901. During his 48 years he signed his name to the plans of many important railways and he put more railway mileage on the map of Western Scotland than any other railway engineer. Among his projects were the intricate Glasgow Central Railway built under the streets of the city, the Lanarkshire & Ayrshire Railway, the line from Glasgow to Clydebank *via* Yoker, and the Strathendrick & Aberfoyle Railway. He took time off from the West of Scotland to engineer the Foxdale Railway in the Isle of Man, and in a moment of aberration he built a *coach road*: it was the exciting one from Aberfoyle over the hills to the Trossachs. Among projects of his that did not come off were the Glasgow, Berwick & Newcastle direct railway and the Fort Augustus to Inverness railway.

On 23 October 1889 a party of railway and contractors' men went to a spot outside Fort William opposite the Glen Nevis distillery. There, in the presence of at least half the populace (all the shops had been closed at noon), John Aird handed Lord Abinger the silver spade with which he dug the first sod. That was the end of ceremonial for the time being; the gruelling task of building the West Highland began, and it was to continue for five years.

Lucas & Aird's men must have felt at home with the West Highland contract. The firm had specialized in colonial railways, and the West Highland had many of the characteristics of a colonial-type railway. In view of the sparse traffic likely to be offered the directors wanted it built as cheaply as possible; it was intended to carry light loads at moderate speeds. The territory which the contractors set out to master was as tough as any they had encountered overseas. There were passes over 1,000 ft above sea level through which the railway had to be led. There were innumerable gorges to be spanned, rivers to be bridged and miles of boggy moor to be crossed.

The inaccessibility of the country was its most daunting feature. First of all the great army of navvies required for large-scale civil engineering enterprises in the days before universal power tools and earth moving machinery had to be assembled and camps established for them and their equipment in remote places. It was perhaps unfortunate that the contract started at the onset of winter, when nights were long and the weather restricted use of the limited daylight.

For administrative purposes the work was divided into Railway No. 1 from Craigendoran to Crianlarich and Railway No. 2 from Crianlarich to Fort William. Construction began at five points. The southernmost camp was at Craigendoran with easy access both by rail and sea. Arrochar at the head of Loch Long was the site of the second camp, and the third was at Inveruglas on Loch Lomondside, 3 miles south of Ardlui. A pier was built at the lochside to which heavy materials were brought in boats and barges. A smaller pier at Ardlui was used to accommodate light materials and personnel. Crianlarich was the location of the next camp, served by the Callander & Oban line. The fifth camp was on the shore of Loch Linnhe at Fort William. Work over the entire route was in charge of G. M. Tarry of Lucas & Aird. Railway No. 1 was divided into three sub-sections, each with its own resident engineer, inspectors and labour force. The sections were: 1, Craigendoran to milepost 12; 2, milepost 12 to milepost 24; 3, milepost 24 to Crianlarich.

Railway No. 2 was divided into two, Crianlarich to Gorton and Gorton to Fort William. On Railway No. 1 no point was more than 8 miles from a base camp, but on Railway No. 2 at first there was no permanent camp between Crianlarich and Fort William. At an early stage a large base camp was established at Inveroran, the northernmost point reached by the coach road. (This was also known as Achallader Camp.) All the camps were linked to headquarters at Helensburgh by private telephone so that a close check could be kept on progress.

Among the materials ordered for delivery by sea at Helensburgh and Fort William and by rail to Tyndrum were

12,000	tons of 75 pound steel rails at	£6.5.0	per ton
5,500	tons of chairs	£4	per ton
450	tons of spikes	£8	per ton
450	tons of fish plates	£7.17.6	per ton
110	tons of fish bolts and nuts	£11	per ton
30,000	Scots fir sleepers at 2s 5d each		
51,000	Scots fir sleepers at 2s 6d each		

THE NAVVIES

The itinerant Irish navvies who flocked to the building of the West Highland were a rough, motley crew. They did not take well to the lonely, isolated camps, and many of them left after a few weeks for the lusher pastures of Lancashire where the Manchester Ship Canal was being cut. With the onset of winter Lucas & Aird's labour troubles increased.

The navvies' pay varied according to the type of work they did and where they did it. South of Ardlui the average weekly wage was 15s, north of Ardlui it was 21s. Part of it was paid in basic foodstuffs, which the navvies cooked for themselves. This apparently was an attempt to prevent them from spending all their money on liquid sustenance. First aid posts staffed by permanent nurses were set up at all the camps, and the men contributed a small amount each week to an insurance fund which entitled them to disablement benefit if they were injured on the site.

Remembering that the West Highland railway was intended to bring prosperity to the Highlanders, local clan chiefs and public men pressed the contractor to employ Highland labour. But there were few able-bodied men available along the route, and men in the more remote parts and in the Western Isles were too poor to pay their fares to the sites. Again, the Highlanders were not accustomed to working in large organized groups. Nevertheless, Lucas & Aird advertised for Highland labour, and the following is a typical announcement.

> In order to afford work for Highlanders, and acting on the suggestion of Maclaine of Lochbuie, Messrs Lucas & Aird, Contractors for the

> West Highland Railway, desire again to state that they are prepared to employ at piecework or day's wages a large number of competent rock men or labourers. Comfortable hutting is provided, but Messrs Lucas & Aird will gladly give every facility for those who prefer it to erect Turf Dwellings. Every information can be obtained by application to the Head Office at Helensburgh or the following Agents . . .

In order to attract more Highlanders, Lucas & Aird then offered to pay the fares of applicants who were destitute, and in a short time succeeded in building up a considerable force. A report on recruitment sent by the contractors to Maclaine of Lochbuie on 30 June 1890 throws light on the quality and behaviour of the Highland railway navvy.

Helensburgh and Arrochar Section
Passages paid 34, no passages paid 46; total 80.
Appear contented to stay, work steadily and compare very favourably with other labourers. A large proportion are good rock quarriers, and none as yet has given any trouble.

Inverarnan Section
Passages paid 33, no passages paid 28; total 61.
Sixty-seven arrived all together, but 6 have left during the month. Furnish good and steady labour, useful with the shovel, but only a few on this section are good rockmen. As a class they are very steady.

Tyndrum Section
Passages paid 42, no passages paid 43; total 85.
There are some youths and elderly men, but the great proportion are strong, hard-working men who quite hold their own with the labourers from the South. They are very steady, and can be depended on for being at their work all through the week if the weather is favourable.

Fort William Section
Passages paid 69, no passages paid 5; total 74.
Good labourers, many of them excellent rockmen. They are frugal, living mostly on oatmeal, and saving all the money they can.
Total of men employed on above, 300.

That the qualities of the Highland navvies were appreciated beyond their homeland was shown when railway enterprises in other parts of the country began to compete with Lucas & Aird for their services. A rival advertisement in *The Oban Times* ran:

> Forfar and Brechin Railway. Wanted. Good Navvies. Comfortable quarters. Subs daily.

'Subs daily' meant that the navvies could draw their weekly wage in daily instalments.

To their credit the civil population of the West Highlands took the welfare of the temporary navvy invasion very much to heart. Churches, clubs, councils and groups of many kinds co-operated to make life easier for the railway builders. The Rev Mr Elder, minister of Tarbet, built a reading room and canteen on the church glebe and undertook to provide coffee at any hour of the day. In Fort William the Rev Canon MacColl established a reading and recreation room and headed the committee of townsfolk delegated to run it. One of the rules barred the entry of 'intoxicated or swearing men'. Even amid the lonely wastes of Achallader Camp, a group of public-spirited enthusiasts presided over by the Marquess of Breadalbane formed the Blackmount Literary Association, which had as its object 'the intellectual improvement of the members and to excite a spirit of inquiry combined with healthy amusement among men employed upon the West Highland Railway during the winter season'. A concert given by the Blackmount Literary Association was thus described in *The Oban Times*:

> The first part of the programme consisted of choice selections on the bagpipes by Mr. D. MacLachlan, Argyll and Sutherland Highlanders, whose steady playing evinced his proficiency, while Mr. Cropper, Inverarnan, led the second part with pianoforte selections of no mean order, and played the accompaniment to the vocalists, after which a service of fruit took place.

Not quite traditional navvy fare!

The Highland Temperance League's agent went round the camps on pay days and hard on his heels was the representative of the Post Office Savings Bank. The Home Mission of the Free Church of Scotland sent missionaries. One of these reported:

> In prosecuting the more direct mission work among them (the navvies) it is found necessary to visit the men in their respective huts on the Sabbath, and to conduct services in such—an undertaking which, while it involves considerable effort on the part of the visitor, is found to be productive of encouraging results. While the men do not care to come out to services in a church, or even in a hall, they are usually ready to respond to the invitation to join in one conducted in their own temporary dwelling. But for such attentions on the part of those who seek them out the men would be almost destitute of the means of grace.

PROGRESS

As the railway progressed the labour force rose to 5,000. Month after month the navvies pushed the lengthening permanent way round the mountainsides and through the glens. 'The unhallowed hoof of the iron horse is beginning to show traces on the hillside', reported a summer visitor to Loch Lomond in 1890. The quiet passes echoed to the bark of explosives. For the most part the rock through which the contractors had to hack their way was old, twisted mica-schist interspersed with veins of quartz. It was impervious to drills and dynamite had to be used to remove it. Steam shovels were used in making some of the earth cuttings, but there was frequent trouble due to the scoops encountering large boulders among the soil.

Wherever possible, and remembering the need for economy, the line was taken in wide sweeps round projecting spurs. In this way tunnels and some of the heaviest excavations were avoided. In 100 miles of mountainous country the engineers found it necessary to build only one tunnel—that on Loch Lomondside 47 yd long.

The broad policy was to balance embankments against cuttings and to use excavated stone to build the piers of bridges. The West Highland was thus saved the cost of purchasing and transporting the materials. The first two miles from Craigendoran to Helensburgh Upper involved a 1 in 58 climb, partly on a mile-long embankment 30 ft high and partly in a deep cutting. Some 140,000 cubic yards of material were required to form the embankment and of this 74,000 cubic yards of earth and 32,000 cubic yards of red sandstone came out of the corresponding cutting. Three parallel lines of light railway, with two engines working on each, were used to convey the filling material from the cuttings to the embankment. The operation was in charge of a Mr Bloomfield Smith.

A few miles further on the promoters, if they hadn't had to count every penny, would have taken the railway across Whistler's Glen on a viaduct. Instead the contractors put down two long culverts and used the many thousands of cubic yards of material taken out of the Gareloch hills to fill the depression. Rail level was 57 ft above the culverts, one of which was lined with bricks from an old wall demolished near the site. Nature co-operated, and the stone taken from the cutting at Rhu could be carried a few miles along the line and used to build the piers of the Garelochhead viaduct. Masons dressed the newly-cut stones on the spot. When the contractors

(C) *Class K2/2 2-6-0 No 61764* Loch Arkaig *at Fort William shed in March 1959 with BR Class 5 4-6-0 No 73077 in the background*

61764
61764
73077

BRITISH RAILWAYS
FORT WILLIAM STATION
MACBRAYNES
61787
MGG 187

found their way into Crianlarich from the south barred by a great mound of mountain clay, they cut their way through it and used the spoil to make an embankment across Strathfillan at the north end of Crianlarich station. Stone for the piers of the viaducts at this point—one across the Callander & Oban Railway, the other across the Fillan—was brought down the Callander & Oban from the Ben Cruachan quarries.

Above Loch Long where a shelf had to be gouged out of the mountainside to carry the rails the incline was too steep to support the contractors' equipment. Temporary piers were built at the loch-side, and plant and material brought in by sea were passed up to the railway builders on inclined roads worked by steam winches and wire ropes. The inclines varied from 1 in 3 to 1 in 15.

The movement of material for bridges and the erection of the bridges on difficult sites called for much ingenuity. The bridge contract was let to Alexander Findlay & Company of Motherwell. In all, 4,000 tons of steel had to be moved into the West Highlands to go into 19 viaducts with three spans or more, 102 bridges of one and two spans, and numerous cattle creeps. The contractors employed different techniques to suit varying conditions. Three miles north of Ardlui the deep gorge of the Dubh Eas called for a viaduct of seven spans, the centre span being 118 ft long. The piers were founded on rock and built up in concrete layers 9 in. thick. Access to the tops of the piers was obtained by building a light service bridge over the gorge and suspending it by means of union screws and sheer legs on either slope of the gorge. The metal work for the Dubh Eas viaduct was landed at the Loch Lomond pier and conveyed 6 miles to the site, where the sections were riveted together and launched out over the piers. Findlay & Company charged £16 per ton for the bridge work. This included cost of shipment to a base camp and erection on the site, but it did not include transport from the base camp to the site. That item normally accounted for another £2 per ton.

A different technique was used in the construction of the viaducts on the Horse Shoe Curve. Economy dictated the building of the Horse Shoe in the first place. Three mountains stood almost shoulder to shoulder immediately east of the railway, Ben Odhar, Ben a Chaistel and Ben Doran, with Ben a Chaistel recessed about a mile to the east of its two neighbours. The mountains were separated by two glens running in from the east. If cost had not been a prime consideration, the railway would have been taken direct from the slopes of Ben Odhar across the valley to Ben Doran on a long (and

(D) *Period piece at Fort William: Class K2/2 No 61787* Loch Quoich *at the old station with a MacBrayne AEC lorry and Morris 8 GPO van. The MacBrayne Pier is to the left. The old Station has been demolished and resited nearer Mallaig Junction*

expensive) viaduct. But the slimness of the West Highland's purse resulted in the line being carried in a U formation round the flank of Ben Odhar, across the face of Ben a Chaistel and back along the side of Ben Doran. The railway clung to the mountainsides all the way round the U except where it crossed the two intervening glens and at those points curved viaducts were necessary, one of five spans and the other of nine spans.

The girders for the five-span viaduct were built on the site and temporary rails were fitted to the bottom booms. Corresponding wheels were fixed in small frames securely anchored in the ground, and the girders were lowered so that the rails under the booms fitted on to the wheels. The five spans were linked together and tackle was used to pull what was virtually a train of girders out on to the tops of the piers. Once the spans had been built and placed on the wheels the launching of the bridge was completed in a matter of hours.

The engineers found that a viaduct was required at Craigenarden, one of the prettiest spots on Loch Lomonside, and fearing that a lattice girder erection would be a blemish on the landscape they designed the only arched viaduct on the line. Craigenarden Viaduct, 6 chains long and with eight arches of 36 ft span, was built of whinstone. To enhance the scenic effect the parapets were castellated and balusters were run up the piers.

CRISIS

Progress at the northern end was slower than in the south because the Fort William section could be served from only one point. The West Highland bought a strip of the foreshore at Fort William for £25 an acre, and began clearing the site for a station and approach lines. A minute recorded on 5 March 1890 said:

> It has now become necessary to displace certain persons of the labouring classes from their present houses in Fort William and the Engineers were instructed to prepare drawings for the necessary new houses in compliance with the provisions of the Act on the most economical plan possible.

By the end of June 1891 the railway had reached the northern end of Loch Treig, and to celebrate the event the board invited merchants, landowners and other supporters in Lochaber to a complimentary dinner at the new hotel at Invergloy. The guests were taken from Fort William to Inverlair by train and then by four-in-hand to Invergloy. Representatives of railway, contractor and engineer combined to make the day memorable for the visitors, yet that must have been a day of tension for the hosts. Just beneath the surface a serious crisis was bubbling.

Less than three weeks after the dinner the crisis broke. At every camp from Helensburgh to Fort William Lucas & Aird began to pay off men. At the beginning of the month the labour force had been close on 5,000; by the end of the month there were only 1,200 employed on the line, and they had been retained to maintain plant. All construction work ceased. Wild rumours swept the West Highlands. The railway had been abandoned! Construction had proved too difficult! The West Highland had run out of money! *The Oban Times* commented:

> It is, of course, known that only reasons of the gravest possible urgency would induce a firm of such high standing and exhaustless resources as Messrs Lucas & Aird to take the extreme step of recalling their employees while their contract is as yet only about half finished.

The stoppage was the culmination of a dispute that had arisen between the West Highland board and Lucas & Aird in 1890. By the terms of their contract Lucas & Aird had agreed to construct the railway for the lump sum of £393,638 4s 2d payable in monthly instalments. The practice was for Formans & McCall's inspectors to survey the work in hand month by month and submit a certificate of work done to the West Highland board. The amount on the monthly cheque handed to Lucas & Aird was based on the engineer's certificate. The dispute arose because excavated material was classified as rock or soil, and the contractor found that he was dealing with material that was neither rock nor soil, but soil mixed with boulders. The removal of this took more time than the removal of soil, but since it was classified as soil the certificates recorded less work done. The contractor put his case to the West Highland board and asked for a review of prices. But in January 1891 he was informed that the West Highland directors were not prepared to depart from the terms of the original contract. Lucas & Aird made several attempts to get better terms and it was when these attempts failed that they withdrew their labour.

The West Highland was brought face to face with an ugly situation that could have been avoided by the exercise of a little tact. Its first move was to rush to court for an interdict against Lucas & Aird to prevent them removing their plant from the railway. The magistrate granted an interim interdict pending a full hearing of an action which the railway now brought against the contractor.

The case was heard in August 1891 at Dumbarton Sheriff Court. The West Highland case was that the contractors had agreed to build the railway for a fixed sum after they had examined the proposed route and assessed its difficulties. If they could work within this amount they were entitled to all the profit they could make, but if they discovered snags during the construction they had no right to demand more money. Lucas & Aird's case was that

> the line as actually laid down and constructed has been so materially altered by the pursuer's engineer from that shown in the original plan that it is substantially an entirely different railway from that which the defenders contracted to make.

The Sheriff of Dumbarton decided for the railway. An independent engineer was appointed to assess the work done by Lucas & Aird up to the time of their withdrawal, and the West Highland opened negotiations with another contractor for the completion of the line. Meanwhile the fine summer months passed without a foot of permanent way being laid. Worse still, the labour force was dissipated. Particularly unfortunate was the fact that the Highland navvies returned to their distant homes and many of them did not come back to the railway.

Before long common sense prevailed. Lucas & Aird, Charles Forman and the West Highland chairman did some hard bargaining round the boardroom table, as a result of which the original contractor agreed to carry on. Work was resumed throughout on 14 October 1891, on the understanding that the contractors would be paid £10,000 in addition to their agreed fee on the completion of the line. A formal agreement to this effect was signed on Christmas Eve 1891. The set-back had proved costly for the West Highland. The navvies were reluctant to return to the moors and mountains in the middle of winter and it was the spring of 1892 before full-scale working was resumed.

TROUBLE ON RANNOCH MOOR

The great new railway took shape. The lengths of line built out from the base camps merged—with one exception. By the end of the third year a continuous line (except for some of the heavier bridges) ran all the way from Craigendoran to a bleak spot on the fringe of the Moor of Rannoch, some 60 miles from the Clyde. The northern section built out from Fort William had been pushed through the Spean gorges and up Loch Treigside to end in the wilderness at the northern edge of the Moor.

In June 1892 Charles Forman and John Aird conducted a party of West Highland directors and their friends by special train from Fort William to the end of the line. But in the middle between the two broken-off ends of the line was a gap of nearly 20 miles in which little work had been done, and filling the gap was a sombre morass of peat moss and heather. Telford in his day had surveyed a road across the Moor of Rannoch by the almost identical route taken by the railway, but he had abandoned the project. How the railway engineers conquered the Moor is one of the highlights in the West Highland story.

John Aird employed the technique that Stephenson had used on Chat Moss 60 years before. He decided to float the railway across the worst of the bog. First of all the contractors dug longitudinal ditches on either side of the railway 40 ft from the centre line of the track; then at intervals of 30 ft they cut cross-drains. Tons of turf and brushwood were brought to the edges of the Moor and taken out to the workings on the contractors' light railway.

First a layer of turf, then a layer of brushwood, was laid along the line of the railway, followed by further layers. Often the filling sank out of sight at once, and many applications were required before something resembling a permanent way appeared above the level of the bog. All the soil and mountain till that could be obtained from cuttings along the route were tipped on to the path across the Moor, and when no more material was left thousands of tons of ash were brought up from the industrial south to help consolidate the roadbed. The work trains which brought the spoil from all parts of the system were taken out over the Moor on a temporary standard-gauge light railway.

North of Rannoch station a depression nearly 1,000 ft across gave the railway builders a lot of trouble. The bog was 20 ft deep and it was not practicable to find the great volume of material that would be required to fill it and raise an embankment to a height of some 50 ft above it. A viaduct was the only answer, and the engineers decided on a nine-span steel structure, each span being 70½ ft long. The area of the pier foundations was timbered and the soft moss was scooped out down to the firm boulder clay. Granite for the piers was obtained from the convenient Cruach Rock cutting, less than a mile to the north of the site. Rannoch Viaduct, 684 ft, was to be the longest on the line.

The Moor swallowed everything that was offered. Progress was slow at the best of times, and in the depths of winter when work was impossible not a foot was gained for days on end. And the

Moor was swallowing money as well as material. By the summer of 1893 the promoters in their office at 4 Princes Street, Edinburgh, realized that the authorized capital would not cover the construction of the line. The financial crisis that ensued had become acute when Mr Renton, one of the directors of the West Highland, gave part of his private fortune to save the situation. With the help of a fine summer, saved it was. The brushwood no longer sank. A dry, springy carpet stretched across the Moor and on this elongated raft the rails were laid. The last length of rail was dropped into position on 5 September 1893 and Mr Renton was given the privilege of driving the last spike. The railway navvies manhandled a huge boulder to the north end of Rannoch station and out of it sculptured an excellent head of Renton, using only the tools of their trade.

At the half-yearly meeting of the West Highland Railway, held on 28 September, the shareholders were told that 95 per cent of the earthworks and 88 per cent of the mason work was complete. All but 2½ miles of permanent way had been laid, 95 per cent of the track had been fenced and 90 miles of telegraph poles had been erected. 'Given a favourable winter,' said the Marquess of Tweeddale, 'we hope to open in the spring.'

But the winter was far from favourable, and the spring of 1894 found the contractors still wrestling with problems. The railway was like a large liner that had been launched and towed to the fitting-out basin; a lot of fitting-out remained to be done. Station buildings had to be finished, signalling installed, fencing completed and minor bridges built before the inspecting officer from the Board of Trade could be invited to give his accolade.

There were fifteen stations: Craigendoran, Helensburgh Upper, Row (later Rhu), Shandon, Garelochhead, Arrochar and Tarbet, Ardlui, Crianlarich, Tyndrum, Bridge of Orchy, Rannoch, Tulloch (Inverlair), Roy Bridge, Spean Bridge, and Fort William. There were passing places at Glen Douglas, Gorton and Corrour. (The decision to establish a station at Whistlefield had not yet been made.) The longest distance between stations was 18 miles between Rannoch and Tulloch, but this was divided into two sections by Corrour passing place. All the stations except Row, Tulloch, Roy Bridge and Spean Bridge, which had side platforms, had island platforms. The station buildings were finished after the style of Swiss chalets, overhanging roofs and exterior walls faced with wooden shingles brought from Switzerland adding to the atmosphere. Originally the stations were painted in two shades of green and the platforms were covered with red blaize—an attractive combination.

RANNOCH

(21) *Rannoch station, looking north*

(22) *Cruach Rock snowshed*

FROM THE FOOTPLATE

(23) *A J36 on Rannoch Moor*

(24) *A J37 heading south towards Gorton*

(25) *A West Highland driver in* LNE *days*

(26) *A typical West Highland footplate scene. Tablet on the handbrake handle, milk for delivery at lineside cottages*

Single-line tablet was installed throughout by Saxby & Farmer. The tablet instruments usually were situated in the stationmaster's office, the signalboxes at the ends of the platforms containing only the lever frames. A technical journal had this odd comment to make about the West Highland inter-station telephones.

> One of the peculiarities of the instrument is that the tone of voice undergoes a change in the course of transmission and when heard resembles nothing more than the shrill and unmusical tone of voice used by the manipulator of puppets in the Punch and Judy show.

The telephones were said to amplify the voice to such a degree that the speaker could be heard clearly 10 or 15 ft away from the receiver.

The animal population of the West Highlands had to receive special consideration. No fewer than 200 creeps were built, ranging from simple wooden sheep-creeps 4 ft wide, costing £70, to plate girder cattle-creeps costing £230. Where the line passed through deer forests a special fence, 6 ft high, was devised, the lower wires of 7 gauge being 5½ in. apart and the upper wires of 6 gauge being 10 in. apart. In addition a single strand of barbed wire ran 42 in. above the ground. Otherwise 4 ft wooden fencing was used.

Throughout the late spring and early summer of 1894 strenuous efforts were made to have the line ready in time for the fast-approaching tourist season. Coloured posters extolling the new railway appeared in North British stations. A press announcement gave 12 July as the opening date and added that Princess Louis, Marchioness of Lorne, would perform the opening ceremony. But July came and went and the line remained unopened.

Meanwhile staff were recruited from all over the North British system, and railway families moved into their West Highland homes to embark on a life very different from that which they were leaving. William Arnott, district superintendent at Perth, was appointed district superintendent of the West Highland, with an office in Fort William. P. Jamieson, agent at Longwitton in Northumberland, became agent at Rannoch—at a salary of £65 per annum. A signalman was appointed at the same station for a wage of 16s per week. Wages on the West Highland were lower than those for the same job on the North British but, as a contemporary railway journal pointed out,

> To be a clerk in Glasgow on £80 a year is to be a nobody; to be a stationmaster with £60 per annum, free house coal and gas is to be a notable figure in a small community.

The last stages of construction were marred by a number of

unpleasant incidents. In June a labourer was knocked down and killed by a light engine at Gorton. A few days later, at 6.15 on the morning of 25 June, a ballast train consisting of two engines, thirty-five wagons and a van left the rails at a contractors' service siding in Glen Falloch. A permanent-way inspector was seriously hurt and the two engine crews were lucky to get away with light injuries. The derailment turned out to be the work of three labourers who had pulled over the hand points 'just to see what would happen'. The men were taken to court and subsequently sent to prison.

Heavy rain in July brought about the collapse of earthworks near Tyndrum and an engine rolled down the embankment, killing its fireman and injuring the driver. In the following week a driver was killed on Garelochside. 'Recent accidents,' said a press report, 'have suggested the safe and prudent course of not opening the line for traffic till every part of the works has been minutely examined.'

Political as well as physical difficulties beset the West Highland in the last hectic weeks before opening. When the engineers proposed to supply Bridge of Orchy station with drinking water by tapping a nearby mountain stream the noble owner objected. He went to court in Edinburgh and was unsuccessful in an effort to prevent the West Highland from entering his land and taking the water. But in an appeal to the House of Lords his fellow-peers overturned the Edinburgh decision. All this for a few gallons of water in country where water was anything but a scarce commodity! The gentry in an Upper Helensburgh street complained that they could *see* the railway from their gardens and asked the West Highland to heighten their garden walls. Three years later the railway gave them £110 between them and told them to build up the walls themselves.

Then there was a last-minute dispute between the people of Fort William and the railway. The West Highland had been allowed to bring its line along the shore of Loch Linnhe to the pier which stood at the south end of the town. It was the route, indeed, which the townspeople had invited the Glasgow & North Western Railway to use. Too late they realized that the railway cut the town off from the shore, as it ran parallel to and immediately behind the buildings of the main street. It was a monumental blunder in town planning. In the years to come Fort William was to think of the beautiful lochside esplanade it might have had if the town fathers had kept the line away from the water. In 1894 a special meeting of the Police Commissioners in Fort William pointed out that the railway had cut off access roads to the shore and that the station and signal box were not in the places indicated in the original plans. The company poured some oil on the troubled waters by providing wicket gates and level crossings at certain of the shore access roads.

'THE FORT'

When the railway engineers came to Lochaber in 1889 they found Fort William a small, backward town. It had developed a modest tourist trade partly because it was on the Royal Route from Glasgow to Inverness, partly because it nestled at the foot of Britain's highest mountain, Ben Nevis. The town had its origin in the days when William of Orange had many enemies in the Highlands; it was established in 1690 as one of a chain of military installations guarding the Great Glen. Cameron of Lochiel, William's most formidable opponent in these parts, was recovering from a sword wound at the time, and McKay of Killiecrankie notoriety seized the opportunity to establish a fort unmolested on Loch Linnhe on the site of an older fort. The entire fortifications on the landward side were completed in a fortnight and a man-of-war sailed up the loch and delivered a score of guns for its defence. McKay climbed to the battlements, unfurled the standard of the King and insulted the Highlanders by naming the place Fort William.

It was a name that stuck in the throats of the men of Lochaber, and several attempts were made to change it. In a span of 200 years the town was known variously as Duncansburgh, Maryborough and Gordonsburgh, and in comparatively recent times there was a move to have it re-christened Invernevis. Local folks spoke of it as *an gearasdan*—the garrison; today it is known colloquially as 'the Fort'. In the end the entire fort except one building was blown sky-high by a London-based railway contractor, and it fell to a London-based railway company to deliver the *coup de grace* forty years later.

The route of the West Highland into Fort William passed through the disused fort. The railway surveyor found the walls unbreached and entry to the fort was still gained through the archway that McKay had built two centuries earlier. The barrack blocks were occupied as dwelling-houses, and cabbages grew in the fosse. The site was wanted for an engine shed, and John Aird set about demolishing the ancient fortifications. Cannon balls were dug out of the walls, coins were unearthed and a male skeleton was found in the ramparts. The entrance archway, on the instruction of the

West Highland directors, was dismantled and rebuilt at the gateway to the town cemetery, which was the spot where the first Cameron Highlanders had been sworn in.

Thus the gateway to a fort built largely to suppress the rebel Camerons became a monument recording the service given by the clan to the Crown. Within the fort, the building that had been Government House was retained, and the railway company took special steps to preserve the Governor's Room intact. It had been in that room on 12 February 1692 that Colonel Hill had signed the order for the Massacre of Glencoe. The West Highland and its successors provided a caretaker to look after the historic apartment and for over forty years it remained undisturbed amid the bustle of a busy locomotive depot. When the LNE at last demolished the old building, the panelling of the Governor's Room and the stairway leading up to the room were removed to the West Highland Museum in the town.

CHAPTER 5

The Early Years

THE LINE IN SERVICE

Major Marindin took several long looks at the West Highland on behalf of the Board of Trade, suggesting improvements and alterations. On his final visit on 3 August 1894, he rode in state in one of the new first-class saloons hauled by two of Matthew Holmes's West Highland bogies. At long last authority to open the line was received on 7 August. The directors had organized their ceremonial opening for Saturday 11 August 1894, but in order to squeeze as much revenue as possible from the ebbing tourist season they opened the public service on the very day permission was received from the Board of Trade.

The first revenue-earning train left Fort William for Glasgow at 6.10 a.m. on 7 August. In spite of the early hour the townsfolk turned out in large numbers to watch its departure. Many of them bought tickets for Spean Bridge and Roy Bridge with the intention of returning on the first down train, and for some it was their first journey by rail. Such was the demand for places that extra coaches had to be added. Charles Forman was among the important guests, and several of Lucas & Aird's navvies were passengers. Groups of people were watching at all the stations; time was kept as far as Ardlui, where it was held to await the down train which had been delayed at Craigendoran for the detachment of a vehicle with a hot box.

The first timetable showed three passenger trains each way between Glasgow Queen Street High Level and Fort William, timed as follows:

Queen Street	dep.	7.30	12.40	4.50
Fort William	arr.	12.15	5.20	9.40
Fort William	dep.	6.10	11.15	4.25
Queen Street	arr.	11.00	4.00	9.08

The trains normally consisted of two third-class and one first-class

West Highland saloons, except for the first down and the last up train which normally carried one through carriage each for Edinburgh and King's Cross. This service was maintained for three months, then on 1 November the timetable was recast to suit the requirements of the winter traffic. On the same day steam heating was introduced—and not a moment too soon! The winter timings were:

Queen Street	dep.	7.55	3.50
Fort William	arr.	12.47	8.47
Fort William	dep.	7.20	3.55
Queen Street	arr.	12.52	8.43

One freight in each direction was sufficient to handle all the traffic offered.

The West Highland published its timetable showing the new through London—Fort William service in the press on the day it opened for business. Not to be outdone, the Caledonian Railway

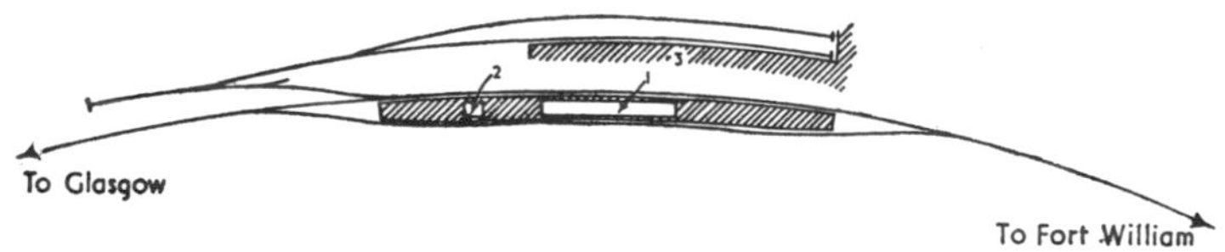

Tyndrum Upper station. Example of standard 'island' station

1. main station offices
2. signal box
3. cattle loading bank

Sidings to loading bank are on much lower level than main passenger platform and running lines

published its own London—Fort William service alongside the rival announcement. The West Coast service was from Euston to Oban and then by MacBrayne steamer to Fort William. Oddly enough, in spite of the boat journey, the West Coast combine could have their passengers in Fort William right on the tail of those who had travelled in the through coach from King's Cross.

The West Highland had high hopes of developing a local service between Craigendoran and Garelochhead serving Helensburgh Upper, Row and Shandon. Garelochside was a residential area highly favoured with the cream of the Glasgow professional and business community. Passengers to town hitherto had travelled either by private coach or by North British steamer to Helensburgh to join the trains. Now the West Highland offered four trains a day between Craigendoran and Garelochhead, with connections for Glasgow at Craigendoran. The innovation was not a success, mainly because the West Highland stations were sited high on the hills behind the lochside villages and were approached by long, steep roads. As the local correspondent of the *Railway Herald* put it, 'Sound heart and lungs and experience in hill climbing are essential to a man who hurries from the breakfast table to catch a train at one of the lochside stations. It is easier to go to a pier.' Potential passengers complained that the first up train left too late and the last down train left too early.

To increase the scope of the service, railway tickets were made interavailable with steamer tickets. Greenock Town Council petitioned the North British for a restoration of the Greenock—Helensburgh steamer service (which had been abandoned by the North British because it did not pay) so that people on the south shore of the Clyde estuary could have easy access to the West Highland. But when the Greenock merchants were sounded on the prospects of their sending freight over the West Highland, they stated bluntly that the new railway was of no use to them; it was cheaper to send freight to Fort William by boat.

The Garelochside train service won unwanted publicity on 4 September 1894, when 14-year-old Helen Hamill, a servant girl, placed a stone in the path of the 7.35 from Helensburgh at Woodend Farm Crossing. The engine and two coaches finished up in a cornfield. The delinquent Helen was removed to Dumbarton court where 'she emitted a declaration' and was sent to prison.

Tourist tickets on the West Highland were made available for travel on the Loch Lomond steamers. Southbound passengers could detrain at Ardlui or Arrochar and Tarbet and continue their journey by boat to Balloch, thence by rail to Glasgow. The same facility was available in the reverse direction.

By the West Highland Railway Act of 1889 the railway undertook to build a station at Portincaple. This was a hamlet beside Loch Long, opposite Loch Goil and several hundred feet below the railway where it emerged from the cutting above Garelochhead. It was further intended to operate a ferry between Portincaple and Loch Goil. When the railway was built and there was no sign of Portincaple station materializing, the handful of local people protested. The West Highland then announced that a decision on the station would be postponed until the line was opened. A further memorial was dispatched to the railway office whereupon the secretary was 'instructed to intimate to the Memorialists that the

Company were not prepared at present to erect a station at that place'. The station—named Whistlefield—was eventually opened on 1 May 1896.

The West Highland, in company with other lines that had built railways through sparsely-populated territory at high cost, charged fares at the full Parliamentary rate. But it was quick to introduce cheap excursions. Weekend fares to all stations were offered before the end of September, the return fare from Glasgow to Fort William being 9s 2d and from Edinburgh 11s 8d. On 13 September 1894, a local holiday in Glasgow, the first day-excursion was run to Fort William. The train started from Bridgeton Cross (now Bridgeton Central) at 6.30 a.m. and called at Queen Street Low Level and various suburban stations west of the city centre, thereby setting a pattern for almost all day-excursion traffic in the future.

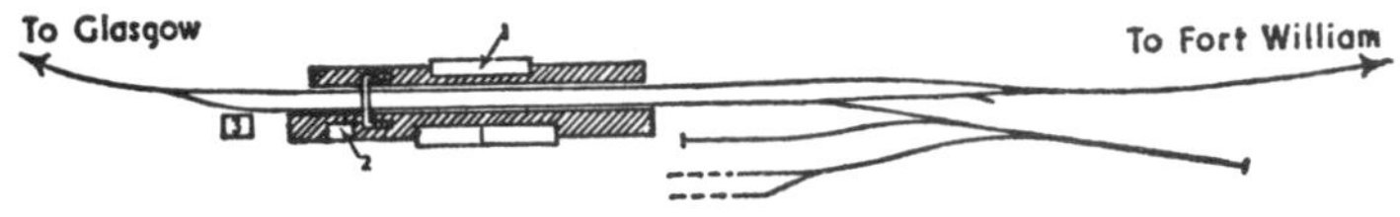

Tulloch, a two-platform station

1. station buildings
2. signal box
3. water tank

The official opening of the West Highland was on 11 August 1894—a significant date. August 12—the Glorious Twelfth—was still a key date in the British calendar of social events, and the trunk lines from the south to Scotland still carried their heaviest passenger traffic on 10 and 11 August each year. With many thousands of acres of grouse shooting along its metals, the West Highland hoped to make capital out of the shooting season. The sport was first class, but its development was limited by the lack of accommodation in these barren regions for the potential sportsmen. Nevertheless the traffic developed sufficiently to justify the employment of temporary clerkesses at the Moor of Rannoch outposts—Corrour and Gortan as well as Rannoch station—whose duty it was to handle the administration of the shooting season traffic. This involved the dispatch of grouse to the markets in the south as well as the reception of the sportsmen. The girls were employed from 12 August until 12 October at a wage of 12s per week.

In order to facilitate sporting and other traffic the West Highland had the foresight to build a road from Rannoch station eastward across the Moor to Loch Rannoch. The contract had been given to

ON THE ROAD TO THE ISLES

(27) *Lochailort station showing concrete construction of platforms*
(28) *Two Lochs head a Glasgow—Mallaig train out of Glenfinnan in 1958*

(29) Glenf

(30) Morar viaduct

ct

(31) *Borrodale bridge*

IN THE FAR WEST

(32) *A K1 crosses Loch nan Uamh viaduct on a Glasgow—Mallaig train*

Lucas & Aird originally, but was later transferred to William Wilson of Kirkcaldy who built the road for £4,896 3s 9d. The West Highland was obliged to pay Lucas & Aird 10 per cent of this amount. A venison slide was erected at Rannoch. This device, which was like a children's chute, extended from the road (which was at a higher level than the railway) to the loading bank. Deer carcases were brought by cart to the road end and slid down the chute to the waiting vans.

Additional passenger traffic came from an unexpected source. When the West Highland opened there was, 15 miles or so west of the line where it crossed the Moor of Rannoch, a community as wild and lawless as a pioneer settlement in the Yukon. This was Kinlochleven, a motley town that had sprung up at the end of Loch Leven and was the base for the construction of the first of the great Highland hydro-electric schemes. It was an incredible place of saloons and gambling dens, where men flocked to work like gold prospectors of old. There were no policemen in Kinlochleven, except the two who came to escort the postman on his once-weekly round. Nor were there in those days any roads into Kinlochleven. The navvies had to go in by boat or trudge round the unmarked shore of Loch Leven from Ballachulish.

With the coming of the West Highland Railway the navvies found that they could go by train to Corrour and walk by an ill-defined path across the Moor to Kinlochleven. It was a dangerous and foolhardy journey. Some of the men who went there were refugees from justice who hoped to lose their identity in the rough and ready colony in the west. On one occasion the Glasgow police traced a wanted man to Corrour station, but a search of Kinlochleven revealed no sign of him. When the Moor was combed the searchers found not only the body of the wanted man, but the skeletons of three others.

THE FIRST WINTER

It was unfortunate that the West Highland's first winter was the worst of the nineteenth century. The great frost that ushered in 1895 was long remembered. Contemporary newspaper headlines tell their own story: *Seas and Lochs Icebound. Railways and Roads Obliterated. Coldest Days of the Century. Many Deaths in the Great Storm.* The severe weather came in three phases. The first dated from 29 December 1894 until 11 January 1895, when a snowstorm of exceptional severity was followed by a lull and a rapid rise of temperature. On 29 January a second storm even more violent than the first swept the country. Another brief period of calm was followed on 5 February by a terrifying blizzard that reached a climax on 6 February.

If conditions were bad in the cities of Britain they were unspeakable on the Moor of Rannoch. The West Highlands were ravaged daily by scouring blizzards that made a mockery of timetables. Day after day the trains that left Glasgow for Fort William got no further than Tyndrum or Bridge of Orchy. Southbound trains rarely covered more than the first 18 miles of their journey. Tulloch was about their limit; the difficult miles between Tulloch and Rannoch were impassable for days. Gangs of railwaymen reinforced by civilian labourers were sent out to attack the drifts on Loch Treigside but to little avail. As a drift was cleared the storm piled up new ones.

On the first Monday of 1895 the district superintendent at Fort William took the precaution of sending out an engine and plough in advance of the first up goods. The engine got as far as Tulloch, and the goods following it came to grief in a newly-formed drift near Tulloch Farm. The 7.30 passenger train reached Roy Bridge, where it was held until mid-day and sent back to Fort William. Meanwhile the first down train, which should have reached Fort William, was still 75 miles short of its terminus, held fast by big snowslides in the hills above Loch Lomond.

In the lull between the first and second phases of the storm some headway was made in clearing the line, but with the renewal of the blizzard the work of a week was undone in an hour. Snow dug out of the cuttings and piled up by the lineside was swept back into the cuttings and layers of fresh snow drifted over it. By now the district superintendent had pin-pointed the danger spots and concerted attacks were made on them by ploughs and diggers. The worst spot of all was Cruach Rock cutting a mile and a half above Rannoch. On a wild Sunday night forces were sent out from Fort William and from Glasgow to tackle the Cruach region simultaneously from both ends. The engine and plough from Fort William climbed all the way up to Corrour only to be caught and held immovable in a huge drift. Two engines from Glasgow struggled as far north as Tyndrum, where they ran into a big drift and became derailed somewhat precariously on the brink of a snow-covered slope. During Monday the engines were re-railed and succeeded in getting through to Rannoch.

Then, when the successful clearing of the line was in sight, came the final and worst phase of the storm. The renewed blizzard was followed at once by a gale-force wind and intense cold. The whole country found itself encrusted in a tough skin of ice. The drifts that filled the cuttings and covered the tracks froze into a solid rock-like mass. The position for the West Highland was serious. There were booking offices on the line where not a penny-piece had passed through the windows for days. Revenue from passengers and freight had dwindled to vanishing point. *The Engineer* commented:

> The experience of the present severe weather on the new West Highland line connecting Helensburgh with Fort William has been anything but pleasant, and the cost entailed in digging trains out of the snow has been very great, and certainly not of a nature to encourage promoters to carry through additional Highland railways.

The railwaymen could do nothing else but continue their effort to clear the line. A relief unit out of Fort William was battling its way up Loch Treigside when the engine left the rails at a bridge over a gully. A ballast train following it was lost in the snow for several days. In the south the snow fighters met with more success, and before long the line was clear from Craigendoran to beyond Bridge of Orchy.

In the midst of all the anxiety came a piece of comic relief. The roaring game of curling was a popular one in the West Highlands and a Fort William curling team, taking advantage of the new railway, arranged a match between themselves and a team from Dall, Loch Rannoch. The match was due to take place on a small loch near Rannoch station on 6 February, the day the whole series of storms reached a grand climax. Undaunted by the frightful weather the curlers went out from Fort William by the morning train and managed to get through to Rannoch on the recently cleared line. But they had no sooner gained the shelter of Rannoch station than the storm broke in full fury, and the line over which they had travelled was blocked. The Dall team had already arrived by the moorland road. In spite of the weather, neither team would agree to abandon the game. Even when the loch on which they had intended to play was found to be unusable, they trudged through the blizzard for a mile to Loch Laidon, and there in the partial shelter of Cruach Hill the game began. But they were soon glad to seek refuge in Rannoch station.

There was no news of any train anywhere. The curlers were marooned on the Moor. Lucas & Aird had not got around to dismantling their hutments at Rannoch and the players found shelter in a large store hut which still, fortunately, contained stores of

NORTH BRITISH RAILWAY.

S 31/8

District Traffic Superintendent's Office,
GORDON SQUARE,
FORT-WILLIAM, 31st Aug 1894

Mr. Whitfield
Rannoch *Station.*

DEAR SIR,

My S. 16/8 of 16th inst.
Walter Lumsden
having been tested by an Inspector and found competent for the duties of **Block Telegraph Signalman** at
Rannoch Station
you may allow him to assume duty in that capacity *vice*
Spare Signalman Jardine
whom send home as soon as the workmen's trains are altered which will be in a day or so.—
Please acknowledge receipt on the annexed form.

Yours truly,
Wm Arnott
per W. Gray
District Traffic Superintendent.

foodstuffs and supplies of fuel. There was no drinking water, but several cases of lemonade were broached; it had frozen solid, but the refugees soon had the bottles thawing in front of a blazing fire. The men passed the long hours of the night by holding a *ceilidh*, a Gaelic sing-song.

During Thursday forenoon an engine with a gang of 30 men arrived from the south. Conditions were still bad on the heights of the Moor and the engine was held at Rannoch to await an improve-

Mary Robertson

(1942)

NORTH BRITISH RAILWAY.

3/5466

District Traffic Superintendent's Office,
~~Gordon Square~~
FORT-WILLIAM, 9th Aug 1901

Mr. Hogarth
Rannoch Station.

Dear Sir,

Miss Mary Robertson
Supernumerary clerk

Please enter the above-named in Paybill at 12/-
per week from 12th August
to 12th October.

Yours truly,
Geo Innes
District Traffic Superintendent.

ment. The men joined the curlers in the store hut. Later in the day a second relief train arrived from the south, and by nightfall two more trains had arrived in Rannoch with no hope of being able to continue their journey northwards.

The population of the moorland settlement was now about 200, and there was anxiety about dwindling food and drink supplies. Fortunately Friday brought an improvement in the weather, and the gangers were able to reach the south end of Cruach Rock cutting. They had to quarry out the ice and frozen snow in blocks. Before the end of the day they met the gang working from the north end, and the line was open again. For several weeks trains crossing the Moor passed through a series of clefts cut in the snow. Smooth white walls rose on either side of the carriages, and it was not until spring was well advanced that the snow buttresses crumbled and disappeared. Meanwhile the West Highland took the precaution of advancing the departure time of the 3.50 Glasgow—Fort William passenger train to 2 p.m., so that it would pass the Cruach Rock danger spot in daylight.

The lesson of that first winter was not lost on the West Highland. North British engineers set about designing permanent snow defences. These took the form of continuous sleeper fences erected on hill faces above the railway where experience had shown that drifting was likely. Danger spots on the Moor of Rannoch were lined with snow fences. Later, at the worst place, Cruach Rock, a snow-shed was built: for a length of 205 yd corrugated sheeting was placed over the notorious cutting. The roof principals were made of old rails spanning the 27 ft 6 in. between the walls. The centre sheets of the snow-shed directly above the rails could be removed in summer. Over the years the defences have worked reasonably well; there have been snowblocks, some of them serious, but none has been on the scale of those of the first winter.

THE BANAVIE BRANCH

The West Highland Railway Act gave the promoters powers to build a branch from near Fort William to Banavie on the banks of the Caledonian Canal. The branch was not ready for the official opening of the main line, largely because of difficulties involved in building a substantial viaduct over the Lochy. The branch left the main line at Banavie Junction a mile east of Fort William, and ran 1¾ miles to a station and pier on the Caledonian Canal. The West Highland hoped to establish passenger and freight business with the vessels plying on the canal. The pier was alongside the station but a considerable distance above it, and wagons were taken through the station and back-shunted up a gradient of 1 in 24 to the canal bank.

The first train set off from Banavie on its 2¾-mile journey to Fort William at 5.40 on the morning of 1 June 1895. By southern standards it was a modest occasion, but the railway-conscious West Highlanders had other ideas. The diminutive branch was opened with due ceremony, and the engine that brought the first train into Fort William in the dawn light was decorated with bunting.

The West Highland had no intention of stopping at Banavie. The great aim was to get westwards to the shores of the Atlantic and north-east to Inverness. In spite of the bland assurances of friendship given to the Highland Railway representatives on the day of the West Highland's opening, the West Highland had surveyors in the Great Glen only a week or two later. They were searching for a route to Inverness. It was odd that the Highland Railway should have *its* surveyors in the Great Glen on the self-same Saturday morning. They were looking for a Highland route to Fort William.

In 1894 the West Highland tried to put a branch across from Inverlair (Tulloch) over the 32 miles to Kingussie on the Highland Railway, but the Highland had no difficulty in thwarting the attempt. The West Highland contented itself by exhibiting at Tulloch what was perhaps the most optimistic notice ever erected on a railway station: 'Tulloch *for Kingussie*.' The timetable designated Tulloch 'for Loch Laggan and Kingussie'.

MINOR MANIA

A minor railway mania seized the West Highlands with the coming of the railway. Railways were projected hither and thither, and more often than not the indefatigable Charles Forman was behind them. He surveyed an extension of the West Highland down the east shore of Loch Linnhe from Fort William to Ballachulish, over the route that Walron Smith planned for the G & NW. At the same time he planned a Caledonian-sponsored branch from the Callander & Oban at Connel Ferry up through Appin to Ballachulish.

Other Forman enterprises within a 30-mile radius of Ben Nevis included a line from the West Highland at Spean Bridge to Fort Augustus in the Great Glen, and a continuation up Loch Ness to Inverness. Of Forman's projected grand cross-country route from Oban to Inverness, all the links between Oban and Fort Augustus were authorized. The Spean Bridge to Fort Augustus line was built by an independent company (of which we are to hear more), the Callander & Oban built the Connel Ferry—Ballachulish link, but the West Highland did not use its powers to take its branch from Fort William to Ballachulish.

Meanwhile, further south two Forman schemes came into direct conflict with each other, which was not surprising considering that he simultaneously engineered a Caledonian and a North British scheme to reach the same objective. Inveraray, the county town of Argyll, lay isolated among mountains near the head of Loch Fyne, and attempts were made to get railways to it from two directions. On behalf of the Callander & Oban, Forman planned a line running south from a junction with the parent system at Dalmally, a distance of 14½ miles; the cost of £142,568 was to include a pier at Inveraray, through which the railway hoped to benefit from the then intensive Loch Fyne herring-fishing trade.

(1042)

NORTH BRITISH RAILWAY.

S 13/H

District Traffic Superintendent's Office,
~~General Supt~~
FORT-WILLIAM, 13th Aug 1903

Mr. Hogarth
Rannoch Station.

DEAR SIR,

Mary Mitchell
Summer Clerk, Corrour

Please enter the above-named in Paybill at 12/-
per week as from 10th inst for the season

Yours truly
G. Innes
District Traffic Superintendent.

At the same time Forman surveyed a West Highland branch that was to leave the main line at Arrochar, pass round Loch Long, and cross to Loch Fyne by the Rest and be Thankful, so to reach St Catherine's opposite Inveraray. From Glasgow to Inveraray by the West Highland route was 54 miles, by the Caledonian and Callander & Oban 107¼. Inveraray was a feudal enclave dominated by the castle. The Duke of Argyll favoured the West Highland scheme if only because it decently kept out of his preserves. But the Dalmally line passed under the castle windows and the duke had no difficulty in inducing Parliament to throw out the bill. The West Highland had enough on its plate in the north-west without adding the Inveraray branch. It was never built.

The wave of optimism that swept Lochaber when the railway came spawned two transport schemes, one basically sound, the other plausible but with more than a touch of fantasy. From time to time schemes had been proposed for building a railway to the summit of Ben Nevis. The Ben was the highest mountain in Britain and already very much a 'tourist' mountain. Moreover, since 1883 there had been a permanent observatory on the summit, inhabited all the year round and connected with the base by an easily negotiated pony track. Much more difficult peaks in Europe and elsewhere had been given rack railways that had paid their way and brought prosperity to their base towns. Everybody who climbed Ben Nevis wrote his or her name in the visitors' book at the observatory, and these books provided a ready-made census of potential traffic for a mountain railway.

In 1893 Charles Forman considered building a railway up Ben Nevis. When the West Highland was opened, a London company took up the challenge and planned to construct a line starting near the West Highland station and, following the pony track for the first 2,000 ft, reach the summit by striking east round the shoulder of the mountain. The line was to be 4¾ miles long and have a maximum gradient of 1 in 2.62 for 600 yd. The company expected to spend £30,000 on the venture (the price inclusive of a large hotel on the summit), and estimated that the revenue from 15,000 passengers a year at fares of 1s 6d return and 1s single would enable 6 per cent to be paid on the capital. The scheme was revived several times between 1894 and 1913, but nothing came of it. If ever a mountain was ready for a railway it was Ben Nevis. It was a pity both for the future prosperity of the West Highland Railway and Fort William that the line was not built.

The other transport scheme that engaged the attention of the West Highlanders and others envisaged the establishment of an Atlantic terminus at Fort William. At that time the steamship route from Liverpool to Quebec was 2,625 miles and the time taken on the voyage was 6 days 12 hours. From Fort William to Quebec *via* Skerryvore and the Ross of Mull was 2,083 miles and the estimated time of the voyage was exactly 5 days. From London to Liverpool was 5 hours by rail, London to Fort William was 14 hours by rail, so that the Fort William—Quebec route was 1 day 3 hours shorter than the existing Liverpool—Quebec route.

And Fort William had other claims. Loch Linnhe was a large

natural harbour with a bottom of firm blue clay and no rocks. It was deep enough to take the largest liners at any state of the tide, and it was safe and perfectly sheltered by the surrounding mountains. Loch Eil nearby was available as an additional anchorage. Furthermore, there were 1,200 acres of flat ground by the lochside, and plenty of local stone for the building of wharves and warehouses. On paper Fort William looked a likely choice for a new Atlantic port. The big ships went to Southampton, but it is intriguing to picture the *Queen Mary* arriving at Fort William and her 2,000 passengers trying to make their way down the West Highland, perhaps in December with Rannoch Moor not on its best behaviour.

TWO DERAILMENTS

On 14 October 1895 an alarming accident involving the 4.20 p.m. from Fort William occurred at Shandon station. The train was double headed, with Driver Thornton in charge of the leading engine and Driver Thomson on the train engine. A storm had been gathering in the West Highlands that afternoon, and by the time the train got to Garelochhead the night was wild and black. Thomson picked up the Garelochhead—Shandon tablet and the train steamed off on the next stage of its journey. The line curves through deep cuttings and dense woods at this part and somewhere in the featureless blackness of the 2½-mile section Driver Thornton became disorientated. He did not know where he was. Thornton had been 11 hours and Thomson 14 hours on duty, and it may have been that the faculties of both men were impaired. Thornton strained through the darkness for a sight of the Shandon up distant, but he never saw it for its lamp was unlit. Presently the up home came into view, but Thornton took it to be the distant (distant and home both exhibited red lights then), and he made only a slight reduction in speed.

Thornton could not have chosen a more inopportune night on which to lose himself, for John Crawford, the Shandon signalman, had been very remiss in his duties that day. Before dusk he should have trimmed all his signal lamps, but he considered that the top of a signal ladder on a windswept hillface was no place for him when he could be making himself comfortable at the porter's room fire. The result was that the up and down distant lamps went out, and in those days there were no repeaters in the cabins to indicate that a lamp had failed.

To complicate matters, after the last down train had passed Crawford had been unable to tear himself away from the fire to reset the road for the next traffic move—the 4.20 up train. Even after he had received the train-entering-section signal from Garelochhead and he knew the 4.20 was on its way, he remained in the staff room. It was only when he heard the train rumbling round the hillside that he hurried along the platform to the box. First of all he had to reverse the points at the south end of the station. By that time the train was running into the down (wrong) side of the island platform, but Crawford did not see it and he pulled the points under it.

Then under the bemused signalman's nose followed a disconcerting spectacle. The train split in two. The two engines and one coach ran round the right side of the island platform and the rear half of the train ran round the left side; and the two portions between them dragged the second carriage up the ramp on to the platform where it overturned. Thornton's engine was 164 ft past the points when it stopped. Luckily the train was lightly loaded, and only one passenger required hospital treatment. But the West Highland had to face a heavy repair bill that it could ill afford.

On 6 May 1896 Thornton was involved in another derailment of a very different kind. His train was the 7.35 a.m. from Glasgow and he had reached milepost 97¼ safely and was steaming easily along the last lap towards Fort William. It was an exceptionally hot day, the sun temperature a foot above the grass in Fort William being no less than 128 deg. F. Suddenly Thornton noticed a bad kink in the rails in front of him. Before he could do anything the tender and entire train, but not the engine, left the rails. The Board of Trade report on the accident trounced the West Highland for badly maintained track; which was disconcerting for the owners of a new railway.

DISAPPOINTMENT

That the West Highland had made life easier for the people of Lochaber was beyond doubt, but the line was not the panacea for the ills of the Highlands that its promoters had thought it would be. The tourist trade boomed, and summer passenger traffic was even better than the directors had anticipated. But in winter there were few travellers in the West Highlands and the trains ran for the most part with only a handful of passengers. The meagre freight traffic developed very slowly and the pattern remained almost static for over 30 years; then the British Aluminium Company changed the face of Lochaber (see page 126).

The West Highland cattle and sheep farmers had been assured that the new railway would give them direct access to the markets of Perth and Stirling, *via* the Crianlarich spur to the Callander & Oban Railway. Cattle traffic to those destinations was indeed secured, but it was routed *via* Glasgow, because the Crianlarich spur was not ready. After the autumn cattle sales of 1895, the town authorities of Perth and Stirling protested to the West Highland over its failure to provide the promised direct (and cheaper) route. The Crianlarich spur was brought into use on 20 December 1897. Round about the same time the people of Oban agitated for a direct service to and from Oban and Glasgow *via* the West Highland and the Callander & Oban. They eventually got it—in 1949.

Crianlarich became the main servicing point for all trains and their passengers. It was a standard island station, but in addition to having the usual building for the station offices, and a signal box, it was provided with a privately-owned refreshment room that became famous in the annals of the railway. Here originated the celebrated breakfast and luncheon baskets which were supplied to passengers during the Crianlarich stop. On the up side of the island platform were a short siding, a turntable and a small engine shed. On the down side were three sidings, one of which served a cattle

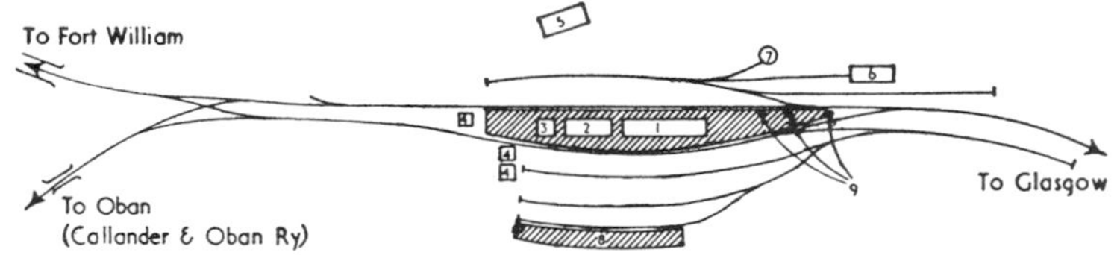

Crianlarich Upper station

1. main station offices
2. refreshment rooms
3. signal box
4. water towers
5. main water reservoir
6. engine shed
7. turntable
8. cattle loading platform
9. water columns

(E) *The most spectacular of many viaducts on the West Highland: Glenfinnan, with North British Locomotive Co Class 29 Bo-Bo D6101 crossing in April 1967*

loading bank. Immediately north of the platform end the spur to the Callander & Oban diverged to the left. It was worked by tablet, a North British instrument being housed in the C & O box. Special attention was paid to the watering of the engines. Before the end of the steam era, when it was common to see two double-headed trains in the station at one time, all four engines taking water simultaneously, a large main reservoir on the hillside overlooking the up road fed three water towers at rail level. At both ends of the platforms water columns were arranged in pairs, so that both pilot and train engine could take water at the same time.

It very soon became apparent that Fort William station was cramped and unable to cope satisfactorily with the peak summer traffic. But there was nothing the West Highland could do about it, for the station was crushed between Loch Linnhe and the buildings of the High Street. There were three platforms, two of which were docks. The third platform line ran alongside the sea wall, carried on beyond the station, crossed the end of MacBrayne's pier and terminated on a jetty just beyond. The three platform lines converged on to the single main line immediately beyond the platform ends. The short trains of the early days were easily accommodated, but increasing traffic brought longer trains and one of these at any platform completely bottled up the station and prevented all movement. Things became really hectic when trains ran out of course and Fort William had a Glasgow—Mallaig and a Mallaig—Glasgow to handle at the same time. Both had to reverse in and out of the station and usually a certain amount of 'topping and tailing' was called for. Much time was lost in conducting these operations in the cramped space available.

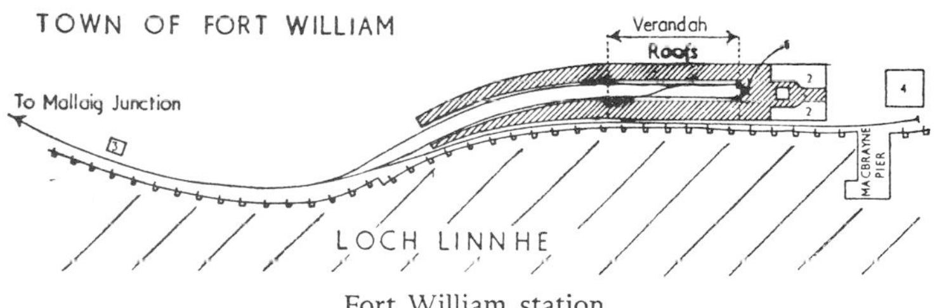

Fort William station

1. bookstall
2. main offices
3. signal box
4. MacBrayne depot
5. lever frame controlling crossover points in station

(F) Crianlarich was the most important station between Craigendoran and Fort William, having a refreshment room, engine shed and junction with the Callander & Oban line. NBL Class 29 Bo-Bo D6107 is seen at the head of an Oban-Glasgow train in May 1968

In the early years the revenue of the line showed a steady rise. Here are the combined passenger and freight traffic receipts for the years specified.

1896	£45,146	12	10
1897	£54,703	14	9
1898	£62,553	4	10
1899	£69,626	3	4
1900	£89,760	16	4
1901	£92,260	8	4

But the line never climbed out of the red. Once working expenses had been paid the North British had to dip into its own coffers to make up the interest on the guaranteed West Highland stock.

In 1899 the North British had to find £34,000 to pay interest due to West Highland stockholders. Maintenance costs on the new railway were light at first but these increased with the passing of the years. North British shareholders became restive over the West Highland. 'I would not venture to prophesy,' lamented the parent company's chairman in 1907, 'whether it (the West Highland) will *ever* pay an adequate return.'

CHAPTER 6

The Road to the Isles

THE MALLAIG EXTENSION

The West Highland Railway as planned had an outlet to the western seas. When feudalism robbed the railway of that outlet the West Highland lost one of the main reasons for its very existence—to provide communication with the far-west fishing and crofting communities and with the peoples of the Western Isles. True enough Fort William was on salt water but, by an accident of geography, Loch Linnhe was far from the fishing grounds. The fishing villages of the west were 40 miles overland from Fort William but close on 100 miles away by water. The West Highland, if it were to survive, could not let its terminal remain at Fort William. The railway had to get to the sea, if only to channel to the main line the fish traffic that alone would give the line a chance of paying its way.

John Aird and Cameron of Lochiel had a look at the country west of Fort William. They liked Loch Nevis as a base for a port; it was deep and sheltered by surrounding mountains and it was close to Skye. But south of Loch Nevis was a tough mountain barrier that would be costly to pierce, so they settled on Mallaig Bay, 4 miles south of Loch Nevis. A railway from Mallaig to the nearest point on the West Highland would be 39 miles and 53 chains long.

In March 1892 the Government sent a committee consisting of Major-General Hutchinson, Rear-Admiral Sir G. S. Nares and Mr Henry Tennant to the West Highlands to inquire into the need for transport and harbours. These gentlemen found that the landowners who had been so obstructive in the recent past were now inclined to modify their views. The more progressive among them even offered their land for a railway at below market prices. The crofters were so enthusiastic that 400 of them offered to work on the construction of the line and devote one-sixth of their wages to the purchase of shares in the railway.

The investigating trio also picked Mallaig Bay as the best place for a railway terminal. They suggested that a breakwater be built to enclose 30 acres of water and that a connecting line be constructed to the West Highland at Banavie. They considered that such a railway built through extremely difficult and sparsely-populated country would have no chance of paying its way and suggested the payment of a £100,000 grant to the builders. Meanwhile the North British railway separately had reached the conclusion that the Mallaig Extension would not pay and the directors were not prepared to recommend its construction to their shareholders unless the Government gave adequate financial guarantees.

The West Highland promoted its West Highland Railway (Mallaig Extension) Bill in January 1894, with the object of building a railway from a point on its Banavie branch to the coast at Mallaig. At the same time the Lords Commissioners of Her Majesty's Treasury were empowered to pay certain grants and dividends to the builders and to holders of Mallaig Extension stock. This gave rise to the quite separate West Highland Railway (Guarantee) Bill. The position was that the promoters had to get their West Highland Railway (Mallaig Extension) Bill passed in the usual way and then await Parliament passing the West Highland Railway (Guarantee) Bill, which would guarantee some of the finance for the project. Without the Guarantee Bill the Extension Bill was useless, and the railway could not be built.

The West Highland Railway (Guarantee) Bill required the promoters of the Mallaig line to satisfy certain conditions. First of all they had to present their bill to Parliament and have it passed. In addition they had to submit plans for the harbour at Mallaig and have them approved by the Government. They were further required to enter into an agreement with the North British Railway whereby that company would maintain and work the line in perpetuity in return for half the gross receipts. Now that Government backing was assured the North British stood behind the West Highland and the promotion of the line was pushed with vigour.

The Highland Railway opposed the Mallaig Extension. It was about to take its Dingwall—Strome Ferry line out to the coast at Kyle of Lochalsh, some 20 miles north of Mallaig, and wanted at all cost to avoid competition from a rival line. Moreover its existing mail contract was worth £27,000, and it visualized losing part of this traffic to the newcomer. As on similar occasions in the past, fish featured prominently in the arguments for and against the line. Cameron of Lochiel spoke of west coast fish being dumped into the sea because there was no means of transporting them south. But Lord Portman told the House of Lords that the fish were thrown back because they were too small! The west coast crabs, the committee were assured, were pathetic creatures compared with the robust crabs handled by the Highland Railway. There was no lack of witnesses to prove that Mallaig would be a dangerous place for a harbour. Donald McDonald, whom the Highland Railway introduced as the man who knew more about Skye than anyone else, declared, 'Mallaig is no harbour at all. It is just a pretty wee bay.'

The committee listened patiently to the arguments, but they were not impressed. The truth was that the time had come when the people of the west must get their railway. To save useless legal expenses the Highland forthwith withdrew its opposition and as a goodwill gesture the North British gave it £500 towards its Parliamentary expenses. The West Highland Railway (Mallaig Extension) Act was passed on 31 July 1894.

Not all dealings between railway promoters and landlords were rancorous. Lord Lovat had been a relentless opponent of the Mallaig Railway but, when the fight was over and the railway was victorious, Lord Lovat's solicitors, Macdonald & Graham of Inverness, wrote in these terms to the secretary of the WHR:

> Before allowing the settlement which has just taken place to pass out of memory, we hope you will not take it amiss if we send you a private expression of our appreciation of your uniform courtesy and ability throughout the whole course of the negotiations. Keen and tenacious to a degree over what you considered your just rights you never pushed your views too far but, after due discussions, met ours in a fair and broad spirit. Without reflection upon others who have to do with railway affairs, we must say that so far as our experience goes your methods formed a pleasant contrast to the narrower and obstructive tactics which we sometimes observed elsewhere. It will be a pleasure to us to meet you again and fight as keenly as ever with the same happy results.

A POLITICAL PAWN

Meanwhile, the vital Guarantee bill was having a rough passage in the House of Commons. Unhappily, the Mallaig Railway became a pawn in the game of party politics, a political issue of some magnitude. The urgent need of the people of the West Highlands for a railway was forgotten amid the squalid arguments of the politicians. Mallaig was a long way from Westminster. The gist of the situation was that the Tories approved of public subsidies for transport, the Liberals did not. The anti-subsidy faction set themselves up as guardians of the public purse and expressed horror at the 'free gift' being handed over to the railway promoters and their shareholders.

The principal architect of the opposition to the bill was a Scottish radical member, J. H. Dalziel, who represented Kirkcaldy. Dalziel hated the North British. His constituency was wholly in North British territory, and he maintained that the company used its monopoly to hold the district to ransom. In the Guarantee bill Dalziel saw a plot by the rich and rapacious North British to exploit the West Highland and so extend its own influence at the taxpayers' expense. Unfortunately, the chairman of the North British played into Dalziel's hands by delivering an incredibly tactless speech at a shareholders' meeting. Here are the fatal words:

> It is of the utmost importance that that company (the West Highland) should be connected with the coast, and the directors of the North British believing it to be of paramount importance in their interest that this extension is made have agreed to work the line. If the Government carry out their promise the company as a matter of fact will obtain a railway 40 miles in length for the moderate sum of £100,000. In any case we think this is a gift one should not look askance at, but rather is an opportunity to take full advantage of the generosity of the Treasury.

With relish the radicals seized on those careless phrases 'in their interest' and 'a gift'. There were members from comfortable English constituencies who could not have pointed out Mallaig on the map if their lives depended on it, who now thundered against the Mallaig Railway. It was a heaven-sent stick with which to beat the Government. 'The plain truth,' insisted Dalziel,

> is that from the moment of its inception the Bill has been a flagrant political manoeuvre. The only interest the taxpayer is to have in the undertaking is to be allowed to pay. Notwithstanding that the capital is to be subscribed on the strength of the Government guarantee no provision is made for the Government having any voice upon the board of management as is the case in regard to the Caledonian Canal, or having any substantial guarantee that the company's affairs shall be wisely and economically conducted. As it is not pretended, even by the promoters, that the line will be a commercial success we have the spectacle of public funds being pledged to the extent of a quarter of a million of money without even providing for a report as to the operation of the company to whose exchequer we are so liberally to contribute.

An election in Inverness was fought with the Mallaig Railway as a main issue. At campaign meetings candidates were questioned on their attitude to the railway, and there was no mistaking the fact that audiences favoured the candidate who pledged support for the Guarantee bill. The Tory candidate even managed to produce at the last minute that hoary electioneering device, the 'stunt' letter. This particular letter was said to have been written by the Tory Chancellor of the Exchequer to the secretary of the West Highland Railway, and in it he stated that he fully recognized the importance of the Mallaig Railway. The implication was that the return of the Government candidate would ensure the passing of the bill. The rival candidate complained, 'I doubt whether the records of Parliamentary elections provide a more shameless and open-faced political bribe to the electors.'

The efforts of Dalziel and his friends forced the withdrawal of the Mallaig bill. There was anger and dismay in the Highlands. Anticipating that the Guarantee bill would be passed with alacrity, many of the men who had built the West Highland had stayed on in Lochaber. Lucas & Aird, confident that the contract for the Extension would be theirs, put both men and equipment into a proposed base camp at Corpach, overlooking the spot where the first sod would be turned.

When news of the failure of the bill reached Lochaber, the navvies marched from Corpach into Fort William, where they joined the townsfolk in a demonstration against the railway wreckers. Effigies of Dalziel and another Scottish M.P. who had opposed the bill were made and labelled respectively *Kirkcaldy Brat* and *Highland Traitor*. The effigies were kicked through the main street of the town at the head of a procession some hundreds strong to the public refuse dump where they were ceremonially burned. Lucas & Aird struck camp and took their men and equipment to a new railway venture in the south of England.

The set-back to the railway could only be temporary. The Guarantee bill came up in Parliament again in 1896 and this time it was passed. By the terms of the Act the Treasury undertook to guarantee the shareholders 3 per cent on £260,000 of the West Highland (Mallaig Extension) capital, and to make a grant of £30,000 towards the £45,000 pier at Mallaig. The new railway was given preferential treatment in the matter of rating. Section 2 of the Act said:

> The railway shall not be assessed to any local rate at a higher value than at which the land occupied by the railway would have been assessed if it had remained in the condition in which it was immediately before it was acquired for the purpose of the railway.

Under the terms of the Act the railway's annual rate bill was

£147 1s 11d. If it had been assessed *as a railway* the amount payable would have been about £9,000. English members were aggrieved by the benefits conferred on the Mallaig Extension promoters. English railways, they protested, had to find their interest out of their earnings, whereas the Highlanders who had done nothing to help themselves (*sic*) were being mollycoddled.

But English spleen did not prevent the Highlanders from getting the railway for which they had fought for so long. Lady Margaret Cameron of Lochiel cut the first sod in a field at Corpach on 21 January 1897. The Act specified 31 July 1902 as the time-limit for the completion of the line, so that the contractors had 5 years 6 months and 10 days in which to build 40 miles of track.

'CONCRETE BOB'

A fresh team embarked on the construction of the Mallaig Railway. The engineers were Simpson & Wilson, and the contractors were Robert McAlpine & Sons, both of Glasgow. The head of the firm of contractors was the same Robert McAlpine who had walked across the Moor of Rannoch in 1889. He was known in civil engineering circles as 'Concrete Bob'.

He was an enthusiastic advocate of the relatively new building medium, mass concrete, and on the Mallaig Extension he was given a glorious opportunity to do wonderful things with concrete. For the next five years McAlpine was to be the central figure in the greatest concentration of concrete construction in the world. The Mallaig line had to be built on the cheap, and concrete was from 10 per cent to 30 per cent cheaper than masonry. (Even if he had wanted McAlpine could not have repeated Lucas & Aird's tactics and used local stone for his bridge piers, for the stone on the Mallaig Railway was virtually unworkable.) Again, the flooring of a concrete viaduct did not have to be painted or replaced; there was no ironwork to rust. And concrete bridges were more in keeping than steel bridges with the scenic splendour of the west.

McAlpine appointed his son Robert, aged 28, to take full charge of construction, and his younger son Malcolm, aged 19, was made his assistant. The route of the Mallaig line was much more accessible than had been the main line. The first 12½ miles along Loch Eil were approachable at every point by sea. A pier was built at Locheilhead and workshops established beside it, and further camps were set up at Mallaig, Morar Beach, Lochailort and Arisaig. The labour force consisted of Irishmen, Lowland Scots, Highlanders,

Scandinavians and men from the islands who spoke only Gaelic.

The largest camp was established at Lochailort; eventually it housed 2,000 of the 3,500 navvies who worked on the line. The old schoolhouse was converted into an eight-bed hospital, staffed by two nurses and a resident doctor; it was the first hospital to be set up on a construction site in Britain. The navvies were housed in huts with beds for 40. They did their own cooking over a hotplate situated in the middle of a large central hut. The navvy's favourite cooking utensil was his shovel, which he kept spotlessly clean and brightly polished when not in use. A large, well-stocked provision shop was provided at Lochailort and a chain of 18 local shops was established along the line. These were supplied by Cooper & Co., a high-class Glasgow firm of provision merchants, and their contract with McAlpine required them to sell only the best quality foodstuffs. The camp bakery provided fresh bread daily. The navvies were paid 4½d or 5d per hour, but a bonus system based on actual work done augmented their earnings.

A writer in McAlpine's house magazine gave this picture of the navvy of the Mallaig line era.

> The regular navvy was proud of his calling and a good man was never out of a job. If their methods were old-fashioned they were skilled in a way which is fading in fashion to-day. They were without many of the mechanical aids known so well to the modern contractor, but as tunnellers, timbermen, platelayers, horse handlers, or in the plain use of a pick and shovel many of them were artists in their own way. Even in their dress they stood out from other men—cloth cap, silk muffler knotted round the neck, heavy grey flannel or checked shirt, corduroy trousers and stout leather hobnail boots. The trousers were supported by at least one stout belt instead of braces which would constrict shoulder movement, and fastened under the knee with leather 'Yorks' to keep them up out of the mud. The more prosperous navvy sported a real moleskin waistcoat.

The navvy's lot on the Mallaig Extension was not an easy one. By 5 a.m. Lochailort camp was a buzz of activity, with men streaming out of the huts to wash in cold water pouring directly into the wash basins from mountain burns. Then came the surge round the hotplate as breakfasts were prepared, followed by the trudge to the working area. Often the weather was wet and disagreeable. It is little wonder that McAlpine, in spite of the good conditions offered, could not retain labour. Navvies came for a few weeks, and left again for the more hospitable south. Tradesmen were particularly difficult to obtain. At one time a force of over 400 joiners was needed for the concrete work, and great difficulty was experienced in attracting and retaining good men. There was a shortage of labour, too, at Locheilhead pier, and supplies were held up because ships could not be unloaded. The owners of a steamer that brought a cargo to Loch Eil in the winter of 1896-7 claimed £314 8s 4d demurrage. The half-yearly reports submitted to the West Highland board by Simpson & Wilson regularly lamented the slowness of progress due to shortage of labour.

At the outset McAlpine had been confident that the line would be ready for the summer traffic of 1900, but unforeseen difficulties slowed construction. On the stretch of line along Loch Eil the track rose no higher than 32½ ft and the contractors' materials were taken by boat to the exact spot where they were required. It was when the railway left Loch Eil that the skill of the builders was taxed, for it had to be taken through rough country calling for stretches of gradient at 1 in 48 and 1 in 50 as well as constant severe curvature. The engineers had hoped to get through to Mallaig with only two tunnels; in the end they needed eleven.

The hard rock encountered greatly slowed progress. Many experiments were carried out to find out the best type of steel drill. At times the steam-operated air compressors could not produce enough air to drive all the drills working in the tunnels and cuttings.

A solution to the problem came to young Malcolm McAlpine in the best Archimedes-in-the-bath tradition when he was sitting in a dentist's chair in Helensburgh. He noticed that the dentist made the drill work by pressing a knob on the floor with his foot. On asking how the device worked, Malcolm was told that the knob operated a valve in a water pipe under the floor, causing a flow of high-pressure water to impinge on a Pelton wheel which provided the rotary motion for the drill. A water turbine! Malcolm asked Andrew Reid, his chief engineer, if a water turbine could be used to provide power for the air compressors. The engineer decided that this was feasible, and an Edinburgh turbine specialist was invited to supply suitable machinery with a compressor coupled to it.

To obtain water for the turbine a dam 7 ft high was built across Loch Dubh. A 21 in. steel pipe carried the water from the dam for 140 yd to the turbine which revolved at 900 r.p.m. The air produced was then conveyed to the workings by a system of cast iron or malleable iron screwed pipes. By the end of 1897 the turbine was working night and day and the air was powering rock drills over two miles of cuttings and tunnels. The engineer reported that the turbine was doing four times the amount of work of the steam compressor it replaced.

It was ironical that young Malcolm McAlpine should have been one of the few serious cases admitted to the hospital at Lochailort. He was superintending a blast in a rock cutting when a sudden explosion showered him with shrapnel-like fragments of rock. He fell to the ground seriously wounded. The doctor at the hospital found that the youth had a fractured pelvis, broken ribs and serious internal injuries caused by rock fragments penetrating his body. That afternoon a telegram was dispatched to his father in Glasgow telling him of his son's grave injuries and adding that he was not expected to live.

Robert McAlpine (senior) got in touch at once with Glasgow's most distinguished surgeon. Professor Sir William Macewen, who agreed to go to Lochailort. By that time the last West Highland train had long since left Glasgow, so the contractor ordered a special. When it reached Craigendoran with its two passengers it was found that the West Highland was closed from end to end and no apparent arrangement had been made to open it. The engine driver had been instructed not to proceed beyond Craigendoran without further orders. Robert McAlpine argued and pleaded with him and eventually, when the contractor said that he would take full responsibility for what happened, the driver set off. Tales have been told about the train's night-long journey. It is said that it covered the length of the West Highland without the benefit of a single tablet and with the driver and fireman manipulating point levers where necessary. What is certain is that the train reached Fort William about 5 a.m. The doctor and contractor roused a coachman, and after seven hours of jolting over the terrible road to the Isles, they reached Lochailort in the early afternoon.

By that time Malcolm was very low. With none of the refinements to which he was accustomed in his own operating theatre, Macewen performed a major operation. Then he sat by his patient for four days and nights. At length he decided that the only hope of saving Malcolm's life lay in getting him to Glasgow. And the transport of the sick man highlighted graphically the lack of communications that the railway was planned to alleviate. Malcolm could not be taken by road; the jolting would have killed him. There was nothing for it but to take him by stretcher to the still distant railhead. Professor Macewen trained eight railway navvies in the art of stretcher bearing and on the morning of the fifth day after the explosion the men set off bearing their injured employer over the rough country. At the end of 2 miles they came to the shore of Loch Eilt, where the stretcher was placed on a boat and towed 3 miles to the other end of the loch. Then followed a gruelling 4 miles overland to Glenfinnan where a halt was made for the night. A window had to be removed in the Glenfinnan hotel to allow the stretcher to be taken into the building.

The stretcher party set off next morning at first light. Two miles took them to the westernmost point reached by the railway, where an engine and wagon were waiting. A long chain coupling was provided between the engine and the vehicle. Navvies sat facing each other in two rows, one on the buffer beam of the engine, the other on the frame of the wagon, their legs touching and braced to take shocks during the slow, careful journey. At Locheilhead the stretcher was transferred to a steamer and taken down the loch to Banavie where a special was waiting to rush the patient to Glasgow. His navvies travelled with him and when the train reached the city they carried him on his stretcher through the streets to Professor Macewen's nursing home. Sir Malcolm McAlpine celebrated his 87th birthday on 19 June 1964.

BORRODALE BURN

The Mallaig line bridges were built of concrete, most of them in standard spans of 50 ft. The most spectacular viaduct was the one at Glenfinnan which used twenty-one standard spans. There was another at Arnabol Glen, and at Loch nan Uamh there was a viaduct of eight 50 ft arches. A 90 ft span was required to take the line across the River Morar almost under the Falls of Morar. At Borrodale Burn 'Concrete Bob' faced his biggest challenge. The defile in which the burn ran was wide, and the original intention was to put piers in the stream and build a series of standard arches. The owner agreed to this provided that McAlpine clad the piers in granite. Since that was a highly expensive procedure the contractor decided to cross the gap in a single span. Never before had a mass concrete span of such dimensions been built.

Borrodale Bridge has a clear span of 127 ft 6 in. and two side spans of 20 ft each. It is 86 ft high and has a rise of 22½ ft. It created world-wide attention. The American *Engineering News* featured the bridge in an article in 1899. In 1909 an American civil engineer, H. Gratton Tyrell, published a table putting Borrodale Bridge in its proper perspective. The table, which listed major mass concrete bridges built between 1893 and 1909, showed that in the five years before Borrodale only three concrete bridges had been built, all of them road bridges and all the design of the German

RAILWAY PIERS

(33) *Banavie Pier station in 1935. The embankment of the Caledonian Canal is behind the station. The station itself was not renamed. Notice the original West Highland name board*

(34) *Fort Augustus Pier station when in use about 1905*

STATION SCENES

(35) *Rolling stock of the 'big four' companies at Arisaig in 1938. The goods train has been divided to make a passage for the sheep*

(36) *Panorama at Mallaig, 24 May 1952. The engines, left to right, are 'Loch Laidon', 'Loch Eil', 'Loch Rannoch' and 'Loch Sheil'. Steam crane in the centre*

engineer Leibrand. In the eleven years following the building of Borrodale fifty-two concrete bridges were built.

Labour troubles and bad weather continued to hinder progress. In the engineer's report to shareholders on 4 July 1899 it was stated, 'The Contractor has not made good progress owing to the difficulty of getting men.' By January 1900, 33 miles of track had been laid and of the remaining 7 miles 6 were formed ready for the rails. But that same month the engineer again reported: 'We regret to state that in spite of all our efforts there is not a sufficient force of men on the works to insure the completion of the line in time for next summer's traffic.' The last winter was the worst of all for weather. In December 1900 the rainfall in the district was 29 in. above normal. With each delay the radicals began sniping in Parliament. The President of the Board of Trade was frequently under fire about progress on the line, or lack of it. But even in the middle of 1900 he was able to take refuge in the fact that the time limit for completion was still two years away.

In all McAlpine had to excavate 100 cuttings. In complete contrast to the rock work, he had to use the Rannoch Moor floating technique to get the line across bog at Keppoch Moss, north of Arisaig. Mallaig harbour was also his responsibility, the harbour works being constructed of concrete blocks. Stations were built at Banavie, Corpach, Locheilside, Glenfinnan, Lochailort, Morar, and Arisaig, and there was a private station—Beasdale—for Arisaig House between Lochailort and Arisaig. The station platforms and buildings were of concrete. Banavie, Corpach, Locheilside and Morar had one platform only and no loops. In the double platform stations the station buildings were on the down side only, the up side being provided with a small wooden shelter. In the interests of economy sleeper crossings were provided at the platform ends instead of the conventional overbridge. The signalling was by the Railway Signal Company, which also provided wooden signal boxes of its own design.

Mallaig station alone had an island platform. The station was built on a shelf of rock jutting out into the water, and a stout stone wall was erected on the seaward side to protect the platforms from the gales that would at times sweep in from the western seas. The point where the Mallaig railway left the Banavie branch was named Banavie Junction, and the original Banavie Junction was re-named Mallaig Junction. This had the effect of shortening the Banavie branch to three-quarters of a mile. The original Banavie station became Banavie Pier: the name was changed in the timetables and official documents, but not on the station itself. It still exhibited its original West Highland name-board 'Banavie' forty years after a new station of the same name had been provided less than 1 mile away.

VICTORY AT LAST

When the steamer *Clydesdale* cleared Stornoway harbour just after 11 o'clock on the night of 31 March 1901, she had on board the first passengers ever booked through from Lewis to Glasgow and Edinburgh by the new iron road to the isles. At daybreak when the vessel entered the brand-new harbour at Mallaig the passengers crossed to the waiting train where they were joined by people just in from Portree in the *Lovedale*. At 7.20 a.m. the first ever up train on the Mallaig Extension departed for the south. Some two hours later it crossed the first down train, the 5.55 a.m. from Glasgow bringing passengers for their first experience of the new railway.

The train from the south had stopped only at Arrochar and Tarbet, Crianlarich and Spean Bridge, and arrived at Fort William at 9.50, where a fresh engine was attached at what had been its rear. At 10 a.m. the train pulled out to Mallaig Junction, rumbled over the Lochy Viaduct and at the new Banavie Junction ran on to the metals of the Mallaig Extension. As the train worked its way round the elbow bend of Loch Linnhe and Loch Eil, and crossed the Caledonian Canal on a swing bridge pivoted on one bank to leave the whole channel clear for shipping, the passengers had excellent views of Ben Nevis towering in all its brute mass above Fort William. A stop at Corpach was followed by a lively sprint along the shore of Loch Eil on track unaccustomedly straight and level for the West Highlands.

But at the end of Loch Eil mountains closed in on the railway, and the engine's exhaust became more and more laboured as the track pushed its way up a narrow glen and into the heart of some of the most glorious scenery in the world. Within ten minutes the train burst out of the confines of the pass into the natural amphitheatre at the head of Loch Sheil, encircled by mountains except where the long tongue of Loch Sheil pushed its way in from the west. The railway entered dramatically from the right and crossed the arena on a gracefully curving and dazzling white viaduct of twenty-one arches. Down below by the lochside the passengers could see the lighthouse-like monument that marked the spot where Prince Charlie unfurled his standard in 1745.

(G) *The attractive canopy at Mallaig station has been demolished, leaving a stark platform. Here, before such depredations, Class 27 D5356 waits to leave with a Glasgow train on 6 April 1971*

WEST HIGHLANDER
5407

Glenfinnan Viaduct curves in a crescent of 12 chains radius for 1,248 ft across the Finnan Valley. The track is supported on slender white pillars 100 ft above the ground, each pair being surmounted by a semi-circular arch with a span of 50 ft. The concrete that went into the making of the viaduct (see page 96) had as one of its constituents crushed rock from the cutting through which the railway passed to enter the valley. It is a beautiful structure, but it is best seen from high up in the surrounding mountains. Then it looks like a Roman aqueduct in a remarkable state of preservation. The Scottish author, J. J. Bell, a staunch friend of the West Highland Railway, described the viaduct as 'a thing so delicate that the fairies might have built it'.

In Glenfinnan they tell a story (perhaps apocryphal) about an incident at the building of Glenfinnan Viaduct. Some of the vertical pillars had hollow interiors, and before the superstructure supporting the rails was built the tops of the columns were open to the sky. It is said that a horse which was being led with a cart over planking resting temporarily across the top of a column slipped into the interior; animal and cart plunged 100 ft down the hollow shaft. Because of the difficulty of removing the carcase the remains were buried inside the pillar.

A brief halt at Glenfinnan station and the train was off again through a narrow wooded glen that took it to the shores of Loch Eilt. The railway began high above the loch and dropped rapidly on a series of reverse curves until the train was running at water level.

The Mallaig Railway is never far from water, salt or fresh. From Loch Eilt it follows the river Ailort to the point where it meets Loch Ailort. Then it crosses the wooded peninsula of Ardnish, past little Loch Dubh and across Glen Mamie on a viaduct to emerge at Loch nan Uamh—the Loch of the Caves. It is when the line meets the Atlantic at Loch nan Uamh that the climax of the journey is reached. In high summer a mass of luxuriant growth sweeps down the hillsides to the edges of the sea. The trees are almost tropical in their brilliance. Where the belt of lush green meets the contour of the many bays is a fringe of rock covered with bright orange seaweed, and beyond that an expanse of blue water ribbed with green. There is a hint of the South Seas about the scene. The islands sparkling out on the polished surface of the ocean might well be Pacific islands; Eigg with its unreal, block-shaped Sgur has a volcanic look about it. Further up the coast at Arisaig palms flourish and there is a garden full of sub-tropical plants.

It is hard to believe that the wilderness of Rannoch is on the

(H) *LMS Class 5 No 5407 leaves Fort William with the SLOA West Highlander railtour for Mallaig on Sunday 27 May 1984, the first public steam working over the West Highland for twenty-two years*

same railway line three hours away. The Gulf Stream, bringing its warmth direct to the west-coast bays, confers many benefits on the Mallaig Extension. There are winters when the villages on the Mallaig line have dawn-to-dusk sunshine for days on end. It is not uncommon for the morning up train to begin its journey in mellow warmth and amid fields sprouting spring flowers and end it six hours later in a city still firmly in the grip of winter.

The first down train on that April opening morning made its way to Lochailort and Arisaig and then on to Morar of the silver sand. The train rattled along rocky galleries and plunged through short tunnels emerging in the intervals into a world ablaze with colour. Each twist of the line revealed enchanting new vistas. That stretch between Lochailort and Arisaig accounted for a disproportionate share of the half-million pounds that went into the making of the Mallaig Extension. In 8¼ miles there were no fewer than nine tunnels. From Morar the train slipped round the toothed coast with the mountains of Skye looming up ahead, to stop at 11.45 in Mallaig station. The *Clydesdale* and the *Lovedale* were waiting to receive their passengers. By 4.30 that afternoon the *Lovedale's* were disembarking at Portree, having taken 10 hours 35 minutes to travel from Glasgow to the capital of Skye. Travellers who had come all the way from London, leaving King's Cross at 8.15 the previous night, were landed at Stornoway at 8 p.m.—not quite a round of the clock.

In the first summer timetable Mallaig was given through-carriage and sleeping-carriage services with King's Cross, but these were not continued in subsequent years. Fort William became the terminus of the sleeping cars. An early innovation was a *weekend* return fare from Mallaig to London, 60s 6d for the 1,202 miles. This compared with the tourist return of 70s 6d and the ordinary return of 83s 8d. The ordinary return fare from Mallaig to Glasgow was 23s 7d, but mindful of its duty to the fishing community, the company issued a special fisherman's ticket at 18s 6d.

An immediate result of the opening of the Mallaig Extension was that it put Fort William and its amenities within easy reach of the people living in the 30 mile stretch of country between Locheilside and Mallaig. Before the railway came the district's transport consisted of one coach, which left Arisaig for Fort William on Tuesdays, Thursdays and Saturdays and returned on Mondays, Wednesdays and Fridays. The journey from Arisaig to Fort William took 7½ hours, and the single fare was 10s plus 1s driver's fee. The potential traveller had now a choice of from two to four trains a day (according to the time of the year); the journey time was under 90 minutes and the fare a fraction of the cost by coach.

Fish had been the magic word in all the long arguments leading up to the completion of the Mallaig Railway. Fish became and remained a staple item of West Highland freight, and for many years the red North British fish vans at the tail of a passenger train were a familiar sight on the line. But the traffic never attained the volume that the promoters had expected, and the east coast's supremacy was never seriously challenged. The best prices for prime fish in top condition were obtainable at Billingsgate and the fish dealers aimed at getting their fish shipped to London with all speed. To get fish caught on Friday night and Saturday to the London market for Monday morning meant that it had to be sent over the West Highland Railway on Sunday. What southern economists failed to understand was that Sunday working was completely unacceptable to the Highlanders, railwaymen and civil population alike. So powerful was religious feeling in these areas that the people, notwithstanding their desire for a railway, would have organized a boycott of the system if the company had transgressed their religious code. So weekend fish had to wait until Monday.

Militant Sabbatarianism was one hazard of railway operating in the Highlands that was not mentioned in the various prospectuses. What happened at Strome Ferry on Sunday 3 July 1882 is part of the story of the Highland Railway, but it is worth telling here if only because it gave a pointer to any railway company that attempted to handle the fish traffic of the district. On the last Sunday in May 1882 a fish train was loaded up at Strome Ferry on the Dingwall & Skye line and dispatched to London. When the fact became known there was rage and consternation in the area. On the following Sunday the railway company, aware of the popular feeling, arranged somewhat clandestinely to load and dispatch a train from Strome Ferry in the early hours of the morning. About 1 a.m. two vessels, the *Harold* and the *Locheil,* with 6,700 boxes of fish between them, slipped up Loch Carron and berthed at the railway pier. What happened next was described in the following day's *Glasgow Herald.*

> At that moment a body of about fifty natives armed with clubs and bludgeons presented themselves on the quay and stated they would not allow the unloading of the vessels to go on. It was the Lord's Day and they would not permit such a desecration of the Sabbath for fear of a judgement from heaven. The crowd forcibly ejected a man in

> charge of the steamers and, on the crews of the steamers and the railway officials persisting in unloading the fish, threatened them with personal violence. A fight ensued and those belonging to the steamers and the railway company were completely overpowered and compelled to give up hope of unloading the vessels.

Later that morning, when Highland Railway headquarters in Inverness were informed by telegraph of the situation at Strome Ferry, a special train was sent out, stopping at Dingwall on the way to pick up six policemen. They found Strome station and pier invested by some 150 angry and determined men. The police charged the crowd six times and were beaten back to stand cowed and impotent outside the station door. The Highland Railway then requested the military authorities for 'a detachment of bayonets' but the request was refused. Strome stayed in rebel hands until someone shouted 'Twelve o'clock', whereupon the demonstrators disappeared into the darkness. The fish, no longer fresh, left for London.

On the following Sunday the company ran three fish specials out of Strome while 300 policemen (sixty of them brought specially from Glasgow) held the rebels in check. At Fort George a troop train stood ready to rush the local garrison of Cameron Highlanders, reinforced by Gordon Highlanders brought in from Edinburgh the previous day, to the trouble spot. The lesson of the episode was plain to see. Fish, the mainstay of the economy of all the West Highland lines, could not be carried on these lines on a Sunday with impunity.

THE £ S D OF THE MALLAIG LINE

The railway brought immediate tangible benefits to the inhabitants of the district. There was a substantial drop in the prices of the necessities of life. Coal imported on the railway was cheaper than local peat, and coal supplanted peat as the almost universal domestic fuel. The tourist trade was good in that first year. There was a large-scale international exhibition in Glasgow in 1901, and some of the visitors made their way to the newly opened north-west. One visitor in 1902 was the general manager of the SE & CR and he has left this comment:

> I visited Fort William, Banavie and Mallaig. I found between these stations a very sparse population, and for some years to come there is very little chance of an increase in receipts. The company will have to look to the summer and excursion traffic which at the most can only last about three months. The beauties of the district seem to be

well advertised, and the traffic will no doubt be much augmented when the splendid scenery through which the line passes becomes better known.

Eleven years later Lt-Col E. Druitt, after making the annual inspection of the line on behalf of the Government which the West Highland Railway (Guarantee) Bill required, reported as follows:

The work in formations, banks, cuttings and tunnels is standing well, and shows no signs of weakness. The permanent way is in good order. Station buildings and passenger accommodation are well maintained. Generally speaking the maintenance and upkeep during the past twelve months have been very satisfactory. The North British Company continue to advertise the attractions of the railway with a view to developing the tourist traffic and endeavour by every reasonable means to promote the earning power of the line.

In spite of the uproar caused by the opponents of the Guarantee bill the Treasury was never called on to pay more than £4,000 under the terms of the guarantee in any one year between 1901 and 1914. The following table sets out the profit and loss account on the railway year by year, and shows the amounts paid by the Treasury.

Year	*Receipts*			*Expenses*			*Loss*			*Paid by Treasury under guarantee*		
	£	s.	d.	£	s.	d.	£	s.	d.	£	s.	d.
1901-2	8,525	1	7	19,385	9	8	10,833	8	1	3,789	19	9
1902-3	8,465	7	7	14,789	11	8	6,324	4	1	3,790	9	10
1903-4	8,856	13	8	15,606	17	3	6,750	3	7	3,594	6	10
1904-5	9,233	10	5	15,518	18	9	6,285	8	4	2,537	19	11
1905-6	9,126	13	1	15,113	5	0	5,986	11	11	3,228	18	11
1906-7	9,567	11	0	15,227	6	3	5,659	15	3	3,010	8	11
1907-8	9,602	6	10	15,477	15	3	5,874	8	5	3,033	10	7
1908-9	10,360	2	0	13,954	11	7	3,594	9	7	2,696	10	3
1909-10	9,983	7	9	13,195	10	7	3,212	2	10	2,852	9	9
1910-11	10,892	9	0	15,202	4	7	4,319	15	7	3,431	19	4
1911-12	11,044	3	8	13,061	15	8	2,017	12	0	2,325	6	8
1912-13	12,126	5	6	16,163	13	9	4,036	8	3	1,780	7	10
1913-14	9,691	1	4	17,469	3	8	7,778	2	4	1,600	11	4

During the period, the railway showed a trading loss of £72,672 10s 3d. The contribution made by the Treasury was £36,672 19s 11d. The following tables show an analysis of the receipts and expenses in two consecutive years.

Receipts from the Banavie Jc—Mallaig Sec

	1912-13	1913-14
Passengers	£5,644 8 5	£3,175 3 2
Parcels	£3,164 9 5	£2,842 12 2
Goods and Minerals	£2,753 8 5	£3,180 2 5
Livestock	£259 11 9	£211 9 4
Mails	£160 0 0	£160 0 0
Parcel post	£137 17 2	£116 3 5
News contract	£6 11 4	£6 11 4

Expenses

	1912-13	1913-14
Loco. dept	£5,281 1 0	£5,904 13 3
Maintenance	£7,942 19 2	£8,472 9 2
Traffic	£2,939 13 7	£3,089 11 3

In 1902 the North British Railway (General Powers) Act abolished all West Highland railway debenture and other stock guaranteed by the North British, and it was replaced with 3 per cent North British debentures. The West Highland thus became a railway without shareholders. Then the North British Railway Confirmation Act of 1908 gave the North British authority to absorb the entire West Highland undertaking. On 31 December 1908 the 142 miles of track comprising the original West Highland line, the Mallaig Extension and the Banavie branch passed to the ownership of the North British Railway. The system represented an investment of £2,370,000.

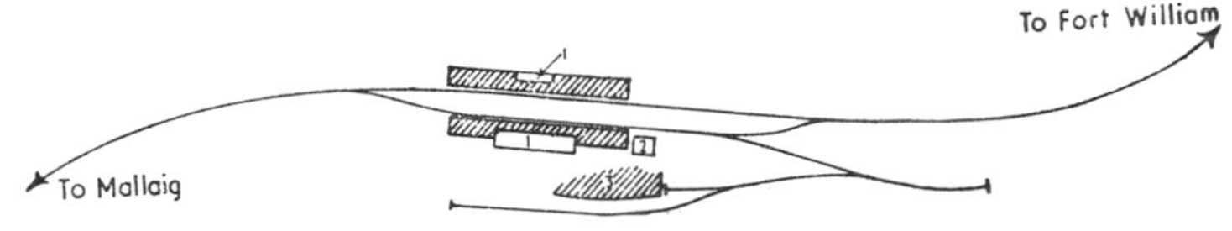

Glenfinnan station

1. station buildings
   On all Mallaig Extension stations with two platforms, the main buildings were on the down side, the up platform having only a hut
2. signal box
3. loading bank—end-on only to short siding
   No passenger footbridges; sleeper crossings only, at platform ends

CHAPTER 7

The Battle for Inverness

THE REMARKABLE VALLEY

'Strange as it may seem to you this day,' prophesied Conneach Odhar, the Brahan Seer, early in the seventeenth century, 'the time will come, and it is not far off, when full-rigged ships will be sailing eastwards and westward by Muirtown and Tomnahurich.'

The Seer was saying that sea-going vessels would be crossing the dry mainland of Scotland from Fort William to Inverness. The country between the two towns seemed to have been made by nature for a canal. It was as if the Creator had rolled back the mountains, as Moses had rolled back the Red Sea, to form a 60-mile valley stretching diagonally across the country from sea to sea. Telford, when he came to look at it, frequently wrote in his notes the phrase, 'this remarkable valley'. Over the years its inviting geographical features lured transport men to it. But it was to become a valley of lost transport causes, a glen of weeping for the people who set their hearts and fortunes on its conquest.

The Caledonian Canal was begun in 1804 and it was then designed to take the largest ocean-going ships. There was a heavy timber traffic in those days from the Baltic to Liverpool, and the timber ships were sometimes wrecked or delayed for weeks on end by contrary winds as they rounded the storm-swept north of Scotland—even if they escaped being harassed and destroyed by the French fleet. The Caledonian Canal was to provide a short, safe and easy passage for the Baltic timber boats as well as for traffic between Britain's east and west coasts.

Telford said he would make the canal in seven years for £350,000. But eighteen years passed before a partially completed channel was opened for traffic and nearly forty years before the canal was fully completed, and it had absorbed a million of money. By that time, steam, unknown when the canal was begun, was triumphant on land and sea. Anyway, the much bigger sea-going ships of 1843 could not even enter the canal conceived four decades earlier. Baltic timber was now taxed 300 per cent and Britain was importing timber from Canada. Above all, Waterloo had been fought and won and the French were no longer a menace on the seas. What had been planned as a great national highway had become a secondary shipping channel of use only to fishing vessels and small coasters. The Caledonian Canal was obsolete before it was opened.

Two years after the canal came into full operation the railway engineers were in the Great Glen seeking a route to Inverness. They might have got it and been first into Inverness from the south had the financial crash of 1845 not put paid to their schemes. In 1882 the Glasgow & North Western Railway engineers came to the remarkable valley. But by then the Highland Railway was established in Inverness and Highland policy was to resist every attack on its citadel. As we have seen in an earlier chapter, it easily defeated the North Western's attempt to reach Inverness. Ever after the Highland, realizing how vulnerable it was to attack up the Great Glen, was specially vigilant when any rival railway showed interest in the route. It had been suspicious when the West Highland Railway was promoted, and its suspicions, despite protestations of innocence, were justified. *Inverness* was the name engraved on the North British chairman's heart.

TEMPORARY TRUCE

The first West Highland—North British sortie into the Great Glen took place in 1893, when the Edinburgh-based consortium sought to take a line from Fort William to the Highland capital. The Highland Railway's immediate answer was a proposed line of its own from Inverness to Fort William.

It is possible that these were little more than claim-staking exercises. Neither side could have wanted to embark on a Great Glen railway, for both were heavily committed elsewhere. The North British had its West Highland line still to finish and the Mallaig Extension was in prospect. The Highland was in the process of building its very costly direct line from Aviemore to Inverness *via* Carr Bridge, and further developments were maturing in the Far North. The Aviemore—Inverness line was a by-product of the G & NW attempt to get to Inverness ten years earlier. The strongest argument for a West Highland route to Inverness was that it was shorter than the existing Highland route. By building the Aviemore cut-off the Highland was shortening its route and at the same time robbing future Great Glen schemes of what had been their main advantage.

Nothing came of the 1893 plans, but as soon as the West Highland Railway was open in 1894 the Highland and West Highland again produced rival schemes. The Highland looked for widespread local support in its defence against attack from the south. The railway considered itself a truly *Highland* railway, with its headquarters in Inverness, and with a duke and a brace each of marquesses, barons and baronets as well as local landowners on its board. The Highland Railway considered that the Highlanders owed it a debt of gratitude for having given them a railway, even if they had to pay the highest permitted fares for the privilege of using it. That this view was not universally accepted was made plain by Highlanders who welcomed the possibility of another company coming to Inverness.

Contemporary correspondence in the press—much of it anonymous—painted the Highlands as a feudal domain dominated by the big landowners, some of them directors of the Highland line. 'Against the Highland Railway scheme from Inverness to Spean we cannot organize opposition here like the people of the South,' lamented *Sutherlandshire* in the *Glasgow Herald*.

> Our landlord is sure to be a director, and we must keep quiet or suffer. We depend on the free south in its own interest and ours to see that the Highland Railway Company do not command every avenue to the Highlands. If the Highland Railway Company gain their ends the progress of the North and South will be retarded for a century.

This correspondent thought that the lot of the Highlanders would be easier if the West Highland pushed on not only to Inverness but into Highland Railway preserves in the Far North. 'Let there be a junction ten miles or so south of Inverness and from there let the railway extend northwards to the Muir of Ord (for the markets) and on in a straight line to Bonar Bridge and over the Oykel to Dornoch.'

Another correspondent had faith in neither the North British nor the Highland. He wrote:

> I have a strong sympathy with the people of Inverness who are of the opinion that it would be an advantage to the whole district if another company was to come in and provide competition. The history of the Highland Company has been that of close conservation to what might be termed aristocratic ideas of management. They have not catered in any popular sense for the million.

Of the North British he added, 'The policy that guides it gives with a most grudging hand any benefits the public obtain. It does not seem to me desirable that the future extension of the railway enterprise in the Highlands should be kept to either of these two companies.' This correspondent saw the solution to the north's transport problems in a *Caledonian* invasion of the Highlands. The Caledonian, he said, should build a grand scenic line from Oban round the coast by Ballachulish to Fort William and on through the Great Glen to Inverness.

The 1894 phase of the struggle for the Great Glen was short-lived. It ended when in December, William Whitelaw, chairman of the Highland Railway, received a letter from Lord Tweeddale, his opposite number on the North British, suggesting that the parties concerned should meet 'in an amicable spirit' to discuss their problems. Only eight members of the Highland board attended the Highland Railway meeting at which the North British letter was discussed, and the diehards wanted to continue the fight. But reason prevailed and representatives of the Highland, West Highland and North British met in Edinburgh in February 1895. As a result, both sides withdrew their current bills from Parliament, and undertook not to promote railways in the Great Glen during the next ten years. The Caledonian and the Callander & Oban entered into the spirit of the thing and in the same month withdrew a bill by which they had hoped to reach the southern end of the Great Glen from Oban.

BURTON'S FOLLY

The peace of the Great Glen was shattered in 1896 by the appearance of a private company calling itself the Invergarry & Fort Augustus Railway, which proposed to build a railway linking Spean Bridge with Fort Augustus. This was a perfectly genuine local line with no association financially or otherwise with the two big contenders for power in the glen. It was to some extent a one-man show; the principal instigator and chairman was Lord Burton, and he put up more than half the capital. His supporters were well-meaning but foolhardy local patriots (and their friends in the south) who were devoted to the idea of giving their district a railway.

The Invergarry & Fort Augustus was an incredibly ill-conceived venture, the classic example of the railway that should not have been built. The line, 24 miles long, was to run from Spean Bridge, where there was nothing but a bridge and a few cottages, to Fort Augustus, which boasted a Benedictine monastery, a handful of houses, and a pier on the Caledonian Canal. The intervening country was devoid of industry and supported only a few hundred people. Of Fort Augustus itself a local guide book said: 'It may not be without interest to note that it is exactly in the centre of the deer forest country and that, if the very fertile land east of Inverness be excluded, 99 per cent of the country within 50 miles is deer forest and only 1 per cent arable.' And that was the country through which the Invergarry & Fort Augustus hoped to build an expensive railway—and make it pay.

Although the Invergarry & Fort Augustus was purely a local promotion, the very fact that it had a physical connection with the West Highland at Spean Bridge was enough to raise the Highland Railway hackles. All the West Highland had to do was to acquire running powers over the Invergarry & Fort Augustus to Fort Augustus and it was halfway up the glen and within 30 miles of Inverness. The Highland Railway attacked the Fort Augustus bill vehemently, and the North British and West Highland, bound as they were by the treaty of the previous year to oppose any railway in the Great Glen, also fought; but less vehemently.

The usual dreary, protracted Parliamentary battle ended on 14 August 1896 with victory for the Invergarry & Fort Augustus. The intrepid Lord Burton was free to build his railway. Commenting on the new situation in the Great Glen, a financial journal said:

> . . . the Highland Company forgot that independent promoters might do what the North British, *père et fils* had promised not to do, and although the West Highland and its parent in obedience to treaty arrangements, opposed the Fort Augustus project, their grief at the success must have been a good deal less poignant than that of the Highland.

Formans & McCall were the engineers of the Invergarry & Fort Augustus and James Young of Glasgow was the contractor. The line was to have intermediate stations at Aberchalder, Invergarry and Gairlochy. Not content with reaching Fort Augustus village, the promoters were determined to set up a port of their own on the Caledonian Canal, itself by now partly moribund. So they devoted a large slice of their capital to taking the line three-quarters of a mile beyond the village on a costly extension involving the construction of a swing bridge over the canal and a substantial viaduct over the Oich, as well as pier and station buildings on Loch Ness. At other parts of the system rock cuttings were required, there was one tunnel through hard rock, and there were considerable viaducts spanning the Spean and the Gloy.

THE LAST BATTLE

The advent of the Invergarry & Fort Augustus was the signal for both the North British and the Highland to jettison their treaty obligations. By December 1896 both companies re-entered the field with schemes to link Fort Augustus with Inverness, and they were joined by the Invergarry & Fort Augustus which produced a scheme of its own. The battle was resumed with renewed fury. The contestants poured out money in survey fees, the great trek of witnesses to London was repeated, and some twenty QCs and many lesser legal lights were engaged to represent the respective parties. Mr Pope, who had performed so satisfactorily on behalf of the Highland in the G & NW affair a decade before, was retained again by the Highland. The Highland Railway (Inverness & Fort Augustus Railway) Bill, the Invergarry & Fort Augustus (Inverness Extension) Bill and the North British and West Highland Railway Companies Bill were presented in Parliament on the same day. It was the only time in Parliamentary history that three railway bills all covering the same ground were read on the same day.

The Highland Railway went to London on the defensive; it had little enthusiasm for the line it was promoting. The Great Glen crisis could not have come at a worse time, for the Highland board were beset with troubles. There was a serious domestic situation. For several years the Highland, judged from the standpoint of the dividends it paid, was prosperous, but an inquiry showed that dividends were being paid out of capital, and not out of earnings. When the company was forced into adopting more orthodox book-keeping methods, its true state of health was revealed. Between 1894 and 1897 the Highland Railway stock fell from 115 to 82½. On top of that the assault up the Great Glen coincided with an attack from the east: the Great North of Scotland Railway chose that moment to make its fifth attempt to obtain running powers into Inverness from its outpost at Elgin. It was a time of travail for the Highland.

Mr Samuel Hoare presided over the committee that considered the three bills. The examination and cross-examination of witnesses went on day after day throughout the spring and early summer of 1897. Mounting legal fees drained away money none of the contestants—least of all the little Invergarry & Fort Augustus—could afford; and there was nothing to show for it. The North British spent £13,449—the equal of ¼ per cent of the dividend—in its efforts to thwart the Highland's attempt 'to occupy the district from Fort Augustus to Inverness in a manner prejudicial to the interests of the company'. Lord Tweeddale considered the money well spent.

Inverness Town Council by a vote of 15 to 3 decided to petition both Houses of Parliament to sanction the Invergarry & Fort Augustus bill. While admitting that it was useful to have the Highland Railway headquarters in Inverness, the business men on the Council thought that they did not get a square deal from that company. Also, the Invergarry & Fort Augustus scheme undertook to run a line to Inverness harbour clearing away some old slum property in the process. Wick Chamber of Commerce, too, opposed the Highland bill. 'We have to pay smartly for whatever benefits we have received from the company,' said their spokesman. 'Until the Highland company has opposition they will extract from their customers pounds instead of pence.'

In the end the Highland won, but it was refused running powers over the Invergarry & Fort Augustus. The bill then went to the House of Lords for consideration by Lord Brougham's committee. The domestic upheaval in the Highland headquarters had produced a new general manager, Charles Steele, and he went to London to plead for the bill in the Lords. Steele made the mistake of threatening the committee:

> If we are not authorised to make the line from Inverness to Fort Augustus, or if it is authorised with concessions to other companies, the Highland Company will not be able to consider any of the contemplated lines north of Inverness which are the only lines that could develop the industries in the North.

Lord Brougham threw out the bill. If the impoverished litigants went back to the Great Glen wringing their hands, they left the London lawyers rubbing *their* hands.

FRUSTRATION

Now the Invergarry & Fort Augustus Railway proprietors were left in peace to squander their money on their pathetic little railway. They started off boldly on 2 February 1897 with the ceremonial digging of *two* first sods—one at each end of the line. (They had to get Lord Lovat's permission to enter the land where the Fort Augustus sod was cut.) Although the line as planned was single throughout, the optimistic proprietors had bought enough land for double track.

George Malcolm, who had been a co-founder with Mr Boyd of the West Highland, had given his professional services in getting the Invergarry bill through Parliament. When he presented his account amounting to £366 10s 3d the generous proprietors airily wrote a cheque for the nice round figure of £500 and dispatched it to their benefactor. The chief constable of Inverness informed the Invergarry that he had appointed two extra policemen to the district owing to the influx of the railway navvies, and enclosed an account for £21 11s 6d, being the cost of pay and uniform for the two constables. The railway paid up without demur, but refused to pay an account for £12 5s for two 'cabin cells' erected at Fort Augustus to receive recalcitrant navvies.

The line slowly took shape. It started at the west end of Spean Bridge station, curved through a wood and struck north-west to the bank of the Spean, here a wide river flowing in a deep ravine. The passage of the gorge demanded four lattice spans, one of 120 ft, one of 50 ft and two of 60 ft, carried on piers rising 76 ft from the river. Once across the Spean the line passed by Gairlochy through undulating wooded country for 4 miles to the river Gloy, and crossed this on a three-span lattice girder bridge of two 50 ft and one 100 ft spans. The track then climbed gently through a thick forest of pine and fir to emerge on moorland leading to the summit of 370 ft at Letterfinlay. It then dropped down into the Great Glen and ran along the hillside parallel to but above the chain-lochs, Lochy and Oich and the connecting length of Caledonian Canal, to Invergarry village. Then it passed through the 67 yd Oich tunnel, and crossed the four-span Calder Burn viaduct to reach Aberchalder. The final stretch took the track across a patch of moorland and along the shore of Loch Uanagan to Fort Augustus town station, then across the canal and the Oich to the pier station on Loch Ness.

The I & FA spent lavishly and built on a grand scale. The first and last miles absorbed between them one-third of the railway's capital. The tops of the piers of the Oich viaduct were elaborately castellated and the stonework was embellished with a design involving a cross—expensive frills which a wealthier line would have dispensed with. Costly retaining walls were required where the line clung to the hillside above Loch Lochy, one being 338 ft long and from 5 to 25¼ ft high. While it was still being built a massive landslide brought tons of rock, soil and trees down on to the newly-formed permanent way, completely obliterating it.

The hamlet of Gairlochy was provided with facilities that would not have disgraced a small town: in addition to the station there

45 YEARS OF GLENS

(37) *Two Glens on a Glasgow train at Fort William about 1914*

(38) *Glens among the mountains in* LNE *days*

(39) *Two Glens prepare to leave Ardlui on a Glasgow—Mallaig train in May 1959*

FORT WILLIAM

(40) K1 No. 62034 *about to leave Fort William for Glasgow, Queen Street, 24 May* 1952

(41) *Steam in the shadow of Ben Nevis. 'Loch Arkaig', 'Loch Treig', 'Glen Spean' and 'Glen Gloy' at Fort William shed,* 12 *June* 1936

were four lines of sidings and loading banks for goods and cattle.

Invergarry was given an island platform in the Swiss style favoured by the West Highland. A large verandah was provided on the down side and a private waiting room was installed for the use of the occupants of nearby Invergarry House. Generous goods and cattle sidings waited for traffic that was never to materialize; at Letterfinlay summit an unnecessary passing place and signalbox were built and never staffed. Some years later the house at Letterfinlay was listed in an inventory of I & FA property as 'intended for signalman'. Fort Augustus was given two terminal platforms, and a through platform from which the line continued to the pier station.

The North British extended Spean Bridge station and put in a dock platform at the west end for use of the I & FA trains. It also laid the double junction at Spean Bridge at a cost of £303 0s 5d to the Invergarry company. The junction signalling instruments were at first installed in the I & FA box at the junction, but the inspecting officer of the Board of Trade insisted on their removal to the North British booking office in Spean Bridge station. The line was equipped with Webb & Thomson staff with the following block sections:

Spean Bridge—Gairlochy	2 m.	52 ch.
Gairlochy—Invergarry	12 m.	24 ch.
Invergarry—Fort Augustus	8 m.	7 ch.

The Fort Augustus pier branch was worked by a one-engine-in-steam key controlled by Fort Augustus box. Aberchalder, between Invergarry and Fort Augustus, was novel in being a passing place without signals. All approaching trains had to stop and the driver operated the points by inserting a key token in a one-lever ground frame.

By April 1898 the directors felt confident enough to conduct the press over the works. The man from the *Dundee Advertiser* admired the straight stretches at the eastern end of the line and expressed the opinion that they would 'greatly facilitate matters when the time comes for running at express speed'. In August 1899 the line was inspected by the directors. The North British provided them with a saloon on which they were taken 6 miles from Spean Bridge to the river Gloy. The Gloy viaduct was not complete so the visitors had to de-train and make their own way across the river. On the far side they joined a wagon which the contractors had fitted out with seats, and the contractors' engine took the passengers on to Loch Oich tunnel. Since the tunnel also was unfinished, they had to walk through to where another improvized passenger train was waiting to take them on to Fort Augustus.

It is an odd thing, but on the day before the directors inspected the bits and pieces of their line, it was privately inspected by an officer of the Caledonian Railway and that company's consulting engineer. Nothing more was ever heard of that strange visitation. But what a fire there would have been in the heather if the Caledonian had come to the Great Glen.

The I & FA shareholders were paying for their shares by instalments as the line was built, the company calling for cash as it was required to meet current expenses. A financial crisis broke when certain shareholders refused to answer a periodic call; two prominent former supporters of the scheme, each with £5,000 in partly paid-up shares, decided to cut their losses, and refused the request for further instalments. They forfeited their holdings. Charles Forman had demonstrated his faith in the line by agreeing to take up £20,000 of I & FA stock. But when in 1898 he was called on for a cash payment of £4,000, he asked the company to place that sum against the amount owing to his firm for professional services. Another shareholder who was also a creditor of the I & FA told the secretary to waive his account in lieu of a cash payment. The supply of ready money dried up, and Lord Burton had to provide funds from his private purse—not for the last time.

The Invergarry & Fort Augustus could have offered a service in 1901. That it did not begin for another two years was due to shameless bureaucratic processes which forced the proprietors again and again to go to the courts or to the House of Commons over relatively trivial matters.

The trouble stemmed from the fact that, in spite of private loans, after spending £322,000 on the line the company had no funds left for the purchase of engines and rolling stock. Clearly somebody had to be found to work the line for it, and the obvious candidate was the North British. Of course the Highland Railway objected to that, and the usual Parliamentary circus followed. The North British was not over-anxious to accept the job. Its terms to the Invergarry & Fort Augustus were 60 per cent of the gross revenue subject to a minimum of £3,000 each half-year. 'My company does not feel disposed to work the railway at a possible loss,' said Mr Jackson, the general manager of the North British.

William Whitelaw, the Highland chairman, had no such scruples. At a meeting held in March 1902 the Highland board agreed to work the Invergarry for £2,000 per half-year. Whitelaw was quite prepared to accept a small loss as the price of gaining control of the Invergarry and so keeping the North British out of the Great Glen.

He also made a statement of which the significance was missed at the time. First-class local passenger traffic was then an important source of revenue for railways in the Highlands. The gentry did most of their social visiting by rail; obsequious stationmasters and porters were at hand at all stations to pander to their every need; private waiting rooms and even private stations were not unknown. Whitelaw informed his shareholders that in the previous year there had been a drop of over 1,000 first-class local journeys. 'The loss,' said the chairman,

> is almost entirely due to the extraordinary development of motor cars. We are not likely to recover this traffic, but I do not think we will lose much more on long distances through motoring. People are beginning to get a little bit sick of the general squalor of long-distance motoring.

The writing was on the wall.

The North British had conducted negotiations with the I & FA over the use of Spean Bridge station fully expecting to be operating the Invergarry line itself. The arrival of the Highland on the scene changed the atmosphere. When the North British seemed likely to be obstructive, the Invergarry decided to make its own approach road to the station, and build its own separate entrance and station offices. This piece of folly was avoided when the North British, realizing that it was to its own advantage to encourage traffic to and from the West Highland and the Invergarry, not only offered accommodation to the small company but gave it the use of North British staff without charge. (The North British benefited to the extent of £7 17s 6d when a second-hand Highland turntable was consigned from Inverness to Spean Bridge for installation there.) The Invergarry directors voted a £10 annual gratuity to the stationmaster at Spean Bridge.

The Invergarry & Fort Augustus lost no time in applying for a provisional order to confirm the working agreement with the Highland. The line was ready and waiting to earn money; all that was required was the official stamp on the inter-railway agreement. Alas! the Invergarry & Fort Augustus had filled in its application on the wrong form. It had applied in terms of the Private Bill Procedure (Scotland) Act, whereas it should have proceeded as for an ordinary private bill. It was July before the Parliamentarians reached this conclusion, and the important business of holidays for the legislators brought a halt to further discussion. So the new railway had to lie fallow during the tourist season of 1902.

It was November before the bill was given Parliamentary attention, and it was not passed until 30 June 1903. The Highland Railway just had time to work two engines and rolling stock all the way round by the Caledonian and West Highland to Spean Bridge and set up in business to capture what they could of the summer trade. The Invergarry & Fort Augustus had enough money left to invest in the luxury of a gold whistle, and this was blown on 27 July 1903 by a local lady who set off the first train. The opening-day luncheon in Fort Augustus was presided over by William Whitelaw, who in a graceful speech wished the new railway well.

Six months later when Whitelaw had the first balance sheet on his desk he realized what he had let his shareholders in for. In its first half-year of operation the railway had produced a total revenue from all sources of £907.

A HOPELESS STRUGGLE

The first timetable provided four trains each way daily between Spean Bridge and Fort Augustus. Most of the trains were booked to do the journey in one hour exactly, with stops at the three intermediate stations. Two of the up trains originated at Fort Augustus pier station, and one of the down trains terminated there. Unfortunately, the Invergarry & Fort Augustus had obtained its Act too late for the services to be incorporated in the timetables of connecting companies, and at first no through tickets could be issued for journeys between stations on the line and points throughout the country.

To advertise itself the I & FA spent £50 on photographs which were framed in elaborate panels and exhibited at certain stations on the Highland Railway. It offered advertising space free in its first guide, and the guide itself was distributed free. The right to put chocolate and weighing machines at its stations was given to the Sweetmeat Automatic Delivery Company Ltd for a fee of £2 per machine, and the letting of advertising space on the railway was given to Slaughter & Co. of Edinburgh. The I & FA owned the Lovat Arms Hotel at Fort Augustus, and leased it to David Rattray, who promptly complained 'of the loss caused to the hotel by the evening train taking prospective guests away from Fort Augustus'. He wanted the last up train cancelled.

MacBrayne normally withdrew his mid-morning return sailing from Inverness to Fort Augustus in September, but the Invergarry asked him to retain it in September 1903 so that the railway could benefit from any traffic brought by the vessel. MacBrayne agreed, but only after the Invergarry had agreed to subsidize the sailing by a payment of £100. £50 of this was contributed by the Highland. Displeased with the arrangement the Invergarry directors instructed their secretary to 'see the Turbine people' with a view to obtaining a fast turbine steamer of their own for service in Loch Ness. This breathtaking command was quite in keeping with a railway that thought in terms of two first sods and a gold whistle. The Parsons steam turbine had been applied for the first time to a passenger vessel only two years previously and was just beginning to revolutionize water transport.

The more settled traffic pattern of 1904 showed all too clearly that the railway was to have a struggle to exist. Local people used it to get to Fort William *via* the West Highland, for the fares were only half the steerage fare on the Caledonian Canal boats which had enjoyed a monopoly. But the summer tourist traffic that was to fill the empty coffers did not materialize in anything like the expected volume. Travellers by choice still went to Banavie and sailed all the way up the canal; few showed any desire to take the railway short cut to Fort Augustus.

The 1904 accounts made grim reading for the Invergarry directors. During the half-year ending 31 July 1904 they spent £3,776 17s 1d on capital account, mainly for repairs and improvements to the permanent way. Even after deducting £303 13s 2d obtained from the sale of surplus construction materials, the capital account still claimed £3,473 3s 11d. That amount, with the half-yearly £2,000 due to the Highland for working expenses, made a total outlay of £5,473 3s 11d. The revenue for the half-year, including rents from railway properties, was £976 14s 3d. The Highland complained that, after all, £2,000 did not cover the cost of working the line, and asked the Invergarry to make good the deficit. Lord Burton agreed to pay the Highland £1,000 if it would guarantee to work the line for ten years and during that time refrain from asking for additional payments. The Highland refused.

The Highland Railway tried to stimulate trade in 1905 by applying for permission to run steamers from the railway pier at Fort Augustus to Inverness in connection with the trains. This move was opposed by David MacBrayne, the sole steamboat operator on that section of the canal. Incredibly, it was also opposed by the Invergarry & Fort Augustus, on the grounds that if the Highland operated steamers on the northern section of the canal it might be deprived of extending its own line to Inverness!

By 1905 it was plain that the tourists preferred the well-established Royal Route. Contraction, not expansion, became the policy of the Invergarry & Fort Augustus. At the end of the 1906 summer timetable the service between Fort Augustus town and pier stations was withdrawn, never to be resumed. During its brief service this stretch of line could not have earned more than a few hundred pounds. The heavy investment in bridges, piers and buildings had gone for nothing; they were left to rust and moulder away.

Troubles now assailed the Invergarry from all directions. The factories inspector for Inverness insisted that the company provide life-saving apparatus at the pier it no longer used. (That it hoped to use it again was indicated by the fact that it spent £800 on repairing the pier foundations.) The local sanitary inspector complained that the cesspool at the Lovat Arms was causing offence, and money was spent in providing the appropriate remedy. The Sweetmeat Automatic Delivery Co. struck a blow to morale by removing their machines from the I & FA stations; and in the minute book appeared the plaintive note, 'The Secretary reported that the Assessor had again valued the Railway at Nil.' (It had been valued at £900 while under construction.)

But Slaughter & Co. remitted a cheque for £1 19s 3d to the Invergarry, that being the profit for one year on the letting of advertising sites, and on 1 July 1904 the directors felt confident enough to open a new station and passing place at Invergloy between Gairlochy and Letterfinlay. A belated mail contract signed with the Post Office on 1 August 1905 brought an annual revenue of £75.

Death and desertion had robbed the I & FA of some of its most faithful shareholders, among them Lord Abinger and Charles Forman, and the burden of meeting the crushing annual deficit fell on fewer people. Lord Burton made by far the largest contribution. It was difficult to escape the conclusion that the Invergarry owed its existence, albeit indirectly, to the drinkers of a particular brand of English beer.

The Highland Railway persevered for another year; then on 31 October 1906 it informed the Invergarry it would withdraw its engines and rolling stock on 30 April 1907. Lamenting the decision, William Whitelaw said:

> I think the Highland Company have done all that could reasonably be expected of them. They have worked the line within the estimated cost for four years and given it every possible opportunity. It has not shown any sign of expansion of traffic and we have been experiencing a loss of £2,000 a year.

The Invergarry was forced to go cap in hand to the North British, seeking whatever terms it could get. The agreement between the I & FA and the NB, signed in the head office of Bass Radcliffe & Gretton at Burton on Trent, two clerks employed by the firm acting as witnesses, read like a treaty imposed by the victor on the vanquished. It was to be valid for three years from 1 May 1907. The North British agreed to move in on that date, providing it could move out again on 31 January of any year after giving six months' notice. It had the right to inspect the railway, put it in working order to its own satisfaction and instal additional sidings if considered necessary; all this at the expense of the I & FA. The North British would pay for routine maintenance, but landslides and failures of culverts would be the responsibility of the Invergarry. All I & FA servants would pass into North British control and the NB had the exclusive right to make all future appointments. All monies would be collected by the North British, which would retain 60 per cent and remit 40 per cent to the I & FA within two months of each half-year *provided* that the North British share was not less than £2,000 per half-year. If it fell short of £2,000 the Invergarry would be required to make up half the deficit.

The Invergarry directors found themselves wallowing in a maze of accounts, claims and counter-claims. The Highland Railway sent an account for £2,062 11s, the loss incurred in working the railway for the year ending 31 January 1907. Once again there was a whip-round among loyal shareholders, and money was contributed as follows:

Lord Burton	£1,112	8	9
Forman's Trustees	£234	5	0
J. C. Cunningham	£139	1	3
G. Malcolm	£13	17	6
J. Lambrick	£3	2	6
Lord Abinger's Trustees	£3	2	6
G. W. T. Robertson	£2	10	0
Robert Angus		10	0
	£1,508	17	6

A cheque for £1,500 was sent to the Highland in part payment of the debt. Next the North British rendered an account for £565 16s 1d, the charge for putting the line in order. The Highland Railway wanted £26 9s 6d from the North British for the tickets, luggage labels and picture postcards it had left at I & FA stations, but the North British maintained they were worth only £6 9s 2d, and that is all it would pay. The luckless Invergarry was presented with the bill for the difference of £20 0s 4d. By the time the accountants had made sense of the financial mess the Invergarry was found to owe the Highland £400 and the North British £1,027 18s 1d. The accounts were shared as follows:

	H.R.	N.B.
Lord Burton	£260	£523 1 1
Forman's Trustees	£80	£266 9 6
J. C. Cunningham	£60	£238 7 6

The North British took over on 1 May 1907, according to the agreement, although services did not start until 4 May. The agreed service was four trains each way in summer and two in winter. The deficit to be shared by Lord Burton and his friends at the end of the first half-year of NB rule was £627 15s 1d. Burton died in 1909, and the yoke of chairmanship of the I & FA fell on J. C. Cunningham. Then, at the end of the summer of 1910, the North British gave notice that services would be withdrawn on 31 January 1911.

The people of the district were fantastically loyal to their railway. They wanted it and were not to blame that their numbers were too few and their journeyings too infrequent to make it pay its way. Public meetings were held up and down the Great Glen in efforts to find ways and means of saving it. On one evening meetings were held simultaneously in Spean Bridge, Invergarry, and Gairlochy, and at all three assurances of financial support were given. The money situation had been aggravated by the death of Lord Burton who had been plugging leaks with his private fortune. Now the trustees of his estate refused to divert money to the little railway in the Highlands. The North British under pressure undertook to work it for another summer. On 31 October 1911 it withdrew, leaving the line to its fate.

The Invergarry board resigned themselves to the fact that the position was hopeless. Following several bitter meetings they took the sad decision of putting out tenders for scrap. But they were to find that they had to fight almost as hard to abandon the line as they had fought to build it. When they tried to sell their property at its scrap value Inverness County Council moved in with an interdict to prevent the sale. When they took their case to the First Division of the Court of Session the Lord President reminded them that they were a main line in their own right and not simply a branch line that could throw in the towel when it liked. 'Once a railway has been established,' lectured the Lord President, 'it is to a certain extent an asset of the public as well as an asset of the particular company, and this is different from a successful railway company discontinuing an unprofitable branch.' The Invergarry representative was informed that the line could not be sold for scrap in any case, since the proprietors had not taken the statutory steps to abandon it.

The company could not sell the line for scrap, and nobody would lease or buy it. While it lay bound in red tape, private citizens, local and county councils and Government departments haggled over its fate. With an eye on the nearby Mallaig line, the Invergarry pleaded for a Government grant to enable it to give a service to the community; the profit motive was now forgotten.

A long series of letters passed between the Invergarry, the North British and the Board of Trade in an effort to find a solution. The North British made a cash offer of £22,500 for the £344,000 railway. This the Invergarry refused, still hoping to get a better price for the line as scrap. When after nearly two years of negotiations Sir George Younger (Ayr Burghs) asked the President of the Board of Trade what he was doing about the Invergarry & Fort Augustus, the President gave this reply:

> As I think the Hon Baronet is aware, the Board of Trade have for the past two years been in communication both by letters and interviews with the Invergarry Company and the North British Company and various individual bodies (including the County Council of Inverness) who are interested in the matter with the view of arriving at some arrangement for the continuance of the working of the railway. I regret that these efforts have not been successful and I should be glad to do anything in my power to secure the reopening of the line, but I greatly fear that the Board of Trade have exhausted their good offices in the matter.

Meanwhile, the Lochaber District Committee of the Inverness County Council had made an interesting discovery. Their accounts for road repairs in the Spean Bridge—Fort Augustus area had risen by £600 and this they attributed to the increase in motor traffic following the closure of the railway. The Lochaber District Committee suggested to the parent body that a grant of £600 be made to the Invergarry & Fort Augustus to induce it to re-open the line.

The 1913 negotiations resulted in the North British agreeing to work the line again for a trial period, and it was reopened on 1 August. The results were no better than before and the Invergarry directors pressed for it to be scrapped. By this time, however, Inverness County Council had obtained a provisional order to raise £5,000, the difference between the top figure the Invergarry was willing to accept and the £22,500 the North British was prepared to pay for outright purchase. The deal was concluded at Fort Augustus and the man who represented the North British was the same William Whitelaw who had already opened and closed the line on behalf of the Highland. He had become chairman of the North British in the previous year. So in the end it was the ratepayers of the Great Glen who saved the railway. On 28 August 1914 the royal assent was given to the North British Railway (Invergarry & Fort Augustus Railway Vesting) Order Confirmation Act, and the Invergarry became lock, stock and barrel the property of the North British.

By that time the Great War had broken out and in a matter of months the Highland Railway was bending under the burden of wartime traffic it had not been designed to meet. If only there had been a second route to Inverness to share the vital naval traffic to the northern bases! If only the three parties to the 1897 *fracas* had, instead of pouring their money down the legal drain, made a joint-purse pact to build a joint line between Fort Augustus and Inverness, the nation would have had a strategic railway of first importance in the Great Glen. It was easy to be wise after the event.

If anybody deserved to have a railway it was the people in the lower half of the Great Glen. Today railways skirt both ends of the glen, but in the glen itself there is not a foot of line. It would be pleasant to think that somewhere among the quiet alleys of legal London there was a plaque inscribed, 'From the gentlemen of the legal profession to the Railway Promoters of the Great Glen, in gratitude for their munificence.'

CHAPTER 8

Trains and Timetables

A STEADY PATTERN

The main features of the West Highland timetable devised when the Mallaig Extension was opened in 1901 survived and were recognizable 60 years later. The early-morning and mid-afternoon all-the-year-round trains from Glasgow remained, although they had been re-timed. These were the only down passenger trains on the Glasgow—Fort William section in the winter timetable. For a period before 1914 the summer traffic supported two down trains between the early and late trains. These were timed to leave Glasgow at 10.9 and 12.43 but were later consolidated into a single train leaving at 11.23. This train is now recognizable as the 10.5. The first down and the last up trains in the summer ran through from London King's Cross; these served Edinburgh in each direction, but not Glasgow.

The timetable for the Mallaig Extension changed pattern from time to time. Usually there were four trains in each direction daily between Fort William and Mallaig, with an additional service each way on Saturdays. In 1914 a non-stop train ran from Mallaig to Fort William at 6.50 a.m., catering mainly for the outer-islands steamer passengers, followed by a stopping train. The 1925 timetable showed four up trains and two down trains on the Mallaig Extension; both down services were through trains from Glasgow, and three of the up trains went through to Glasgow. In that year an 8.30 p.m. was put on from Fort William to Mallaig.

The original local service from Craigendoran to Garelochhead was extended to Arrochar and Tarbet and included Whistlefield. The basic service on this section was four trains a day each way. They were poorly patronized, largely because of the unfortunate distance of the stations from the villages they purported to serve. By 1964 a railbus was catering for the mere handful of passengers, and services ceased on 14 June that year with the closure of Rhu, Shandon, and Whistlefield stations to passenger traffic. In 1914 an attempt was made to bring Crianlarich into the commuter belt by providing a morning and evening train to and from Glasgow. This was the 8.5 a.m., which worked through to Springburn; the return service left Queen Street (Low Level) at 5.12 p.m.

After the second war an afternoon train was put on from Glasgow to Crianlarich on Saturdays, timed to leave at 3 p.m. or 2.50 p.m. This offered a circular tour, whereby passengers could return from Crianlarich *via* Callander; they could also alight at Ardlui or Arrochar and Tarbet and return to Glasgow by the Loch Lomond steamer as far as Balloch, and thence by train. Experience showed that few used the train beyond Ardlui and this station was eventually made the terminus. For some years the Loch Lomond circular tour was highly popular and the train was well loaded. In the early sixties the traffic fell away, and in 1964, when Ardlui pier was closed, custom all but vanished.

The establishment of comfortable residential outposts on the shores of the Gareloch, Loch Long and Loch Lomond had been one of the dreams of the original West Highland promoters. It remained a dream.

THE 'NORTHERN BELLE'

One of the most interesting trains ever to visit the West Highland Railway was the LNE's *Northern Belle*. This made history when it left King's Cross at 11.20 p.m. on 16 June 1933 and cruised for some 4,000 miles before returning to King's Cross at 7.58 p.m. on 30 June. The *Northern Belle* was made up of eight day-cars, six sleeping-cars and a van, and it accommodated 60 passengers and a crew of 20. Included in its amenities were a passenger lounge, a hairdressing saloon, a cocktail bar and two shower baths. The inclusive fare for the cruise was £20.

The *Northern Belle* eventually reached Balloch pier at the foot of Loch Lomond, where the passengers embarked on one of the loch steamers for Ardlui. The night and day portions then left separately for the West Highland line, the day portion arriving at Ardlui station in time to meet the steamer. The train then ran right through to Mallaig. On the return journey a ten-minute stop was made on Glenfinnan Viaduct. One of the passengers kept a log of the cruise, and here is an extract:

> At Ardlui we board the day portion of the *Northern Belle*. But before lunch there is a small ceremony to be performed. For this is Derby Day, and the *Northern Belle* sweep, for which the whole of

the passengers and the staff have entered, has to be drawn. The result of the race comes aboard the train in the afternoon, and the winner of the sweep is announced—one of the train staff. Passengers seem as pleased as if they had won it themselves. On the return from Mallaig the *Northern Belle* stands for ten minutes on Glenfinnan Viaduct. Passengers have heard a good deal about the incomparable views between Fort William and Mallaig and the alternative offered—a motor trip to Loch Ness in search of the Monster—attracted only two passengers, one of these being a Dutch lady who, with kindly forethought, had obtained from the kitchen staff a supply of bread to feed the beast. Alas! she was disappointed. In the evening dinner is served on the train as she stands beside Loch Linnhe.

In April 1935 a similar cruising train organized by *The Scout* magazine took 140 boys to the West Highlands. The train was stabled at Banavie Pier station for two days while the boys climbed Ben Nevis.

EXCURSION TRAFFIC

On 10 June 1931 the LMS and LNE sent the first-ever train to Oban over the West Highland and Callander & Oban. That year MacBrayne's had introduced the new vessel *Lochfyne* on the Oban to Staffa and Iona run, and a special train was run from Glasgow Queen Street to Oban with passengers for the cruise. The train left Glasgow at 6.10 a.m. and arrived in Oban at 9.27, thus completing the trip in 83 minutes less than the best-timed Glasgow Buchanan Street to Oban train.

In subsequent years joint excursions were operated from Glasgow to Crianlarich *via* the West Highland, returning *via* Callander, but no regular service was established on the short route to Oban until after nationalization. The summer timetable of 1949 contained the first-ever regular return service from Glasgow to Oban *via* Loch Lomond and Dalmally. The train was well advertised and trumpeted as one of the fruits of nationalization. But the public refused to use it, and it was soon withdrawn. It was revived in the sixties as a diesel multiple unit, operating Mondays to Fridays, with an appeal mainly for the tourist traffic.

The LNE and LMS frequently co-operated in running circular tour trains to Crianlarich, out *via* the West Highland and back *via* Stirling or vice versa. These proved very popular, especially when operated as evening excursions at a fare of only 3s for the round trip of 135 miles.

The Six Lochs Rail Cruise was a British Railways variant of the Crianlarich circle. This operated as a diesel multiple unit from

Edinburgh and Glasgow to Fort-William and Mallaig

	Sleeping Car (1st and 3rd Class) London to Fort-William on Sunday to Friday nights inclusive. TC London to Fort-William – RC Glasgow to Fort-William					Sats only	Sats only		Buffet Car Glasgow to Fort-William. Through Train Glasgow to Mallaig	Ex Sats		Sats only	Sundays			
	p.m	a.m.	.	p.m	.	a.m	a.m	p.m	p.m	p.m	.	a.m.	.	.	.	.
London (King's X) — lev.	7 E 5	—	—	1030	E	—	—	—	1130	—	—	4 25	—	—	—	—
Edinburgh (Wav.) . lev.	4a25	.	.	9 a 5	.	.	10 0	.	2 0	.	.	4 p 0	.	.	.	.
Glasgow Queen (Low) —	—	7B50	—	1032	FB	—	1B10	—	—	5 B 6	—	6 B 7	—	—	—	—
Glasgow St. (High) .	5 55	.	.	.	.	1125	.	.	3 46	.	.	.	.	.	.	.
Dumbarton — — — — —	6 22	8B24	—	11F3	B	1154	1B38	—	4HB3	5B37	—	6B36	—	—	—	—
Craigendoran	.	9 0	.	1130	.	12 6	2 0	.	4 22	5 56	.	6 57	.	.	.	.
Helensburgh (Upper) — —	6 39	9 6	—	1136	—	1213	2 6	—	4 29	6 3	—	7 3	—	—	—	—
Rhu	.	9 11	.	1141	.	.	2 11	.	4 34	6 8	.	7 8	.	.	.	.
Shandon — — — — — —	—	9 17	—	1147	—	—	2 17	—	4 40	6 14	—	7 14	—	—	—	—
Garelochhead	.	9 25	.	1155	.	.	2 25	.	4 46	6 24	.	7 24	.	.	.	.
Whistlefield — — — — —	—	9 30	—	12 0	—	—	2 30	—	4 52	6 29	—	7 29	—	—	—	—
Arrochar and Tarbet . .	7 17	9 51	.	1221	.	1253	2 51	.	5 16	6 50	.	7 50	.	.	.	.
Ardlui (Loch Lomond) —	7 34	—	—	—	—	1 10	—	—	5 38	—	—	—	—	—	—	—
Crianlarich . . . . arr.	7 55	.	.	.	.	1 31	.	.	6 0	.	.	.	.	.	.	.
Crianlarich — — — lev.	8 1	—	—	—	—	1 37	—	—	6 6	—	—	—	—	—	—	—
Tyndrum	8 14	.	.	.	.	1 50	.	.	6 20	.	.	.	.	.	.	.
Bridge of Orchy — — — —	8 29	—	—	—	—	2 5	—	—	6 35	—	—	—	—	—	—	—
Rannoch	8 58	.	.	.	.	.	.	.	7 2	.	.	.	.	.	.	.
Corrour — — — — — —	9 14	—	—	—	—	—	—	—	7 18	—	—	—	—	—	—	—
Tulloch (Loch Laggan) .	9 35	.	.	.	.	3 8	.	.	7 39	.	.	.	.	.	.	.
Roy Bridge — — — — —	9 47	—	—	—	—	3 22	—	—	7 51	—	—	—	—	—	—	—
Spean Bridge	9 57	.	.	.	.	3 32	.	.	8 0	.	.	.	.	.	.	.
Fort-William — — — arr.	1014	—	—	—	—	3 49	—	—	8 17	—	—	—	—	—	—	—
Fort-William . . . lev.	1028	.	.	.	.	RC Glasgow to Fort-William	.	4 50	8 30	.	.	.	.	.	.	
Banavie — — — — — —	1035	—	—	—	—		—	4 57	8 37	—	—	—	—	—	—	—
Corpach	1039	.	.	.	.		.	5 1	8 41	.	.	.	.	.	.	.
Locheilside — — — — —	1052	—	—	—	—		—	5 13	8 53	—	—	—	—	—	—	—
Glenfinnan M (Loch Shiel)	11 6	.	.	.	.		.	5 27	9 7	.	.	.	.	.	.	.
Lochailort — — — — —	1127	—	—	—	—		—	5 48	9 28	—	—	—	—	—	—	—
Arisaig	1146	.	.	.	.		.	6 7	9 47	.	.	.	.	.	.	.
Morar — — — — — — —	1159	—	—	—	—		—	6 21	10 1	—	—	—	—	—	—	—
Mallaig ¶ . . . . . arr.	12 6	.	.	.	.		.	6 28	10 8	.	.	.	.	.	.	.

* Saturdays only † Except Sats. § Mondays only ‡ Except Mondays

¶ See Ferry Service, Mallaig and Armadale, at foot of Page

B Change Craigendoran E Sunday to Friday nights inclusive

F From 1st October leaves Glasgow (Queen Street) 10-24 a.m. and Dumbarton 10-58 a.m

H From 15th September leaves Dumbarton 3-2 p.m

M Connection from Glenfinnan Pier to Dalilea and Acharacle off 5-55 a.m. Glasgow to Mallaig

RC Restaurant Car TC Through Carriage

For Steamer Sailings to Portree and Stornoway, apply D. MacBrayne Ltd. 44 Robertson St., Glasgow C.2.

Mallaig—Armadale Ferry Service.

The Ferry service between Mallaig and Armadale (Skye) operated by Messrs. Alexander McLennan (Mallaig) Ltd., will be as under, for the period 16th June to 30th September:—

Mallaig	dep.	9-45 a.m.,	12-20 p.m.,	3-45 p.m
Armadale	dep.	10-45 a.m.,	1-0 p.m.,	4-45 p.m

Last LNE summer timetable, 1947

Mallaig and Fort-William to Glasgow and Edinburgh

	a.m	a.m	a.m	.	a.m.	Sats only p.m	Ex Sats p.m	Sats only p.m	p.m	.	Sats only p.m	p.m	Sundays .	.	.	.
					Buffet Car Fort-William to Glasgow				Sleeping Car (1st and 3rd Class) Fort-William to London; TC Fort-William to London; RC Fort-William to Glasgow		RC Fort-William to Glasgow					
Mallaig ¶ lev.	—	6 35	—	—	7 46	—	—	—	1 0	—	—	5 42	—	—	—	—
Morar	.	6 46	.	.	7 55	.	.	.	1 9	.	.	5 51	.	.	.	.
Arisaig	—	7 1	—	—	8 8	—	—	—	1 22	—	—	6 8	—	—	—	—
Lochailort	.	7 24	.	.	8 27	.	.	.	1 41	.	.	6 27	.	.	.	.
Glenfinnan M (Loch Shiel)	—	7 50	—	—	8 52	—	—	—	2 2	—	—	6 48	—	—	—	—
Locheilside	.	8 11	.	.	.	.	.	.	2 17	.	.	7 3	.	.	.	.
Corpach	—	8 30	—	—	—	—	—	—	2 30	—	—	7 16	—	—	—	—
Banavie	.	8 37	.	.	.	.	.	.	2 35	.	.	7 21	.	.	.	.
Fort-William arr.	—	8 46	—	—	9 24	—	—	—	2 42	—	—	7 28	—	—	—	—
Fort-William lev.	.	.	.	.	9 36	.	.	.	2 55	.	5 20	.	.	.	.	.
Spean Bridge	—	—	—	—	9 56	—	—	—	3 14	—	5 39	—	—	—	—	—
Roy Bridge	.	.	.	.	10 3	.	.	.	3 21	.	.	.	.	.	.	.
Tulloch (Loch Laggan)	—	—	—	—	1021	—	—	—	3 41	—	6 2	—	—	—	—	—
Corrour	.	.	.	.	1043	.	.	.	4 4	.	.	.	.	.	.	.
Rannoch	—	—	—	—	1057	—	—	—	4 18	—	—	—	—	—	—	—
Bridge of Orchy	.	.	.	.	1122	.	.	.	4 46	.	.	.	.	.	.	.
Tyndrum	—	—	—	—	1139	—	—	—	5 4	—	7 21	—	—	—	—	—
Crianlarich arr.	.	.	.	.	1148	.	.	.	5 13	.	7 30	.	.	.	.	.
Crianlarich lev.	—	—	—	—	1154	—	—	—	5 19	—	7 36	—	—	—	—	—
Ardlui (Loch Lomond)	.	.	.	.	1212	.	.	.	5 37	.	.	.	.	.	.	.
Arrochar and Tarbet	7 18	—	10 6	—	1231	1 0	2 45	4 50	5 55	—	8 11	—	—	—	—	—
Whistlefield	7 42	.	1028	.	.	1 21	3 8	5 15	6 17	.	.	.	.	.	.	.
Garelochhead	7 47	—	1034	—	125/	1 28	3 15	5 20	6 22	—	—	—	—	—	—	—
Shandon	7 53	.	1041	.	1 4	1 34	3 22	5 26	6 28	.	.	.	.	.	.	.
Rhu	7 59	—	1047	—	—	1 40	3 29	5 32	—	—	—	—	—	—	—	—
Helensburgh (Upper)	8 4	.	1052	.	1 15	1 45	3 35	5 37	6 40	.	.	.	.	.	.	.
Craigendoran arr.	8 8	—	1056	—	1 19	1 49	3 40	5 41	6 44	—	8 56	—	—	—	—	—
Dumbarton arr.	8E27	.	1120	E	1E37	2E21	4E10	6E0	7EH6	.	9E29	.	.	.	.	.
Glasgow Queen Street High L	—	—	—	—	2F4	—	—	—	7L30	—	9N40	—	—	—	—	—
Glasgow Queen Street Low L	8E59	.	1154	E	.	3E 3	4E46	6E41	.	.	.	.	.	.	.	.
Edinburgh (Wav.) arr.	1125	—	2B15	—	3 50	4U47	6 23	9 8	9 26	—	—	—	—	—	—	—
London (King's X) arr.	9p23	A	2a49	.	5a5	5a5	6a5	.	6a50	.	.	.	.	.	.	.

For Steamer Sailings from Stornoway, Portree, and Inverness in connection with Trains, apply D. MacBrayne Ltd., 44 Robertson Street, Glasgow, C.2

* Saturdays only † Except Saturdays § Mondays only ‡ Except Mondays

¶ See Ferry Service Armadale and Mallaig on Page 56

A 9-15 p.m on Fridays and Saturdays B Saturdays 1-28 p.m E Change Craigendoran

F Stops Cowlairs 1-55 p.m H From 15th September arrives Dumbarton 7-17 p.m

L Stops Cowlairs 7-21 p.m N Stops Cowlairs 9-32 p m

M Connection from Acharacle and Dalilea to Glenfinnan Pier into 1-0 p.m Mallaig to Glasgow

RC Restaurant Car TC Through Carriage U 5-11 p.m in October

Spean Bridge, Invergarry and Fort Augustus. (Road Motor Service).

The Train Service has been withdrawn from Gairlochy, Invergloy, Invergarry, Aberchalder, and Fort Augustus, but Parcels and Miscellaneous Passenger Train traffic previously dealt with at these stations will continue to be accepted. The undernoted Motor Service is in operation:—

	a.m	.	.	a.m.	.	.	a.m.	.	.	p.m	.	.	p.m	.	.	p.m	.	.	.
Spean Bridge lev.	8 56	—	—	10 0	—	—	1155	—	—	2 55	—	—	4 25	—	—	8 15	—	—	—
Gairlochy Road End	8 58	.	.	10 3	.	.	1158	.	.	2 58	.	.	4 28	.	.	8 17	.	.	.
Invergloy	9 12	—	—	1017	—	—	1212	—	—	3 12	—	—	4 42	—	—	8 32	—	—	—
Invergarry	9 32	.	.	1037	.	.	1232	.	.	3 32	.	.	5 2	.	.	8 52	.	.	.
Oich Bridge (Aberchalder)	9 38	—	—	1043	—	—	1238	—	—	3 38	—	—	5 8	—	—	8 58	—	—	—
Fort Augustus arr.	9 50	.	.	1055			1250		.	3 50	.	.	5 20	.	.	9 10	.	.	.

	a.m	.	.	a.m.	.	.	a.m	.	.	p.m	.	.	p.m	.	.	p.m	.	.	.
Fort Augustus lev.	8 10	—	—	9 40	—	—	1040	—	—	1 50	—	—	5 25	—	—	6 25	—	—	—
Oich Bridge (Aberchalder)	8 25	.	.	9 52	.	.	1052	.	.	2 2	.	.	5 37	.	.	6 37	.	.	.
Invergarry	8 33	—	—	9 58	—	—	1058	—	—	2 8	—	—	5 43	—	—	6 43	—	—	—
Invergloy	8 58	.	.	1018	.	.	1118	.	.	2 28	.	.	6 3	.	.	7 3	.	.	.
Gairlochy Road End	9 12	—	—	1032	—	—	1132	—	—	2 42	—	—	6 17	—	—	7 17	—	—	—
Spean Bridge arr.	9 15	.	.	1035	.	.	1135	.	.	2 45	.	.	6 20	.	.	7 20	.	.	.

Glasgow (Buchanan Street) to Glasgow (Queen Street) allowing the passengers time off at Callander, Killin, and Crianlarich, and became one of the most popular trips ever run to the West Highlands. Frequently on Sundays and holidays two six-coach sets, all seats filled, were dispatched, and the 'Six Lochs' also became a favourite with charter parties.

Another variation on the Crianlarich circle was the Amateur Photographers' Excursion run on 25 May 1957. This train allowed stops for photography at Garelochhead, Crianlarich, Killin, and Kingshouse platform and, in addition, it was run slowly at three points to enable photographers to obtain pictures from their carriages. A photographic information bureau was provided on the train, and prizes ranging from photographic equipment to runabout tickets were offered for the best prints submitted to British Railways. A public exhibition of the pictures taken on this excursion was held in Glasgow Central station.

An enterprising excursion involving a visit to Oban and Fort William in one day has been offered on several occasions. A diesel multiple unit was run *via* the West Highland from Glasgow to Crianlarich, where the train divided, one half going to Oban and the other half to Fort William. The Oban passengers sailed to Fort William and the Fort William passengers sailed to Oban. The respective MUs then converged on Crianlarich, where they were united for the return journey to Glasgow.

The Scottish Region Television Train made its first appearance on the West Highland. Its special feature was that each vehicle had a television set mounted above the central gangway door at each end, and passengers were invited to a studio in the van to provide entertainment for their fellow-travellers. The TV train on one occasion was chartered by an education authority, and several hundred children were given a most practical and no doubt palatable West Highland geography lesson.

THE PATTERN CHANGES

The pattern of passenger and freight traffic changed little in the period between the opening of the line and the mid-twenties. The coming of the British Aluminium Company to Lochaber transformed the scene. The manufacture of aluminium demands above all a supply of cheap electricity. The B A C not only built new plant at Fort William, but created a complex hydro-electric generating system in Lochaber to power the plant. The scheme involved turning

K4's IN ACTION

(42) *'The Great Marquess' climbing in Glen Falloch when new*

(43) *No. 3443 heads a Glasgow train out of Fort William in 1939*

(44) *A K4 handles a nine-coach train single-handed on the ascent of Glen Falloch*

NORTH BRITISH CLASSES

(45) *A J36 on a Fort William–Mallaig train near Corpach i 1914*

(46) *A J36 on the Moor o Rannoch in 1938*

(47) *J37s at Mallaig*

Loch Treig into a reservoir from which water was conducted through Ben Nevis by a tunnel which emerged 1,000 ft up the face of the mountain overlooking the Fort William factory. Pipes took the water down to the turbine house at the factory.

For the first time the West Highland found itself with a large industrial enterprise on its territory, and tonnages and revenue reflected the new situation. Freight booked at Fort William, which had been between 10,000 and 15,000 tons a year, and had been as low as 7,428 tons, jumped to 27,114 tons in 1926. By 1928 it was 34,402 tons and by 1931 47,117 tons. Because of the influx of power scheme workers into the district passenger figures showed a corresponding increase. From 23,434 passengers booked at Fort William in 1923 the figure rose to 31,095 in 1926 and 43,250 in 1928. The figures tailed off once the major task of constructing the power scheme and factory was completed, but the new industry brought the railway a substantial permanent gain. In 1934 Fort William booked 27,992 passengers and 42,987 tons of freight. A steady traffic developed in bulk alumina between the Fort William factory and the British Aluminium Company's factory at Burntisland in Fife.

As part of the Lochaber power scheme the level of Loch Treig was raised by 33 ft and the original line at the north end of the loch was submerged, necessitating the construction of a diversion and tunnel. The scheme was serviced from a temporary station at Fersit near the foot of Loch Treig. The contractor's narrow-gauge line passed over the main line at this point on a spectacular wooden trestle bridge. The power scheme changed the lineside scenery. The water that pours through the Ben Nevis tunnel no longer plunges and tumbles down the Falls of Treig and through the gorges of the Spean.

SUNDAY TRAINS

An outstanding feature of the West Highland scene in the thirties was the development of an intensive Sunday excursion traffic. The first tentative Sunday excursions in the late twenties met with some opposition in Fort William; excursionists found shops closed and house window-blinds lowered as a protest against their intrusion. But a large influx of industrial workers changed the atmosphere in the district and by the early thirties the trading community at least welcomed the excursion trains. On a fine Sunday, upwards of 1,000 people came into the town by train and their arrival had an appreciable impact on the local economy.

The coming of the Sunday trains coincided with the discovery by the masses in the industrial Clyde belt of the glories of the open air. It was the age of the hiker and hosteller. Sunday fares were remarkably cheap even by the standard of the time. The return fare from Glasgow to Fort William was 7s, to Mallaig 9s; nearly enough, 3 miles for a penny. At the height of the season there could be as many as six trains on the line on a Sunday. Glasgow usually dispatched two and sometimes three, one of which went through to Mallaig. Edinburgh accounted for another, and on certain dates West Highland trains originated at miscellaneous points on the LNE, Grangemouth, Peebles, and stations in Fife among them. The Glasgow trains started from Bridgeton Cross and after calling at Queen Street picked up passengers at the Glasgow suburban stations and at Singer and Dumbarton.

But those were also the years of the great industrial depression on Clydeside, and hundreds of hikers could afford to go no further than Arrochar and Tarbet. There was no Sunday winter service on the West Highland or on the Glasgow—Helensburgh line, but one year the regular hiking clientèle induced the LNE to put on a train from Arrochar to Glasgow on Sunday evenings. Engine and stock had to be worked empty from Glasgow, and the line opened throughout for this one train. Since the returning week-enders seldom numbered more than 30, and the fare from Glasgow to Arrochar and back was 3s 9d, the train's earning capacity seldom could have reached £3.

The thirties were certainly happy days on the West Highland. The merry Sunday trains crowded with bronzed, healthy young people will be remembered with pleasure and affection by all who used them. On 3 September 1939, that fateful Sunday, the hikers turned up for their trains as usual. They were running all right, but they were engaged exclusively in the grim business of evacuating schoolchildren from Glasgow. It was the end of an era. No Sunday excursion trains ran on the West Highland again until 1949, and by then a new generation of hikers and campers had been won to road transport. The Sunday trains were withdrawn in 1957, victims in part of a current economy drive.

Before the war the Sunday trains were not in the public timetable; after the war the Sunday service appeared in the timetable.

THE WAR YEARS AND AFTER

Like railways everywhere the West Highland was transformed with the coming of war. With Southampton and London under constant threat from enemy bombers, alternative safe ports had to be established elsewhere, and the Gareloch was chosen as a site for one of them. The placid beauty of the loch was swept away. Hillsides were sheared of trees, villas were pulled down, every kind of mechanized appliance scooped and clawed at the soil to make way for the docks, cranes, and workshops and all the paraphernalia of a major seaport. This time there could be no plea of destruction of amenity; the country had to have a port to survive. But the older residents of Garelochside must have smiled wryly when they reflected on the fuss that was made fifty years before when the West Highland cut a thin, discreet path along the hillside.

A double line was taken from Croy, between Rhu and Shandon, on a steeply falling gradient to the new port in Faslane Bay. The branch was worked by Royal Engineers railway-operating troops on military principles, and War Department locomotives were used. From the opening of the port in May 1942 until August 1945 the Faslane branch received sixty-five passenger trains and 104,877 loaded wagons from the West Highland. To help in the handling of this traffic a loop and siding accommodation were provided at Faslane Junction, the Helensburgh Upper loops were extended, and a new yard was brought into operation at Craigendoran. The port is now used by Metal Industries Ltd as a shipbreaking centre.

On the outbreak of war the Mallaig Extension was placed in a prohibited zone and travellers had to have a good reason and a special pass to use its trains. A naval base was established at Corpach and new loops and sidings were put in. The capacity of the line was increased by the placing of a new signal box at Camusna-ha, 4¼ miles from Mallaig Junction. Fort William's cramped station and yards proved inadequate for the wartime traffic, and the situation was alleviated by the building of additional loops and sidings at Mallaig Junction.

Even the moribund Fort Augustus branch took on a new lease of life. The increased traffic in timber and ammunition from a base set up at Fort Augustus was enough for the sole surviving service, a weekly coal train, to blossom into a daily freight. The military authorities planned to use the Fort Augustus branch as an alternative route to the north in the event of the Highland line being put out of action, and reserve sidings were put in at Spean Bridge and Fort Augustus. The planners must have regretted that the line did not extend to Inverness.

Immediately after the war, the Loch Sloy power scheme brought an increase in traffic to the line. Water had to be piped from Loch Sloy, lying deep in the mountains immediately to the west of Loch Lomond, through the mountains to a point above Inveruglas on Loch Lomond. The pipelines then ran steeply down the mountain face and passed under the railway to reach a turbine house by the lochside. The line was diverted for about a quarter-mile to allow a bridge carrying the track over the pipelines to be built. At the same time Inveruglas station was constructed—close to the site of the turbine house—to serve the camp where a large part of the labour force was quartered. A halt was also established in Glen Falloch. Prisoners of war living at Faslane were picked up at the halt near their camp by the morning work train which then collected British labour at Arrochar and Tarbet, and dropped them all at Inveruglas and Glen Falloch as required. All three stations were removed when the power scheme was completed.

'SAVE OUR RAILWAY'

The West Highland remained remarkably intact. The Banavie branch closed on 2 September 1939. The Royal Route had lately fallen from favour, and the Caledonian Canal steamer ran only on alternate days, with the trains from Fort William making a connection. The outbreak of war saw the end of the steamer service, and there was no need for the connecting train. The Fort Augustus branch saw its last passenger train on 30 November 1933. It was the 12.5 p.m. ex-Fort Augustus, and like all passenger trains on the West Highland then and now, it exhibited express headlights. And it took 83 minutes to cover the 23¼ miles! The local people fought hard for its retention, but the figures did nothing to justify the continuance of the service. In the last full year of operation only 1,911 passengers travelled on the branch and the revenue was £179. The once-weekly coal train was run until 31 December 1946 when the line was closed. The track was lifted shortly afterwards, and all that now remains of the Invergarry & Fort Augustus Railway is a shunting neck at Spean Bridge.

When, in the sixties, the era of massive railway closures dawned, the feeling of unease in Fort William changed to alarm when rumour had it that the existence of the whole of the West

Highland line from Craigendoran to Mallaig was threatened. There could not be two railway routes to the Islands, so it was said, and one had to go. It was disconcerting to see chalked on the streets of Fort William the plaintive appeal, 'Save Our Railway'. And these were the same streets along which the good folks of the town had kicked the effigies of politicians who had opposed the railway, the same pavements over which they had carried their torches in triumph when the railway's case was won. Now every foot of railway for which Lochaber had fought was to be swept off the map.

In the nick of time an unprecedented agreement made between British Railways and Scottish Pulp (Development) Ltd saved the railway and guaranteed its continued existence for at least 22 years. Scottish Pulp undertook to set up a large factory at Corpach and lay it out for rail transport. On their part British Railways agreed to maintain the line, deliver locally-grown timber to the mill, and take away the finished products. A traffic of 200,000 tons a year was visualized. 'It is hoped,' said the official announcement, 'that the knowledge that rail facilities will be available on a long-term basis will encourage other industrial development in the area.' The Fort William populace was saved the necessity of kicking along their streets the effigy of the personage most closely associated with the threat to their line.

The position of the West Highland was further strengthened by the closure of the Callander & Oban line east of Crianlarich in the autumn of 1965. All Oban trains now leave Glasgow Queen Street and run to Crianlarich *via* the West Highland. The completely re-cast Oban timetables at long last provide a faster and cheaper service from Oban to Glasgow, although passengers to Edinburgh are faced with increased mileage and fares.

CHAPTER 9

West Highland Life

THE LOCAL SPIRIT

When the West Highland was new the clean, cut rocks were like the raw flesh of a recent wound on the countryside. The fresh earth of the embankments was bare and there were bald spaces where the contractors had hacked their way through woods to gain access to sites. But nature soon reasserted herself. The rocks browned and mellowed and heather and wild flowers in profusion carpeted the embankments. The railway grew into the soil.

Although the West Highland had a separate existence for only fourteen years it soon acquired a spirit of its own, a spirit that amalgamation and nationalization could not quench. The pay envelopes that arrived every week at the West Highland stations might have been inscribed 'N.B.R.' or 'L.N.E.R.', but the men who signed for them thought of themselves as West Highland men. They were a race apart. From the day the railway opened the trains dominated the lives of the people (railway and non-railway) at the places along the line. They turned out then every day to greet the trains and they still do so. Fort William station is almost a community centre where people foregather to gossip and await the arrival of the evening papers by the 4.35 from Glasgow.

The regular traveller on the line knew and appreciated the 'West Highland touches'. There was the late afternoon train rumbling across the Moor of Rannoch in the evening light with the engine now and again emitting gentle pop whistles. That was the driver telling knowledgeable passengers that he had spotted a herd of deer. More often than not if you looked forward you would see an arm pointing from the footplate, and if you followed its direction you would spot the splendid creatures silhouetted against the setting sun. There were the succulent, baked, brown trout that appeared unannounced on the high-tea tables of the friendly West Highland dining-car when the printed menu spoke of nothing more exciting than haddock or sole. There were the Scots firs seen piled at the back of the tender on south-bound runs in the week before Christmas, to say nothing of the odd salmon in the tool box.

There were times when even the most important trains made social stops of which the timetable breathed not a word, when driver, fireman or guard (and maybe all three) gossiped over the fence to an appreciative ganger and his family. They did that on the Mallaig boat connection one morning when someone who mattered was on board. The driver, carpeted, confessed his fall from grace and escaped with a few days' suspension. The fireman, interviewed separately, denied all knowledge of the unauthorized stop and was dismissed.

LIGHTHOUSEMEN OF THE LAND

When the railway was new, trees were planted round the exposed, isolated cottages by the line to act as windbreaks. To the modern traveller, a clump of trees away ahead is the first indication that he is approaching one of the lonely Moorland outposts. The men of the Moor and their families have intrigued visitors ever since the line was opened. Rannoch was a station in its own right and appeared in the tables. Corrour and Gorton, according to the minutes, were built as passing places and became private stations only incidentally. Corrour was used by the public almost from the beginning: for instance, the navvies for Kinlochleven de-trained there.

Corrour featured in the public timetables from 1934, but the author has been unable to trace any mention of Gorton. It is possible that Lord Breadalbane persuaded the railway to prevent passengers alighting at Gorton, but there is no proof of this. As late as the LNE period, the authorities tried to make a mystery of Gorton, and permission to leave the train there was not readily obtained. A journalist on a Glasgow newspaper who wanted to write a feature on the railway community on the Moor was refused permission. Later, when a writer and photographer entered the forbidden territory uninvited, the published result of their clandestine visit resulted in 'please explain' letters being sent to railway personnel on the spot. A happier result followed an accidental visit by an English journalist who made the acquaintance of Gorton when his train was delayed there. After his account of the settlement appeared in a national paper, innumerable parcels of toys arrived for the children of the line. At one time a special engine and brake made a Christmas visit to the lonely stations and cottages, and a railway official from Glasgow, disguised in the familiar red cloak and white beard, distributed gifts to the railway children.

The education of the children living in isolated houses along the line presented a problem to the authorities, and their solution varied with the school population of the Moor at any given time. At one period the children were picked up from their homes in Argyllshire every school day by the first down passenger train in the morning, and taken all the way across the western corner of Perthshire to their classrooms in Fort William, Inverness-shire. They returned by the last afternoon up train. In a school week they spent sixteen hours travelling and covered some 425 miles.

During the early thirties a school was established in an old passenger carriage on Gorton platform. The Argyll authorities found a lady teacher for it, but there was no place for her to stay in Gorton, so she had to travel up from Bridge of Orchy every morning. At one time there were eleven pupils. Travellers who passed in the trains caught a fleeting glimpse of childish faces lifted momentarily from their books looking curiously at them from the windows of the school. The children of Gorton never set eyes on a motor car for weeks on end, but they had a guard rail in front of their schoolroom door; that was to prevent them tumbling on to the line if they made too exuberant an exit.

The water on the Moor of Rannoch is unsafe, and all Gorton's domestic water has to be imported. It was once the duty of the fireman of the first up train of the day to deliver from his tender twelve bucketfuls for use at Gorton. Now the water comes from Fort William in hygienic containers. Food supplies come in bulk from Glasgow once a week, and are delivered by train to the customer's door. In addition the wives of the railwaymen are provided with market passes which enable them to ride on goods trains to Fort William once a week.

Sudden illness presents another problem for the people on the Moor. They tell tales of an engine dashing in the night with a doctor on the footplate to the succour of a railwayman who was taken suddenly ill. On one such occasion word was received in Fort William late at night that a surfaceman's wife was seriously ill in a lineside house on the north-western edge of the Moor of Rannoch. While the traffic department was opening up the line the locomotive department sent an engine out to Tulloch where arrangements had been made to pick up a doctor. The engine duly delivered the doctor at the house on the Moor and, when he had made his examination, took him back to Tulloch. It was a wild winter night with a touch of sleet in the air. The engine had to run tender first —something that is avoided at all costs on the West Highland—and the chilling blast of the icy mountain air tore through the cab. All on the footplate were chilled to the marrow, and the fireman's hands were so numbed that he could hardly hold the shovel.

The spiritual needs of the railwaymen were not forgotten. When the railway came to the West Highlands it entered tracts of country where the Reformation had never penetrated. The first Protestants in the district were the men who came from the south to work on the line. Churches were improvized in station waiting-rooms, the local signalman acting as beadle for the minister, who came often long distances perhaps one Sunday in four to preach to his small railway flock. Later as the Protestant population increased the station churches were attended by any civilians who could reach them.

The relief man on the West Highland had to be a 'lad o' pairts', able to turn his hand to anything. His standard equipment consisted of a portable bed, a cooking outfit, a fishing rod and a snare wire. Thus equipped he could answer an emergency anywhere on the line and be able to live in tolerable comfort.

There is a story told about the relief man who was sent to one of the settlements on the Moor of Rannoch to take over from a family who were going on holiday. The train which set down the relief also picked up the holiday family, and there was time only for a brief exchange of words. The newcomer had a free run of the house and when he went into the kitchen he found a note containing instructions—not for handling the railway's business, but for tending the animal population of the place, which consisted of miscellaneous poultry, a few cats, a dog and three goats. On the first day the goats escaped on to the Moor and attempts by the relief man to retrieve them met with hostile demonstrations.

There used to be a celebrated goat at Gorton. Its peculiarity was that it found the grass that grew on the track much sweeter than anything offered on the Moor or in the patch of garden beside the house. Drivers got into the habit of watching for it, and time and again they saw the beast making hair-raising escapes from under their wheels. Then one night the last down passenger arrived at Fort William and when the driver was looking round the fore end he found a tuft of shaggy hair adhering to the wheel guard. He was wondering just what he had hit when he remembered the Gorton Goat. The damage was not mortal but the goat ever after displayed a bald patch on its hindquarters.

Tablets are exchanged manually on the West Highland, often at spectacular speeds. There have been few accidents to personnel, although the first signalman to come to Ardlui was pulled under the wheels of a train and killed while exchanging a tablet. The sweep of a train along an island platform, the flash of hoops as nimble hands effect the change is a characteristic sight on the line. It is not uncommon to see a railway family gathered at the door of their cottage to watch one of their members change the tablet.

In steam days the practice was for firemen to hang the tablet carriers by the hoop on the handle of the hand brake while they were in section. There was an occasion when the last train of the day arrived at a signal box on the Moor of Rannoch without a tablet. The driver reported that the carrier had swung off the hand-brake handle with the swaying of the engine and had fallen on to the track. It was a Saturday night and darkness had fallen; there was no point in searching the line immediately. The signalman decided to wait until Sunday when the line would be closed to all traffic and he could stroll up the track at his leisure keeping an eye open for the tablet. When he woke on Sunday morning he found the landscape with an even covering of deep snow!

A fireman tells the story of how he came to Glasgow on holiday and treated himself to the unaccustomed luxury of a visit to the cinema. As he was taking his seat in the darkened auditorium he heard a voice behind the screen say 'and the train cannot leave a station without it'. When he looked at the screen there was a signalman standing on a station platform holding up a tablet. 'I nearly put my hand out for it,' said the fireman, relating the tale afterwards.

'THE GHOST'

A casual visitor to Fort William might well have overheard an engine-driver's wife complain that her husband was 'on *The Ghost*'. She would have been referring to the only regular named train the West Highland has known, and even that name has never appeared in a timetable. *The Ghost* is the express freight that leaves Sighthill, Glasgow, about 2.15 a.m. and runs through to Fort William. Its time of departure and intermediate stops have varied over the years, but it was common in steam days for it to stop only at Crianlarich for water. It regulates the domestic scene in railway houses up the length of the West Highland Railway. The working day begins for many West Highland signalmen when the bells offering *The Ghost* ring out, for all the boxes are switched in at its approach. As the train makes its way north the railway rouses itself for the work of the day.

Many are the tales they tell in West Highland bothies about *The Ghost* and its journeyings. The Inspecting Officers of the Board of Trade would have been happy to have issued reports about some of the things that happened to it if only they had learned about them. But there was a feeling on the West Highland that what happened on the line was no business of Glasgow's, let alone London's. What on a more orthodox railway would have produced a stodgy printed report became on the West Highland the stuff of legends passed from mouth to mouth.

There was the morning about daybreak when *The Ghost* came panting up off the Moor and the driver shut off to let his fireman pick up the tablet at Corrour. When he saw the fireman toss the hoop over the handbrake handle he opened up smartly, and with the gradient falling in front of him had put on a bit of speed by the time the wagons at the back end of the loose-coupled train took up the slack. The brake van was given a nasty tug. It was sharp enough to snap the coupling between the van and the rest of the train, but not sharp enough to waken the guard who was sound asleep in the van. Now, although most of the train was over the summit and on a falling gradient, the detached van was still on the rising gradient. It followed its train for a second or two, then slowed and stopped, and gently began to run back the way it had come. The last the Corrour signalman saw of it was as it fast disappeared down the line in the direction of Rannoch.

The van was next seen bounding out of the rock cutting above Rannoch station and soaring on to the viaduct. Plainly, it was, as they say of ships in distress, not in command. The rule book was explicit about such a situation: the Rannoch signalman was duty-bound to derail the runaway. But when he saw it charging down off the viaduct at speed he knew that to do so would mean killing the guard. Any grand notion he had of leaping aboard had to be abandoned when he saw the speed at which it rattled through the station. So he let it alone.

Gorton was duly warned that the runaway was approaching, but the signalman there, too, could not bring himself to cause its deliberate derailment. It swept through at upwards of 35 miles an hour. Now it was on the long descent to Bridge of Orchy. The stationmaster concluded that if it negotiated all the curves and was still on the rails by the time it reached him, the rising gradient south of the station would check it. He, too, let the van run through, but he followed it on foot and found it at a dead stand about two miles along the line. The still slumbering guard responded to a sound shaking. 'Do you know where you are?' asked the stationmaster. 'No,' admitted the guard, peering about him. 'You're at Bridge of Orchy,' the stationmaster informed him. 'Ach, don't be daft,' said the guard, 'we were there two hours ago.' 'Well, you're back again!' replied the stationmaster.

The van had run back 25 miles.

There is an old joke about the West Highland train that was late 'because she had the wind against her'. It was a joke that sometimes fell flat; the younger generation of footplatemen scoffed when they heard the old-timers' tales of minutes lost because of wind. It was not until the early days of the diesels that dramatic visual proof of the effect of wind on a locomotive's performance was offered. On a March day in 1962 the afternoon up passenger had threaded its way round the Horse Shoe and was emerging on to the length of track leading up to the summit at the county march. A full gale was blowing from the west, and as the train came out of the shelter of the Horse Shoe the driver saw the speedometer needle drop back from 35 to 15. His first thought was that the communication cord had been pulled, but a glance at the vacuum gauge revealed that vacuum was being maintained. The wind, pressing on the sides of the coaches and grinding the wheel flanges against the rails, was the culprit.

ACCIDENTS

In spite of the natural hazards of operating the West Highland accidents have been rare and the few that have occurred were relatively minor. The 8.40 a.m. Sighthill—Crianlarich goods came to grief in a rock fall on Loch Lomondside about mid-day on 8 August 1906. It had been raining heavily all morning and the rocks must have loosened and plunged on to the line after the passing of the forenoon up passenger. Andrew McKinnon, the driver of the goods, never had a chance. He had just passed through Craigenarden tunnel and was nosing round a blind curve near the Pulpit Rock when the obstruction appeared almost under his buffer beam. The engine struck the rocks heavily and the wagons piled up against it and were smashed to pieces. McKinnon was badly hurt, and had to be taken by motor car to hospital in Helensburgh. The line was blocked for 24 hours, during which time passengers were shuttled between

Arrochar and Tarbet and Ardlui by the Loch Lomond steamers.

The West Highland has witnessed two head-on collisions between trains; both took place in stations, but neither was serious. About 7 a.m. on 6 December 1909 the first up local from Arrochar and Tarbet to Craigendoran collided with a down freight that had been held to cross it at Glen Douglas. The driver was slowing down to make a conditional stop, otherwise the impact would have been greater than it was. Two coaches, both empty, were telescoped, but because of the absence of casualties the accident received little attention.

The other head-on collision occurred at the north end of Bridge of Orchy station on 17 April 1954. A K1 No. 62012 on a southbound goods struck B1 No. 61064 heading a northbound goods. There was extensive damage to the front ends of both engines, and the north end of the station was completely blocked by derailed wagons. The block occurred at one of the most critical points on the line, for there was no parallel road beyond Bridge of Orchy on which to organize the customary bypass bus service. Moreover, it was Easter Saturday and the morning train from Glasgow, double-headed and with ten coaches, was following the down goods. With the north end points at Bridge of Orchy out of action, there was no way of running an engine round a ten-coach train. The down passenger was, therefore, sent forward from Crianlarich with one engine and seven coaches, a formation that could be handled in the down sidings at Bridge of Orchy. The passengers were conducted round the wreckage and entrained in a special which departed for Rannoch hauled by a K4 running tender first.

On 27 January 1931 the 4.5 passenger train from Fort William to Glasgow met with a peculiar mishap on the Moor of Rannoch. The train, a heavy one, was double-headed and had six fish vans at the rear. The last vehicle, a 9-ton van, carried only 22 cwt of fish. When the train left Corrour on the falling gradient of 1 in 200 both engines were steaming, but some 600 yd south of the station Driver McIntosh on the train engine shut his regulator. Driver Young on the pilot engine kept his regulator open until the train had breasted a short stretch rising at 1 in 83 about 3 miles out from Corrour. The train then coasted briskly across the Moor on a falling gradient of 1 in 86.

At that part of the Moor the track wound in easy curves round pools and rocky outcrops. Only 11 minutes were allowed for the 7¼ miles between Corrour and Rannoch, and it was here that southbound trains whipped up speeds substantially in excess of the

40 m.p.h. maximum permitted on the line. By the time the 4.5 had run three-quarters of a mile down the slope the speed was climbing into the 50s and Young made a brisk brake application. The sudden check caused two wheels of the last van to lift momentarily off the rails.

In the 7¼-mile section there were only 70 yd of imperfect track, and the van was on the bad patch at that moment. There was an irregularity of curvature amounting to no more than a quarter of an inch, and the wheels, instead of settling back on the rails, dropped on to the sleepers. The derailed vehicle bumped along behind the train for 3½ miles as it wove round the reverse curves, rattled through the Cruach Rock snow-shed and dropped down the 1 in 53 into Rannoch station. The drivers knew nothing about the incident until they looked back after stopping at Rannoch: here the rear van had become completely derailed at the points and pulled the next vehicle with it.

The accident was attributed to the effect of the sudden brake application on a lightly loaded four-wheel vehicle riding on imperfect track. In future the railway company made a point of attaching fully-loaded six-wheeled vans at the rear of trains.

On Saturday 18 July 1953, the start of the annual Glasgow Fair holiday, traffic on the West Highland was exceptionally heavy. The 3.46 from Glasgow to Mallaig was made up of nine coaches and one large van in charge of K1 No. 62011 and B1 No. 61277. Southbound traffic was equally heavy, the 2.52 from Fort William to Queen Street having ten coaches and two vans. The trains were booked to cross at Ardlui. The appropriate tablets were picked up at Arrochar and Tarbet and Crianlarich respectively, and as one train steamed along Loch Lomondside and the other rumbled down Glen Falloch towards the rendezvous it did not seem to have occurred to anybody that *both* trains were too long for the Ardlui loops. The 3.46 was the first to arrive, and the stationmaster made the disconcerting discovery that the train overlapped the points at both ends of the station. Meanwhile, the even longer 2.52 had turned up and was being held at the up home.

The B1 was uncoupled from the front of the down train, run up over the points at the north end of the station, and set back into the up siding. That left space for the 2.52 to squeeze into the up side of the island platform. The train was brought in under caution, and the engine was stopped halfway along the platform. The next move was to have the K1 cautiously edge its train along the down platform until the buffers were almost touching the carriages of the up train. It was then found that the rear van had just cleared the fouling point at the south end of the station by inches. The 2.52 was able to run through; once it was clear the B1 was restored to the down train. Both engines then took water and left 39 minutes late.

CHAPTER 10

Locomotives and Rolling Stock

NO WORKSHOPS

The writer who sets out to record the history of the West Highland Railway locomotives is faced at the outset with the daunting fact that the railway had no workshops, no locomotive superintendent, and in all its history only two classes—comprising 30 engines—were designed specifically for use on its metals. To give an account in detail of all the classes that ran on the railway would be to produce a re-hash of North British locomotive history. For all that, there is much that is worth mentioning about the engines that served there.

THE WEST HIGHLAND BOGIES

Matthew Holmes was in command at Cowlairs when the North British Railway was called on to produce motive power for the West Highland Railway. A light machine capable of handling modest loads at modest speeds on continuous heavy gradients and severe curves was what was required. Holmes simply took his standard highly successful inside-cylinder 4—4—0 and adapted it to the needs of the West Highland. The result was NBR Class N—the West Highland bogie. The engine weighed 43 tons 6 cwt in working order. The standard 6 ft 6 in. driving wheels were reduced to 5 ft 7 in. and the wheel base of 9 ft 1 in. was cut to 8 ft 2 in. Two brake blocks were fitted to each driving wheel. The cylinders were 18 in. by 24 in., and a boiler of new design was used.

Six of these engines were built in 1893 (693—698), and by the time the railway was opened six more were ready for service—55, 393, 394 and 699-701. Twelve more were turned out in 1896—227, 231, 232, 341-346 and 702-704. Not all were sent to the West Highland. A modification of the standard engine that Holmes might well have considered eminently suitable for a West Highland engine was an improved cab. The Holmes cutaway cab did not quite fit in

STRANGERS WITHIN THE GATES

(48) *C.R. No. 123 in a blizzard at Glen Douglas in 1963*

(49) GNSR *'Gordon Highlander' with Caledonian coaches and observation car in Glen Falloch*

MORE NORTH BRITISH LOCOS

(50) *A West Highlan bogie and train of Wes Highland stock at Rhu i the early days*

(51) *C15s for the Craigen doran — Arrochar loca service at Craigendoran Note the express heac lamps*

(52) *Farewell to steam o the West Highland. En thusiasts' special haule by 'Glen Douglas' and J3 at Bridge of Orchy 1 Jun* 1963

with the Moor of Rannoch on a night of wind and rain. Yet the old drivers swore that the Holmes cab was more comfortable than the enclosed Drummond cab and the Reid cab of later days.

The West Highland bogies worked freight as well as passenger trains. Some of the freight trains were worked by Holmes Class C 0—6—0s which were almost new in 1894. The class was associated with the West Highland for 70 years; as Class J 36 some of their number were still at work at the demise of steam on the line. Of the West Highland bogies, seven survived to become Class D35 of the LNE, the last but one going to the breaker in October 1924. The odd man out was No. 695, one of the 1893 batch. This engine was enlarged and rebuilt by W. P. Reid in 1919, and became the sole representative of LNE Class D36. As rebuilt it was given a new boiler with Robinson superheater, new 19 in. by 26 in. cylinders with piston valves, and a side-window cab. It far outlived its fellows; it continued to do interesting work on and off the West Highland until it was scrapped in 1943, with 50 years of toil in difficult terrain behind it.

As new designs came from Cowlairs for general use on the North British system, some were tried out on the West Highland and if their performance was acceptable they were given regular duties. Two new classes were introduced to the line in 1906. One was Reid's Class K 'Intermediate' 4—4—0, and the other was his Class B 0—6—0. Both were more powerful than the two classes that had monopolized traffic since the opening of the line. The 4—4—0s were useful in saving double-heading of trains that had become marginally too heavy for a single West Highland bogie.

In 1913 came the engine whose class name is synonymous with West Highland—Reid's 'Glen'. The 'Glen' was not designed as a West Highland engine. It was a mixed-traffic design, but the happy decision to name it after West Highland glens, and the fact that many—though not all—of the engines made their way to the line at some part of their existence, left it with the reputation of being *the* West Highland class. For more than twenty years the 'Glens' bore the brunt of the passenger duties, and for many more years they were to be seen assisting engines of a later generation.

Also at work on the West Highland were some of Drummond's famous express passenger 4—4—0s of 1877, the 476 class. These had been built principally for service on the Waverley route, and their 6 ft 6 in. driving wheels were considered by some to be unsuitable for the West Highland terrain. Nevertheless they were useful engines, and on busy summer Saturdays when locomotive power was scarce they could take over a train single-handed and give a good account of themselves. The last of the class was scrapped in 1923.

The 'Glens' with North British numbers

34	*Glen Garvin*	298	*Glen Shiel*
35	*Glen Gloy*	307	*Glen Nevis*
100	*Glen Dochart*	405	*Glen Spean*
149	*Glenfinnan*	406	*Glen Croe*
153	*Glen Fruin*	407	*Glen Beasdale*
221	*Glen Orchy*	408	*Glen Sloy*
241	*Glen Ogle*	490	*Glen Dessary*
242	*Glen Mamie*	492	*Glen Gour*
256	*Glen Douglas*	493	*Glen Luss*
258	*Glen Roy*	494	*Glen Loy*
266	*Glen Falloch*	495	*Glen Mallie*
270	*Glen Garry*	496	*Glen Moidart*
278	*Glen Lyon*	502	*Glen Fintaig*
281	*Glen Murran*	503	*Glen Arklet*
287	*Glen Gyle*	504	*Glen Aladale*
291	*Glen Quoich*	505	*Glen Cona*

No. 256 *Glen Douglas* has been preserved and restored to North British livery. Until 1925 No. 492 was called *Glen Gau*.

The 'Glen' was followed in 1915 by Reid's superheated Class S, and this class too, as J 37, remained at work on the line until steam was withdrawn in 1963. The local trains between Craigendoran and Arrochar and Tarbet were handled for the most part by Class L and Class M 4—4—2 tanks, later Class C16 and C15. Class C15 also shared the working of the Fort Augustus branch with Drummond R Class 4—4—0 tanks. In 1940, 9135 (later 67460) was fitted for push-pull working and in the 1950s 67475 and 67474 followed suit.

During the Highland occupation of the Fort Augustus line the traffic was handled by Highland Railway Skye bogie No. 48 and 4—4—0 tank No. 52.

In early LNE days the names Doncaster and Gresley meant little to the West Highland old hands. Railway politics notwithstanding, the West Highland was still the West Highland. English innovations were not welcomed. If an engine arrived from the south with a newfangled footplate fitting, there was always an understanding relative in the works who would provide a good old North British counterpart to be fitted surreptitiously at Fort William. Visiting inspectors *had* to pass Craigendoran, and as soon as their presence was noted on West Highland metals the news was flashed to Fort William. Then there was brisk activity at the shed as the orthodox fittings were retrieved and the forbidden North British parts hidden under the coal—along with the hastily removed 'Jemmies'.

The West Highland Jemmy usually consisted of a short length of wire with a fishplate fastened to each end. The wire, when set across the orifice of the blastpipe and weighed down with the fishplates, was said to be a wondrous aid to steaming. But the sharp blast thus induced did not do the tubes any good, and the Jemmy tended to cause back pressure. The more fastidious driver, by answering a Peterborough firm's advertisement that appeared in the railway press at one time could, for the modest outlay of 1s 6d, avail himself of 'The Driver's Friend', a professionally made Jemmy guaranteed to improve the steaming of any locomotive. The device, claimed the advertisement, 'will fit any blast pipe, and can be put in or taken out in two seconds'. That 'taken out in two seconds' was significant; trouble awaited the driver whose engine was found to be equipped with a Jemmy, whether hand-made or mass-produced.

THE COMING OF THE K'S

By the early thirties passenger-train loads had increased, and in the height of summer double-heading was almost universal. By then the vast resources of the LNE were behind the West Highland, and from the varied stock of locomotives under his control Gresley decided that his H2 class built for the Great Northern Railway would be the most likely to solve the West Highland's problems. As Class K2, thirteen of the engines were allocated to the West Highland. These humble, mixed-traffic machines had conferred on them the dignity of Gaelic nameplates, and in deference to the climate in their new territory they were taken to Cowlairs and given single-window cabs. They were named and numbered as follows:

4674 *Loch Arkaig*
4682 *Loch Lochy*
4684 *Loch Garry*
4685 *Loch Treig*
4691 *Loch Morar*
4692 *Loch Eil*

4693 *Loch Sheil*
4697 *Loch Quoich*
4698 *Loch Rannoch*
4699 *Loch Laidon*
4700 *Loch Lomond*
4701 *Loch Laggan*
4704 *Loch Oich*

The 'Lochs' could take 220 tons compared with the 'Glens'' 180 tons. One result was that the normal five-coach passenger train which had had to be double-headed when a string of fish vans was put on its tail was now handled by one 'Loch'. The K2s were particularly useful on the Mallaig Extension, where they soon supplanted the 'Glens' on the passenger trains. On the Craigendoran —Fort William section the heaviest trains were worked by K2s assisted by 'Glens'.

The K2 was to some extent a stop-gap engine; plainly something still more powerful was required. A K3 would have done the job if its axle-load had not been too heavy for the West Highland. Gresley had produced an engine to meet the special traffic demands on the East Coast route between Edinburgh and Aberdeen. Now, in 1936, he turned his attention to producing a special engine to cope with the peculiar demands of the West Highland. The result was the K4.

The first K4, 2—6—0 No. 3441 *Loch Long*, emerged from Darlington Works and was sent to King's Cross for tests early in May 1937. The following table compares some of the features of the K3 and K4.

	K3	K4
Dia. of coupled wheels	5 ft 8 in.	5 ft 2 in.
Wt of engine	72 tons 10 cwt	68 tons 8 cwt
Wt of tender	52 tons	44 tons 4 cwt
Heating surface	2,308 sq. ft	1,732 sq. ft
Grate area	28 sq. ft	27.5 sq. ft
Tractive effort at 85 per cent boiler pressure	30,031	32,939

No. 3441 had three cylinders of 18½ in. by 26 in., which were cast in one piece. Walschaerts valve-gear was employed in the outside cylinders and Gresley's system for the inside cylinder. The boiler barrel was 5 ft 6 in. in diameter and 11 ft 7 in. between tube plates. The boiler pressure was 180 p.s.i. A Robinson 24-element superheater was provided, and narrow firebars gave 56 per cent air space.

Loch Long was put to work on the West Highland in the summer of 1937 on both passenger and freight trains, and the drivers soon realized that they had been given a tool of unprecedented quality.

The K4 became the talk of Eastfield and Fort William sheds, and there was keen competition among the men to get their hands on the regulator. *Loch Long* could take 300 tons unassisted, and it used no more water than a K2 with two-thirds of the load.

The success of *Loch Long* prompted Gresley to put five more K4s in hand at Darlington. With an eye to public relations, the policy of naming the engines after Highland lochs was discontinued in favour of the more romantic practice of naming them after clan chiefs. All the engines were turned out in apple green. The first of the five, No. 3442, appeared from Darlington Works in June 1938 and arrived at Fort William in time to help with the summer traffic.

To appreciate the story of 3442's name plate you have to know something of Lochaber history. The new engine was serviced at a shed within sight of Inverlochy Castle, and it was there in 1645 that James Graham, Marquess of Montrose—the one they called The Great Marquess—soundly defeated a Campbell army under their chief, the Duke of Argyll. Montrose had been away in Campbell country killing Campbells and looting their property, and while he was so engaged word came to him that the Duke of Argyll had invested Inverlochy. Montrose hurried back to Lochaber, swooped on the castle and put two thousand Campbells to the sword.

When No. 3442 arrived at Fort William the local folks were puzzled to find that the engine bore the name *Mac Cailein Mor*. Mac is Gaelic for 'son of', Mór is 'great'. *Cailin* (the spelling is that of Innes of Learney, Lord Lyon King at Arms) was the founder and chief of the Clan Campbell. The new engine might well have been named *Duke of Argyll*. Why on earth had the LNE chosen to honour a man who had been no friend of Lochaber? The tale that went round Fort William was that the railway company had intended all along to honour the Marquess of Montrose but that some Sassenach (and the word can mean a Lowland Scot as well as an Englishman) had told them that *Mac Caelien Mor* was Gaelic for *The Great Marquess*. Anyway, the plate as it stood was wrong: there was a vowel too many in *Cailien* and the accent was missing over the vowel in *Mor*. No. 3442 disappeared into the shops and duly emerged safely named *in English—The Great Marquess*. The vanquished of Inverlochy had become the victor, the villain the hero. No. 3445 of the class was named *Mac Cailin Mór* and the erstwhile rival clan chiefs joined forces to improve the services on the West Highland line.

There were those who were not reconciled to a Campbell being commemorated in Lochaber. Clan history apart, had it not been a

Campbell who had done his utmost to keep the railway out of his part of the Highlands? But *Cameron of Lochiel* was a happy choice for No. 3443, for a Cameron of Lochiel had put his weight behind every railway scheme in the history of Lochaber. No. 3444 was named *Lord of the Isles,* and No. 3446 took the title *MacLeod of MacLeod.* It is perhaps a pity that the name-pickers did not go the whole hog and call it *Sir Rory Mór, MacLeod of MacLeod.* That would have been an engine name to remember.

In 1945 No. 3445 was rebuilt at Doncaster by Edward Thompson as a two-cylindered engine with cylinders 20 in. by 26 in., and the boiler pressure was increased to 225 pounds. The engine became the prototype of the K1 class which was turned out from 1949 in large numbers for mixed traffic duties by Peppercorn. *Mac Cailin Mór* as Class K1/1 spent some two years in East Anglia before returning to Eastfield where it was joined by a batch of March K1s. The engines of this class associated with the West Highland were 62011, 62012, 62031, 62034 and 62052. *Mac Cailin Mór,* 62031, 62032 and 62052 were transferred from Eastfield to Fort William in June 1954.

The K4s did away with some, although not all, of the double-heading. They always worked alone; they were not allowed to be piloted. The Sunday excursion trains were often loaded to nine vehicles, the maximum for a K4. The engines came to the West Highland about the same time as the LMS Class 5s were introduced on the Oban road. The maximum load for a Class 5 on the Oban line was then 265 tons. West Highland drivers must have felt much satisfaction when they climbed out of Crianlarich with nine vehicles behind their K4s and caught sight of a Class 5 running parallel with them on the other side of Strathfillan with a lighter train—and piloted by an ex-Highland 'Castle'. The K4s in their shining green looked magnificent against the majesty of the West Highland landscape. The sight of one of them fighting its way up Glen Falloch with nine LNE teak coaches behind it, or winding round the wooded slopes above Loch Long with a train of LNE green and cream special excursion stock, was a memory to treasure for a lifetime.

After nationalization Fort William became a sub-shed of Perth, and LMS Class 5s from the parent shed began to appear on the West Highland. The earliest members of the class to arrive were in poor shape, and some lamentable performances were recorded. But it is only fair to add that when Class 5s, both LMS and Standard, were put on the line in tip-top condition they gave excellent results.

The advent of the 4—6—0 saw the older classes relegated to

minor duties, and some entirely disappeared from the West Highland. The K4s no longer handled passenger traffic south of Fort William, but west of the town they continued to perform feats that were entrusted to no other engine. On 26 July 1954 *MacLeod of MacLeod* took over at Fort William the 5.15 ex-Glasgow, a train of eight coaches and two vans that had arrived double-headed some 45 minutes late, and ran it to Mallaig with a loss of no more than five minutes. The tare load of that train was 291½ tons, and with its passengers it must have been 20 tons over the permitted maximum for a K4.

In May 1953 an attempt was made to replace the K2s on the Mallaig road with four Ivatt 2—6—0s—43132, 43133, 43135 and 43137—but the experiment failed. The engines were withdrawn in June of the same year. By the middle 50s the 'Glens' were making only fleeting appearances on the West Highland, but in May 1959 *Glen Falloch* and *Glen Loy* returned to stage a glorious swan-song. For a week they worked between Glasgow and Fort William, their exploits providing material for a most enjoyable television film.

By the early 1960s once-famous West Highland classes were vanishing, not only from the West Highland, but from human ken. The last of the C15s was withdrawn in April 1960, to be followed in March 1961 by the last C16. Before the year was out the 'Glens' (except for the preserved *Glen Douglas*), the K4s and the unique K1/1 had disappeared from the scene; *Mac Cailin Mór* was condemned in June; *Loch Long, Cameron of Lochiel, MacLeod of MacLeod* and *Lord of the Isles* were condemned in October; *Glen Loy* was withdrawn in November. The very last of the K4s, *The Great Marquess,* was condemned in December, but was preserved privately. Of the old guard two 'Lochs' remained—*Loch Arkaig* and *Loch Rannoch*—pottering about on Cowlairs ballast trains; but their days were numbered.

STRANGERS WITHIN THE GATES

On 10 May 1956 an unusual visitor to the West Highland was Class 6 No. 72001 *Clan Cameron.* This engine headed the 3.46 from Glasgow Queen Street to Fort William and returned with the 9.31 a.m. from Fort William the following day. The exercise was a rehearsal for a special, due to be run on 16 June from Glasgow to Spean Bridge in connection with the gathering of the Clan Cameron at Achnacarry. The driver, fireman and guard on that occasion all had the surname Cameron. In spite of a start ten minutes late, and twenty minutes lost on the road, the 'Clan' had its seven coaches in Spean Bridge on time. In case of accidents the railway authorities stationed K4 *Cameron of Lochiel* at Crianlarich ready to take over.

In the closing years of steam, the enterprise of the railway societies was instrumental in bringing several interesting strangers to West Highland metals. Perhaps the most incongruous visitor was Caledonian Railway No. 123—a 7 ft single on the West Highland gradients! This grand old veteran made one of its trips in a raging blizzard. On an earlier occasion No. 123 partnered No. 256 *Glen Douglas* on a trip from Glasgow to Oban *via* the West Highland and the Callander & Oban. That was the first time a 'Glen' had tasted Callander & Oban metals. In their day, of course, the 'Glens' had been prohibited, a fact apparently forgotten by the powers that be. Another interesting combination on the West Highland was GNS No. 49 *Gordon Highlander* hauling the two Caledonian restored coaches. In 1961 *Cameron of Lochiel* was retrieved from mundane duties in Fife and performed excellently on a last K4 run from Glasgow to Fort William.

Other classes that appeared on the West Highland from time to time were J38 and J39 0—6—0s and V1 2—6—2 tanks, the latter on Arrochar local trains. During the second war Class 07 2—8—0s helped out with the heavy freight. The special workings from Glasgow to Oban *via* Dalmally raised some problems for the operating department, for the 'Glens' were prohibited from using the Oban road. The odd pairing which gave the combination of power and route availability was an ex-Great Eastern B12 4—6—0, No. 8502, and the rebuilt West Highland bogie No. 695 (in LNE days, 9695). These engines handled the pioneer trip to Oban in 1931 and were subsequently employed on Crianlarich circular excursions. When the regular daily train from Glasgow (Queen Street) to Oban was instituted in 1949 it was hauled throughout by a B1.

The LMS Class 5s and Standard Class 5s were joined by ex-LNE B1s, and in the last days of steam these engines took most of the traffic on the Craigendoran—Fort William section. It was pleasant to see the final 4—6—0 designs of two great pre-grouping companies in partnership, lifting a heavy train away from Ardlui to begin the ascent of Glen Falloch. Such entertainments were short-lived. In December 1961 the railway authorities announced that it was hoped within a few months to replace the forty-five steam engines on the West Highland railway system—and this included the Callander & Oban as well as the West Highland—with twenty-three Type 2 diesel-electrics and four diesel shunting engines.

LOCOMOTIVE PERFORMANCE

On the West Highland the speed of a train is governed by the nature of the line rather than by the power at the head end. Train timing loses much of its excitement if the timer knows in advance that over large tracts of territory speed will not climb out of the 30s and in 100 miles may never reach 50. For that reason logs of West Highland runs are rare. The following extracts from two logs meticulously recorded by A. J. S. Paterson in the last decade of steam are of particular interest.

The first log records part of a run from Glasgow to Fort William by the 10.21 a.m. on 6 August 1954. The engine was Class 5 No. 44908, and the five coaches weighed 167¾ tons tare, 180 tons gross. After an average run from Glasgow to Craigendoran Junction, the train left Craigendoran station 2 min. 05 sec. late. Uninspired footplate work brought the deficit to 4 min. 10 sec. by Garelochhead and 5¼ min. by Arrochar and Tarbet. The Fort William crew who took over from the Eastfield crew at Ardlui faced a challenge; because of the late running of the up train the 10.21 left Ardlui 19 min. 39 sec. late.

The new crew showed more spirit than their predecessors. The train left Crianlarich 16 min. 16 sec. late, and this was down to 14 min. 11 sec. by Tyndrum. It was at Bridge of Orchy that the fireworks started. From a dead stand at the station, 44908 was climbing steadily at 40·9 m.p.h. a mile out, and this on gradients of 1 in 80 and 1 in 170. The following mile, with gradients of 1 in 240 and 1 in 114, was taken at a top speed of 50 m.p.h. Then followed a 3-mile stretch of 1 in 60 and 1 in 66 with speed falling in the first mile to 42·9, in the second to 37·5 and finally to 32·2 at milepost 55.

A recovery to 45 m.p.h. at milepost 57 brought the train to Gorton showing a gain of 1 min. over scheduled time on the difficult 8-mile section. A further minute was clipped off the time from Gorton to Rannoch and 2 min. were picked up between Rannoch and Corrour. A detailed log of the run from Bridge of Orchy to Corrour Summit follows.

A fast run down Lochtreigside and through the Spean gorges, plus smart station work, had the train in Fort William only 4 min. 28 sec. late.

The second log records a run on 7 August 1954 from Mallaig to Glenfinnan Summit. The train was the 2.45 p.m. Mallaig to Glasgow (Queen Street) made up of 5 coaches weighing 168 tons tare. The

LOG 1

Station	*M.P.*	*Sched.*	*Actual*	*Speed*	
Bridge of		28.00	26.39		14 m. 55 s.
Orchy *dep*	½			24·3	late
	50		29.57	29·0	
	½		30.51		
	¾		31.14	39·1	
	51		31.36	40·9	
	¼		31.56	45·0	
	½		32.14	50·0	
	¾		32.34	45·0	
	52		32.52	50·0	
	¼		33.09	52·9	
	½		33.29	45·0	
	¾		33.49	45·0	
	53		34.10	42·9	
	¼		34.32	40·9	
	½		34.56	37·5	
	¾		35.20	37·5	
	54		35.44	37·5	
	¼		36.10	34·6	
	½		36.38	32·2	
	¾		37.05	33·3	
	55		37.33	32·2	
	¼		38.01	32·2	
	½		38.29	32·2	
	¾		38.55	34·6	
	56		39.19	37·5	
	¼		39.42	39·1	
	½		40.04	40·9	
	¾		40.24	45·0	
	57		40.44	45·0	
Gorton *pass*		44.00	41.31		13 m. 47 s.
	57¾		41.59		late
	58		42.19	45·0	
	¼		42.39	45·0	
Rannoch		55.00	51.39	45·0	
pass	64¾		51.57		12 m. 44 s.
	65		52.32	25·7	late
	¼		53.09	24·3	
	½		53.46	24·3	
	¾		54.23	24·3	
	66		54.57	26·5	
	¼		55.57	26·5	
	½				
	¾		56.22		
	67		56.45	39·1	
	¼		57.09	37·5	
	½		57.34	36·0	
	¾		57.59	36·0	
	68		58.24	36·0	
	¼		58.50	34·6	
	½		59.17	33·3	
	¾		59.42	36·0	
	69		60.05	39·1	
	¼		60.29	37·5	
	½		60.54	36·0	
	¾		61.17	39·1	
	70		61.40	39·1	
	¼		62.04	37·5	
	½		62.27	39·1	
	¾		62.52	36·0	
	71		63.14	40·9	
	¼		63.37	39·1	
	½		64.00	39·1	10 m. 40 s.
Corrour *pass*	71 54c.	70.00	64.24		late

LOG 2

Station	M.P.	Sched.	Actual	Speed	
Mallaig *dep*		00.00	00.00		43 s. late
	39		02.03		
	38¾		02.57	16·67	
	½		03.42	20·0	
	¼		04.22	22·5	
	38				
	¾		05.35	24·0	
	½		06.03	32·2	
	¼		06.29	34·6	
Morar *arr*			07.43		
Morar *dep*		09.00	08.17		Time
	36				
	35		12.09		
	¾		12.29	45·0	
	½		12.47	50·0	
	¼		13.07	45·0	
	34		13.27	45·0	
	¾		13.47	45·0	
	½		14.12	36·0	
	¼		14.42	30·0	
	33		15.18	25·0	
	¾		16.02	20·5	
	½		16.48	19·6	
Arisaig *arr*			18.07		
Arisaig *dep*		22.00	19.51		1 m. 26 s.
	31		22.35		early
	30		25.07	21·5	
Beasdale	29		26.47		
pass			27.27		
	28		28.32		
	27				
	26		32.16		
	25		34.29		
	24		36.34		
Lochailort			37.16		
arr					
Lochailort			38.58		
dep		41.00	41.55		
	23		43.33		
	22		45.10		
	21		45.32	40·9	
	¾		45.55	39·1	
	½		46.17	40·9	
	¼		46.39	40·9	
	20		47.02	39·1	
	¾		47.29	33·3	
	¼		47.57	32·2	
	19		48.32	25·5	
	¾		49.10	23·5	
	½		49.50	22·5	
	¼		50.34	20·5	
	18		51.17	20·9	
	¾		52.01	20·5	
Summit			52.57		

engine was K4 2—6—0 No. 61998 *MacLeod of MacLeod*. From a late start of about ¾ min. the engine got away smartly and was doing 22-23 m.p.h. at the first summit 2 miles out, after negotiating gradients ranging from 1 in 50 to 1 in 150. Departure from Morar was on time. The engine, driven over Keppoch Moss at 45-50 m.p.h., rushed into the ½ mile of 1 in 90 followed by a stretch of 1 in 50 beset with severe reverse curvature. Speed had dropped to 19·6 by the next summit, although an excellent climb had put the K4 1½ minutes to the good by Arisaig.

The 8 miles to Kinlochailort, packed as they are with sharp curves and steep gradients (including two miles of 1 in 48), were taken with the usual caution. The engine quickly reached 40 m.p.h. on the 3 miles of level track east of Lochailort, but soon it was battling with stretches of 1 in 50 and 1 in 48 by the side of Loch Eilt. Speed never fell below 20½ m.p.h. and Glenfinnan Summit was cleared in 13 min. 59 sec.

The start from Glenfinnan station was over 12 minutes late due to the late arrival of the down train. Some brisk running along the easy length beside Loch Eil brought the train into Fort William only 7 min. late.

ROLLING STOCK

The carriages specially designed and built at Cowlairs for the opening of the West Highland Railway were imaginative and ambitious vehicles for their time. Matthew Holmes had the idea of giving as many passengers as possible a window seat while at the same time catering for those who preferred orthodox compartment-type accommodation. The vehicles had single compartments at each end with a large saloon in the middle. Each compartment seated four passengers on one side and three on the other, the space usually allocated to an eighth passenger being occupied by a door leading into the saloon. In the first-class vehicle the compartments were 7 ft deep and the intervening saloon was 21 ft long. The saloon itself was sub-divided by a light partition in which was a swing door.

The outstanding feature of the carriage was the space given to windows. The first-class saloon windows were 4 ft 6 in. long by 2 ft 4½ in. deep. Walnut mouldings and gold beading were much in evidence. 'The fittings,' said a contemporary description, 'include a folding basin with water tap and mirror and a carafe and tumbler arranged in the manner adopted in the best of steamship cabins.'

Contractors' photographs of the new railway decorated the walls. Messrs Laycock of Sheffield installed the brown spring blinds, the torpedo ventilators and the Gold system of carriage heating. In the third-class coach the end compartments were 5 ft 10 in. deep, and the central saloon was 24 ft long. The observation windows were somewhat smaller—4 ft by 2 ft 4½ in. The first-class coach seated a total of 42 passengers, the third class 60 passengers.

The vehicles weighed 22 tons, were 50 ft 1 in. over the buffers, 8 ft 0¼ in. wide and 11 ft 9 in. high above rail level. They were mounted on standard North British four-wheel bogies. They compared very favourably with the six-wheel 15-ton East Coast Joint Stock vehicles that catered for the through passengers from King's Cross to West Highland destinations. In 1895 an East Coast bogie composite was introduced for the West Highland service. A peculiarity was that it had coupé ends. During the first North British occupation of the Invergarry & Fort Augustus one of these coaches was used in winter only to provide the passenger service. Main line comfort including steam heating and lavatory accommodation was offered to 12 first-class and 25 third-class passengers.

The West Highland saloon carriages were not entirely successful in their original condition. The trouble stemmed from the fact that none of the windows was designed to open, and the torpedo ventilators sent a thin jet of fresh air into the vehicles almost at roof level. The result was that the interiors became uncomfortably hot. The observation windows were broken by opening half-lights which, if they improved the temperature, spoiled the appearance of the coach and impeded the view.

In 1906 the North British built large, handsome corridor carriages with which to challenge the Caledonian's *Grampian Express* for the Glasgow—Aberdeen traffic. Seven years later a modified version of this vehicle was designed for the West Highland. It had side corridors but no vestibules; this was to allow gable windows to be fitted in the end compartments. On the trial run of these vehicles to Fort William on 24 April 1913, William Whitelaw and directors and friends joined the train. The idea of the coupé compartment was good, but only a very limited number of passengers could enjoy a rear view of the receding scenery. As recently as 1951 one of these carriages was used daily to transport railway employees from Queen Street to Cadder yard and back. The staff train appeared in the public timetable as far as Bishopbriggs and railway enthusiasts made a ploy of occupying the coupé compartment for the trip up Cowlairs Incline. The view across the tender on to the footplate as the engine—sometimes a J36—blasted its way up through the tunnel could be enthralling. It was not until the rebuilt ex-LNE beaver-tail cars from the Coronation sets were sent to the West Highland in the late fifties that an observation car worthy of the name was seen on the line.

Dining-cars were late in coming to the West Highland. The first ones—old Great Northern vehicles—began operating on 8 July 1929. Their advent meant the curtailment of one of the West Highland's most delightful customs. During the servicing stop at Crianlarich passengers could have a snack at the dining-room on the platform, or they could collect a meal basket which the guard had ordered for them in advance. The Crianlarich basket became an institution. Some of the travellers took their baskets to the seclusion of their compartments, but others preferred to explore its mysteries in the open air. Many a passenger who had entrained the previous night in London enjoyed his first Scottish breakfast sitting on a platform seat at Crianlarich, his appetite whetted by the pure, crisp air of a Perthshire morning. The stopping time at Crianlarich varied between 5 and 11 minutes. The demand for the famous baskets became less as the dining-cars grew in popularity, but breakfast, luncheon, and tea baskets were still being offered at the outbreak of war in 1939. The arrival of the trains was greeted with enthusiasm by the Crianlarich hens. The sound of an approaching train was the signal for every fowl in the railway cottage gardens to go squawking and clucking over the rails, oblivious of the danger of churning wheels, to solicit crumbs from the open-air diners. The dining-room still functions at Crianlarich, but the 4-to-6-minute stop of the diesel-hauled trains puts some restriction on its use.

EPILOGUE

Now the diesels are in the glens. Glen Falloch no longer echoes to the crack of twin exhausts as a double-header roars across the Dubh Eas. No more do the sparks patter like hail on the carriage roofs. No more does the shriek of a K2, responding to a lineside 'whistle' board, rise to the rocky tops of the mountains. No longer can a traveller stand on Rannoch platform of an evening and hear the thin whistle of a 'Glen' far away out on the Moor.

These were sounds to remember.

Chapter 11

Postscripts

AUTHOR'S INTRODUCTION TO SECOND EDITION

One summer day a few years ago I found myself sharing a compartment in a West Highland train with an elderly American couple and a young lady from Kent. It was a sparkling morning, and our English traveller frequently poked her camera at the passing scene. Eventually she opened her bag, extracted a book and handed it to me with the query, 'Have you read this?' I would have answered with a simple *yes* had not the Americans (who were in the know) broken into broad grins which demanded an explanation. The book I had been offered was my own *The West Highland Railway*. 'This has made my day,' declared my lady reader, and I could see she meant it.

It is very gratifying for an author to be told that he has achieved precisely what he set out to achieve. My aim in writing the book had been to try to capture the peculiar magic of the West Highland Railway in print, and when the book first appeared in the shops I was not convinced that I had done so. Then came a steady and continuing flow of letters from people who had experienced the West Highland's magic and were at pains to tell me that they had found it again in the pages of my book.

A church organist wrote from Surrey, 'I would like to send a few lines to say how much pleasure your book has given me over the past two years—so much so that I recently bought another copy in the Pan edition for conveniently slipping in the pocket.' 'Thank you very much for giving such a great deal of pleasure,' wrote Lord Garnock. 'Having been brought up in a part of the world traversed by that remarkable line it gave me a great deal of pleasure to read a whole book devoted to the West Highland and certainly brought back many memories.' A retired passenger guard who had seen 51 years of service with the GNR and LNER wrote to say how in his young days he had been fascinated by a nameboard he had seen on a north train leaving King's Cross: *Edinburgh, Glasgow, Fort William, Mallaig*, but it was 1972 before my correspondent, by then a widower, set off to see the West Highland. 'I was thrilled by all I saw on the whole journey,' he wrote. 'I was lucky enough to meet two ex-railwaymen and their wives who had done the trip after reading your book.'

One West Highland tale I encountered but did not use in my book for want of corroboration was the story of the West Highland baby. It appeared that this legendary infant had been born in a West Highland train and had been named after the guard, the fireman or the driver according to which version you chose to accept. I was more than interested to receive a letter from Dorset written by the doctor who had delivered the baby. He described how he and his wife were returning to England, after spending a fortnight tramping in the West Highlands, when the guard, in an agitated state, inquired through the train if there was a nurse on board. On being asked by the doctor what was wrong the guard replied, 'Oh sir, we're going to have another passenger.' Investigation proved that this was indeed the case. The train was running between Roy Bridge and Tulloch and there was nowhere to put off the mother-to-be. She was taken to a first class compartment. The doctor explained what happened next. 'In the next compartment were the Marquess and Marchioness of Bute. The former had a painful condition for which he had some analgesic tablets. He gave me a number of these. The marchioness and my wife acted as my helpers. They collected all the lavatory towels, kept me supplied with boiling water from the diner and stood guard at the door of the compartment. I was amazed at the contents of the railway first-aid box—everything essential.'

At Crianlarich there was a stroke of luck when a Scots Canadian nurse on her way back to Canada boarded the train. She was nicely in time to assist at the birth. The baby was born about 40 minutes out of Glasgow. The doctor concluded, 'My one regret was that in the excitement I did not take a photograph of my wife at Queen Street attired in tramping kit carrying the baby wrapped in triangular bandages to the ambulance.' The baby was named Evan McLeod Nicholson after the nurse and the doctor.

But what of recent events? The most significant change in the West Highland since the book was first published has been the re-siting of Fort William station. The railway, of course, had cut off the town from Loch Linnhe, a piece of deplorable planning which the townspeople had recognised too late and had been a bone of contention in local politics for 80 years. The new station at the east end of the town was opened on 13 June 1975. The original station and approach lines disappeared within a week. The engine shed and associated yard and sidings likewise disappeared and were replaced by a motive power depot and marshalling yard at Tom-na-Faire near Mallaig Junction. Gorton platform and

LATER DAYS STEAM

(52) *Two Stanier Class 5 4–6–0s crossing the Fillon viaduct at Crianlarich, against the background of Ben More in 1959*

(53) *K1 No. 62012 on Mallaig–Fort William train on the ascent from Keppoch Moss to Arisaig in the summer of 1954*

(54) Class 27 D5382 passes the engine shed at Crianlarich in April 1968 with a freight from Glasgow. Freight traffic over the West Highland remains heavy despite the cessation of traffic to Corpach pulp mill

(55) The old station at Fort William: Class 27 D5356 waits to leave on 8 October 1971. A road now covers the site of the delightfully positioned original station

signal box have vanished, Ardlui has lost its platform buildings due to subsidence and Glen Douglas public platform no longer functions. On the signalling side tokenless block has been installed between Crianlarich and Rannoch to control movements on the single line sections between these places, and foreshadowed the end of yet another traditional facet of railway operation, the exchange of tokens at crossing places.

A MODERN POSTSCRIPT

by Alan J. S. Paterson

It is eight years now since the second edition of this popular book appeared and, but for the much lamented death of its author, there is no doubt that he would have had much to narrate regarding the many changes in the West Highland scene in recent times. In adding these notes to bring the story up to date it occurs to me that the reader may be interested in a personal view of the many alterations north of Craigendoran as they appeared to me during a recent journey over the whole route to Mallaig. During the 1950s and up to the end of steam traction in the early sixties, I had been a frequent traveller on the West Highland, gaining an intimate knowledge of the railway itself as well as the districts which it served. The departure of the steam engine, however, meant for me and many other railway enthusiasts the end of one of the principal attractions of this fascinating line, and other interests claimed my attention thereafter. My journeys, therefore, to Fort William and Mallaig after 1961 were rare, and ceased entirely after 1972. Consequently, it was with a feeling of keen anticipation that I arranged to make a return trip to Mallaig during late May, 1984 for I knew that much had changed in the dozen years since my last run.

THE SOUTHERN SECTION

It is still necessary to rise at an early hour to make the return journey in one day with a reasonable time at Mallaig, and I joined the train from Glasgow (Queen Street) at its first stop at Dumbarton. Although all modern timetable references are, of course, on the 24-hour system, the habits of a lifetime make it difficult to think of the early morning departure from Glasgow as anything but 5.50 a.m. Older times were recalled when the train was notified as running over half an hour late—so often were the timekeeping faults south of the border reflected in long delays on the single line sections of the West Highland, and the problem still seems to exist today, to some extent.

The train arrived behind type 37 diesel electric locomotive No. 37027 *Loch Eil*, bearing on her side panel the West Highland terrier motif which is now widely used to identify and advertise the line's services—it appears, for example, on the public timetable leaflets. This is an ingenious and attractive publicity feature and, as with so many good ideas, one wonders why nobody thought of it before. The name *Loch Eil* recalled vividly the Gresley K-2 which, thirty years earlier, might well have appeared on the corresponding train but there was nothing then in service similar to the second 'engine'—No. 97252 *Ethel 3*—one of the older and now obsolete diesel electric locomotives of which three have been specially adapted to provide electric heating for the carriages. (The apparent 'name' is, in fact, compounded of the initial letters of the words 'Electric Train Heating ex-Locomotive'). At a fairly moderate cost, each of these former type 25 diesels was altered to become a generator vehicle supplying the modern Mark 3 sleeping carriages and Mark 2 daytime coaches, thus ensuring the continued provision of sleeper facilities over the Fort William line, for the type 37 diesel electric engines, fitted only with steam heating, could not cope with the most modern coaches. The train itself consisted of two Mark 3 sleeping carriages, which now run via the West Coast main line from London, another change from the years when the West Highland connections were identified exclusively with the East Coast route from King's Cross. Two Mark 2 day coaches and three older vehicles made up the remainder of the seven-coach train.

It is probably true to say that most of the obvious changes in the West Highland line have taken place on the section south of Arrochar, and to one who knew the railway in earlier times it was depressing to note the absence of the stations at Craigendoran Upper, Rhu, Shandon and Whistlefield, which have now been demolished, leaving few traces of their existence. At Helensburgh Upper the up loop line has been taken out and the station—now unstaffed—looks unkempt and neglected, to a great extent abandoned to the undergrowth now encroaching upon it. This part of the line, running mostly beside and above the Gareloch, is vastly different from what it was thirty years ago, for the suburban sprawl now extends as far as Garelochhead itself. Much of it has been built for defence personnel who have moved into the area to serve the extensive NATO installations, which can be seen at their most obtrusive at the once peaceful wayside crossing of Glen Douglas. But all this housing came too late to save the once familiar 'push-and-pull' train service which ran for many years from Craigendoran to Arrochar and Tarbet in connection with the Helensburgh suburban trains. The new population on the Gareloch depends wholly upon road transport, and the hillside echoes no longer to the scream of a North British whistle as the handsome little tank engine with its two carriages rattles amongst the trees high above the loch.

Garelochhead station, largely untouched, is the first sign that the older West Highland still survives, although the buildings are painted nowadays in a combination of shades of green—not, perhaps, entirely successfully. Nevertheless, as the train swung round the curve out of the station loop and started on the first long climb, to Glen Douglas, all the old thrill was there, of the slowly-changing panoramic views, the fresh scent of highland vegetation, the magnificent sight of primroses and bluebells in veritable cascades down the hillsides. May is a lovely month to see the line at its very best, and in fine weather there is no other route in Britain to compare with its scenic glories. On the occasion of my journey, however, the morning was dull, with a fine, misty rain, and *Loch Eil* was in some trouble getting her train under way on the sharp climb to Whistlefield, slipping continuously and noisily on the wet rails before finally getting a grip.

There are obvious changes on this section, which is now covered with the large-scale plantings of the Forestry Commission, and a landscape once very bleak is well on the way to being heavily wooded. The work of the Commission is also evident further north, most notably on long stretches of Rannoch Moor. Despite criticisms in some quarters as to the visual impact of seemingly endless tracts of evergreens, there is no doubt that the planting of these trees is bringing fresh prospects to an area which badly needs work, and in the long run they will help the railway to remain in being. Whatever may be said of trees, however, they are infinitely preferable to the sinister clutter of military equipment and installations now disfiguring the hillside at Glen Douglas, a dreary reminder in this otherwise peaceful spot of the continuing political tensions under which we all live.

THE CENTRAL SECTION

From Arrochar & Tarbet the original stations are practically intact, with two or three notable exceptions. The impressive buildings at Ardlui, once the largest of any intermediate station on the line, have finally succumbed to subsidence and have long since been swept away. At Craianlarich, fire destroyed the old structure several years ago and a more modern, and much smaller, building has been substituted. Happily for West Highland *aficionados*, the tearoom of long tradition and happy memory was spared the conflagration and survives.

Crianlarich engine shed remains as a prominent feature of the erstwhile steam operating facilities, but the old turntable has gone now. Apart from this, however, the sidings are all *in situ* and Crianlarich is obviously a centre for local permanent way repair work. The original signals remain much as before, save only that here, as elsewhere over the whole route, the original Stevens pattern lower quadrant signal arms have at long last been replaced by upper quadrants. Most, however, are mounted on the lattice posts of North British design. More modern signalling has replaced the older type at Tyndrum (Upper) and Bridge of Orchy, where the station loops have been arranged for double direction running. At the former station the train ran through the down side in the normal way, passing an up goods train headed by one of the un-named type 37 locomotives, but at Bridge of Orchy we ran through the up side, although passing no other train at that point.

There is much evidence of new planting by the Forestry Commission all the way from upper Glen Falloch, through Tyndrum and on past Bridge of Orchy. This is, of course, the district so closely identified in Gaelic literature with the celebrated bard Donnchaidh Ban—Duncan Macintyre (1724–1812)—whose poetry sang the praises of Glen Orchy as none other. It is a scene dominated by the striking outline of Ben Doran, a mountain closer to the poet's heart than all others—'An t-urram thar gach beinn aig Beinn Dobhrain' (pre-eminent over every mountain is Ben Doran)—and whose natural beauties he extols in many lovely verses. Descending slowly round the Horse Shoe Bend towards Bridge of Orchy one is constantly reminded of the old bard as the whole splendid panorama unfolds. It is one of the great moments of the railway journey to Fort William.

On Rannoch Moor the old crossing place at Gorton has now wholly vanished, but at Rannoch station the passing loop still remains and all is much as it used to be in former days. The long climb up to Corrour, the summit of the railway, is still distinguished by snow fences—now much eroded by time, fire, and the weather, it must be admitted—and the unique snow shed in the Cruach rock cutting continues as before to draw comment from uninformed passengers. At Corrour there is still a passing loop, where *Loch Awe*, yet another of the ubiquitous type 37 engines, headed the 4-coach 08.40 train from Fort William to Glasgow. This engine carries a name new to the West Highland, for Loch Awe lies in former Caledonian Railway territory on the Oban route and it was never used by the London & North Eastern Railway as a title for one of its engines. Nevertheless it is now an appropriate and attractive addition to the list of named locomotives running to the western highlands.

THE NORTHERN SECTION

The descent to Fort William down Loch Trieg and on through Glen Spean is as attractive as ever, with the dramatic passage of the Monessie Gorge remaining one of the highlights of the entire journey. Tulloch station is practically unchanged, but in contrast Roy Bridge is now no more than an unkempt halt, all its operating facilities having been removed. However, at Spean Bridge the scene was quite different—station buildings renovated, the passing loop still in use, and sidings obviously carrying local freight traffic—generally an atmosphere of activity in pleasing distinction to the closed and unstaffed stations further south. Yet another type 37—No. 37081 *Loch Long*—headed an up goods here, its name recalling an old favourite of steam days, the pioneer Gresley K-4 2–6–0. Just west of the station is to be seen one of the few surviving relics of the ill-fated Invergarry & Fort Augustus Railway in its former engine shed, still intact, and now used for private purposes by a local owner.

Fort William presents probably the greatest changes to one familiar with the old terminus. John Thomas drew attention to how the railway had cut off the town from Loch Linnhe, but in truth it is difficult to see how, in Victorian days, the demand for a centrally situated station could have been met otherwise. The site of Fort William rises steeply from the water's edge to a height of three or four hundred feet and the only flat ground available for the railway was on the loch side. What gave rise to a demand for the removal of the station to another spot in later years was the burgeoning road traffic which, every summer, jammed up the town's main thoroughfare. Present-day planners therefore abolished the old station and replaced it with a by-pass road and roundabouts. While these facilities were much needed and long overdue, it can hardly be said that the aesthetic result has been much of an improvement, the exposed frontage to the loch being bleaker than ever. I was fond of the old station, which was admittedly not a classic architectural feature, but it was pleasant to walk from it along the lineside to the engine shed at the old military fort on a fine summer evening, an innocent pleasure, alas!, now denied to the railway enthusiast. The new station, about half a mile short of the former terminus, is clean and smart, without being outstanding, but it has good facilities for passengers and remains quite conveniently placed for the town.

THE MALLAIG EXTENSION

I found the Mallaig line adequately served by a three-coach train hauled by the inevitable type 37 engine, this time No. 37192, but it was pleasing to note quite heavy passenger traffic. All stations on the extension remain in use in some shape or form, but Banavie, Corpach, Locheilside and Morar have been reduced to unstaffed halts, as has also Lochailort, which has lost its passing loop and sidings. The stations at Glenfinnan and Arisaig retain full operating provisions. The entire line is unquestionably the finest scenic section on the whole of the British Rail network, and has lost little of its charm for those whose principal interest lies in railway operation. In the summer of 1984 it has been the scene of an imaginative experiment by British Rail, in which preserved steam locomotives, beautifully restored to original condition, have been used to haul regular trains during the peak months. Initial public response appears to be gratifyingly favourable, and this marvellous section of railway once again witnesses the sight of a North British goods engine, No. 673 *Maude*, in her pre-1923 livery, in service over the line on which this class was one of the first to be employed when it was opened at the turn of the century. Accompanying her will be two LMS Stanier Class 5 4–6–0s and these, although never used on the Mallaig line in steam days, were nevertheless latterly the mainstay of the traffic south of Fort William.

Morar station, reduced to an unstaffed halt, has an unusual feature in the operation of its level crossing, where the gates are now opened and closed, as required, by the train crew. This very practical solution has allowed station staff to be dispensed with, permitting economies to be made on a route where reduction of overheads is as important as the generation of fresh traffic.

Mallaig station nowadays presents a rather forlorn appearance, having lost its overall canopy roof and most of its sidings. The engine shed is derelict, the turntable removed, and no traffic is now taken to and from the pier at the harbour. But the Caledonian–MacBrayne ferry to Armadale still reminds us of the steamer connections of former days, and the cry of seagulls remains a feature of this remote outpost of the railway system. Here you are on the doorstep of the Hebrides, the Isle of Skye beckons from across the Sound of Sleat, the western seas shimmer as always, and somehow one is aware that, in spite of much change, the West Highland Railway is still the same in spirit.

THE FUTURE

What is the present position of the line? As a result of recent decisions by British Rail, through which a considerable degree of commercial autonomy has been given to local managers, the prospects are surprisingly good. Passenger traffic has increased in the last two years and freight appears buoyant. Large-scale planting of timber along the route appears to offer longer-term prospects and the possibility of re-opening the pulp mill at Corpach where closure of the original plant caused grave local unemployment. Bulk alumina for the Fort William factory is also a probable source of increased traffic from the south. But the development of tourist traffic, possibly in conjunction with circular tours from the Kyle of Lochalsh line, certainly offers one of the best opportunities of increased revenue, justifying the long-term retention of the Mallaig line, always the most commercially vulnerable part of the West Highland system. Besides the experimental use of steam traction, a well-tried feature from earlier years was reintroduced in 1983 in the form of observation cars, nostalgically turned out in LNER varnished teak livery and named *Lochaber* and *Loch Eil*, resulting in a welcome boost to traffic on the Mallaig extension. Sunday excursions were experimented with on that section during the same summer, with encouraging results, while on that part of the route between Craigendoran and Crianlarich a Sunday service was also given by Edinburgh–Oban through trains. Although not perhaps strictly a West Highland service, it is possible that its success may pave the way for an eventual reintroduction of the former Fort William Sunday excursion trains, last run in 1957.

The basic 'all-the-year-round' timetable has been much improved in recent months by re-timings and the introduction of a morning train from Glasgow, running every weekday during the summer and on Mondays, Fridays and Saturdays during the winter. Retention of the London sleeping car service, at one time under threat of withdrawal, but now using Mark III air-conditioned vehicles, has also guaranteed continuation of a much-appreciated local service. These carriages run as part of the *Royal Highlander* over the West Coast main line to London, combining with the Inverness service. The present policy of aggressive 'selling' of rail facilities seems to be yielding good results and the future of this remarkable railway appears as reasonably secure as it can be in the uncertain economic circumstances of today. There is a growing appreciation that the modernised railway has an important contribution to make to local industrial and business life, quite apart from its tourist potential. With proper exploitation of its many advantages there seems to be no reason to doubt that the West Highland line has the capacity to survive into the indefinite future.

CONCLUSION

How then does the modern scene commend itself to one more familiar with the West Highland of thirty years ago? The obvious changes have been noted—substitution of diesel for steam traction, removal of some smaller stations, the reduction of others—but the overall impression is that the whole line is surprisingly much less affected by new conditions than one had any right to expect in the years when Dr Richard Beeching wielded his managerial scalpel. Any railway enthusiast of those times would have placed the West Highland high on the list of railways ripe for closure, and it was astonishing that it survived and is almost intact today, the only loss of route mileage being due to the resiting of Fort William station. The marvellous scenery, of course, never changes and this alone makes the West Highland route unique, or nearly so, in Britain. Combined with the continuing interest of its railway operations, these factors ensure that there will always be attractions not only for the tourist but also for those whose main reason for visiting the district is to see the railway itself. Long may it continue to delight us!

(56) *NBL Co Class 29 D6103 at County Maich Summit between Bridge of Orchy and Tyndrum on 20 April 1968*

Appendix

1: WEST HIGHLAND CHRONOLOGY

12 August 1889	West Highland Railway Act passed
23 October 1889	First sod cut near Fort William by Lord Abinger
20 July 1890	Banavie branch authorized
5 September 1893	Last spike driven on Rannoch Moor by Mr Renton
31 July 1894	West Highland Railway (Mallaig Extension) Act, 57 & 58 Vict., passed
3 August 1894	Final inspection of line by Board of Trade
7 August 1894	Public opening Craigendoran to Fort William
11 August 1894	Ceremonial opening
4 September 1894	Derailment at Woodend Farm crossing
1 November 1894	Refreshment baskets available at Arrochar and Tarbet
1 January 1895	Inverlair: name changed to Tulloch
27 May 1895	Glen Douglas siding opened
1 June 1895	Banavie branch opened
July 1895	Refreshments available at Crianlarich
1 May 1896	Whistlefield station opened
6 May 1896	Derailment at Mallaig Junction
August 1896	West Highland Railway Act, 1896 (Extension to Ballachulish)
14 August 1896	West Highland Railway Mallaig Extension (Guarantee) Act, 59 & 60 Vict., passed
21 January 1897	First sod of Mallaig Extension cut at Corpach by Lady Margaret Cameron of Lochiel
20 December 1897	Crianlarich spur to Callander & Oban railway opened
8 February 1901	Death of Charles Forman
1 April 1901	Mallaig Extension opened
22 July 1901	First sleeping-car service King's Cross—Fort William. Summer only
8 August 1906	Accident at Pulpit Rock
21 December 1908	North British Railway (Confirmation) Act
31 December 1908	North British took over West Highland, Banavie branch and Mallaig Extension by terms of above Act
6 December 1909	Accident at Glen Douglas
1 June 1924	Row: name changed to Rhu
1 May 1926	Gortan: name changed to Gorton
8 July 1929	Restaurant-cars first introduced on 4.30 a.m., 5.45 a.m. and 11.23 a.m. down and 12.10 p.m., 4.5 p.m. and 5.12 p.m. up trains
October 1929	Sleeping-cars start operating throughout year
6 July 1931	Loop put in at Rhu
27 January 1931	Rannoch Moor derailment
1 August 1931	Fersit opened

7 August 1932	Loch Treig diversion brought into operation
31 August 1933	Buffet cars on 9.52 a.m. up and 3.46 p.m. down trains
15 September 1934	Corrour, formerly private, opened to public
1 January 1935	Fersit closed
2 September 1939	Last passenger train on Banavie branch
2 October 1939	Sleeper service withdrawn
27 April 1941	Faslane Junction opened
21 December 1941	New signal box and extended loops brought into operation at Helensburgh Upper
4 January 1942	Craigendoran yard opened
15 November 1942	Camus-na-ha signal box opened
26 March 1943	Corpach naval sidings completed
5 April 1944	Withdrawal of restaurant-cars
26 August 1945	Faslane platform (temporary) opened
29 October 1945	Inveruglas (temporary) opened
10 April 1946	Glenfalloch (temporary) opened
June 1946	Restoration of restaurant-cars
23 May 1949	First regular train Glasgow—Oban via West Highland and Crianlarich spur
17 April 1954	Collision at Bridge of Orchy
9 January 1956	Rhu closed (first closure)
24 September 1956	Television train, first in Britain, runs over West Highland
4 April 1960	Rhu re-opened as unstaffed halt
14 June 1964	Craigendoran (West Highland), Rhu, Shandon, Whistlefield and Glen Douglas closed. Last day of local service Craigendoran—Arrochar and Tarbet
13 June 1975	New Fort William terminus opened, replacing original station in the town
1980	Closure of pulp mill at Corpach with adverse effect on rail freight traffic
1983	Observation cars restored to Mallaig extension—summer service only
1983	Sunday excursions reintroduced on West Highland line
1984	Steam engines return to service as a tourist attraction on the Mallaig route

2: MILEAGES

	Miles	Chains	Opened
Craigendoran Junction	0	0	
Craigendoran	0	17	7 Aug. 1894
Helensburgh Upper	2	8	,,
Rhu	3	70	,,
Faslane Junction	5	20	27 April 1941
Shandon	6	48	7 Aug. 1894
Garelochhead	8	76	,,
Whistlefield	10	30	1 May 1896
Glen Douglas	15	21	7 Aug. 1894
Arrochar and Tarbet	19	47	7 Aug. 1894
Inveruglas	23	26	29 Oct. 1945
Ardlui	27	47	7 Aug. 1894
Glenfalloch	30	33	10 April 1946
Crianlarich	36	23	7 Aug. 1894
Crianlarich Junction	36	31	,,
Crianlarich Junction to C & O		39	,,
Tyndrum	41	24	,,
Bridge of Orchy	48	68	,,
Gorton	57	40	,,
Rannoch	64	36	,,
Corrour	71	54	,,
Tulloch	81	60	,,
Roy Bridge	87	34	,,
Spean Bridge	90	57	,,
Mallaig Junction	98	70	,,
Fort William	99	70	,,
Fort William Pier	99	72	,,
Fort William	0	0	,,
Mallaig Junction	1	0	,,
Banavie Junction	2	26	1 April 1901
Banavie Pier	2	68	1 June 1895
Banavie	2	49	1 April 1901
Corpach	3	52	,,
Camus-na-ha	5	18	15 April 1942
Locheilside	10	25	1 April 1901
Glenfinnan	17	4	,,
Lochailort	26	14	,,
Beasdale	30	76	,,
Arisaig	34	29	,,
Morar	39	5	,,
Mallaig	41	66	,,

NOTES

Most of the dates given in this table and elsewhere in the book are British Railways' official dates. Occasionally, when the official date seems suspect, a second source is used. For instance, the official date for the opening of Whistlefield conflicts with the date given in the contemporary local press. All the mileage points listed are stations, with the exception of Faslane Junction, Mallaig Junction and Camus-na-ha. Glen Douglas and Beasdale were opened as private stations. Gorton and Corrour were established as passing places and no mention was made in the Act of their function as stations. They were in fact used as private stations by local landowners. Glen Douglas and Corrour eventually appeared in the public timetable (see Chronology) but Gorton never did so. Passengers apparently experienced no difficulty in alighting at Glen Douglas and Corrour in their 'private' days, but visitors were not encouraged at Gorton. Beasdale, on the other hand, catered for the public from its opening, and was the only one of the four private stations to keep its own accounts. The traffic books show that there was steady custom all the year round.

In the West Highland Railway Act of 1889 the station subsequently named Arrochar and Tarbet was listed as Ballyhennan after a nearby hamlet.

3: PASSENGERS AND FREIGHT BOOKED AT FORT WILLIAM 1913—1934

Year	No. of Pass.	Goods Tons	Minerals Tons	Total Tons
1913	31,708	6,773	5,618	12,391
1914	26,624	5,346	5,276	10,622
1915	29,745	5,581	5,294	10,875
1916	14,889	7,165	5,223	12,388
1917	13,751	4,833	3,232	8,065
1918	16,645	4,181	3,247	7,428
1919	24,450	9,009	7,987	16,996
1920	28,194	7,516	5,719	13,234
1921	22,184	8,607	5,053	13,660
1922	25,364	9,957	6,292	16,249
1923	26,434	11,083	6,275	17,358
1924	26,011	11,934	5,443	17,377
1925	35,851	20,463	6,651	27,114
1926	31,095	16,507	7,841	24,348
1927	41,200	19,539	10,575	30,114
1928	43,250	24,322	10,080	34,402
1929	41,013	33,815	13,805	47,720
1930	33,478	34,103	8,501	42,604
1931	32,048	37,119	9,998	47,117
1932	31,737	32,811	8,889	41,770
1933	32,743	30,390	7,777	38,167
1934	27,992	34,582	8,405	42,987

4: NUMBER OF PASSENGERS BOOKED AND PASSENGER RECEIPTS FOR ALL WEST HIGHLAND STATIONS, 1930

Station	No. of passengers	Passenger receipts
Helensburgh (Upper)	8,113	£3,224
Rhu	3,065	£762
Shandon	1,272	£196
Garelochhead	3,367	£450
Whistlefield	3,819	£274
Arrochar & Tarbet	10,917	£1,802
Ardlui	887	£161
Crianlarich	2,253	£957
Tyndrum	1,358	£359
Bridge of Orchy	3,215	£916
Rannoch	11,106	£3,807
Tulloch	1,075	£425
Roy Bridge	1,665	£415
Spean Bridge	5,959	£2,004
Fort William	33,478	£12,841
Banavie	2,229	£220

Banavie Pier	115	£5
Corpach	2,829	£251
Locheilside	2,974	£186
Glenfinnan	2,641	£884
Lochailort	2,478	£421
Beasdale	562	£55
Arisaig	5,735	£1,067
Morar	6,207	£548
Mallaig	16,842	£8,242
Gairlochy	1,948	£295
Invergarry	1,020	£604
Fort Augustus	4,301	£1,852

5: INVERGARRY & FORT AUGUSTUS RAILWAY CHRONOLOGY

14 August 1896	Invergarry & Fort Augustus Act passed
2 February 1897	First sod cut
14 July 1903	Final Board of Trade inspection
21 July 1903	Highland and Invergarry & Fort Augustus Railway Act passed allowing Highland Railway to operate the line
22 July 1903	Line opened by Mrs Ellice of Glengarry
1 July 1904	Invergloy platform opened
30 September 1906	Fort Augustus pier closed
30 April 1907	Highland Railway withdrew its engines and rolling stock
1 May 1907	North British took over
4 May 1907	North British ran first trains
30 October 1911	Invergloy platform closed
31 October 1911	Line closed to all traffic. North British withdrew
1 August 1913	Line re-opened by North British
28 August 1914	North British Railway (Invergarry & Fort Augustus) Vesting and Confirmation Act passed. North British purchased line
1 December 1933	Line closed to all traffic except one weekly coal train
31 December 1946	Final closure. Track lifted

6: INVERGARRY & FORT AUGUSTUS RAILWAY

Directors at opening, 22 July 1903

Rt Hon Lord Burton, chairman
Cpt. Edward Charles Ellice, M.P. of Glengarry
Rt Hon Lord Abinger
J. C. Cunningham
George Malcolm, Esq., of Invergarry
John Lambrick, Burton-on-Trent

7: INVERGARRY & FORT AUGUSTUS RAILWAY: MILEAGE

	Miles	Chains
Spean Bridge	0	0
Gairlochy	2	52
Invergloy	8	15
Invergarry	15	6
Aberchalder	19	27
Fort Augustus station	23	9
Fort Augustus pier	24	6

Engine turntables and water columns were provided at Spean Bridge and Fort Augustus. There was a water column at Invergarry.

8: INVERGARRY & FORT AUGUSTUS RAILWAY: PASSENGERS CARRIED AND TRAIN MILES

Highland period

Six months ending	Passengers carried	Passengers miles run	Goods miles run	Total
Jan 1904	12,829	16,923	4,607	21,530
Jul 1904	11,133	14,389	4,246	18,636
Jan 1905	12,625	16,502	3,825	20,327
Jul 1905	9,917	13,305	3,821	17,126
Jan 1906	12,362	16,154	3,858	20,012
Jul 1906	8,948	12,840	3,974	16,814
Jan 1907	12,395	15,304	4,514	19,818
	First North British period			
Jul 1907	7,784	10,194	2,563	12,758
Jan 1908	13,226	16,186	3,626	19,812
Jul 1908	10,111	13,435	3,792	17,227
Jan 1909	12,113	14,801	4,316	19,117
Jul 1909	9,575	13,167	4,112	17,279
Jan 1910	11,704	15,228	4,324	19,552

9: INVERGARRY & FORT AUGUSTUS RAILWAY: PASSENGER AND FREIGHT REVENUE

Highland period

Six months ending	Passenger	Goods
Jan 1904*	£848.16.4	£190.11.6
Jul 1904	£696.10.9	£143.9.5
Jan 1905	£911.4.3	£194.6.9
Jul 1905	£681.3.9	£142.6.1
Jan 1906	£933.14.9	£221.6.5
Jul 1906	£665.6.9	£147.8.11
Jan 1907	£907.6.1	£220.7.2

* Includes 10 days in June 1903

	First North British period	
Jul 1907	£660.18.7	£142.12.10
Jan 1908	£963.13.9	£224.6.11
Jul 1908	£672.1.3	£142.8.7
Jan 1909	£909.5.0	£205.14.9
Jul 1909	£700.18.4	£176.19.11
Jan 1910	£883.9.3	£202.19.3

10: 'LOST ON RANNOCH MOOR'

There is an interesting tailpiece to the story of the survey party lost on Rannoch Moor. In 1927 an article entitled 'Benighted on Rannoch Moor' was published in *Blackwood's Magazine*. It gave a full account of the episode, but mentioned the participants by profession only, and not by name. In 1937 Lt.-Col. the Rt Hon A. C. Murray, director of the LNE, had a copy of the *Blackwood* article bound and presented to the company's museum in Edinburgh. At the same time Murray asked W. A. Fraser, engineer, Scottish Area, LNE, if he could identify the people in the story. Fraser got in touch with J. E. Harrison, who had been Forman's young assistant in 1889, and in his letter of reply dated 27 November 1937 from Skelmorlie, Ayrshire, Harrison gave full particulars of all the men who had taken part in the Rannoch Moor walk. He concluded his letter,

> I always like hearing of others being interested in the story and it is extraordinary how many have written to me about it. The Scottish Mountaineer Club had it in the recent issue of their Journal—by request. I was glad to hear from you and hope you are well—as I am myself—though scarcely feeling equal to another such trip across the Moor.
>
> Yours very sincerely,
> J. E. Harrison
> (only survivor!!)

Ten years later, in April 1947, interest in the episode was again revived when Lt.-Col. Murray sent the article to Sir Robert Burrows, chairman of the LMS. Burrows commented:

> I took it home with me last night and read it with great relish. I know most of the country, but I must confess I have never done the walk. If the walk had been in summer and by young men there would be nothing much in it. The idea of Victorian middle-aged men setting off with umbrellas and ordinary civilised garments to attempt the feat in January is the maddest thing I ever heard of, but very amusing.

Acknowledgements

I am greatly indebted to Mr R. M. Hogg, Curator of Historical Records, British Railways Board, Edinburgh, and his staff, and to Mr C. W. Black, City Librarian of Glasgow, and the staff of the Mitchell Library for placing at my disposal most of the material on which this history is based. Mr Alan Cameron, who received me with great courtesy at the office of *The Oban Times*, made available the unique information contained in the files of his newspaper. Robert McAlpine & Sons readily lent me the only pictures of the Mallaig Extension bridges they possess, and Miss Drysdale of the West Highland Museum, Fort William, supplied the rare prints of the sod-cutting and opening ceremonies. The original WHR appointment notices were unearthed by J. Michie, signalman Rannoch, and the map and gradient profile are printed by courtesy of the Editor of *The Railway Magazine*. Alan Paterson not only read the manuscript but gave me a free run of his copious West Highland notebooks with their valuable logs and station diagrams. J. F. McEwan read the page proofs and made several valuable suggestions. And more than one generation of West Highland railwaymen provided a fund of stories.

THE ILLUSTRATIONS

W. A. C. Smith, plates 5, 28, 47, 48, 49, 52; West Highland Museum, plates 8, 9; W. Hennigan, plate 10; A. J. S. Paterson, frontispiece, plates 12, 15, 32, 51, 52, 53; H. A. Vallance, plates 16, 34; C. Murray, plate 20; D. McMillan, plates 21, 22; J. F. McEwan, plate 27; Robert McAlpine & Sons, plates 29, 30, 31; Boy Scouts Association, plate 33; W. A. Camwell, plates 36, 40, 41; H. J. Patterson Rutherford, plates 37, 45; G. D. King, plate 39; M. Smith, plate 50; Derek Cross, plates 54, 55, 56; the Author, plates 1, 2, 3, 4, 6, 7, 11, 13, 14, 17, 18, 19, 23, 24, 25, 26, 35, 38, 42, 43, 44, 46.

The sketches in Chapter 1 were taken from *Mountain, Moor and Loch*, the original guide to the West Highland Railway, published in 1894.

COLOUR ILLUSTRATIONS

J. M. Jarvis, Colour-Rail, A; W. J. V. Anderson, Colour-Rail, B, C; R. E. Toop, Colour-Rail, D; Derek Cross, E, F, G; Anthony J. Lambert, H.

Author's Notes

The main sources used in the writing of this book are contained in two great storehouses of railway knowledge, the British Transport Historical Records Office, Edinburgh, and the Mitchell Library, Glasgow. All the relevant Acts are available to show exactly what the promoters had in mind. The minute books of the companies unfold in detail the story of the railways as it developed. But the minute books, important as they are, present neither a complete nor a balanced picture. It is easy to conclude from an inspection of the West Highland minutes that there were times when the directors 'forgot' to minute items that they did not want publicised. For instance, the minutes barely mention the trouble between the railway and the contractor in 1891, and certainly nothing of the magnitude of the crisis emerges. The researcher has to go to the court records as reproduced in *The Glasgow Herald* and *The Scotsman* for the technical details, and to the excellent reporting of *The Oban Times* for an impression of the impact on the West Highland community of the stoppage of work.

The annual Board of Trade (and later Ministry of Transport) inspections and resulting reports on the condition and conduct of the Mallaig Extension (mandatory under the Guarantee Act) provide first-class source material. Seldom has a line in this country been the subject of public scrutiny year by year for thirty years of its life. The Invergarry & Fort Augustus Railway minutes were in four volumes; unfortunately, the final and vital volume, which told the Invergarry's own story of the eclipse, is missing. But the most important features of the episode can be gathered from the proceedings of the North British Railway and Inverness County Council. After the passing of the North British Railway (Confirmation) Act of 1908 the affairs of the West Highland tended to become lost amid the business of the North British, and patience and diligence are required to disentangle purely West Highland material from the mass of matter available. NBR and LNE traffic note books give details of traffic at all stations on the system, and by abstracting statistics from the West Highland stations it has been possible to give a picture of the traffic pattern on the line over the years.

The West Highland is our most photogenic line, yet it has been neglected by photographers. The reasons are not hard to seek. The railway is largely inaccessible to travellers on foot. (Let the doubter try to make his way to the track through the neck-high tangle of bracken, boulders and bog to be found even in such civilised spots as Loch Lomondside.) Sections are long and trains are few. For a considerable part of the year the only two up and down trains traverse most of the line in the hours of darkness, daybreak or dusk when photography is impossible. Hence most West Highland pictures are taken from moving trains or at stations. The few taken in section are usually obtained at the rare places where the railway can be viewed at close quarters from the public road. The pictures in this volume have been selected for their West Highland flavour. The West Highland is above all a *scenic* railway and photographs, to do it justice, must illustrate its scenic attractions. A book of this kind is no place for the stock view of a locomotive posed against a coal dump.

BIBLIOGRAPHY

Minute books of the West Highland Railway.
West Highland Railway Accounts and Reports to Shareholders.
The West Highland Railway Act, 1889.
The West Highland Railway (Mallaig Extension) Act, 1894.
The West Highland Railway (Guarantee) Act, 1896.
The West Highland Railway Act, 1896.
North British Railway (General Powers) Act, 1902.
North British Railway (Confirmation) Act, 1908.
NBR and LNER Traffic Note Books.
NBR, LNER and BR public and working timetables.
Records of the House of Commons.
Invergarry & Fort Augustus Railway minutes.
Invergarry & Fort Augustus Railway Accounts and Reports to Shareholders.
The Story of the West Highland. (G. Dow.) 1947.
Lochaber in Peace and War. (W. T. Kilgour.) 1908.
Concrete Bridges and Culverts. (H. G. Tyrrell.) 1909.
Loyal Lochaber and its Associations. (W. D. Norrie.) 1898.
Kilkumein and Fort Augustus. (O. Blundell.) 1914.
Romantic Lochaber. (D. B. McCulloch.) 1939.
The Glory of Scotland. (J. J. Bell.) 1932.
The Land of Lochiel. (T. R. Barnett.) 1927.
Newspapers and periodicals: *Railway Gazette, Railway Magazine, Railway Times, Railway Engineer, Railway Herald, LNER Magazine, The Engineer, Engineering, Journal of Transport History, Blackwood's Magazine, The Scots Magazine, The Green Man, Journal* of the Stephenson Locomotive Society, *The Glasgow Herald, The Glasgow Argus, Glasgow News, The Scotsman, The Oban Times.*

Index

Illustrations are indicated by heavy type

THE FAITHFUL

JULIET WEST

First published 2017 by Mantle
an imprint of Pan Macmillan
20 New Wharf Road, London N1 9RR
Associated companies throughout the world
www.panmacmillan.com

ISBN 978-1-4472-5909-1

1 3 5 7 9 8 6 4 2

A CIP catalogue record for this book is available from the British Library.

Typeset by Ellipsis, Glasgow
Printed and bound by CPI Group (UK) Ltd, Croydon, CR0 4YY

For Steve, with love

PART ONE

1

July 1935

Even as he queued to board the coach at Victoria, Tom thought about turning back. He would tell his mother that he was ill, a sudden stomach upset, and he'd be better off spending the week at home on his own. She'd cluck and fuss but she might just let him go.

A pigeon eyed him from its perch above a newspaper stand, its head cocked, the stump of one foot hovering over a sign for Pears Soap: PURITY ITSELF.

A week at home on his own. Imagine. He could invite Jillie round; a little more comfortable than their usual spot by the back doors of the Gaumont. Tom fought down a sudden stab of desire. He mustn't think those thoughts – he was with his mum and dad, for pity's sake. Anyway, did he really want Jillie at his place, picking up the family photographs, drinking tea from his mum's best cups? Jillie was getting a bit too attached as it was.

The coach doors opened and a cheer rippled through the queue. In a neighbouring bay, a bus moved off to the shouts of 'Stand clear!' Petrol fumes billowed into the still morning air.

'Should leave on time after all,' said Tom's dad, looking up at the clock. The minute hand jerked forward. Five to nine.

His mum turned and flapped a hurry-up hand. 'Come on, Tom,' she said. 'Chop chop.'

This was the moment, thought Tom. He would clutch his guts, retch a few times – it was the weather for stomach upsets, after all – and groan something about a ham roll bought from a milk bar on the Strand. Could he get away with it? He'd never been much good at lying. And now the thought of putting on such a performance began to make him feel genuinely queasy. Everyone would stare, and his mother would fret, and in all likelihood she'd miss the coach too, escort him back to Lewisham and dose him with Milk of Magnesia. He'd end up spoiling the holiday for her and that would be plain cruel because she'd been looking forward to Bognor ever since they'd paid their half-crown deposits before Christmas.

'Just a bit tired,' said Tom, stepping forward to close the gap between them. 'I woke up at five.'

'It'll be the excitement,' she said. 'You were always the same before Scout camps.'

They had reached the coach door. Bea grabbed the handle and hauled herself up onto the boarding step. 'There are still a few seats at the front, Harold. You have got the sandwiches, haven't you?' Tom's dad raised his eyebrows and lifted his old khaki tote bag.

Tom climbed the steps and inhaled the smell of motor oil and disinfectant. Too late now – he was here and there was no chance of escape. Beggsy and Jim called to him from the very back of the coach, loud and larky. Tom gave a short wave but took a seat across the aisle from his mum and dad: Beggsy was a pain in the arse at the best of times.

As the coach moved off into the sunshine of Belgravia, Tom's mood began to shift. The seat beside him was empty; he wouldn't have to make small talk or listen to some droning bore from HQ. The whiff of disinfectant gave way to something different, to peeled oranges and chip paper, towels made stiff by saltwater and sun. Yes, the coach smelt different now. It smelt of promise.

They crawled through Clapham and Wandsworth until finally the roads cleared, and the coach picked up speed as it motored into the open countryside. Skylarks rose above fields and the verges shimmered with bees and butterflies.

At Dorking, Mrs Winters began to stalk down the aisle handing out information leaflets about the camp. And then – in case they couldn't read, Tom supposed – she stood swaying at the front, reciting every line of the leaflet. Most of the coach passengers were travelling in civvies, but Mrs Winters wore her uniform, the skirt a little too tight, coarse black hairs poking through her tan stockings.

'There will be four good meals daily,' she called out. 'The camp is complete with a shop, shower baths and a mess marquee.'

Tom's mum turned wide-eyed towards his father. 'A marquee, Harold!' Harold blinked his heavy lids, gave the faintest nod in response. Bea fanned herself with the leaflet as Mrs Winters continued.

'Cricket matches, rounders, quoits and badminton,' she said, grabbing on to the back of a seat as the coach swerved around a sharp bend. 'Punchballs for those who want to hit something, and boxing matches when two people want to hit each other.'

This caused a great laugh, and Beggsy at the back cheered. Tom's insides crumpled at the mention of boxing matches and punchballs. Boxing, fencing, ju-jitsu – all manner of sports would be laid on, and he wasn't interested in any of them. He didn't want to punch anyone, or prance around with a daft sword. The enforced exercise was just the start, though: there'd be meetings too – speeches, lectures, patriotic songs. Damn it. He should have trusted his instincts, should have bailed out while there was still time.

2

If Charles did that thing with his jaw once more she would have to leave the table. It was bad enough that her mother had invited him to stay yet again, but at least generally they got up late and she didn't have to breakfast with them. Now here they both were, strangely energetic for this time of day – zestful, even – and every time he chewed there was a vile sound, like small bones cracking.

Her mother dropped a fig stalk carelessly onto the tablecloth, took a sip of tea and turned to Hazel. 'I've decided to go up to town,' she said. 'Charles needs to get back for . . . urgent business. And I'd rather like a change of scene. You won't mind, will you, darling?'

Hazel swallowed her mouthful too quickly and the dry toast scraped her throat. 'When are you leaving?'

'We thought midday,' said Francine.

'But what about this afternoon?'

Francine narrowed her eyes and raised a questioning shoulder. Her jade silk dressing gown clung to her skin, sinking into the dip of her collarbone. 'This afternoon?'

'The shopping trip. You were going to buy me some more summer things. Last year's dresses are –' she paused, feeling her cheeks colour – 'you know.'

'Oh, darling.' Francine laughed and gestured towards Hazel's bust. 'Don't be bashful, of course I know. It's just rather hard for me to accept. My little girl growing into a woman.' She turned to Charles and put a hand on his arm. 'Honestly, Charles, if you'd seen her this time last year, she was flat as a board. Then *whoosh* came the monthlies, and now look!'

Hazel could only stare down at the toast crumbs on her plate. At Rosewood House, amongst the other girls, conversations about monthlies were had in whispers, if they were had at all. What was wrong with her mother, broadcasting the subject at breakfast? Oh God, he was probably looking at her, just as Mother had suggested. Hazel hunched her shoulders and curled her spine, hoping that the evidence would somehow disappear.

'She's going to be a great beauty,' said Charles, 'just like her mother.'

The mantel clock struck nine. Francine gave a high laugh that clashed with the chime. A major seventh, thought Hazel. Horrible.

'Flatterer,' said Francine. She traced a painted fingernail down Charles's forearm. 'Don't sulk, Hazel, for heaven's sake. How about this for an idea? I'll buy you some dresses in Selfridges while I'm in town. There'll be more choice.'

'But *I* wanted to choose.'

'Plenty of time for shopping once I'm home. I won't be gone long. Just a few days. Perhaps a week. And in the meantime Mrs Waite might be able to let out some seams.'

Francine put another fig into her mouth and began to chew. The seeds cracked like miniature bullets firing, and Hazel knew that it was pointless arguing, pointless feeling surprised. This was how things were now. Mother wanted Charles more than she wanted her.

The horizon was starting to fuzz and shimmer and that meant the day would be hot and the sea would be warm enough for bathing. Later she would change into her turquoise costume (that, at least, still fitted), walk down to the end of the garden and climb over the wall onto the beach. If the sea stayed calm she might even swim out towards Pagham.

She opened her bedroom window and leaned forward on the sill, listening to the layers of sound – the outgoing tide pulling away from the shore, the scream of a young gull, the blind dog from next door snuffling in the box hedge. And then another layer, growing louder until it eclipsed all other sounds; heavier, mechanical: the hazy drone of aircraft. The planes appeared in the sky to the west, flying over the sea in formation.

Hawker Furies.

Hazel watched them rise and fall, their polished cowlings glinting. The Hawkers flew out every morning now. Sometimes Hazel cycled past the base at Tangmere, and from the farm track you could see the planes, shadowy in their hangars, the pilots and the airmen scurrying around them, their laughter echoing across flat clay fields.

'Ha-zel!'

Francine's voice called up from the bottom of the stairs. Hazel hadn't spoken to her mother or Charles since breakfast, as a punishment for the London trip. Most likely the punishment had gone unnoticed. Charles had been in the hall, making calls on the telephone in a hushed voice, and Francine had been in her room, banging wardrobe doors. What on earth would she be packing? Francine didn't dress like normal mothers; neat summer suits with matching shoes and handbags. She threw things together higgledy-piggledy: peppermint trousers with a striped orange blouse, which might have been passable if she didn't then tie a floral cambric scarf around her neck. Yet she was forever receiving compliments on her style – 'Bravo, Francine, quite the Bohemian,' her London friends would say, or 'So wonderfully daring, Francine.' But London was one thing. In Aldwick Bay, her clothes caused nothing but backwards glances, amused stares.

'Darling, our car is here!'

Hazel slunk from the bedroom and peered over the banister into the hall below. Francine was standing at the wide-open front door, a cigarette burning in the black onyx holder. She was wearing the white sundress with a plunging neckline, pink glass beads and an orange belt that matched the marmalade shade of her hair. Charles leaned against the timber pillar of the porch, his face shaded by the brim of his panama.

'Darling, I won't leave without a kiss. Now stop sulking and come here.'

Hazel walked barefoot down the staircase, kissed her mother on the cheek and muttered, '*Bon voyage.*' Francine smiled and stroked the top of her daughter's head.

'I'll try to call but Charles's telephone can be horribly temperamental. Your father will ring, I expect.'

'There's no need, Mother.' She hung her head and pressed one finger onto the spoke of an umbrella in the stand.

'Oh, do liven up, Hazel. Aren't you pleased that I trust you enough to leave you? When I was sixteen, I was desperate for a little freedom.' She drew on her cigarette and her green eyes seemed to darken and mist, like pieces of frosted sea glass. 'You and Bronwen go out and have some fun. Here –' she reached for her purse and took out two ten-shilling notes – 'walk into Bognor one afternoon. Take tea at the Royal Norfolk. Or go to the cinema, why don't you? I'll be back in a week or so.' She lowered her voice so that it would not be heard beyond the hallway. 'And be nice to Mrs Waite.'

From the kitchen came the sound of a wooden spoon battering the side of a mixing bowl. Mrs Waite would be making some kind of sauce for tonight's dinner. Hazel took the money and thanked her mother. She gave a half-hearted wave as the taxi swept out of the cul-de-sac and onto Tamarisk Drive.

Might as well go to Sweaty Arnold's for a packet of Pall Malls, thought Hazel. She was getting rather good at inhaling. Last time she barely coughed.

Hazel waited until after lunch when Mrs Waite was in her room, resting. She shut the front door quietly and walked down the path, pushing her hair behind her ears and trying to smooth it flat against her head. Hopeless. Muggy days like this always turned it frizzy.

The estate was quiet but for the sound of a hand-mower wheezing up and down a neighbouring lawn. She reached the flint piers which marked the boundary of the estate, where the footway changed from grass-verged pavestones to the rough, gravelled tracks of Aldwick village. The little row of shops was just across the road, shaded by a line of lime trees. Coastguards' Parade, the shops were called, though Hazel had never seen any evidence of any coastguards; there was only the skinny butcher and the bespectacled grocer and

Mr Arnold, the newsagent, whose round face shone perpetually with tiny beads of perspiration.

The day was getting hotter. Cats lazed under shady bushes and Hazel wished she had worn a hat. A small black fly landed on her bare leg, just below the hem of her dress. She bent to brush it away and as she straightened up, she sensed a vibration in the ground, a light thumping. She looked up – Furies again? – but the skies were clear. Drumming, was it? Yes, drumbeats, growing nearer. Then the sound of a bugle piercing the hot air, boots hitting the ground. Marching.

Hazel stepped back from the kerb and retreated a few yards to the entrance of the estate. She leaned against one of the piers, and the knapped flint edges pressed into her shoulder blades. A column of drummers came into view. She had been expecting a British Legion parade, ex-soldiers wearing blazers and medals, a procession of eye patches and missing limbs. But these marchers were healthy men, three abreast, side drums low on their hips. Their uniforms were black, and oversize buckles shone on their belts – great square hunks of steel that flashed in the sun.

Behind the first column were rows of younger men, their marching less precise. Finally, the women and girls, scores of them, each wearing a black beret, shirt and tie, with a grey skirt close-fitted around the hips. One of the girls turned towards Hazel – a young woman, eighteen perhaps. She looked beautiful, Hazel thought, even before she smiled. Hazel smiled back, and the girl reached into a black leather pouch that hung from her belt. She took out a wad of papers, marched over and gave Hazel a handbill. Hazel blushed and mumbled a thank-you as the girl turned and strode back to the column, keeping step all the time with the beat of the drums.

Blackshirts. Hazel had seen them before, small bands dotted around Bognor selling their weekly newspaper, a penny per copy. She'd asked her mother about them. 'Political cranks,' Francine had said, hurrying past with a look of distaste. 'Don't flatter them with your attention.'

How strange to see them here, en masse, marching past Coastguards' Parade towards the beach. The butcher, Mr Gibbons, came out of his shop. He lifted his spectacles and smiled at the sight, but the grocer stayed inside, and through the plate-glass window it looked as though he was shaking his head.

Crank? What did that mean? It was the same as eccentric, wasn't it, a word for people who'd gone a little cuckoo and couldn't get on in society? There didn't seem to be anything cuckoo about these people, thought Hazel. They were full of purpose, so well turned out, so . . . organized.

When the parade had passed, she looked down at the handbill. BRITISH UNION OF FASCISTS. MOSLEY SPEAKS! THEATRE ROYAL, BOGNOR REGIS, 7 P.M. She folded the paper into a small square and slid it into the pocket of her dress.

She could follow the marchers down to the beach but it would be better, she decided, to go home and spy on them from the garden. If she stood on the table in the summer house, there would be a prime view over the garden wall, straight out to the bay.

Cigarettes. She crossed the road and pushed open the door into the newsagent's, trying not to breathe in too deeply. The smell was more pungent than ever.

Mr Arnold got up from his stool and wiped a hand on his trousers. 'How do, miss?'

'A packet of Pall Malls for my mother, please,' said Hazel, 'and a quarter of mint imperials.'

He sniffed and turned to take the cigarettes from the display behind the counter.

'Did you see the march?' asked Hazel.

'Cudn't miss it.'

'I wonder what they're doing here?'

'They've set up a holiday camp by all accounts, over at Pryor's Farm. On the fields behind your estate, miss.' He opened the jar of mint imperials and rattled the sweets into the bowl on the scales. 'Down from London, I s'pose.' He peered at the dial on the scales. 'Dozzle over?' Hazel nodded and he tipped the mints into a white paper bag. 'Ol' Gibbons is going to their meeting in Bognor tonight, but you shan't catch me there. I leave politics to them what's paid to know better.'

Hazel smiled and gave him a ten-shilling note. He sighed, rang open the cash drawer and scraped about for the change.

Walking back, she sucked on a mint imperial and thought about the blackshirt meeting. Perhaps they would march into Bognor, drums beating all the way. It was something different, it might be fun to watch, and that's what her mother wanted, wasn't it, for her to have a little fun, a little adventure? She'd have to persuade Bronny, of course, but that shouldn't be too difficult. They could go to the cinema afterwards. *It Happened One Night* was showing at the Odeon. Clark Gable was Bronny's favourite.

3

At last the parade was dismissed. Tom stood to one side as his column jostled and whooped through the narrow wooden gate leading from the lane to the beach. Finally he stepped through and headed left, away from the crush of excited cadets streaming down the shingle bank.

Tom had been to the seaside once before, on an outing to Margate organized by the social committee at his dad's old factory. He must have been nine or ten. Soggy oysters were what he remembered, thick rough shells that looked as though they were filled with globs of phlegm. He had shaken on plenty of vinegar and the fumes made his eyes water. There was a photograph of that day slotted into the wooden frame on the parlour mantelpiece. It was a picture of him on the promenade, holding his parents' hands, blinking against the wind, the sea a stormy smudge behind them. The following year his dad was laid off, and after that there were no more seaside trips. For a Saturday outing they would take the bus to Hyde Park and follow the crowds to Lansbury's Lido. There was a man called Mr Reeves who was teaching his two sons to swim, and he let Tom join in the lessons. But Tom's own dad refused to go in the water – his scars had never properly healed, and he claimed he would frighten people away if he showed himself in a bathing costume. 'Go on, Dad,' Tom would wheedle. 'If you scare everyone off we can have the place to ourselves.' His dad would smile from the deckchair and shake his head, knock his empty pipe against his thigh.

Now Tom stood and looked to the east, towards the pier at Bognor, and he thought he had never seen a sight so bloody marvellous. Here was a blue sea, not Margate grey, and the sky was cloudless, hazing down so that it merged with the shifting colours of the water. There were plants and grasses sprouting from the shingle, some with yellow flowers, others that looked like flattened cabbages. Everything was unspoilt and natural. It couldn't have been more different from Margate.

'Tom!' His mum waved as she made her way up the bank. Her face was red under her black woollen beret and a single trickle of sweat dripped from her temple. 'Come down to the shore, love. O.M. is going to bathe and there's a photographer.'

Tom shrugged. He hated the way everyone called him O.M., or the 'Old Man', as if they had a kind of intimacy or friendship with him. He wasn't even *that* old in any case. Bea often remarked on how far Sir Oswald had come, for a man not yet forty. 'Such determination,' she would say, with a sideward glance at his dad. 'Such drive.'

'I'm not being in any photographs,' said Tom.

She sighed. 'But love, it would be a shame to miss out. You can change behind the huts. You've got your trunks on, haven't you, under your uniform?'

Tom looked over to a row of five or six white-painted beach huts. Beggsy was there, along with Jim Dove and Fred Tester. They were unbuttoning their black shirts, stepping out of trousers. Fred pulled his shirt over his head to reveal a saggy knitted bathing suit that looked as if it must have belonged to his dead granddad, and Tom knew the other two would rag him something rotten.

'All right. Don't think I'm smarming up to Mosley, though.'

'Smarming up? I didn't say anything about smarming.' She took a handkerchief from her sleeve and wiped her brow. 'You used to be potty about Sir Oswald. That little scrapbook of yours . . .'

'*Your* scrapbook. You let me mix the paste.'

'Now you're just being silly, twisting things. Come along, get that uniform off and enjoy the weather. Mind you, this is a bit *too* hot for comfort.' She fluttered the handkerchief around her face in an effort to stir up the air.

'I wanted a swim anyway. But I'm not posing for any photographs.'

The tide was out and it was a fair walk to the sea. Tom stepped across the shingle, trying not to wince as the pebbles dug into his bare feet. Beggsy and the others were just ahead, Fred hugging himself with both arms to stop the lads from twanging the straps of his suit.

It was a relief to step from the shingle onto the sand. Ahead of him, Beggsy started to run, a wild sprint, wheeling his arms, head thrust down as if he was charging towards the finishing line in a running race. Tom smiled and started to jog. The sand became wet and clammy, grabbing each footprint and sucking it down.

Mosley was already in the water, a fixed grin on his face. Beggsy and Jim stepped through the waves towards Mosley and his hangers-on, letting out short cries of surprise every time a wave lapped higher, over their thighs, their stomachs. They were freezing their bollocks off, thought Tom, but they didn't want to let on.

Tom turned to Fred. His fists were clutched to his chest and he stared down at the water, as if by concentrating hard enough he could make the English Channel warmer.

'Only one thing for it,' said Tom. 'On the count of three.'

Fred grinned. 'You're on,' he said, unfurling his fists and trailing his fingers into the water.

'One, two, three . . .' Tom plunged in and swam underwater, away from the Mosley crowd, the low rumble of the ocean pressing against his ears. He pushed his body on, strands of seaweed collecting between his fingers, his breath running short now, but still he kept swimming.

When he finally surfaced he couldn't see Fred. And then . . . there he was, a distant figure standing in the waist-high waves, one arm raised apologetically. Tom smiled to himself, turned onto his back and swam farther out. Somehow the sea felt warmer here, luxurious. He trod water and gazed back towards the beach. Mosley must have had enough; he was getting out already. Two women offered him towels and he took them both with an exaggerated bow.

From this distance Tom had a clear view of the buildings that backed on to the beach. Big as mansions they were, detached jobs, some with thatched roofs and exposed wooden beams, others built of red brick with slate tiles. They looked fairly new – one of those exclusive estates you saw advertised in railway station waiting rooms. He allowed himself to imagine the possibility, the thrill, of waking every day in one of those houses, wandering down a long leafy garden, climbing the back wall and dropping down to this beautiful beach on the other side. What a life.

A conifer stood in one of the gardens, its golden branches pointing towards the sky. In the shade of the tree was a summer house, white-painted timber with a green-tiled roof. The summer house was probably bigger than his bedroom at home, he thought, now that he'd moved into the box room to make way for Mr Frowse.

A small bird flew into the lower part of the conifer, quickly followed by another. Something in the shape, the squat muscular body, made him think of a bullfinch. Bullfinches, nesting? Would they nest next to the sea like this? Egg-collecting was a young lad's hobby, he told himself, time he grew out of it, but he couldn't suppress the twist of excitement that always came with the prospect of a new find. He'd like to get up into that tree and have a look.

Another movement caught his eye. Someone – a girl – was standing in the summer house, peering out across the beach. Either she was very tall, or she was standing on a chair. She brought her hand to her face and held it there for a second. She might have been laughing, or smoking – it was impossible to tell from this distance – but he fancied that she was watching him, and suddenly he felt foolish to have been staring at this house and garden so intently, to have imagined himself living there.

Tom heard his mother's voice calling from the beach. There she was, waving one arm above her head. He gave a reluctant wave, to reassure her that he wasn't drowning, and swam a slow crawl back towards the shore.

4

'No use knocking.'

The voice came from behind the topiary yew, which was clipped to resemble a peacock. Hazel lowered her hand from the door knocker, and the old gardener emerged from behind the peacock's fanned tail. He was holding a pair of pruning shears.

'Nobody home?' Hazel asked.

Adams smiled, and the dry skin cracked on his lips. 'Gone up to the grandmother's. She's taken ill.'

'The grandmother in Wales?'

'That's right.'

Hazel looked down at the honey bees droning around the lavender bushes. So much for the walk into Bognor, the cinema and Clark Gable. It was a shame about the grandmother, but still, Bronny might've called by, just to warn her that she was planning to disappear.

'Did they say when they'd be home?'

'No idea. Depends whether or not the ol' girl rallies. They think she might, you know . . .' He widened his eyes and drew the blunt side of the shears across his throat.

*

There was nothing to do but wander around the estate, hoping she might bump into someone, but she knew that Patricia was away in the south of France, and Lottie – poor thing – was fell-walking in the Lakes with an earnest god-mother. Hazel passed the social club and the tennis courts, where four women were playing a game of doubles. One of the women called, 'Thirty-fifteen,' and Hazel recognized Miss Bell's voice. She kept her head down. She hadn't practised the piano for days. If Miss Bell saw her she'd only ask how she was getting on with the Scarlatti or the Bartók. God, the Bartók. Just the thought of that piece made Hazel's stomach tighten. The jarring rhythms and the clashing notes. It made no sense whatsoever.

She could still taste the cigarettes, though she'd eaten half the bag of mint imperials. She'd smoked two Pall Malls in the summer house, standing on the wicker table so that she could see over the wall and onto the beach. It was odd watching the blackshirts. For one thing, they were incredibly *white*. Their ribs stuck out and there were shadows under their shoulder blades, especially on the younger lads, scrawny boys who acted as if they'd never seen the seaside before. Most of them couldn't swim, by the look of it, just fooled around in the shallow waves before shivering up the shingle, shaking themselves like dogs.

At home, Hazel told Mrs Waite she'd like her supper early. 'I'm going to Bognor with Bronny to watch a film,' she said. She scratched her nose and turned her face to the kitchen window, fixing her eyes on the pear tree where a blue tit pecked at a half-grown fruit.

'You're to be home before dark,' said Mrs Waite, dolloping

a lump of fish pie onto a plate. 'No later than nine. Did you want me to warm up the tart for pudding?'

'Just the pie, thank you, Mrs Waite. We'll get some sweets at the Odeon.'

The heat had dulled her appetite, but she did her best to force down the fish. The dining-room windows were open, and a slice of sunlight angled in, illuminating one of Francine's paintings that hung above the sideboard. It was an oil landscape painted somewhere on the Downs, greens and browns, with black brushstrokes (birds or bats?) swooping around what might have been a plough or a tumbledown barn. Hazel used to enjoy watching her mother paint – she always seemed to be happy as she took out her brushes and mixed colours on a palette. But Francine rarely set up the easel now; it was in one of the attic rooms, abandoned along with Father's violin and Hazel's packed-away toys.

She pushed the remains of the fish pie to one side of the plate and lay her knife and fork across the food in an attempt to mask the leftovers. Mrs Waite took the plate, tutted, and walked back to the kitchen. A year ago she would have chided Hazel, encouraged her to eat up, but her tactics seemed to have changed. There had been a power shift, and it felt almost as if Mrs Waite had given up on her. 'When I was your age I'd been out to work two years,' Mrs Waite had said recently. Hazel had been unsure how to respond. Should she apologize? But it wasn't her fault; she hadn't wanted to stay on another year at school. And in any case she didn't mind the idea of work, was looking forward to it, if she was ever given the chance. Anything was better than another term at Rosewood House, cooped up with scatty Miss Lytton and her obsession with ancient Rome. Hazel imagined herself escaping Rosewood and finding a job in London. She wasn't sure what kind of job yet. She'd long ago given up on the idea of concert pianist, because to achieve that she'd have to practise for hours and hours a day and she just couldn't be fagged. A piano teacher – that was possible, then again she'd be expected to teach the modern stuff, Schoenberg and the rest, all those discords that actually hurt her ears. Nursing? There was nursing, she supposed. She thought about Charles. Apparently he did some kind of medical work, although he was vague when Hazel once asked which field he practised in. 'Medical and social,' he'd said with an enigmatic air, and her mother had stifled a laugh.

Through the open windows came the distant sound of a bugle. Hazel gulped a mouthful of water and rushed upstairs to get ready. On her mother's dressing table she found a pot of rouge and rubbed a little into her cheeks. She dabbed her finger in the pot again to redden her lips. The rouge tasted like damp flannel. Disgusting. She flattened down her hair, looked in the mirror and smiled. Her smile would have been perfect but for the small chip in one front tooth. It had been Nanny Felix's fault, pushing her too fast on the bicycle so that she toppled over and hit the London pavement. Hazel smiled again, this time with her mouth shut. Her eyes looked more green-blue than blue-green, and her face had lost its chubbiness around the cheekbones. She looked older than sixteen, she thought. With her mother's white hat and the slip-on mules, she might even pass for twenty.

The parade was already halfway along Barrack Lane. Hazel walked as fast as she could without running. Once she had caught up, she carried along the pavement beside the drummers, her hat brim tipped low in case anyone she knew should be passing. It was a warm evening. The sun was still bright, its heat pulsing from the south-facing walls of the red-brick terraces and guest houses that lined the streets leading into Bognor. Families stood in their front gardens and stared, and when the parade reached Marine Drive the crowd of onlookers grew: bemused holidaymakers trailing buckets and spades; old women in headscarves; a group of young lads who mimicked the marchers, then sloped off when the standard bearer turned to glare.

Past the pier and on to the Theatre Royal. A blackshirt with a long neck and a loudhailer paced up and down the promenade opposite the theatre. 'Mosley speaks!' he called. 'Seven o'clock start, free admission!'

Hazel followed the swarm into the foyer and found herself shoulder to shoulder with a crush of uniformed blackshirts and others in ordinary clothes – men in pressed suits, women wearing fashionable hats and colourful summer wraps. The air crackled. Gone was the familiar theatre mustiness, the stuffy politeness. Even the flocked wallpaper and faded velvet drapes seemed shot through with anticipation. Hazel had watched Bronny's dreaded ballet shows here, she'd played piano in the music festival. How odd to find the theatre transformed like this, into somewhere thoroughly grown-up, somewhere almost glamorous. She stood to one side, near the doors, debating whether she might actually dare to go into the auditorium. A small man in a flat cap appeared next to her. As he pulled a wad of handbills from a canvas bag, his elbow jabbed into her arm. 'Sorry, miss,' he said, touching his cap. Hazel nodded in reply, trying to edge away, but still watching him as he stepped forward to press the leaflets into people's hands. She could just see the heading at the top: 'Stop the Fascist Lies', it said, and underneath was stamped a blood-red star. Most people glanced at the handbills in disgust and screwed them into pockets or dropped them onto the carpet. A few seconds later, two blackshirts approached the man and steered him away. He struggled but they held down his arms and forced him into the street, shoving him hard so that he stumbled into the gutter. 'Shame on you!' the man hissed. And then he lifted a clenched fist and yelled: 'Don't listen to the fascists! Evil lies!' He began to sing; a wavering tenor threading across the seaside street. '*So comrades, come rally, and the last fight let us face . . .*'

It was too hot in the foyer, difficult to breathe. A prickling sensation began at the back of Hazel's throat but when she coughed, the prickles intensified, as if there were insects crawling up her windpipe. She coughed louder and her eyes began to water. What was she doing here? She should leave now, walk over to the promenade and buy a lemonade or an ice to cool her throat. She looked at the entrance, but the crowds were still streaming in and it would be awkward to push her way out.

She noticed a sign for the ladies' lavatories. Yes, that was the answer. She could lock herself in a cubicle until the meeting started, then creep away unnoticed.

There was a queue for the lavatories, with three women waiting ahead of her. A blackshirt girl stood at the sinks. She was leaning in towards the mirror, poking tentatively at her eye as if there was a grain of sand stuck in there. On her hand she wore a gold ring with a tawny-coloured gemstone that caught the light from the bulb above the mirror. It was the girl from the parade earlier in the day: the one who'd given Hazel the leaflet. She recognized her sharp jaw, her large dark eyes. Now the girl blinked, looked at Hazel's reflection in the mirror and smiled again, raising her pencilled-in brows.

Hazel half-smiled back, just as the cough started again. She felt light-headed and reached a steadying hand towards the sink.

'Are you all right?' asked the girl. 'You look fearfully pale.'

'Yes, it's just . . .' Hazel trailed off.

'You're here for the meeting?'

'Oh, not really. I'm only passing.' She took a deep breath and felt her head clear a little.

The blackshirt girl rinsed her hands under the tap, then straightened up, turning away from the mirror. Her waved ebony hair shone under the ceiling light. 'Shame to miss Mosley,' she said. 'Quite a *tour de force* once he gets going.'

Hazel thought for a moment. She couldn't go home just yet, and the film would have started by now. Perhaps she would stay after all, buy a drink at the theatre kiosk to settle her throat. 'How long will the meeting last?' she asked.

'An hour or so, I should think. Then questions from the floor. That's when it gets interesting. Are you with your people?'

'No. I was coming with a friend but . . . she's not here after all.'

'Sit with us, why don't you? I'm Lucia Knight.' She spoke her name with a flourish. *Lu-chee-a* – the Italian pronunciation, Hazel supposed. 'And here's Edith now.'

Edith emerged from a cubicle and nodded as she turned on the tap. She was shorter than Lucia, with a thin expressionless mouth and the beginnings of sweat patches at her armpits. 'And your name is?'

'Sorry. It's Hazel.'

'We'll wait for you outside, shall we?' said Lucia. 'When you've finished?'

'Yes . . . yes, all right,' said Hazel, only now realizing that a cubicle was free, and that the woman behind her in the queue was shuffling with impatience.

Hazel let herself in through the kitchen door to find Mrs Waite bent over the gas ring, stirring a pan of milk. Her white hair was plaited and pinned into a loose bun which had begun to sag.

'Your father telephoned twenty minutes ago,' said Mrs Waite, not troubling to look up from the pan. 'All the way from France and you weren't here.'

Hazel made a show of checking her watch, though she knew perfectly well it was almost ten. She apologized, said the film had run on, and that she'd lost a brooch and had to search under the seats.

'You'd better wait in the hall. He'll be calling back presently.'

The milk sizzled to the boil just as the telephone rang. Her father was calling from a hotel telephone and he sounded harassed. He was having dinner with an important client. How long had her mother been in London, he asked, and why was she, Hazel, out so late?

If you care so much, why don't you come back? Hazel wanted to say, but didn't. She told him that her mother had left only that afternoon. The film was very long, that was all, and there was the fuss over the brooch.

'How's Paris?' she asked.

'Hot and dirty.'

'When can I visit?'

'Not just yet, Hazel. The project isn't quite going to plan.

I'm dreadfully busy. Look, I really must go. Take care. I'll try to telephone later in the week.'

Hazel replaced the receiver on the cradle and stood for a moment, tracing her finger along the bevelled edge of the telephone table. Her father had been in Paris for five months now, and it was getting harder to remember him as he was: a whole, breathing person who would come down to breakfast every morning humming a tune, tapping out the rhythm with a spoon as he broke the top of his soft-boiled egg. Now all the music seemed to have gone from him: he hadn't even taken his violin to France. Hazel found that when she thought of her father, she pictured only the lower half of his face, a mouth speaking into the telephone and the dark stubble of his beard, which was always visible, however close his shave.

She walked up to the landing and stood against the door of the linen cupboard, listening to the sounds from downstairs. Mrs Waite rinsed the milk pan, clattering it onto the draining board, then switched on the kitchen wireless. She'd be down there for a while now, sipping her cocoa and listening to the news.

Radio voices drifted up the stairs. Hazel longed to talk to someone, anyone, about the meeting. She put her hand to her chest. Yes, her heart was still pounding, and it wasn't just the run back along Barrack Lane. It had been pounding before she left the theatre.

She wandered into her mother's room. Talcum powder bloomed on the rug like bursts of white pollen, and the air was still heavy with a musky scent. The room was large and square, with an enormous black-varnished bed pushed against the wall facing the window. To the left was Francine's dressing table, strewn with jewellery and make-up, postcards propped against the mirror. A man's gold wristwatch lay next to a string of glass beads. Hazel lifted the watch and looked at the time on the ghost-pale face. Charles's watch, she supposed, stopped at ten past seven. Ridiculous, the little pantomime they acted out whenever Charles stayed. He would go up to the guest room, but Hazel knew that once all the bedroom doors were closed, he crept out to join Francine in the double bed. This was where he undressed. Where he unfastened his watch.

Hazel opened the bottom drawer of the dressing table and felt around for the photograph that was buried under a tangle of stockings. She slid the frame out and clutched it to her chest, then sat on the bed and switched on the side light.

Her father was dressed in army uniform, his shoulders angled slightly but his eyes gazing straight at the lens. Even in the dulled photograph she could see that everything was polished to a high shine: his cap badge, his medals, the leather strap across his tunic. Hazel had no idea what the medals were for. No idea, in fact, where her father had been or what he had done during the war. She simply assumed that he hadn't had too bad a time of it. He always appeared to be perfectly healthy, and cheerful enough. Until last year, of course.

The photograph must have been taken when he was in his twenties. She supposed he was handsome in an understated way: heavy brow and sensible moustache; small dark eyes; well-defined jaw. She stood up from the bed and pushed the photograph back into the stocking drawer. It was odd because Father couldn't be more different from Charles, with his tousled brown hair and his jangly limbs. Charles was . . . sort of *loose*; he would lounge on a sofa or a beach chair, the top button of his shirt undone. Her father wasn't like that at all. She couldn't imagine him lying down in anything but a bed, at night, when it was time to go to sleep.

How serious was it between her mother and Charles, she wondered? He seemed keen, and there was an easiness between them that Hazel found disconcerting. Perhaps it was because they had known each other for so many years. For ever. Apparently they had holidayed together as children – the families were friends – but when Hazel had once asked about that time Francine had snapped shut her cigarette case and told her to stop being so tiresome.

Charles couldn't be after their money, that was certain. From what Hazel could gather, they were getting poorer by the day. Her father was an architect, but he couldn't be a very good one, because his projects so often seemed to fall through. In any case, Charles seemed to have plenty of his own money. Just yesterday he'd been full of the new car he was planning to buy. A Brough Superior, motto 'Ninety in silence'. Her mother had looked through the brochure with gleaming eyes.

Hazel crossed the bedroom to the low bookcase that stood under the windowsill. The shelves were filled with romances and mysteries – Agatha Christies and Georgette Heyers. Tucked amongst them was something far more interesting: a pale yellow, cloth-bound book by someone called T. H. van de Velde. *Ideal Marriage* was the title, which was odd, because the book had appeared just at the time when her parents' marriage was quite the opposite of ideal. Still, Hazel preferred not to dwell on the possibility that her mother or father had actually *read* the book. It was too awful to think of them reading, let alone acting on, Mr van de Velde's words. Words that, even now, she barely understood but knew instinctively to be salacious. Erogenous, effleurage, secretions.

No, the book was meant for younger people, girls like her, who needed the mysteries of sex explained. She had reached Part III: 'Sexual Intercourse, Its Physiology and Technique'.

It was almost midnight when she put the book down and switched off the light. She had found Part III confusing. The section began by discussing the importance of the 'Prelude' to lovemaking, the differing arts of coquetry and flirtation. Coquetry was a little like teasing, van de Velde explained, and must not be used excessively. *Lovers – beware!* So was it better to be direct, to flirt and fawn, the way she'd seen her mother behave after a couple of cocktails? That seemed to be van de Velde's conclusion. *Flirtation may beautifully refresh and renew erotic feeling. For, if conducted to the rules of this oldest human art, through purely psychic stimuli, it produces an unmistakeable physical symptom in both man and woman. This symptom is the lubrication of the genitals which physically expresses the desire for closer contact.* Ugh. Lubrication. Why did it all have to sound so repellent?

Hazel tried to sleep but she couldn't have felt less tired. When she shut her eyes it was Lucia's face she saw, the smile around her lips as she watched Mosley deliver his address. Hazel had felt oddly detached at the start of the meeting, self-conscious, as if she was watching herself from a seat in the upper tier. She couldn't claim to belong with the blackshirts, couldn't even claim any knowledge of their ideas. Politics was rarely discussed at home or at Rosewood House, unless you counted the Senate of Ancient Rome.

The first speaker at the Theatre Royal had been a man called Beckett. He wore small round spectacles and spoke in a quiet voice. His words were measured, with over-long pauses as he let the audience absorb each point. He talked about the dangers of Britain trying to compete with Oriental labour and the threat of cheap Eastern imports. It was the 'roast beef' standard versus the 'handful of rice' standard. The Tories wouldn't be happy until all working men had been brought down to coolie level, whereas Labour would prefer every worker to join the Communist Party and starve to death. Fascism was a third way, he said, the roast-beef way. People cheered and clapped at that. Lucia touched her on the shoulder and whispered, 'He's terrific once he's warmed up. You watch, he'll take off his spectacles.'

Beckett began to outline the third way – a corporate state in which business would be run jointly by management, workers and consumers. And he did take off his spectacles, flung them onto the lectern and stared out into the darkness of the theatre. International bankers, private finance – these crooks were ruining the world's economy, shouted Beckett. The time had come to act in *Britain*'s interests.

Hazel joined in the applause when Beckett stepped down and took his seat on the stage. Mosley now marched towards the podium and the audience began to rise, right arms outstretched in a fascist salute. 'Hail, Mosley!' they chanted. 'Hail, Mosley!' Lucia and Edith jumped to their feet, but Hazel stayed seated. She felt embarrassed, out of place. She wasn't truly part of this, she shouldn't be here. Leaning forwards, she glanced towards the aisle but she'd have to push past several people to get out, and that would only draw attention to herself. No choice but to stay put, she thought. In for a penny . . .

Mosley listened to the chants for a minute or more, nodding in approval, his nostrils flared, his chin jutting forward. Finally, he motioned for the audience to sit.

They were several rows back, but Hazel had a clear view

of Mosley. He began to speak, and there was something extraordinary about the way his dark eyes seemed to glint and entice; widening one moment, narrowing the next, casting out into the audience like a thousand invisible fishing lines, hooking every single one of them. He had a wonderful voice, she thought. Commanding but somehow gentle and utterly in control. She did her best to follow every word, but really she knew nothing about economics. 'International finance' was the phrase that kept cropping up. It was the root of all the country's problems, said Mosley. It was time to make a choice between the man who invests his money abroad and the man who invests not only his money, but his *life*, in British land.

'National socialism' was what Mosley advocated. Hazel seemed to remember her father calling himself a socialist, during a dinner-party argument she'd overheard from the top of the stairs. She had asked him afterwards what socialism meant, and he said that it was a way of making life fairer for everyone. National socialism. Yes, that made sense. A fairer Britain. How could any decent person disagree?

But now, lying awake, she remembered the man with the handbills in the foyer. *Lies*, he had shouted. The anthem he'd sung began to play again in her head. *The internationale unites the human race* . . . Hazel found it hard to untangle her thoughts. Was it possible to package up lies and pass them off as fact?

Whatever the truth, she was sure of one thing. The blackshirts weren't cranks. Her mother was wrong about that.

5

Each time Tom began to doze, Beggsy would snore: a sudden, violent snort that left his nerves jangling. And then Fred let one off in his sleep, and that made Tom smile, despite himself. He wondered if the other lads had heard it too, but . . . No. Just the heavy breathing, the tooth-grinding, the sound of everyone else having a lovely bit of shut-eye, snoring and farting and doing whatever else came naturally, never mind how he was wide awake in the airless gloom and sick of the bloody lot of them.

It was too dark to check the time on his wristwatch, but he reckoned it must be after midnight. The camp was silent. Rules were clear on that point: NO CAROUSING AFTER 11 P.M. Mosley hadn't come back to the camp after the meeting: he had climbed into a Bentley, saluting the crowds through the open window as the chauffeur pulled away from the theatre at top speed. No camp bed in a bell tent for Mosley. Doubtless he was staying in some swish country hotel, or with one of his aristocratic friends, carousing to his heart's content. They were a nobby bunch, the blackshirt high-ups. Tom had become more aware of this fact recently, and it made him suspicious. Winchester College, Sandhurst. They looked after their own, that sort. However much Mosley claimed to be for the people, however much he courted the working classes – the labourers, the unemployed, the street-fighters – surely he didn't really care for them? This corporate state he was so intent on setting up, there'd be fat cats just the same, wouldn't there? And Mosley would be the fattest of the lot, cream dripping from his well-groomed moustache, while the rest of them would still be scrabbling around to keep a decent pair of boots on their feet.

Sleep seemed impossible now. Foolish to even try. He had to get outside, clear his head.

He crept from the tent, unpegged his trunks and towel from the guy rope and draped them over his bare shoulder. It was only a five-minute walk to the beach, ten at the most. There was nothing in camp rules about bathing after eleven, was there?

The moon was rising, and a few shreds of pale cloud hung in the sky. When he looked up he felt dizzy, unanchored. Somehow the stars had multiplied a thousandfold between London and Sussex; there were no street lights to mask them, no drifts of factory smoke or plumes of blackened steam from the railway engines that converged at the Lewisham depot.

Silently he picked his way between the tents to the far side of the campsite, and then on through the gap in the hedge and down the bramble-edged lane that led towards the sea. The air was sharp and clean in his lungs and he knew, with absolute certainty, that if he'd grown up here he would be at least one inch taller, his shoulders a shade broader. He patted the fresh-burned skin that was taut and tender across his chest. He was tall and broad enough, and strong as any lad who spent his working hours racing up and down office stairs, lugging boxes round greasy Fleet Street pavements.

At the end of the lane he turned right, past the row of shops and on through the gate that led to the beach. He'd forgotten how loud the shingle would sound, the slide and crunch of pebbles and tiny white shells as he made his way towards the sea. Perhaps there would be less noise if he walked barefoot.

He sat on the stones and took off his loosely laced boots. The tide was out. Dotted along the shore were cuttlefish corpses, brittle white bodies like tiny ghosts. He looked at the sea, so vast, so black, and then up again at the endless sky, and he wondered whether bathing was a good idea after all. The expanse of the Channel unnerved him. Perhaps it was enough simply to have left the tent. He felt cooler now, at least.

Behind him, a little to the west, was the garden with the summer house and the golden conifer that overhung the wall. He remembered the birds he'd seen flying in and out earlier in the day. It wouldn't harm just to take a look, easy enough to climb the flint wall, and then up into the lower branches. If the moon stayed bright, he should be able to spot the nest. The birds themselves usually gave the game away. Rubbish parents, birds. If you approached a nest after dark, they would fly quietly off, abandoning eggs or chicks, watching from a higher branch or a nearby tree until it was safe to return.

Tom put his boots back on, tying the laces tight for climbing. When he reached the wall he found a foothold where the cement had crumbled between the flints. He wedged his boot in and grasped the top of the wall, but as he hauled himself up he felt a sharp pain in the palm of his left hand. Dropping back onto the shingle, he angled his hand towards the moonlight to get a look at the damage. A plump bead of blood swelled from a cut and slid down his wrist. He took a step backwards, gazed up at the wall and the silhouettes of jagged flints which stood proud at three-inch intervals. He tried to shake the blood off, then pressed a corner of his towel to the cut, blotting the flow, wondering whether to give up, to walk back to the camp and forget about the eggs. Shame to have come all this way, though . . . He dropped the towel and found a foothold further along, placed his hands carefully between the flints and heaved himself up so that he was astride the five-foot-high wall, facing the conifer with his back to the summer house. He edged closer to the tree, tested the branches and gripped the one that seemed sturdiest.

A sound made him jump, the squeak of wood on wood. Branches creaking, he supposed. And then he smelt smoke. Tobacco smoke. Tom froze. Someone in the garden? He turned around, almost losing his balance, and there on the threshold of the shadowy summer house stood a girl. One arm was clenched around her waist, the other was held away from her body, wrist bent and a cigarette between her fingers.

He looked down to the shingle on the beach side of the wall: he would jump down and scarper before she had the chance to raise the alarm. But just as he was about to leap, she spoke.

'Are you one of the blackshirt crowd?' Her voice was hushed, a little shaky, but there was a sharpness, a determination. She had some nerve, he'd give her that. Most girls would have screamed by now.

He stopped, heart racing, muscles still tensed for the jump. 'I was looking for a nest, miss,' he whispered.

'What nest?'

'Er . . . bullfinches?' And at that moment two small bodies flapped up from the branches, disappearing into the garden next door. Thank you, he thought. 'I collect the eggs.' He coughed and deepened his voice. 'At least I used to, when I was younger. Old habits, you know.'

She came out of the summer house, shut the door, and took a step backwards on the path, widening the distance between them. She would run up the garden now, thought Tom, tattle to her parents or whoever it was she lived with. How old was she anyway? Older than she looked? She took a drag on the cigarette and a momentary glow lit up her face. Old enough to be married? She might have a husband in the house. At the very least an angry father with a service revolver, a war memento stashed in a bedside cabinet.

But the girl didn't run away. She dropped the cigarette and trod on it with the sole of her sandal. He felt self-conscious standing on the wall, poised to jump as though he had something to hide. Slowly, he bent his knees and attempted to crouch so that he was closer to her level.

'Don't look so worried,' she said. 'I do believe you. About the birds.' She glanced down to his pyjama bottoms. Of course she wasn't scared of him. Who'd be scared of an intruder who came dressed in his pyjamas?

'All right . . . Thanks.' He turned away, thinking that their conversation was at an end, that he was free to leave. But again the girl spoke, and it seemed for all the world as if she actually wanted to keep him there a moment longer, to chat quite normally as if they'd just met at the Saturday dance.

'I was at your meeting this evening,' she said.

She tilted her head up towards him, and the moon was bright enough for him to get a good look at her face. She was about his age, he reckoned, maybe a little younger. Her fair hair was cut quite short, just below her ears, and it was very curly. Not the carefully styled curls that the girls all wore in town. This was more of a corkscrew frizz, no style to speak of. She had a very wide, friendly mouth. He liked how she looked. If you ignored the hair, you could say there was a touch of Ginger Rogers.

'At the theatre?'

Damn it, why did he mention the theatre? Now he'd good as admitted that he was a blackshirt. She could report him yet, and the police would come calling at the camp, first light tomorrow.

'Yes. I sat with Lucia and Edith. They've invited me to visit your camp.'

'Can't say I know them. We've come from all over.'

In fact the names did ring a bell. Lucia and Edith. Bossy posh girls. They'd been in charge of rallying the greyshirts for the tug-o'-war tournament that afternoon, and Lucia had drafted him in as referee.

'Where are you from?' she asked.

'Lewisham. That's in London.'

'Yes, I do know. I used to live in Bloomsbury.'

Bloomsbury. Blackshirts had a thing about Bloomsbury types. Loose morals. *Bohemicus Bloomsburyus*, he'd heard them called. *Bloomsbury Bacilli*. 'I work near there,' he said. 'Fleet Street. The *News Chronicle*.'

'A reporter?'

He hesitated. 'Yes. Cub reporter. They don't let me cover the big stories yet. Magistrates' Court, mainly. Drunk and disorderly.'

She smiled and patted the pocket of her cardigan. He wondered if she kept her cigarettes in there. Usually he could take or leave them, but right now he could just fancy a smoke.

'What about the eggs, then?'

For a moment he was baffled. Then she nodded towards the tree, and he remembered why he was here.

'Only, I'm going in now.' She smiled and he noticed a small chip in her front tooth. 'I won't tell anyone about our meeting. My friend's brother is an egger too. You'd better take them before he does. Go on, promise I won't say.'

'N-no. It's too dark really.' He couldn't climb up there now, couldn't be sure she wouldn't squeal in the end. Maybe it was a tactic to keep him on the property while she fetched her father. 'I ought to get back. It's very late. Just that I couldn't sleep.'

'Me neither. I've been tossing and turning, reading . . . but I just couldn't drop off. It was such an exciting meeting, don't you think?'

He shrugged. 'Not particularly. I've heard it all before.'

'Oh. Aren't you a . . . supporter?' She looked disappointed. If she expected him to start swanking about the movement, she'd picked the wrong person.

'It's my mother really. She's the Mosleyite.'

'*My* mother says blackshirts are cranks.'

Tom bridled. Did she think he was a crank? 'I wouldn't go that far. Membership reached forty thousand last year. It's a serious party. You thinking of joining?'

'Perhaps.' There was a distant tap and creak, like the sound of a window being opened. The girl looked over her shoulder towards the dim outline of the house.

'I'd better go,' she said.

'Might see you at the camp, then?'

'Yes. And if you change your mind, you can come back

for the eggs. I like to wander down here, you know, when I can't sleep. You can't imagine how dull this summer has been.'

Tom wasn't sure how to reply. For a moment he dared to picture himself returning tomorrow night, to picture the girl undressing in the summer house, beckoning him in with her wide smile, no, *dragging* him in by the string of his pyjamas, whether he liked it or not. He felt his cheeks flush. Thank God the clouds had blotted out the moon.

As he dropped back onto the beach he felt a throb in his left hand and remembered the cut. Shit. Blood had dripped onto his pyjama bottoms. He picked up the towel and pressed it hard to the wound.

6

Francine sat in the lukewarm bath water, eyeing Charles's toiletries. They were laid out neatly on a glass shelf above the sink: toothbrush and paste; cologne; the silver rectangular box that contained his razor. A few of Carolyn's things were there too: a bottle of skin tonic and some vanishing cream. No sign of any make-up. Carolyn must have taken her cosmetics case (if she possessed such a thing – her style was rather country) when she decamped to Gloucestershire. Shame, thought Francine, because the red lipstick she'd brought on the journey had melted in the heat, and the coral was down to the last scrapings.

He had disappeared at eight that morning, kissing her as she lay dozing in bed, and apologizing again for the unexpected appointment. She didn't mind terribly – he would be gone only a few hours. They had arranged to meet in Soho at one, at a new bistro that had become quite the rage.

She pulled the bath plug and let the water drain around her, enjoying the feeling of rushing emptiness, as if she might be swallowed, too. Her head was fuzzy from yesterday's champagne, and then of course there were the nightcaps they'd drunk back at Bruton Street. Yes, she probably had been a little tight when she went to bed. Still, lunch would clear that. She would have an iced tonic water, with just a dash of gin. Gripping the sides of the bathtub, she eased herself up and stepped onto the carpeted floor. The towel smelt of Charles, lemon soap and cologne, but it was musty too, in need of a wash. This housemaid he employed, Jean. She was hopeless. Couldn't bring up a pot of tea without tripping on the stairs and cracking a saucer.

Casting the towel onto the rail, Francine looked down at her body, pulled in her stomach and ran warm hands over her skin. Her breasts seemed as full and as firm as they had when she was twenty, and her waist was still trim. The figure was holding up for now: it was the face that suffered, once one reached forty. Thank Christ for the marvel of Max Factor.

Francine found a tin of primrose-scented talc in the mirrored cabinet above the lavatory. She patted the powder under her arms and between her legs, then sat on the bed and rubbed talc around her toes. It was so hot again. She would wear her cerise dress today, with the Oriental wrap that Charles had so admired. Assuming Jean had managed to press her things without mishap.

Sunlight beamed through a gap in the curtains, and her eye was drawn to the chest of drawers where Charles's gold cufflinks winked from the little porcelain jewellery dish. He had worn pewter cufflinks this morning, with the cornflower-blue shirt and a light linen jacket. In his breast pocket he'd folded a matching blue spotted handkerchief, finest silk from Jermyn Street. Smart as hell, yet somehow still raffish.

This woman he was meeting today, what would she be like? Charles was given only the most basic details before an appointment. It was better that way, he'd explained, to guard against any form of attachment. Occasionally there would be an advance meeting, if the client was particularly jittery, but this wasn't advised.

Important not to dwell. Francine opened the drawer of the bedside cabinet (Carolyn's side), pulled out a leather-bound New Testament and opened a page at random. It was the Book of James. *He who doubts is like a wave of the sea, driven and tossed by the wind.* Oh, not the sea again. She'd only just managed to get away from all that: the salty Sussex air with its threat of seaweed; those ugly green-brown mounds that would clump, fly-infested, over the shingle come late summer. No, the city was what she craved. How had she ever let Paul persuade her to move away from London? He'd put up a good argument, claimed that Aldwick Bay was attracting all sorts of interesting characters: intellectuals and artists, pens and paintbrushes in hand ready to capture the beauty of the Sussex coast and the Downs, so hidden and unspoilt. It would be better for Hazel, he'd said, to grow up away from the city. The talk of war would not go away, and if the doom-mongers were right, who knew what hell Germany would unleash on London this time? 'And if we don't like Sussex,' Paul had said, 'we can think again. Nothing is permanent.'

Well, he'd been right about that last bit.

In the taxi, she spotted Charles walking down Wardour Street. It was his Gladstone bag she noticed first, though why he needed that lumbering thing she had no idea. There was never anything in it but a half-bottle of brandy. Perhaps he felt it lent him an official air, the look of a learned medical man.

'Pull up here, please.'

The driver huffed, stepping too sharply on the brakes, and

Francine almost slid off the seat. She had planned to ask Charles to join her in the taxi, but if the driver was going to be like that, she'd get out at this very spot and they could walk the rest of the way to the bistro. She paid without speaking, and didn't leave a tip.

'Charles!'

His face broke into a smile when he saw her and she felt her heart lift. He was just too handsome, with those ridiculously blue eyes and the light brown hair that was thick and shiny as a schoolboy's. But it wasn't just his looks, it was his manner, too. Such a change from the diffident boy he'd once been. Charles as an adult seemed surprisingly carefree, so different from Paul – different, in fact, from any other man of her acquaintance. Perhaps it was because Charles hadn't fought in the war. There was a lightness to that, and a sense of equality between them. Equality, yes, that was it. Hadn't they shared their own horror, long before the guns started firing in France?

'Frangipane, darling. How was your morning?' His face was a little red, she noticed. Was it because of the heat, or the exertion of his appointment? A snip of resentment caught her, but she kept her smile wide, tilted back her neck and lifted the brim of her sun hat so that he could kiss her on the cheek.

'Wonderful,' she said. 'Yours?'

'Satisfactory in every way.' He ran his finger down her arm, tracing the lotus-flower pattern on the silk wrap.

'*Every* way?'

'Naturally, I can't know for sure. But all the signs were . . . promising.'

When they reached the restaurant on Old Compton Street the waiter apologized and said their table wasn't quite ready. They were shown to a small, sloping anteroom with velvet-upholstered armchairs that listed on the crooked floorboards. The waiter offered cocktails on the house, and as they waited for their drinks they played the guessing game. There were five categories and she had never scored full marks.

'Auburn hair,' she said.

He raised an eyebrow. 'Correct.'

'Straight not shingled.'

'Correct.'

'Twenty-eight-inch waist.'

'Hmmm . . . close.'

'Blue eyes.'

'Wrong. Brown as mud.'

She laughed, leaned across to his armchair and prodded his shoulder. 'How do I know you're telling the truth, anyway? You could say what you liked and I'd never be any the wiser.'

'A matter of honour,' he smiled. 'And if you don't believe me, you could ask Dr Cutler to show you her files. She records everything in great detail.'

'I'll bet she does.'

Francine had met Dr Cutler only once – a diminutive woman with a severe bun and wire-framed pince-nez. Hard to believe that someone who looked so coiled and Victorian could be so avant garde in her thinking.

'Do excuse me,' said Charles. 'Nature calls.'

Francine crossed her legs and picked up a copy of *Punch* from the small table. Above the hubbub from the restaurant she heard a muted rustling sound. A smatter of soot fell from the chimney onto the screwed-up newspaper in the grate. Then came a frantic beating against brickwork and, with a light thump, a speckled bird tumbled into the hearth. It was a starling. The bird lay dazed for a fraction of a second, before flapping off towards the closed sash window, crashing into the glass with a horrible thud and landing on the windowsill. Francine sprang up from the chair. She would open the window and free the poor thing. But then the bird rose again and flew straight towards her. She screamed.

'Open the window!' Francine shouted as Charles shot through the door. The bird was on the carpet now, one wing tucked in, the other outstretched and held at a strange angle. Charles bent to lift the bird from the floorboards, cupping it in both hands, gently at first, then tightening his grip. There was a sharp, jerky movement and then a snapping sound: light, almost delicate, like an eggshell breaking. It took Francine a second to realize that Charles had wrung the bird's neck.

'But it might have flown away,' she said. 'You just . . . killed it.'

Charles smiled. 'Darling, it was injured.' He walked over to the window, lifted the lower sash and tossed the corpse down into the alleyway at the side of the restaurant.

'And how is Paul?' Charles asked. He cut a thin wedge of Camembert and placed it on a cracker.

Francine took a sip from her gin. Generally, they didn't speak about their spouses; it was an unwritten rule. 'There was a letter, a fortnight ago, I suppose. He'll be in Paris until October at the earliest. Apparently the clients are proving difficult.'

'So I have you to myself for at least three months.'

Francine flushed. 'I'm completely yours, darling. But once

he's home we'll have to be more careful.' She sighed and stabbed a grape with a dessert fork. 'Hypocritical goat.'

Charles put his hand over hers and stroked it. She drained her drink and let an ice cube slip onto her tongue.

'Is Paul serious about the divorce?'

'I'm not convinced he can afford it. And it would be unfair on Hazel. He feels that, I'm sure. He wants the best for her. I just wish he'd agree to a truce, and then we could jog along, make the best of it. If one or other of us has a dalliance, what's the harm? It's how most marriages survive, isn't it? Look how marvellously it's worked for you and Carolyn all these years.'

'This separation might make him see sense. When Paul comes home from Paris and sets eyes on your irresistible face, you can be sure he'll melt.'

Francine crunched the remains of the ice cube. 'And is that what you want?'

'*Want* doesn't come into it. It's about making the best of our situations. As you said yourself, Frangie.'

They sat in silence during the taxi journey back to Mayfair. Francine's thoughts returned to the starling, the blue-black shimmer of its speckled feathers. Odd that such a drab-seeming bird could be so beautiful at close quarters. There had been flocks of starlings in the hawthorns at Lostwithiel, she remembered. Always a mess of droppings on the ground underneath.

The taxi swayed through the streets of Bayswater, and she felt a little sleepy after the gin, could almost imagine herself back in Cornwall, lazing in the Lostwithiel garden, the hammock under the oak tree pitching gently back and forth, back and forth . . .

'Bruton Street,' the cabbie called. Francine fumbled for her handbag, but she needn't have worried. In no time Charles had paid the fare, and now he was holding the car door open, waiting for her to climb out.

Was it the echo of Lostwithiel that had made her feel suddenly desolate? She rarely allowed herself to think of those times, still less discuss them with Charles. This was another of their unwritten rules, and one she was happy to embrace. What was the use in talking about that summer? Unpicking the events would only reopen the wound. Really, she must not give in to memory.

7

Hazel had been awake for several minutes before she remembered the boy. She had dreamed of Lucia, and Edith too, the three of them diving in the water off the rocks at Pagham. The dream had migrated to a beach in France, and Edith disappeared, buried under a sand dune, a paper kite stuck atop the mound like a bizarre headstone. The boy didn't feature at all, and when she remembered the midnight conversation at the bottom of the garden, she couldn't help wondering whether the boy on the garden wall was actually a dream, and the swimming with Lucia and Edith was perfectly real.

She heard Mrs Waite's slow tread up the stairs, the three quick raps on the bedroom door.

'It's after nine,' called Mrs Waite. 'I've left your breakfast out.'

The mention of food made Hazel suddenly ravenous. She had eaten such an early supper yesterday, and then nothing whatsoever after the meeting. All she could taste now was the musty after-effect of the cigarettes that she'd smoked – without coughing – in the moonlit summer house. How fortunate that she'd been smoking when the boy appeared. The Pall Mall had lent her courage.

Hazel stayed in her room until she heard the click of the latch on the front gate. Mrs Waite would be walking to the shops to place the orders.

In the dining room, she found four triangles of cold toast propped in the rack and a pot of stewed tea. She ate quickly, not bothering to butter the toast. It would be better to go out now, she decided, before Mrs Waite arrived home. She raced up to her room, dressed in cycling shorts and a tennis shirt, and put her purse into her haversack. At the top of the stairs she paused, then ran into her mother's bedroom. *Ideal Marriage* was on the bookshelf, exactly where she had replaced it last night. She dropped it into the haversack. In the kitchen, she scribbled a note: *Gone bicycling with Bronny. Having a picnic lunch. Back this afternoon.* She cut some cheese and two slices of bread, wrapped the food in greaseproof paper, and took the garage key from the hook by the kitchen door.

The campsite at Pryor's Farm was only a two-minute cycle along Nyetimber Lane, but she couldn't turn up this early. Eleven, they had agreed, and it was still only ten.

Hazel pedalled up Pagham Lane and left her bicycle against a stile that led into a cornfield. Harvest mice scurried and rustled ahead as she brushed through the waist-high stalks. She and Bronny had often tried to catch a harvest mouse. Hazel had once caught hold of a tail, but her nerve failed her at the last moment – it seemed too cruel – and she let it slip from her grasp.

In the far corner of the field was a sycamore tree. She sat underneath it and opened the book. *Different Kinds of Kisses*, was the next heading. A man, during the Prelude, was at liberty to kiss any part of a woman's body, however intimate, and vice versa. Kisses could be delicate, fluttering, brief or lingering. Kisses could become violent; they could even take the form of a bite. *Women are conspicuously more addicted to love-bites than are men. It is not at all unusual for a woman of passionate nature to leave a memento of sexual union on the man's shoulder in the shape of a little slanting oval outline of tooth-marks.*

Did Charles and her mother bite each other? She remembered how she had watched Charles when he first came to stay last year. The weather had been heavenly, hot as high summer though it was early May, and he was sunbathing after a swim, wearing only a pair of navy trunks. She would have noticed any love bites, surely? She had been lying on a towel in her bathing costume, with a sun hat tipped over her face, but she had a perfect view of him through the tiny holes in the woven straw. The beauty of it was, he hadn't a clue she was looking at him. The pinholes were like so many microscopes, and she could examine his smooth tanned skin, the sand sprinkled in the fair chest hairs, the fleck of seaweed that lay below his navel. At one point Charles propped himself up on his elbows and waved to her mother, who was still in the sea floating idly on a raft they'd moored to a groyne. Then, unmistakably, he turned to look at her. Examined *her* body. She had closed her eyes, anxious, suddenly, that her face wasn't quite masked by the hat, and she felt her skin burn under his gaze.

A green sycamore seed twirled down and landed on the book. She brushed it away, and checked the time on her watch. Almost eleven o'clock. Lucia and Edith would be waiting.

By the flagpole, Lucia had said. A Union flag flying twenty feet high. Hazel found the flagpole easily enough, but she couldn't see anyone standing next to it. A few young boys were playing nearby, spelling out HAIL, MOSLEY on the rain-starved grass using buckets full of pebbles. Beyond them, a crowd of children queued to buy ice cream from a wagon, coins rattling in their hands. Opposite the flagpole was a large marquee, and scores of blackshirts were sitting at picnic tables and benches outside the tent. Hazel felt like a perfect idiot. Everyone would be staring at her. The boy might be there, too, watching, wondering what on earth she was up to. She could at least have worn a dark-coloured blouse, instead of this silly white tennis top that marked her as an outsider. She scanned the field but there was no sign of Lucia. It was ridiculous to have come here where she didn't belong, expecting to meet two girls she barely knew. She decided to run, run as fast as she could, back to the hedge where she'd hidden her bike. But just as she turned, there was a call from one of the tables.

'Hazel! Over here!'

Lucia was waving, her long arm swaying in a wide arc. Hazel made her way to the marquee, keeping close to the edge of the field, and Lucia raced up to meet her.

'There you are,' she said. 'I didn't think you'd come.' She was wearing a different uniform today: black slacks instead of the grey skirt, and a silver badge pinned to the breast pocket of her shirt. 'But I kept hoping. Join us, won't you?'

They walked over to the crowded tables. Edith was next to another girl who held a paper parasol above their heads. No one else seemed to be taking any notice of her; perhaps she wasn't such a spectacle after all.

The talk was of the meeting last night, of how well the speeches had been received, and not just by the blackshirts but by the people of Bognor Regis who had come along out of curiosity. 'People like you,' said Lucia.

A whistle sounded and Edith groaned.

'Back to babysitting duties,' she said, brushing biscuit crumbs from her hands.

'Babysitting?' asked Hazel.

'The little greyshirt boys. We're supposed to be keeping them amused. Obstacle courses, gymnastics practice, that kind of thing,' Edith sniffed. 'Most of them are here without their parents and they're prone to run wild, just as they do in the slums of Shoreditch or wherever it is they're from. Military discipline is what they need, according to Mrs Winters. Catch 'em young and all that.'

'But I'm let off the hook until after lunch,' announced Lucia, rising from the bench.

'Really?' asked Edith, her voice suddenly sharp. The other girl, Alexia, snapped shut the parasol and they both looked up at Lucia, their eyes narrowed against the sun.

'I told Mrs Winters that Hazel might be visiting. She said I should show her around the camp. Make her welcome.' She turned to Hazel. 'You can stay for an hour or so, can't you? We'll have a wander down to the woods.'

Hazel nodded and lifted her haversack from the grass. 'I've nothing to get back for,' she said. 'Nothing at all.'

As they walked towards the copse at the bottom of the campsite, Lucia linked her arm in Hazel's. Hazel knew the copse well; it belonged to old Pryor, and when they first moved to Aldwick she and Bronny had often trailed down there to play in the stream. Yet today it felt like Lucia's territory, the way she trod the path, somehow leading the way though they walked side by side.

A magpie landed on a low branch and Hazel thought of the blackshirt boy, his muscles flexed as he crouched on her garden wall.

'I met someone else from your camp yesterday,' said Hazel.

'Oh, yes? What's her name?'

'It was a chap, actually. From Lewisham, I think he said.'

'And how did you meet him?'

It was a mistake to mention the boy, Hazel realized. She couldn't talk about their meeting like that, the fact that he was hunting birds' eggs in her garden at midnight. She didn't want to get him into trouble.

'Oh, it was just a brief chat. After the meeting.'

Lucia laughed and waved her hand dismissively. 'Well, don't expect me to know him. There are hundreds of boys here, and they all look identical in their uniforms.' And then Lucia was in full flow, chatting breathlessly about camp life, how the food was jolly good considering, but the beds were like boards and she had a crick in her neck from the lumpy pillow.

Lucia began to talk about fascism, opening and closing her eyes in an exaggerated blink, her voice wavering with emotion. Her eyes were almond-shaped, glossy like a deer's. It was almost as if she was in a state of bliss. She told Hazel that this was just the beginning and that the British Union was a wonderful force for good. Just look at the national socialists in Germany, she said. Unemployment falling every day and the country positively bursting with patriotic pride.

'I expect you've heard all sorts of rubbish about the blackshirts, haven't you? The press are against us, even the *Daily Mail* now, and the *Mirror*. Yet only a few months ago we could do no wrong. What newspaper do your people take?'

Hazel frowned. 'My father used to take the *Guardian* but . . . he works in France now.'

'Oh? Never mind,' said Lucia.

Never mind *what*? wondered Hazel. Was it to do with the *Guardian*, or the working in France?

'Anyway, I'll give you a copy of our paper before you leave. I'm sure you'd enjoy it.'

Hazel hesitated for a moment and Lucia laughed. 'What a bore I must sound!' she said.

'I'm not bored,' said Hazel. And it was true. She wasn't bored in the least. The way Lucia spoke was so vivid, so interesting. She made politics sound thrilling, and Hazel felt foolish for allowing her world to be so narrow and ill-informed.

They had reached a shallow stream where a rope swing hung from a tall ash tree. Instead of crossing the stream, Lucia stopped abruptly. She turned to face Hazel and grasped both her hands.

'The thing is, Hazel, I can't help chattering on. It's just that when one feels strongly about something, well, all one wants to do is spread the word. I can't tell you how wonderful it is, being part of the Union. Everybody is so passionate, working together for a common purpose. And to know in one's heart that something is right . . . it's simply the most glorious feeling.' She laughed again, squeezed Hazel's hands tighter. 'I felt it when we met at the theatre yesterday, Hazel. I knew you would be the most terrific friend. And in fact it was *before* we met, do you remember? It *was* you yesterday, wasn't it, leaning against the pillar in the blue dress, watching thc parade? I felt, somehow . . . a connection.'

Hazel swallowed drily. It was odd to feel Lucia's hands in hers, their warm palms pressed together.

'Yes, that was me. I was on my way to buy cigarettes.'

Lucia dropped Hazel's hands and took a step back. There was something scolding about her expression, but then it softened and her lips broke into a conspiratorial smile. 'Cigarettes? Do you have some now?'

'In here.' She patted her haversack.

'Let's share one, shall we? Edith and the others are dreadful prigs about smoking.'

Hazel began to unbuckle the haversack. 'So's my friend Bronny.'

'The one who couldn't come to the meeting?'

'Yes. Her grandmother's ill so she had to go to Wales. I'm at school with her.'

'Boarding?'

'No, day school.'

'Pity for you. I loved my boarding school. Miss it like hell.'

'What do you do now?'

'I work in town, at the B.U.F. headquarters. Voluntary, of course. My father would think it terribly vulgar if I were paid.'

'Is he a blackshirt?'

Lucia laughed. 'No. My mother was. She died last year.' For a moment the brightness of her voice dimmed.

'I'm very sorry . . .'

'Don't be.' She twirled the ring on her finger. 'I find it best not to think about it. What about these cigarettes, then? I've spied the perfect place to sit.' Lucia pointed to a fallen tree trunk on the other side of the stream. 'Wish me luck.' She laughed again and took a running jump at the dangling rope. Somehow she managed to look graceful as she swung across and dropped down onto the dusty bank. 'Your turn!' she called, slinging the rope back over the stream.

Hazel swung off, but as she landed on the bank she tripped on a half-buried rock and flung her arms outwards to save herself. The haversack thumped to the ground, landing upside down so that everything tumbled out: the cigarettes, the uneaten slices of bread, the book.

She scrambled to her feet, her hands stinging. Lucia rushed to her side.

'I'm fine,' Hazel said, trying to laugh as she grabbed at the scattered contents. But Lucia had picked up the book before she could reach it.

Lucia looked at the title and smiled, her eyes alight. 'Isn't it enthralling?' she said. 'Have you reached chapter eight? Quite filthy.'

'You've read it?' Hazel couldn't stop herself blushing, but Lucia didn't seem in the least embarrassed.

'Esther Levine had a copy at school. Stole it from her parents' house. We had to pay Esther, of course. Two shillings for one week's loan. She bought gin with the proceeds and sold it by the double. Quite the entrepreneur. Typical of her race, one might say.' She paused. 'What's your opinion of the Jew, Hazel?'

'Which Jew?' asked Hazel absently. She could think only of the book, of wanting to cram it back into her haversack, into darkness.

Lucia screeched. '*Which Jew?* Oh, you're too adorable.' She shook her head and began to leaf through the pages. 'Now, where was it . . . Ah, yes. It's all very well *reading* this stuff, but don't you think one is left with more questions than answers?' She pointed at the text and read aloud. '*By sexual intercourse we refer exclusively to normal intercourse between opposite sexes. It is our intention to keep the Hell-gate of the Realm of Sexual Perversions firmly closed. Ideal Marriage permits normal activities the fullest scope, in all desirable and delectable ways. All that is morbid, all that is perverse, we banish: for this is Holy Ground.*'

Lucia shut the book and held it out towards Hazel. 'What can he mean, do you think? "The Hell-gate of the Realm of Sexual Perversions"? Now that's the book *I* want to read.'

Hazel found that she could not meet Lucia's gaze. She wanted to be with someone familiar, with Bronny in her bedroom, playing a game of Sorry, or with Miss Bell, practising piano. Notes played in Hazel's head, a chromatic scale ascending.

'I don't understand most of it, if I'm honest,' said Hazel, stuffing the book into her haversack. 'It's just . . . well, it's interesting, that's all, because we'll have to get married in the end and so . . . we might as well know what to expect.'

'I'm not getting married for ages,' said Lucia. 'Never, if I can help it. Mother wanted me to come out. Parade me around the debs' ball like a show pony. At least that's one fight I'm spared.' She shuddered and sat on the fallen trunk, patting the space next to her. A ray of sunlight fingered through the canopy, flashing on her silver badge. Hazel could see the emblem closely now. It was a curious design, she thought: a bundle of sticks and an axe, bound together with rope.

Hazel made a show of looking at her wristwatch. 'I promised our housekeeper I'd be home by now. Sorry, but . . . take a cigarette for later?' She edged one from the packet and held it out.

Lucia shook her head. 'No, you keep them. Another time. But we must pop back to the camp first. I was going to give you the newspaper. And if you'd like to leave your address, I can sign you up for our postal list? It doesn't commit you to membership or anything. Just an expression of interest.' She stood and flicked a fragment of moss from her slacks.

It would be quicker to cut through the bottom of the wood to the hedge where she had left her bicycle, thought Hazel. But to disappear now might look as if she was running away. She would take the newspaper and sign up for the list because it would be rude to leave suddenly when, after all, Lucia had been nothing but friendly. It was amusing about the book. There really was no need to feel embarrassed.

8

When he saw her walking back from the wood with Lucia, he dodged behind a water tank next to the cookhouse rather than walk up to say hello. Lucia was talking at the girl non-stop, lecturing no doubt, and he knew that he wouldn't be welcome if he interrupted. As they passed twenty yards ahead, he peered out to have a proper look, to see her face in daylight. Her hair was a little tamer than last night, and it shone a kind of reddish-gold. He supposed that was what they meant by strawberry blonde. Her shirt was tight and he could see the outline of her figure, her bust and the dent of her waist.

Tom wondered whether she'd really meant what she said, about going back for the eggs.

At night, when the others were fast asleep, he finally made his decision. Madness, that's what it would be, to go anywhere near that garden again. He'd allowed himself to dream a little, to conjure a kind of romance, the type of soppy tale his mother brought home from the Lewisham library. But real life wasn't like those novels. He worked for a newspaper, didn't he? Knew how messy and fucked-up real life was. Sometimes, for a half-hour skive, he would sit in the public gallery at the Old Bailey, listening to the trials. Mind-bending, what people were capable of. Carnage.

In real life, lads like him didn't get friendly with girls like her. There would be a catch. The most likely catch being that her father would be standing on the other side of the garden wall, cigarette in one hand, garden spade in the other. No, the father wouldn't hold the spade. He'd have some lackey standing by to do his dirty work, to chase him off and make sure he never came close to his precious daughter again. And all the while the girl would be watching from her bedroom window, enjoying the drama of it, the thrilling slice of scandal, something to giggle over with chums when she went back to her finishing school or her exclusive secretarial college or wherever she was bound after the hols.

He pictured her standing at the door of the summer house, one arm around her waist. *You can't imagine how dull this summer has been.*

Blood sang in his ears, and an insistent pain throbbed where the flint had pierced his skin.

There was always Jillie. Jillie with her devoted eyes and her tendency to titter at everything he said, whether or not he'd meant it as a joke. She was decent enough, pretty despite the spots. But the weekend before he left for Sussex she'd come over all serious as they canoodled behind the Gaumont; she said she loved him more than anything, would let him do whatever he wanted. He was grateful and couldn't believe his luck, and afterwards she seemed grateful too, wouldn't stop kissing him as they walked back through Manor Park, squeezing his hand and saying 'I love you' till he felt so sickly and smothered he might as well have had lilac blossom stuffed up his nose. If he stayed with Jillie, next thing she'd be expecting and he'd be married by eighteen, just like it'd turned out for Ted Field. Poor bugger was stuck in his mum's back bedroom with a wife and baby. That was his life now, no going back.

Perhaps it would be better to break it off with Jillie, to let her down as kindly as possible. He'd tell her he needed to concentrate on his studies. True enough: he wanted nothing more than to go to evening classes, to learn typing and shorthand, because then he might be in with a chance of becoming a reporter. It was another dream, he knew that, but it wasn't unheard of for lads like him. Archie Kent, the *Chronicle*'s chief court reporter, had been in the workhouse before starting as a tea boy on a local rag in Essex. Tom wondered whether he might even approach old Kent and ask for some advice. If he was polite enough and keen enough, Kent might let him into the press box at the Old Bailey. Tom had often watched the reporters from the public gallery. Eyes down, scribbling for their lives, the quick bow and the dash out of court when it was time to file their copy.

Yes, he'd give Jillie the heave-ho, and that wasn't the only thing he needed to break off. He'd been agonizing over it for a while now, ever since that first conversation with Bill Cork last year. Bolshie Bill everyone called him, big in the union, always trying to drum up new members. Tom had decided to join, and when he got chatting to Bill and told him that he belonged to the blackshirts, that he was doing his bit towards a fairer Britain – a corporate state that would hammer the greedy capitalists and the corrupt politicians – Bill almost had a choking fit. 'You're being taken for a ride,' he said. 'Fascism isn't socialism. It's for jingoists and anti-Semites. It's the gospel of hate.' Tom hadn't known how to respond, had felt humiliated, but the more he read and the more he thought, the more certain he became that Bill

Cork was right. Fascism wouldn't look after the working man: far from it.

He wondered how he would break the news to his mother. Well, she would just have to bear it. There were worse things than a communist for a son.

9

Bea hadn't told Harold it was her birthday, and she knew he was unlikely to remember without the trail of hints that she generally left in the preceding days. Still, it would dawn on him eventually, and then he would feel guilty. He could be quite sweet when he felt guilty. Chocolates and so on.

It was her fiftieth birthday. Half a century – amazing to think. That fortune teller on Blackheath had got it all wrong, hadn't she? Read Bea's palm when she was seventeen and assured her she'd be married by twenty and would travel abroad – most likely America. *Your lifeline is strong. I see success and money.* What a hoot. Bea was twenty-eight when she and Harold married, and this field in Sussex was probably the furthest they'd ever travelled. You had to laugh.

'Something amusing?' Harold was next to her, squinting through his spectacles at yesterday's paper.

'Not really. Just recollecting.'

'Right-o.' He eased himself from the bed. 'I'll have a shave before it gets busy.'

Bea watched him leave the tent. His leg must be bad this morning, because his gait was more uneven than usual; he swung one arm in a semicircle to help him balance. But he hadn't moaned too much about the camp bed, despite his reservations about coming on the holiday. Perhaps he was even enjoying himself a little.

Lying back on the mattress, Bea stared up at the grey-white canvas. Spiders had appeared overnight, tiny money spiders weaving their webs in the seams. Well then, she might as well make a wish for money. She shut her eyes and imagined the perfect windfall. Fifty pounds should do it: enough to keep them comfortable over the winter, a proper feast at Christmas, a little Whitsun holiday in Broadstairs or thereabouts, and a nice sum for Tom to kit him out with new boots and a warm overcoat for work. They had him trekking the streets in all weathers, that blessed newspaper.

A shame Tom had ended up in a tent with Samuel Beggs, thought Bea. That boy was a proper ruffian, however much his mother insisted he'd turned a corner thanks to the black-shirts. Fortunately Tom didn't seem particularly enamoured of Samuel Beggs. Then again, he didn't seem enamoured of anyone or anything – he'd been in a strange mood for weeks now. More than likely it was just a phase. Her little brother Jack had turned sulky at a similar age. He'd glare if you asked him something perfectly harmless like 'Pass the salt.'

Tom had certainly been busy. There were so many activities, she barely saw him except for mealtimes, just long enough to sneak a dab of Vaseline on his cheeks. He was looking quite suntanned already, ever so handsome in fact. Almost a man. When Tom was a small boy, people would remark how like Harold he was, and it was true, he did have the same gentle nose, the heart-shaped face. But when she looked at him, Bea could see only Jack. Tom's eyes weren't quite such a startling amber, but he had Jack's straight white teeth and the dimple in the centre of his chin that all the girls adored. She sat up with a lurch of dread. That's to come, she thought, and it probably won't be long now. Tom will bring a girl home, and Bea hoped to God it would be a decent girl, not one of these modern sorts, with lips smothered in Tangee and eyebrows plucked to non-existence. If she *was* a decent girl, perhaps it wouldn't be such a bad thing. After all, a girl with manners might be an asset to the family. She might remember people's birthdays.

The tent flaps opened and Harold stooped back inside, one arm behind his back. 'Happy birthday,' he said, swinging his arm forward with a flourish. He held out a bunch of flowers: buddleia and valerian, two stems of hollyhock. 'Tom has the card.'

'Thank you, love.' She took the offering and smiled. Wild flowers from the lane. Well, at least he hadn't forgotten. Dipping her head she inhaled deeply, and tried not to recoil at the strong smell of cats. 'Though what we'll do for a vase . . .'

'I thought we might go for a drink this evening? There's a pub in Aldwick. Or we could walk into Bognor.'

'Not tonight, Harold. It's the beetle drive.'

'Ah. Tomorrow then?'

'One night this week. I'm sure there'll be time.'

Mrs Hunter had very small feet, and she wore the most beautiful shoes: black heels, with a dainty velvet bow at the front. Bea's own feet had swollen in the heat, and they puffed over the sides of her worn black courts like bread dough in a small loaf tin. Bea crossed her ankles and stowed her feet under the chair where they would not be seen.

The title of the meeting was 'Why Women are the Backbone of the B.U.F.', and Mrs Hunter left them in no doubt that all the women present were utterly crucial to the cause.

As Mrs Hunter warmed to the theme, her audience listened in careful silence. Outside the marquee, there were distant shouts and cheers, the sound of a tractor engine sputtering. But it was easy to ignore all that, with Mrs Hunter speaking in her quiet and friendly way.

'Sir Oswald has made it very clear that women are of exceptional assistance in the attempt to build a fascist Britain. In our efforts to combat the Jew, who could be better placed than the ordinary housewife? It is a plain *fact* that our local traders are being driven out of existence by the Jew, crushed and exploited by their alien presence. You, of all people, must act by boycotting Jewry in your midst!' Mrs Hunter's lips, which had thinned and twisted as she spoke of the Jews, relaxed into a smile. 'We shall entertain no talk of violence or unpleasantness. The inflammatory lies you have heard about events in Germany have been put about by communists and degenerates. Herr Hitler is in essence a peaceful man.'

Bea shifted in her seat. She had never liked this Jew talk, and lately it was getting more insistent. What would Mrs Hunter say if she knew that she, Bea, worked for a Jewish man? If Bea boycotted Mr Perlman, she would be two pounds a week poorer, and then that would be it, they'd be on the bread line. Tom's wages were hardly adequate to put a decent meal on the table. The money from the lodger was a help, but it added extra pressure, knowing she had to cook for Mr Frowse. The one time she served up a cheap cut, he left half his meal on the plate, went out and came back smelling of fried fish.

Of course there'd always been muttering about the Jews, that was just part of everyday life. Housewives grumbled to neighbours across garden fences; husbands carped as they queued for their dole. But it was only grumbling, nothing more sinister. It was a jokey thing, Bea told herself, saying that Jews were on the make, the way people said that the Irish were dozy or the French smelt of onions. Doubtless foreigners had their own jibes about the English, and where was the harm in that? Muttering was one thing, but boycotting – *combating* the Jews – that was another.

Bea wondered whether to raise her hand, to challenge Mrs Hunter. Because she knew there had been violence in Germany; it wasn't all communist lies. She'd seen the photographs plain as anything in Mr Perlman's paper.

But when Mrs Hunter finished her speech everyone applauded with gusto, and Bea didn't have the nerve to raise her hand. Perhaps she was being over-sensitive. She pulled a hankie from the sleeve of her blouse, sneezed and wiped her eyes. The country air must be getting to her.

It was all so complicated, thought Bea, and that was the problem with politics. You had to throw in your lot with one party, but you couldn't all believe in exactly the same thing. That was acceptable, wasn't it? You focused on the policies you did support – in her case, it was the fact that Mosley was the leader least likely to start another war with Germany. Peace was all Bea wanted. Tom safe at home. She thought of Jack, how proud he'd been when he came home from the recruiting office, brandishing his papers. The twist of Indian toffee he'd bought to celebrate. She hadn't eaten a toffee, not a single one, since the day Jack left for France.

Elevenses was served after the meeting: fruit scones with jam and whipped cream from the local farm.

Bea sat at a table in the corner, on the edge of a conversation. Samuel Beggs's mother was sounding off about foreigners, spitting out scone crumbs as she spoke: 'I'd put 'em all out to sea in a big ship, and then I'd pull the plug.' A woman at her side cackled.

Bea thought of Ivy and felt a shiver of loss, though her friend was ten years dead. What would Ivy have made of the blackshirts? They'd have wanted her on their side, that was certain. Ivy was a magnificent speaker, wouldn't think twice about standing on an upturned fruit crate in Lewisham market to harangue passers-by on the issue of women's suffrage. She was forever getting up a march, and Bea was always at her side, wearing her knitted green-and-purple scarf, chanting 'Votes for Women!' till her throat was hoarse.

How straightforward life had seemed in those days before the war. Bea had marched, she had chanted and canvassed – and she had never once questioned the cause. Votes for women! Yes, that had been a noble campaign, each one of them united in a common purpose. Men, too. Harold believed in women's suffrage: that's how she'd met him, when she was selling buttonholes at a rally in Hyde Park. Afterwards he'd bought her tea and shortbread at a cafe near the Albert Hall.

'Penny for them, Mrs Smart?'

It was Mrs Beggs, looking at her with slanted eyes.

'Just reminiscing. Were you a suffragette before the war, Mrs Beggs?'

She threw her head back in horror. 'Not likely! How old d'you take me for?'

The other women laughed and Bea felt a flush creep up her neck.

'I was twelve when the war broke out,' Mrs Beggs went on, patting her hair. 'Seventeen when I had Samuel.'

'We've a fair number of ex-suffragettes in the movement,'

said Mrs Wright. 'Mrs Richardson for one – fearless woman. Marched right into the National Gallery and took a meat chopper to that nude painting, didn't she?'

Bea nodded. '*The Rokeby Venus*,' she said. 'How they repaired it I'll never know.'

Mrs Beggs looked unimpressed. 'Some of them suffragettists were off their nuts, if you ask me. Anyway, who needs Mrs Richardson when you can have O.M.?'

There was more laughter, and a long wolf whistle. The cackling woman sang the opening lines to 'You Made Me Love You', and the table chorused in reply, '*I didn't want to do it.*'

Bea dolloped a large spoonful of cream onto her scone and stared out of the marquee into the field beyond. She pictured Mosley on the beach at Aldwick Bay, his broad shoulders bare and tanned. Extraordinary that he should have stripped off like that. So informal, yet so *right*: a show of solidarity towards the whole lot of them, young and old, rich and poor. Ivy would have admired Mosley, all right. And she would have supported his crusade against war, of that Bea was certain.

10

Hidden in her diary were two postcards; they had arrived before lunch and by a stroke of good fortune she'd got to them before Mrs Waite.

The first was from Bronny, a picture of St David's Cathedral on the front, and on the back a long message in impossibly small handwriting, detailing the tedious journey, the smell of boiled plums in the hospital, and her grandmother's long-haired terrier, Oscar, who bared his teeth and snapped whenever she tried to pet him. *I'm praying we'll be home by Saturday*, she signed off. *Mummy says she can't miss the hospital fete.*

The second postcard was plain, the type one could buy in packs of two dozen from the stationer. Lucia had drawn the blackshirts' emblem on the front in thick black ink: the sticks and the axe bound together with rope. She must have posted the card yesterday, after their walk in the wood. On the reverse she'd written a message, diagonally, so that Hazel had to tip the card into a diamond shape to read the writing. *Absolutely gorgeous to see you this afternoon. Edith and I plan to bathe tomorrow at four. See you at the beach huts? Fondest regards, Lucia.*

Hazel chewed her lip and looked at the clock. Almost

three. Was it a mistake to have given Lucia her address? Mother would be vexed if letters and literature started arriving from the blackshirts. Hazel would have to claim that she'd been talked into it inadvertently, that she'd found herself chatting to one of the newspaper sellers in the town, given her address without realizing what she was signing up to.

Lucia seemed determined that they should be friends, yet Hazel wasn't sure what was behind it, whether Lucia really liked her, or whether she was simply trying to recruit new blood for the movement. Well, whatever the reason, Hazel didn't much care. Goodness knows it had been ages since she'd met anyone interesting, and now there were two interesting people in as many days. A pity the boy hadn't come back last night. She'd been so sure he would reappear.

She changed into her bathing costume, pulling her beach dress over the top. It was a plain dress of white poplin, and there was an oil stain on the hem, but it would have to do. On the landing, she took a towel from the airing cupboard. When the doorbell rang, she jumped.

Hazel opened the front door, expecting the grocer's boy, and wondering why he hadn't gone round the side as usual, but there stood Lucia on the doorstep, wearing dark glasses and a pair of scarlet beach pyjamas.

'Surprise! I know I'm a little early. Thought I'd call for you *en route*.'

'Lucia, I was just getting—'

'It's all right, isn't it? My card arrived?'

'Yes . . . but I'm not quite ready.'

'Are your people here?' Lucia lifted her sunglasses onto her head and peered beyond Hazel into the hallway. She had put some kind of pomade on her hair, so that it was sleek and almost flat to her head in the old flapper style.

'No. Everyone's out. Is Edith with you?'

'Attack of the monthlies.'

'Oh . . . I see. Well, come in. I was just finding a towel.'

Lucia stepped inside and glanced around the hallway. 'Adorable house,' she said. 'Do you come here every summer?'

'Actually, we live here all year. We moved down a while ago. From London.'

'How perfect. Although I think it would drive me a little demented, living somewhere so quiet. I'd miss town.'

'I miss it every day. I'd like to move back,' said Hazel.

'Oh yes, you must. Really! I'm longing to flat-share. It's beastly at home, just Father and me.'

They stood facing each other. Hazel felt unsure, suddenly, of what she should do next. If it had been Bronny calling round, they'd go straight up to her bedroom. But Lucia was different. A proper visitor.

'Would you like a drink?' Hazel asked. There was lemonade in the larder, and if pushed she could make a pot of tea.

'You're sweet, but shall we head to the beach? It's such a glorious afternoon, I don't want to waste a moment indoors.'

Lucia shaded her eyes and squinted towards the shore, where a dozen or so boys scampered around the waves. 'Damn,' she said. 'I'd forgotten about the swimming lessons. Let's walk further on, Hazel, or Mrs Winters will rope me in.'

The wind was getting up, and high stems of marram grass whipped at their legs as they picked their way along the beach. Lucia's halter-neck top had a faint gold print like the scales of a mermaid and her skin was bronzed and smooth. Hazel couldn't have felt less glamorous with her freckled arms and her old beach dress. Still, at least her bathing costume was passable. Turquoise was the perfect colour for fair-skinned blondes; she'd read that in *Miss Modern*.

They reached an empty stretch of beach between two low-growing clumps of kale.

'Now for the conjuring act,' said Lucia.

She shook her rolled-up towel and a black bathing costume dropped out. Hazel realized with alarm that Lucia was going to change into her costume right now, on the beach.

'Be a sport and screen me with the towel, would you?' asked Lucia.

She'd just have to go along with it. What choice was there? Lucia was older, of course, more confident, and if Hazel acted coy she would look like a baby. So she nodded and took the towel, held it out with arms stretched wide and her head twisted to one side.

'Oh, don't be bashful on my account,' laughed Lucia. 'We're all girls together.'

She took off her trousers and drawers first, then bent down to wriggle into the legs of her costume. Next she untied the halter knot of the pyjama suit and pulled it over her head, flinging the top in a crumpled pile with the trousers. Even with her eyes turned away, Hazel could see the pale curve of Lucia's breasts. How carefree she was, thought Hazel. Standing there, half-nude, casually looping her arms into the straps of her costume, now fastening the clasp of the little belt around her waist . . .

'Finished!' she said. 'Your turn.'

Hazel unbuttoned her dress and stepped out of it.

'Oh, bravo.' Lucia raised her sunglasses and gazed at Hazel. 'You came prepared . . . and what a sublime shade of blue.'

*

They swam against the incoming tide, cresting the waves, lazing on their backs in the deeper water with their eyes closed to the sun. The sea had seemed cold at first but now they felt miraculously warm – you could almost be in Cannes, Lucia said – and they began speaking to each other in French, giggling at their poor pronunciation. *J'adore la plage. La mer, c'est magnifique.*

Hazel soon ran out of French phrases, and Lucia became quiet, still drifting on her back with her eyes shut. Hazel looked up at the gulls that wheeled and squawked overhead. At first she mistook the high-pitched scream for a young gull, mewling for its mother. Then the cry came again, and she turned her head to see a small hand in the distance, disappearing under the water.

Instinctively she began to swim, to swim with all her strength towards the ripples where the hand had been. It wasn't too far, perhaps twenty yards, and she reached the spot just as a young boy's head surfaced and his arms raised again, thrashing in panic. He looked no older than seven or eight and the skin around his lips was a strange grey-blue. Hazel grabbed him around the waist and cried out herself in surprise as his weight pulled her under too. Water gushed into her mouth, closed over her head, a deafening rush of bubbles.

They sank fast, and her feet grazed against a limpet-covered rock on the seabed. She pushed up and they began to rise, but the boy clamped himself to her, his body cold and slippery with panic. They were sinking again.

It was as if he was trying to kill her and in that moment she despised him. You will not win, she thought. You will not win. Her breath bubbled away, up and up towards the light, but she could not follow it, and now she had none left, and a pain began to rasp in her chest and there was a strange singing in her ears.

Think. She must think.

Under the arms, that was it. Grab him under the arms. How many times had she watched the demonstrations, the lifesaving teams on the sands each summer? The boy's grip began to slacken and she manoeuvred herself underneath him, hooked one arm under his, then pushed up again from the rock. Their bodies surged to the surface. As she gasped fresh air she heard a woman shouting, and the *whoosh* of a laboured breaststroke.

Hazel turned onto her back, and tried to keep the boy's limp body above water, his head half-resting on her chest. Now that she had managed a few snatched breaths she was strong enough to swim again. She kicked on her back for several yards until she was sure she must be back in her depth. Yes, her foot now balanced on a slimy rock. She held the boy to her as he spluttered and shook.

'Is it Leonard? Is it Leonard?' The shouting woman was shrieking now, half-swimming, half-walking towards them. Hazel hadn't the energy to respond, even if she had known his name. She could think only of the pain in her lungs and the violent tremble that ran through her body.

'I think it is Leonard, Mrs Winters,' Lucia called. She had swum to Hazel's side, and she was reaching out towards the boy. 'We just got there in time. Here, I'll take him now, Hazel,' she said in a breathless whisper. 'You must be exhausted.'

'Bring him in,' said Mrs Winters. 'Quick, Lucia, quick. I can't imagine what he was thinking. Striking off on his own like that. Wait till I get him back to camp.'

They waded to the shore. Mrs Winters herded the other

boys into a group and told them all to get dressed. Leonard vomited onto the stones, then lay on his side with his knees up, shivering, as Hazel crouched beside him and rubbed his back.

Lucia walked off, reappearing with their towels. She had thrown her clothes on, and the scarlet silk clung to her wet costume like dark blood. Draping her towel over Leonard, she helped him to stand. 'I have to take him back,' she said to Hazel. 'Do you need anything? A doctor? There's one at the camp, I believe.'

'I'm fine, just getting my breath.'

'Little rascal would've drowned if it hadn't been for us. Here –' she placed Hazel's towel and dress next to her – 'your things. I'll come and see you this evening, shall I?'

'It's fine. Honestly no need. I think I'll go straight to bed.'

'Tomorrow, then. Take care.' Lucia blew her a kiss as she walked away.

Hazel wrapped the towel around her shoulders and lay back, using her beach dress as a pillow. The sun felt warm on her skin. Her breathing was easier now and she was desperate to sleep. She ought to go home, she thought, but she would stay here just a moment, close her eyes.

'Are you all right?'

Hazel sat up. Someone stood above her, his face eclipsing the sun. She recognized his voice. Hushed, deep. It was him, she was sure of it.

'I saw what you did,' he said.

'I should have got there sooner. I thought it was a gull crying out . . .' Her eyes were level with his knees. Shell fragments and sand grains clung to his skin.

'I wanted to help, but I was too far away. Couldn't reach you.'

She shivered, remembering the drowning boy's arms clamped around her neck, heaving her down. The towel fell from her shoulders and he crouched to drape it back around her. She felt his fingers on the top of her arm. There was a cut on his palm, she noticed, the edges whitened by seawater. Their faces were level now. The wind gusted and she could smell his skin, hot and salty.

'You saved his life, though I think your friend might take the credit.'

'Lucia?'

There was a call from the far end of the beach. 'Smart!' Mrs Winters was waving him over. Hazel could just see Lucia disappearing through the gate, clutching Leonard by the top of his arm, a gaggle of greyshirt boys following behind.

'Better go,' he said, standing up. 'Sure you're OK?'

'Yes. Perhaps I'll see you later?'

He paused and brushed sand from his arm. 'The garden?'

'I thought you might come last night. I . . . I waited.'

'You did?' He crouched again, splayed his fingers on the stones to steady himself. His knee pressed against her thigh and the contact sent a startling ache through her body.

'I'll come tonight,' he said. And then he reached for her hand and brought it to his mouth.

It seemed to Hazel as if all the air had been sucked from the summer sky, as if the waves had folded into themselves and fallen still. The boy kissed the skin close to her wrist, kept his lips there for a second or two, and it was only when Mrs Winters called again that he let her hand drop, stood and turned away, unspeaking.

She lay back and closed her eyes. The ache was still there, but it was a bearable pain, a pain that was somehow necessary. The seagulls' cries began to detach from her consciousness, the waves *shushed* her and she fell into a dream, a black dream in which she was underground, following a tiny beam of light. She did not hear the approaching whine of the aeroplane, but when it was overhead the engine's howl shook her from sleep and she blinked up at the underside of the fuselage. The Fury was polished to an impossible shine, the dazzle so bright it seemed to imprint on her eyes, and even when she squeezed them shut she could not blot out the glare.

11

Francine stood in front of the wardrobe mirror and held the yellow dress up to her body. It was pretty, rather girlish, with a bow in the centre of the high neckline. Hazel would be pleased with it, she felt sure. She hoped she'd guessed the size correctly. Alarming how Hazel had transformed over this past year. Not just her figure, but her manner, too. She wore a permanent sullen look that seemed to accuse her mother, silently, of goodness knows what. The days of idolatry were over, and in truth Francine couldn't help feeling relieved that Hazel no longer worshipped her as she once had. Sometimes it was sweet, but as the years went by it became irritating, that doe-eyed gaze of adoration, and the way Hazel would slip away from Nanny Felix and follow Francine around the house or the garden – even the bathroom, for heaven's sake – always wanting a song, or a game of snap, pestering her to listen to the latest tune she was attempting to learn on the piano. The girl had needed a brother or a sister, that was plain enough. But a brother or a sister simply hadn't come along. And now, of course, it was far too late for all that.

She folded the yellow dress back into the tissue paper and took out the crimson satin nightgown. She would wear it tonight; it would be a surprise for Charles when he came back from his appointment, if she was still awake. Such a bore that he had to go out this evening after all. They had arranged dinner at Veeraswamy, but at lunchtime wretched Dr Cutler had telephoned to say that the meeting with the Chislehurst client – cancelled last month – was now back on. The client was a ditherer, kept changing her mind, but Dr Cutler had said she was somebody important whom they couldn't possibly afford to turn down. So at six Charles had taken a taxi to Charing Cross, promising to be home by midnight, and once again Francine found herself alone, with no one but Jean scuttling around the basement kitchen, attempting to cook up a light meal. A simple soufflé, Francine had suggested, perhaps some asparagus.

She lay the nightgown on her pillow, stroked the satin and sighed. Footsteps passed on the street outside and Francine moved across to the window to look down onto the pavement. She watched a young woman in high-heeled sandals click-clacking on the arm of a dashingly tall man. Were they married, she wondered, or engaged? What fun they would have, this balmy evening in Mayfair. How wonderful to be young and in love.

Her stomach groaned and she realized she had not eaten since their late breakfast. She would have the soufflé . . . and then what? There were the friends from her dancing days, Harriett or Flick, or perhaps Deborah Leigh. She could telephone the old gang, whip up an impromptu gathering. But it had been months – over a year, probably – since they had been in touch. Harriett and Jeremy's wedding anniversary, wasn't it, a rainy garden party in Hampstead the previous summer? It was around the time of Paul's first trip to Paris. She had gone alone to the party, drunk too many brandy cocktails, and found herself staying overnight in Harriett's guest room. Had she heard from Harriett since that weekend? She couldn't remember receiving a Christmas card.

Francine took an address book from her handbag and went downstairs to the telephone. She'd try Flick first. Flick was always game. But there was no answer at her flat, and when she rang Deborah's house, a maid answered, informing her that the family would be in Hertfordshire until late August. Was it worth trying Harriett? Francine remembered Harry's cool eyes the morning after the garden party, some upset over a broken decanter. No . . . she shut the address book, picked up the phone and asked for the Bognor Regis exchange.

The operator put her through, and in no time Mrs Waite had picked up, her curious faux telephone voice bringing a smile to Francine's lips though she had heard it a hundred times. There was the unavoidable small talk – yes, it was still hot in Aldwick though the wind had got up, no, still not a drop of rain and the lawn was looking parched. Once the pleasantries were dispensed with, Mrs Waite went to fetch Hazel from her bedroom.

'Hello?'

'Darling. Are you having a good week?'

'The telephone works, then?' said Hazel. She sounded cross, not a hint of pleasure or gratitude at hearing her mother's voice.

'Oh, yes. All fixed. Are you having fun, darling? Have you been into the town with Bronny?'

There was a hesitation, a crackle on the line, and Francine wondered if they'd been cut off. 'Hazel?'

'Sorry, yes, everything is fine. It's still very hot. We went bathing this afternoon.'

'Bathing? Lovely. Shall I ring again tomorrow?'

'There's no need, you know.'

'Perhaps you're right. The day after that, then. I'll ring on Friday. But I wanted to tell you about the summer dress I found you in Selfridges, and a super little hat . . .'

Hazel listened and muttered a grudging thank-you. She asked Francine when she would be home.

'Monday, I should think. I have engagements over the weekend.' Francine decided against mentioning the tickets Charles had bought for *Anything Goes* at the Palace. She'd come home sooner if it wasn't for that, but she did so love Cole Porter. 'You'll be all right, won't you, until Monday? You haven't fallen out with Bronny?'

'No. I'll be fine, Mother.' Hazel sounded brighter. 'I'm having a perfectly good time.'

'Well, that's marvellous. Goodbye, darling.' Francine blew a kiss into the receiver, but the line was already dead.

She sat heavily on the stool at the telephone table. There was a greasy smell drifting from the open door that led down to the kitchen. She picked up the address book and fanned herself with it, then flicked through the pages until she reached *X, Y, Z*, a single entry for Martha and Richard Yelland. The Yellands had moved to America, the last she heard. New York, or Boston.

At the very back of the address book was a pouch where Francine had stored a few Kodak prints. She took them out and looked at each one: Hazel with a crab net on the rocks at Pagham; her mother and father under the yacht-club awning, two or three years before they died; Hazel with Cocoa, the little cat who had disappeared over the back wall one day and never returned. Finally, there was the photograph taken in Siena, where she and Paul had spent a fortnight in 1920. She'd forgotten about this picture, and the sight of it unnerved her. How odd to see the two of them together, smiling. Their bodies touching. They both looked so happy.

A knot of regret tightened in her gut. A large gin would loosen that. Music on the gramophone. Never failed.

The clock in the drawing room struck seven.

She shoved the snapshots back into the pouch and shut the address book. Photographs could make one feel so maudlin. She must concentrate all her energies on the present. She had Charles, hadn't she? It didn't matter that they could never be married, that he was tied to Carolyn and her bountiful wealth. She and Charles loved each other, had always loved each other, even during the many years apart.

But if only Charles were here *now*. Loneliness began to creep, like a sharp fingernail sliding across her heart, and Francine couldn't bear it.

'Dinner is ready, Mrs Alexander.' Jean appeared in the hallway, anxiously shifting from one foot to the other. Such unfortunate large feet, lumped on the end of those sparrow ankles.

'Thank you, Jean. I'll take it in the drawing room on a tray. And bring me a glass with ice, would you?'

Francine opened the drinks cabinet, took out a bottle of gin and set it on the side. She pulled a record from the stack next to the gramophone. The first track happened to be Duke Ellington, 'Cocktails for Two'. Ah well, she thought – the least she could do was pour a double.

Francine spritzed her face with soda water and slumped into the armchair. Strangely enervating, dancing alone. How many records had she stepped on? Only one, wasn't it, the

Sophie Tucker? The cracked disc was over by the standard lamp. She'd have to hide that; Charles need never know.

The smell of soufflé lingered and suddenly a sharp taste of bile flooded Francine's mouth. It was so hot in the room; no wonder she felt seedy. Fresh air would help. She stood and swayed across the floor, almost tripping on the tasselled rug. As she forced up the top sash with the heels of her hands, a heavy scent drifted in: the neighbour's plants, roses and lavender, their perfumes mingling as they had in the Lostwithiel garden.

Francine stumbled back to the armchair and closed her eyes, praying for the strength to bat away the memories. It was no good. She was too weak; it was easier to give in, to find herself back in the four-wheeled trap, lurching along the rutted track, packed tightly between her brother and their parents, suitcases stowed beneath their feet. Each moment replayed with perfect clarity, a cinema reel unspooling. From the high lane she could see down the valley into Lostwithiel, the wooded hill and the church spire rising beyond the rows of slate-roofed cottages.

'Charming,' muttered Francine's mother, pressing a hand to her tight-corseted midriff. The muscles in her neck flexed in an effort not to grimace. 'So very rustic.'

The trap stopped at the end of the lane outside a large red-brick villa. Mrs Lassiter appeared smiling at the gate, waving with excitement to see her London friends after so many years. In the lee of the porch, half hidden by a brick pillar, Francine saw the shadowy figure of a boy.

The boy was Charles, the Lassiters' only child, and Francine had overheard her mother talking about him to her father, explaining how difficult Charles had become, tending towards melancholy when left alone. He was rude to his governess, and had once gone missing for the best part of a day, found at dusk playing jacks with two young girls in the squalid backyard of a local tanner.

Francine and Edward were to befriend Charles during their two-week stay. He needed playmates, they were told, and the three children were close in age – each a year apart, almost exactly, with Charles in the middle. Yet somehow, as they sat silently together on the first evening, this closeness in age made them wary. Francine was eleven and she hated being the youngest. She wished that Charles had been a few years younger, because then at least they might have made a pet of him, and perhaps he would look up to his visitors rather than treat them as intruders.

By the third day, however, Charles showed signs of acceptance. They began to go on outings with Miss Heath, the desiccated governess, to the ruined castle at Restormel or to St Austell. When it was too warm for outings they took fishing rods down to the River Fowey where it ran through the town. Miss Heath accompanied them with her sketchbook, sitting on a fold-up chair on the grassy bank of the river, dozing between pencil strokes so that her drawings always looked fragmented, incomplete. Sometimes Miss Heath let Francine draw in the sketchbook, and Francine was grateful for her praise – praise that was never forthcoming from her own governess at home in Highgate.

They were invited back the following year, and the next. Edward and Charles's friendship grew, became almost secretive, and Francine found herself excluded from the fishing trips and the tracking expeditions, left instead to sit and read in the shady garden, eavesdropping on the conversations between her mother and Mrs Lassiter. They spoke about West End plays, and new fashions, and complained good-naturedly about their husbands' shared obsession with the stock exchange.

One afternoon Mrs Lassiter seemed genuinely irked. 'I sometimes wonder whether I shouldn't chalk up the share prices on my forehead,' she'd said. 'Perhaps then he would take notice of me.'

Francine's mother had found the notion hilarious, and she spluttered into her teacup, composing herself when she remembered that her daughter was within earshot.

Francine carried on reading, pretending to concentrate. The wind blew a leaden cloud over the sun. Mrs Lassiter shivered, and they agreed it was time to go indoors. As the maid gathered up the tea table, Charles burst into the garden from the path that led to the bridleway. He clutched his fishing rod to his chest and his face looked red and damp as if he had been running.

'Dear, where is Edward?' frowned Mrs Lassiter.

'On his way, I expect,' said Charles. He cast his eyes down and stomped towards the house.

'Is everything all right?' Francine's mother called out. Charles stopped, his shoulders hunched, then he turned around with an effort of politeness that seemed to pain him.

'Yes, Mrs Ellis. It's just that I forgot my hat and I'm too hot. A touch of heatstroke, I think.'

'Then you must lie down in your room, dearest,' said Mrs Lassiter. 'Close the curtains and Flynn will bring you iced water.'

The maid bobbed and hurried away with the tray.

Edward returned in time for tea, a large trout sliding in the bottom of his bucket. He didn't ask after Charles, and he sulked through dinner. Later, when they were alone in the bedroom, Francine asked Edward whether he'd fallen out with Charles. 'Something and nothing,' said Edward airily. 'He's an awkward cove, we've always known that.'

The following summer Edward said he wouldn't go with them to Lostwithiel; he'd been invited to a school friend's in the Peak District. Edward didn't come the next year either, the year Charles was sixteen and seemed more disconsolate than ever, due to the fact that his mother had 'spawned' (he spat out the word to Francine at the dinner table, hand cupped over his mouth), producing a plump baby brother whom Mrs Lassiter worshipped even more than her prized roses.

A midnight breeze blew through the open window. There was the sound of a front door opening and closing. Francine swallowed down her nausea and sat up from the armchair. It was no use; she would have to shut out the sickly roses, sacrifice the fresh air. Unsteadily she crossed Charles's drawing room and slammed down the sash.

12

Her body was still a little shaky, the muscles tender and tight, but overlaying that was a coil of energy, ready to spring. There was a clarity to Hazel's vision now. She had a sense that everything was brighter; life was magnified and outlined in outrageous definition. She was alive, Leonard was alive, the Lewisham boy was alive. And now she wanted to live her life. Live it properly, not waste it.

She lifted the piano lid, disturbing the fine layer of dust on the glossy black wood. Miss Bell had told her to start practising the Bartók at the most difficult passage. Master that and everything else will come, she said. But somehow that seemed wrong to Hazel, illogical. She began at the beginning – the simple run of quavers, the octave leaps – and when she reached the devilish bars a kind of miracle happened. Hazel kept the tempo, struck every note with perfect, stylish precision. It was a portent: the gods were with her.

In her bedroom she did a headstand on the rug and held it for one minute. She looked at the clock upside down. Still only nine. Reading would help pass the time. She sat with her back against the bedroom door and turned to chapter nine: *Physiological and Technical Considerations*. It sounded dry, but it turned out to be riveting. Equal rights for women was van de Velde's theme. She read the passage twice, to make sure she had properly understood.

> A woman is not the purely passive instrument which she has been so long considered, and is still considered, far too often. And in any case, she *ought not* to be a purely passive instrument! For sexual union only takes place if and when both sexes fully participate and feel supreme sexual pleasure. If, anywhere and in any circumstances, the demand for equal rights for both sexes is *incontestable*, it is so in regard to equal consent and equal pleasure in sexual union, and in the interests of *both*.

Equal rights in sexual relations? The idea amazed her. Bronny had related the exact opposite: a married cousin had told Bronny (after several glasses of Christmas punch) that sex was a second curse, a wifely duty one had to endure. But if this book was to be believed, that needn't be the case at all. And why *shouldn't* it be believed? Van de Velde was a doctor, after all, distinguished in his field. There was every chance that he was right, and Bronny's married cousin was wrong.

She crossed the room, took her notebook from its hiding place over the curtain pelmet and felt around for a pencil in the drawer of her bedside cabinet. On a fresh page she copied out the passage.

At midnight, when she was certain Mrs Waite was finally asleep, she slipped on her dress and tiptoed down the stairs.

She saw his hands first. One hand firmly gripping the top of the wall, and the other more tentative, just the fingers curled to help him balance. Then the whole of him appeared, dressed in flannel trousers and a shirt, untucked on one side. She stepped out onto the path. The wind felt cool and she hugged her bare arms to her chest as she called a quiet hello. He sat in silence on the wall, his legs dangling down. She thought that he would look up into the tree, mention something about the bullfinch eggs, but he simply stared at her. The wind gusted and caught his hair, blowing it into his eyes.

'You've come,' she said.

'Couldn't sleep.'

His voice was a beautiful baritone. Could he sing, she wondered? She would like to hear him sing.

'You can climb down from there if you like.'

He peered past her, up the garden and towards the house. She was about to reassure him, to let him know that no one was watching, that only the old housekeeper was home and she'd be snoring like a drain by now. But then she decided it might be wiser to keep him guessing.

'I won't be trespassing?'

She laughed, a little louder than she had meant to, and the sound lifted on the breeze. 'I'm inviting you, aren't I? Do you smoke?'

'Sometimes.'

'They're in the summer house. I have wine, too, if you'd like a glass. It's Trebbiano. That's from Italy. Have you ever been?'

He shook his head and jumped down, followed her into the summer house. They stood facing each other, the wicker lounger between them.

'I went to Italy once, when I was twelve,' she said. 'Daddy has friends there, in Rome, except they're not friends any more.' She paused, wondering how much she should say, and then decided she should say whatever she liked. *A woman ought not to be a purely passive instrument.* She took her tumbler of wine from the table and gulped another mouthful. It was her second glass, and her limbs had begun to feel odd: dense and liquid at the same time. 'It was silly, all my fault, really. I overheard a conversation between my father and his friend's wife, Adriana. They didn't know I was in the larder. I was stealing strawberries, great fat strawberries, bigger than you could imagine. I kept quiet, of course, watched them through a grille in the larder door. He kissed her. I felt sorry for my mother, felt she ought to know, so I found her and told her what I'd seen and what I'd heard. She slapped me and then apologized, said it was for stealing the strawberries. Then she cried and asked me to tell her again. To remember every last detail. So I did as I was told, and that turned out to be the wrong thing, too.' She paused, took a deep breath and realized what an idiot she must sound. 'Sorry. I'm gushing on. You don't even have your wine yet. And I'm Hazel, by the way. Isn't that funny? We haven't been introduced.'

'Thomas Smart. Tom is what everyone calls me.'

Tom Smart. She thought it was perfect for him. A perfect name.

She handed him a tumbler from the picnic basket that lay open on the floor.

'Help yourself to a cigarette,' she said, pouring his wine almost to the brim. She nodded towards the packet on the arm of the seat. He picked up the Pall Malls, slid one out by an inch and offered it to her. This was it, she thought. The way lovers find each other in the pictures. The leading man offered the lady a cigarette. She wondered why it was always that way around. The man offering first. Her head rushed like the wind in the marram grass. Here they were, just as she had planned. The Prelude. She had made this happen, and it hadn't been difficult at all.

The first match he struck flared and died, and they both smiled, raised their eyebrows. The second match kept its flame, and he held it to the tip of her cigarette. She thanked him with her eyes, inhaled lightly and turned her head to blow the smoke in a thin stream towards the open door.

Now his cigarette was lighted too, and he was drinking the wine, and they looked at each other in silence. It was his turn to speak, she felt. She had chattered enough, carrying on about Italy and her parents like that. Why hadn't he responded? A dreadful thought struck her. What if he wasn't the charismatic young writer she'd taken him to be? What if he was actually a bore?

He dropped the matchstick into the ashtray and looked up. There was no moon, only the dim glow of their burning cigarettes.

Finally, he spoke.

'And did your mother . . . did she confront your father, about Adriana?'

It was a good question. Direct, worthy of a newspaper reporter.

'Oh, yes. There were all sorts of unpleasant scenes. It was patched up for a while but they're apart now. My father is in Paris. They call it a trial separation, but no one can say when the trial ends.'

'Is it just you and your mother, then? I mean – do you have any brothers or sisters?'

'No. You?'

'Neither.'

'And your parents?' she asked.

He smiled. 'One of each. They're not too bad, as parents go. We live in Lewisham.'

'Yes, I believe you said.' So he lived with his parents. That was a shame. She had pictured him in lodgings; a first-floor room with a high ceiling, sparse but clean. His landlady (decrepit, Victorian) would not allow guests, but he would smuggle her upstairs, and if they were discovered she would claim to be his sister, or a cousin, visiting for the weekend.

'Tell me about your job on the newspaper. Is it awfully exciting?'

He swallowed two mouthfuls of wine, rubbed at an eye. 'I may as well say . . . Look, I gave the wrong impression the other night. I don't know why I said it – well, I didn't at first, you just assumed, but the fact is . . . I'm not a reporter.'

'What are you then?'

'A messenger boy. A runner. But I do work for a newspaper. On Fleet Street. That bit was true.' He stubbed his cigarette into the ashtray. 'I expect you'll want me to leave now.'

She thought for a moment. The lie was unfortunate, but it was obvious why he had lied: to impress her. If he wanted to impress her, that had to be a good sign. And his confession was sweet. She liked him more for it.

'I'd rather you stayed.'

'Really? Right.' He cleared his throat. 'Good.'

'I felt sure you'd come last night,' she said. 'I was down here till one.'

'I'm sorry. I wanted to come but . . .'

'You're here now.'

'Yes.'

He put his wine on the table and leaned across the

lounger. She leaned across too, just a little, and she could feel the warmth of his breath. The touch of his lips made her gasp: the sweet wine taste of them, the heat from his skin. He brought one hand up to the side of her face, ran a finger lightly along her left cheekbone. Instinctively, she raised her hand to meet his, and a dusting of ash fell from her cigarette onto his arm. She pulled away, twisted the cigarette into the ashtray. Her heart lifted and crashed as if it were a giant buoy, rising up in a storm. What should she do now? She couldn't remember a word of Mr van de Velde's advice. They kissed again, properly this time, their mouths opening, tongues – astonishingly – touching, and he pulled her downwards, until they were on the lounger, pressed together between the wicker arms, stray spikes of willow scratching at the back of her thin dress.

She kissed his face and his neck. Small, light kisses that raised goose pimples on his skin. Tom's hands ran beneath her dress, his fingernails tracing a delicate path on her thigh. Now his shirt was unbuttoned and she kissed the breadth of his shoulder, the roughness of his chest. Her teeth grazed his skin, and she took an oval of flesh into her mouth, bit down hard. Tom cried out, but she did not stop.

13

Charles untied the blindfold and stepped to one side like a conjurer revealing his best trick. 'Open your eyes,' he said.

Francine blinked into the morning light – the sun was horribly glaring in her fragile state – and gazed up and down Bruton Street. She saw a telegram boy pass on his bike. Two parked cars. A clump of dirty straw blocking a drain cover. What could Charles possibly mean? What surprise?

'Well?' He twirled the blindfold – one of his silk cravats – in an impatient manner that only left her feeling more befuddled.

'I'm sorry, darling. You'll have to give me a clue.'

'Ninety in silence?'

She looked at the mint paintwork of the car parked to her right. It was a Brough. A Brough Superior.

'The car? You've actually bought it?'

'Promised I'd make last night up to you, didn't I? Couldn't bear to think of my Frangie abandoned last night. I thought we could motor down to the coast after lunch. Give the beast a decent run out.'

'How marvellous! Brighton?'

'Aldwick, if you don't mind, Frangie. I could pick up my

watch from the house. I'm absolutely lost without it. I would have caught that train last night, you know, had I—'

'Yes, all right,' said Francine. 'But I'm not missing the Cole Porter.'

'We'll be back for the weekend, of course. Back in style.' He stroked the bonnet. 'And I know a perfect little stopping place *en route*. Very secluded.'

Why did it have to be Aldwick? she thought gloomily, as she went inside to dress for the journey. Brighton would have been so much more fun. It was a tawdry town, of course, but that was part of the charm. It made no pretence at gentility, unlike Bognor and its risible 'Regis'. Still, it would be an adventure to drive to Aldwick in the Brough. Hazel would have quite a surprise.

14

The rounders tournament dragged on, and by some fluke his team was in the final. Tom stood at his outfield post, a position he'd picked because from here he could see the edge of the copse. Every few seconds he looked towards the trees, then upwards to the murky clouds that were gathering from the south.

It was impossible to concentrate on the game, to ignore the raw energy coursing through his body. Every sinew and every nerve was stretched tight with yearning. He thought of her face in the moonlight. Her kiss. The shock of the bite.

He kicked a heel against the yellowing grass, replaying last night's conversation in his mind – awkward at first, and then her story about Italy; the wine they had drunk; the cigarettes; their bodies pressed together in the sunlounger. His hand brushing against her breast, her thigh. The bite. It wasn't the usual kind of love bite: Jillie had given him a couple of those, and he'd inflicted one in return. All spit and suction. Horrible. No, Hazel's bite was something completely different. Proper passion.

She had pulled back from the embrace, though, as if it had surprised or troubled her, then she'd straightened her dress and topped up their wine. They smoked another cigarette, spoke quickly in low whispers, making plans, plotting. They would meet again today, at five, in the copse at the bottom of the campsite, next to a rope swing that hung by the stream. From there they could walk through Aldwick to a cornfield she knew, somewhere they could be alone. She would have to be home for supper at seven, but later he could come to the summer house again. She'd wait for him.

'When do you go back to London?' she had asked. They were sitting on the floor, their backs against the side of the lounger.

'Saturday.'

'And after the camp. Will you write to me?'

'Every day. And I'll come down to Bognor, often as I can. I'll save all my money for the train.'

As he buttoned his shirt, she gave Tom a sly look. 'Will there be another march before you go home? I haven't seen you in your uniform.'

Tom shrugged his shoulders. 'If there is, I'm not sure I'll be marching.'

'Why ever not?' Hazel tilted her head to one side. She looked disappointed and he hesitated for a moment, wondering how much he should explain. He had to be honest, he decided. It had worked last time, when he told her he wasn't actually a reporter. If they were going to be together – and they *were* going to be together – they needed to be completely honest about every single thing.

And so he'd explained his doubts about fascism, how it had all started after the conversation with Bill Cork, and how he was reading about politics for himself, scouring every paper in the staff canteen from *The Times* to the *Sketch*. He stopped and apologized: 'Am I droning on?'

She put her hand over his. 'Not for one second. Tell me everything.'

'It's just . . . if you only like me because of the blackshirts, the uniform or whatever, well, that isn't really me. After this camp I'm going to leave. I've made up my mind. I just haven't had the guts to tell the old girl yet.' She squeezed his hand. He felt a jab of pain but did not flinch. 'Because I want to do something decent with my life, Hazel. My mates at home, it's like their lives are mapped out. They get their girlfriends in the family way, find themselves stuck in dead-end jobs . . . cooped up in a poky room with a wife and a screaming baby.'

She chewed the inside of her cheek so that her mouth looked all lopsided. 'But wouldn't the blackshirts help with all that? Open up better opportunities? The corporate state . . .'

'It's persuasive, I know,' he said. 'It all sounds perfect. But I think it's a kind of trap. The corporate state is just another con to keep poor people in their place.'

'It makes *sense*, though.'

'That's the point. Any argument can make sense if you don't question it, if you're blind to everything else. All these years I've been listening to my mother, accepting her pronouncements. I know she's a good person at heart, a kind person, but she's got this thing, you see, about Mosley. She's indoctrinated, and it's made *her* blind. She'll overlook the bad bits, because she only wants to see the good.'

He told Hazel it was because of his uncle Jack, killed in France at the age of eighteen. Jack had been dead longer than he'd been alive, but still his mum grieved. She came at politics from one angle and one angle only. War. Mosley could get along with the German fascists and the Italians for that matter, would never pick a fight with them. Only Mosley could keep the country from another war.

'So your mother is frightened for you? She doesn't want you to be a soldier.'

'That's about it.'

'She sounds perfectly dear.'

'Hmmm. You can decide when you meet her.'

'And what about your father?'

'Oh, he likes to humour her. I'm not convinced Dad really believes it any more than I do.'

He stopped speaking, regretting the turn that the conversation was taking. Hazel would ask him about his parents' jobs now. He didn't want to tell her that his dad used to be foreman of a biscuit factory, that he was laid off and now the only work he could get was the odd day unloading crates at his mate's market stall, and that his mum kept them afloat with her cleaning job at the jeweller's in Blackheath. If he spouted all that it would open Hazel's eyes to the gulf that lay between them. There might be only so much truth she could take.

But Hazel didn't ask any more about his family. She smiled and kissed his cheek. 'I expect you think we're very rich,' she said.

He didn't reply, just looked out of the summer-house window into the expanse of the garden beyond.

'We're almost broke, according to my mother. I don't suppose we'll be able to live here much longer. What Mother wants is to sell up and move to our London flat. It's a wonderful flat, by the British Museum. It's let at the moment, so they'd have to get the tenants out. I heard her telling Charles. She hates Aldwick, says she always has. Father persuaded her to move here.'

'Charles?'

Hazel paused for a moment. She let go of Tom's hand and reached for the cigarette packet. 'Mother's lover.'

'What's he like?'

Hazel frowned. 'I hardly know.'

They had walked out onto the path together. He put his arms around her and drew her close, so that the curls on top of her head nestled below his nose. She smelt of geranium petals, velvety and clean. For several minutes they embraced, unspeaking, her body soft against his. It felt somehow as if her body *was* his, and that his own heart had swollen outside of itself, melded with her heart, and he knew that this was what was meant by love.

'Catch!' The scream of his teammates came just in time. He threw his head back to see the rounders ball dropping from the sky. It thumped into his hands and he lobbed it to the fielder on last base, ignoring the pain where the ball had thwacked the scabbed-over cut. Lucia gave a shriek of frustration at being caught out.

Clouds rolled darkly overhead. He prayed the rain would hold off and they'd be able to walk to the cornfield as planned. She'd told him about the sycamore tree in the centre, the mice that scurried around the crops, the larks and lapwings and buntings that nested all around.

It was almost six. She wasn't coming. Why wasn't she coming?

The wood was alive with creaks and snaps, and the stream plashed over green-slimed rocks, stagnating in a pool of frothy scum where the water had collected behind a fallen bough. Crouching against the smooth trunk of a young ash, he picked up a stick and drew patterns in the dust.

It had never occurred to him that she might not come.

His mouth was dry and he wondered whether the water in the stream was safe to drink. He didn't like the look of it. The scum was a peculiar shade, as if the stream was an oozing wet wound.

He touched his shoulder beneath his shirt and felt the mark where her teeth had broken his skin.

Hands drilled into pockets, he wandered into Aldwick village and decided to meet his mum and dad at the pub after all. Tom went into the lounge bar and there they both were, sitting at a table next to the unlit fire. A buddleia flower was pinned to his mum's cardigan, drooping on the shelf of her bosom.

He bent and gave her a kiss on her cheek. Her skin was loose and pillowy, fuzzy with down. She smelt of aniseed and carbolic but there was something else he hadn't noticed before. An image of his dead great-aunt came to mind. That was it. She smelt of old ladies.

'This *is* nice,' she beamed. 'The three of us together.'

'A pint?' asked his dad, delving into his trouser pocket for his wallet.

'Thanks, Dad.'

'Sit yourself down, then.' Bea patted the space next to her on the upholstered bench. 'How did you get on with Fred?'

'What?'

'Your birdwatching.'

'Oh, all right. Saw some magpies in the woods.'

Her face clouded. 'It wasn't just the one?'

'No, two.'

'Smashing. Two for joy!'

Tom ran his fingers through his windblown hair.

'What's this?' she cried, reaching for his left hand. 'What have you been up to?'

'Caught it on a branch.'

'You're too old for climbing trees, Tom. Remember what I told you about the Dixons' lad?'

'All right, Mum. I'm not a baby.'

'Stop fussing, Bea.' His dad handed the pint to Tom. 'There you go, son. Your good health.'

By the third sherry Bea's face had reddened to the shade of an autumn apple. She started to reminisce, and his dad joined in too, and the pair of them were jollier than he'd ever known them to be. 'Do you remember, Harold,' she said, 'when Tom was two and we took him to the zoo at Regent's Park? He wasn't a blind bit interested in the animals. Elephants, zebras, lions – he couldn't give a monkey's. And then we were walking to the toilets and he saw a sparrow hopping around by a bin. The excitement! "Birdie," he yelled.'

Tom did his best to laugh along with them. It was nice, sitting here – the pint had helped calm him – but a tangled feeling still swirled in his stomach, the fear that Hazel had played him for a fool.

The pub door banged open and his mum stared for a moment at whoever it was. Colour ebbed from her cheeks. She picked up her schooner and put it to her mouth, holding it there for too long, as if her arm was stuck in that position. His dad didn't seem to notice; he was drawing on his pipe, sucking to get it going, and the smoke trailed around his head in a bluish mist. Tom turned to look at the newcomers. A tall man wearing a panama hat leaned with one elbow on the bar. Next to him stood a woman in flared trousers and a strange belt of dangling pom-poms. She had red hair and painted lips. He supposed she was the kind of person that people described as striking, but Tom felt a kind of pity for her because she was getting old – forty at least – and her get-up was faintly ridiculous. Perhaps that's why his mother had stared.

Bea put down the glass and now she was fiddling in her bag.

'You all right, Mum?' Tom asked.

'Let's get going,' she said, pulling out a handkerchief. 'Shouldn't have had that last drink. I've come over woozy.'

As they left, Tom heard the pom-pom woman talking in a loud voice. 'Perfectly marvellous,' she said as she walked towards the table under the window. 'Warm gin and no ice.' The man laughed and pulled out a chair for her. She winced as the legs scraped across the flagstone floor. 'Just a quick one,' he said. 'Here's how!' They clinked glasses.

Outside, his mum pulled her cardigan tighter, stretching it over her curves. The wind had an edge to it now, choppy and damp. She shivered.

Harold gave Bea a pat on the back. 'Happy birthday, Mother.'

'Yes . . . thank you,' she muttered, and hurried along the pavement.

The lads were playing poker in the tent. Tom joined in for a while, but he couldn't keep his mind on the game. He put his cards down and reached for his towel.

'Going for a shower,' he said.

Fred looked disgusted. 'Again? You had a shower yesterday, didn't you?'

Tom threw his towel at Fred. 'Some of us have standards

to keep,' he said. 'Clean living, that's what the movement's all about, isn't it?'

With a snigger Jim leaped to his feet and did the blackshirt salute. 'Hail, Mosley!' he said, bringing his heels together so that his bare ankles cracked.

When Tom got back from the shower block, Beggsy was lying on the groundsheet, rolling something between his thumb and forefinger.

'All right, pansy?' he said to Tom. He flicked his fingers and a hard green acorn struck Tom on the side of his head. 'Soaped yourself up nice and clean, have you?'

'Fuck off, Beggs.'

'Ooooh!' Beggsy propped himself up on his elbows. 'The pansy bites back.' He stood, took off his trousers, patted his chest and belched loudly. 'Now if you'll excuse me, I'm ready for some shut-eye.' Beggsy flopped onto his mattress, feet hanging off the end of the creaking steel frame.

'Wouldn't mind turning in either,' said Jim. They put out the candles and Tom lay in the darkness, watching a brown speckled moth crawl and flutter around the canvas, trying to escape towards a light which burned in a neighbouring tent. When the light died the moth opened its wings, spread them against the canvas and grew still. Tom waited another half-hour, slid his haversack from under the camp bed and stepped out into the night.

He jogged along Stoney Stile Lane and then slowed to a walk when he reached the parade of shops. Hazel wouldn't be impressed if he turned up sweaty, especially after he'd gone to the bother of a shower.

There would be a good reason why she hadn't met him in

the woods. She'd be waiting for him now, ready to explain. And if she wasn't there in the summer house, she would have found some way to let him know. A note stuffed into a crevice in the flint wall, perhaps. A coded sign on the summer-house door.

On the beach he opened his haversack and took out the uniform. It was creased after being stuffed into such a small bag, but Hazel wouldn't notice in the blackness of this night. Muffled booms of thunder sounded across the Channel, and a cold wind sliced his hair. On the horizon, a bank of light flared. At last, the storm was coming. His pulse quickened at the prospect.

Swiftly he dressed in the black shirt and trousers, threaded the wide leather belt through the loops and fastened the steel buckle. He traced his fingers over the ridges of the emblem embossed in the centre. The *fasces* of imperial Rome; a symbol of strength through unity. Strength through unity – it was a good motto, he had to admit. He'd be strong with Hazel, that was for sure.

When the lightning flashed again the buckle shone, and the *fasces* seemed to rise up from the shadow. He bowed his head for a moment. This was the last time he would wear the uniform. He'd never march again, not as a fascist. He'd tell his mother next week, once they were back in Lewisham. And after work one day he'd find Bill Cork and they'd have a proper debate. He was ready, now, to make up his own mind.

But this last time was for Hazel. It would amuse her, he thought. And then she would peel the uniform away, and she would see him as he truly was.

His hair was still damp from the shower and he ran his fingers through it, pushing the long strands back from his forehead. The wind dropped and the clammy air seemed to smother him, to cling to his face. It began to rain. He licked his lips and tasted salt.

15

The weather was wild tonight. At the window the curtains swayed, and every now and then a whirling leaf flung itself against the pane. Between gusts Hazel could hear strong waves breaking, the suck of pebbles in the undertow. She opened the window and leaned out, her elbows grazing the salt-specked ledge. On the horizon the lights of a ship winked and she imagined the world beyond the horizon; a house on the other side of the Channel where some other girl might be standing, staring north. Hazel felt suddenly insignificant, a pinprick in the world, no more important than this grain of sand digging into her elbow.

'Hazel?'

She turned to see her mother standing at the door.

'Why aren't you in bed?'

'I'm not tired.'

'Well, I am. This headache simply won't budge.' Francine stepped further into the room and shut the door, leaning back on the handle as if it were a crutch keeping her upright. 'Darling, please don't sulk. I thought you'd enjoy the surprise.'

'I was about to go out, that was all.'

'To meet Bronny, you said. And she could very easily have

come along with us for the drive. Why you wouldn't call round for her I can't imagine.'

'She gets motor sick.'

Francine sighed. 'You can see Bronny tomorrow. We're heading back to London first thing. I must say it's a rum affair when you're not welcome in your own home . . .' Her voice trailed away as she slipped from the room.

Later, when Hazel went to the bathroom, she saw Charles on the landing. He wore a towel around his midriff and his chest was bare. Charles nodded and said goodnight. She half smiled, hugging her arms around the too-tight nightie and wishing she'd worn her dressing gown.

The storm would not matter. The gods would be with her once more and Tom would appear. Downstairs, her heart began to hammer as she slid open the bolts at the back door. She stepped onto the terrace, the wind lashing her face and snatching at her hair. A black shape slid from the bushes and she almost cried out. Only a cat. It ran across the lawn, then sprang up over the neighbour's wall.

As she opened the summer-house door a flash of lightning froze the night, and she blinked at the shapes made strange by the storm. She stepped inside and knelt at the tea chest, pulled the book and her cigarettes from their hiding place under the pile of old newspapers and magazines. Rain began to strike the windows. She'd wait as long as she had to. Thunder did not scare her.

Another lightning flash blazed as she lit a cigarette. She stared hard at the garden wall but he was not there and when the lightning died the night seemed black as hell. She drew on the cigarette, hungry for its glow. At last there was a shift in the darkness, a thud on the ground. The door opened.

'Hazel,' he said, but her breath came too fast and she could not reply. She dropped the cigarette in the ashtray and let the book fall to the floor. A half-remembered instruction called from its pages: she must not throw herself at him – *Lovers, beware!* – and yet it was impossible not to step closer, to reach out for him, to press her mouth against his.

He was wearing his uniform. The steel edge of the belt buckle was sharp and cold. Underneath, his skin was warm.

PART TWO

16

London, 1936

She was not in the mood for drumming. It was a warm evening and there was no air in the hall. The red curtains were closed against the setting September sun, filling the room with a rich drowsy light. Hazel looked down at the parquet flooring. There were damp patches where the bugle players had cleared their instruments of spit, and little dents where Mrs Dunn sometimes banged down her standard in frustration at their mistakes. Mrs Dunn was hard on them but she was a good leader and her pride was infectious. When a rehearsal went well, she brought out a tin of humbugs and told them to take two.

They played through the march again and this time they were perfect – even Winnie with her overenthusiastic cymbals – and Mrs Dunn beamed. 'Wonderful, ladies,' she said. 'You'll be the talk of next month's parade. Let's make O.M. proud!' She looked towards the portrait that hung at the far end of the hall above a trestle table. Hazel half expected Mrs Dunn to genuflect before the image, to bless herself with – what? – the sign of the circle and flash?

Next to Sir Oswald's portrait hung a picture of the old

king. So solid and real: hard to believe he was gone. But Edward would be a good king, they all agreed on that. Very modern in his thinking, and he seemed to have some sympathy with the movement. Lucia had been to a cocktail party at his mistress's home in Cumberland Terrace. Mrs Simpson had complimented Lucia on her beaded peach dress and they had chatted for a short while on the merits of Schiaparelli over Chanel. Lucia told Hazel that Mrs Simpson had remarkably thin wrists, which was a sign of good breeding, whatever your thoughts on divorce.

Hazel lifted the strap of the side drum from her shoulder and rubbed at her skin where the leather had dug in.

'Coming for a drink?' asked Winnie.

It was decent of her to ask, and Hazel was tempted. Winnie was good fun. For one thing she was a great mimic, and had Mrs Dunn to a tee: the Yorkshire accent, the thrust of her chin and her habit of repeating, *Put some oomph into it, lass. Ooomph!* But Lucia didn't like Winnie, called her the 'shop girl' on account of her job at the Army & Navy.

'Well then, fancy coming?'

'Not tonight,' said Hazel.

'Going back to your flat?'

'Yes. I could do with an early night.'

'Bugger that,' said Winnie. 'Life's too short for cocoa.'

Hazel laughed and put the drum into its case. Mrs Dunn appeared, shaking the tin of sweets.

'Bravo, Winnie! You might just have cracked it,' said Mrs Dunn. 'Why don't you take two?'

It was busy outside HQ. The Westminster traffic inched along – roadworks on Victoria Street – and the fumes made Hazel cough. She'd eaten the humbugs already and now she wished she'd saved one; a sweet would have helped her throat. Her brogues pinched with every step. The wretched leather refused to soften, however much she wore the shoes or marched in them or rubbed inside the heel with soap.

At first Hazel had been reluctant to join the drum corps but Lucia was very persuasive. 'It's only one rehearsal a week,' Lucia had said. 'It ought to be jolly exhilarating but I don't have a rhythmical bone in my body. Take my place, won't you, Hazel?'

Hazel had never played a drum before, but she supposed she might be able to manage. Perhaps all those years of piano lessons would help. At the very least, she knew how to keep time. And, after all, it was important to show willing. That was only fair in the circumstances.

Mrs Dunn had been delighted with the proposal. 'It simply hasn't clicked for you, Lucia, has it?' she'd said. 'Hazel sounds ideal.'

Now, almost two months after that first practice, Hazel found she looked forward to Thursday nights. She was good at drumming; the uniform no longer felt so uncomfortable. If only she could wear in these wretched shoes.

At Westminster station, Hazel took the stairs down to the Tube platform, holding tight to the handrail and concentrating on each step. There were a dozen or more people on the westbound platform including, at the far end, a woman from the drum corps, one of the intense types who loved to lecture. She ought to join her – Mrs Forbes, was it? – but instead Hazel headed the other way, sat on the narrow wooden bench and lit a cigarette. After a couple of minutes a train arrived and she got into the first carriage. To her surprise it was empty, save for an unshaven man who was wearing dirty canvas shoes and no socks. She chose a seat well away from him and looked down into her lap. A quick march thumped in her head, and her fingers tingled from the vibrations of the drum.

Beyond Gloucester Road station the train came to an unexpected halt in the tunnel. She tried not to panic, took deep breaths between drags of the cigarette. The lights in the train flickered and then died: the carriage fell dark as a cave. Prickles began to scratch her throat, spiky as ants' legs scuttling up and down her windpipe. This ridiculous asthma, or whatever it was; it was so unpredictable, and when an attack came she had no idea how to control it. At the beginning of the year, when she was still living in Aldwick, her mother had taken her to the doctor. He had listened to her chest, asked her to blow into a brown-paper bag and said she had a good deal of puff. At the end of the appointment he pronounced her perfectly fit and asthma-free. 'Drink plenty of water,' was his advice, but Hazel found that sweets and cigarettes were far more soothing. She took another drag, glad of the momentary light from the glowing tip, and glanced over at the man. He appeared to be dozing, thank goodness, his ludicrous tatty bowler slanted over one ear. He clearly wasn't worried at all that they were trapped in a tunnel – the darkness had only sent him to sleep. She coughed to clear her throat, but of course that only made things worse. The cough turned to spasms and gasps; her throat was actually closing up, it was disappearing, and in her panic she began to see flashes of light in the blackness behind her eyelids. Impossible to breathe. Perhaps this was it, she thought. She'd keel over here, on the District and Metropolitan line, because it was too dark and there was no air, and she realized that she had no letters or papers in her bag, not a single name or address, which meant they wouldn't even be able to identify her when she was found at the next stop.

She became aware of a hand on her back.

A voice, musical.

Dare, the voice was saying. *Dare*.

Irish, was it?

There, there. Take a deep breath now. Calm yerself.

The down-and-out was patting her back and soothing her. She should feel frightened that he had approached her, that he had the impertinence to touch her, but any fear was somehow cancelled out by the relief that she would not die alone. She found a breath, and then another, and miraculously she felt her shoulders loosen, just as the lights came back on and the train accelerated hard, sending the man reeling across the carriage. He staggered into a seat opposite and prised a small metal flask from his trouser pocket.

'Are you better now, miss?' he asked.

Hazel was not sure she could speak. She stood as the train slowed into High Street Ken. 'Thank you,' she whispered, nodding in his direction. He smiled, stretched his arm to offer the flask. She shook her head and he took a long swig.

'You've buried it deep,' he said, screwing the flask lid back into place. 'Sure, it'll find a way out.'

She opened the train door and hurried onto the platform. The gall of the fellow! He meant well, she supposed, but already she was horrified at the thought of their odd encounter, his alcohol-sour breath near her ear. A ghost-hand made her shiver, the sensation of his palm on her back. Thank goodness she would never see him again. London was useful like that.

Anyway, she felt better now the cough was easing. Take the steps carefully, dangerous to rush. All she needed was to get into the open air. A cold drink would help. No doubt it was the heat and the engine fumes at Westminster that had set off the attack. Perhaps the doctor was right. A glass of water was all she needed – yes, she'd have a glass of water as soon as she got back to the flat. Lucia had promised to cook dinner. Doubtless it would be something simple but extravagant. Caviar with toast. Belgian chocolates for dessert.

The day of the great parade had come. It was disappointing not to have been chosen for the march proper, but their position at the Salmon Lane meeting was a vital one, said Mrs Dunn. There would be thousands of sympathizers waiting to hear Sir Oswald as he passed through the East End. Salmon Lane was the first of his four planned stops *en route*, and the women's drum corps would form up at the front of the platform where O.M. was to speak. They would drum him in, and when he had finished his address they would strike up again. It was sure to be intoxicating, said Mrs Dunn.

Of course there was going to be trouble – Hazel had learned to expect that. Wherever they went the Reds heckled and yelled obscenities. The journey here had been bad enough. The Tube was packed with communists, red handkerchiefs and scarves tied around their necks. She and Winnie were squashed at the far end of a carriage, trying to ignore the taunts and the jeers. Every so often you'd hear a few lines of the 'Internationale', and then the fists would go up in the air. Clenched fists, threatening. Not like the fascist salute – the hand outstretched in a sign of respect and peace. True, Hazel had felt silly when she first tried it out, self-conscious, but it had become almost natural now, and it was hard to deny the buzz of energy that travelled all the way to your fingertips as you chanted, 'Hail, Mosley!'

Hazel and Winnie had left the Tube at Stepney Green and walked south to Salmon Lane. Quite an eye-opener. Hazel had never been to East London before. Lucia had described it as an alien zone, overrun by Yids. 'Sub-men', she called them, and certainly it looked like a kind of underworld, everything squat and blackened, mean tenement blocks that appeared derelict until you looked up and saw babies' nappies hanging from rusted balconies. Was this how Jewish people lived? It made no sense to Hazel. According to Lucia, these sub-men were secretly filthy rich, siphoning off Britain's wealth.

Everywhere the pavements and the walls were chalked up and whitewashed with Red slogans: *NO PASARAN*, THEY SHALL NOT PASS!, DOWN WITH MOSLEY. She spotted one of their own slogans – a HAIL MOSLEY on a cinema wall – but someone had rubbed out HAIL and replaced it with KILL. Typical of the Reds, said Winnie. It always came down to violence in the end.

At Salmon Lane, they unpacked their drums from the waiting van and formed up as directed, four rows of four, with Mrs Dunn at the front carrying the standard. To the sides of them stood groups of black-shirted guards. They were strong boys from HQ, they wouldn't stand for any trouble. 'We don't start fights, but we know how to finish them,' Ken had said to her with a wink. He was over there now, leaning against the van door, arms crossed. Hazel thought he'd tried to catch her eye once or twice, but she'd done her best to ignore him.

'Not exactly a crowd of thousands, is it?' said Winnie.

Hazel looked out across the wide pavement. There were a

hundred or so spectators waiting on one side of the street, chatting away or looking at leaflets and newspapers. Some were sitting on the kerb, eating sandwiches and sausage rolls in the October sunshine. Against a row of iron railings lurked a gang of Reds. Young men, mainly, but women too – even a few children who were making a racket by dragging their sticks along the railings.

'It's early yet. The march isn't due for an hour.'

'It's going to be interesting,' said Winnie.

Hazel coughed and patted her blouse pocket. 'Do you think there's time for a ciggie?'

Winnie sucked in her breath. 'You're joking, aren't you? Smoking's not allowed in uniform.' She thrust out her chin and did her Mrs Dunn. '*Put out that fag, lass!*' Hazel smiled and Winnie stuck her hand in the leather pouch on her belt. 'Here, have a fruit gum.'

The advance speaker, a man from Limehouse branch, climbed up on the platform. He was good, thought Hazel, passionate enough to hold the pitch and keep the attention of the waiting crowds. More people began to gather, many listening carefully and hear-hearing, others jeering from the sidelines. The Red gang on the edge of the street swelled. They shuffled closer and a cabbage heart was thrown at the speaker. He dodged to the left and it missed his head, flopping instead against the baker's-shop window behind him. He shrugged his shoulders and looked towards the police who were pretending not to notice, eyes straight ahead. Cabbages were gentle fare, they knew, along with rotten eggs and flour. It was the rocks and broken milk bottles you had to watch out for.

Mrs Forbes leaned towards Hazel and spoke in a low voice. 'The Reds have come from all over the country,' she said. 'They've bussed them down from Glasgow, Leeds, Manchester. It's not the locals, you know. Locals here love us. Look how the crowd's grown.'

The street was certainly filling up – hundreds now, perhaps a thousand supporters – and people were starting to clap and cheer the speaker. 'It's time to mind *Britain*'s business,' he shouted. 'Britain for the British!'

Another yellowed cabbage flew towards him, and a woman in a smeared apron leaned from the third-floor window above the baker's. She sloshed a bucket of dirty water towards the platform, managing to drench the speaker's right arm just as the cabbage hit him on the thigh. There were whoops of delight from the Reds, and the blackshirt boys moved forward. Hazel was relieved to hear a policeman's whistle. Five or more officers stepped in, batons at the ready, and the two sides were kept apart.

Another Limehouse member got up to speak. The crowd hushed for a moment, the air thin and tense in the weakening sunlight. Beyond Salmon Lane came a constant drone of noise: chants and screams, whistles being blown, police bells ringing. The officers tested their batons in the palms of their hands.

The second speaker began, yelling about high finance and usury, and the pavement became more and more crushed until in the end Mrs Dunn was right – there must have been thousands of people waiting for Sir Oswald to appear and take the platform. Then, at the end of the road, came a shout from a young Red who'd shinned up a lamp post. 'Barricades are up at Cable Street. Mosley's turning back!' There was an ear-splitting chorus of cheers, and then a woman cried out. She had somehow clambered onto the roof of a street urinal. 'They did not pass!' she called, stomping one foot on the metal roof. '*No pasaran.* They did not pass!' The Reds cheered and began to chant, 'They did not pass! They did not pass!'

A dishevelled blackshirt shouldered his way towards the platform and spoke urgently to the speaker. Sweat and blood dripped from his forehead, pooling around his eye.

Word went round in seconds. The march had been turned back from Royal Mint Street. The blackshirts were marching west instead of east, back to HQ in Westminster. Mosley would not be coming to Salmon Lane after all.

There were countless scuffles now, Reds shouting, 'Fascist scum!' The sound of bottles smashing and women's screams.

'Stand firm, ladies,' said Mrs Dunn. She slammed her standard into the ground. 'Take position.' Hazel raised her drumsticks. Her hands were trembling but somehow she felt strong and her breath was steady.

'One, two,' called Mrs Dunn.

They began to drum but the police blew their whistles and motioned at them to stop. A sergeant produced a loudhailer. 'Meeting closed,' he called. 'Go home peacefully. Meeting closed.'

Winnie grabbed Hazel by the arm. 'I'm going to my aunt's in Bow,' she said. 'Georgie's coming too. Why don't you join us? We'll be safer together.'

Hazel glanced at her watch. 'Thanks, but I ought to get back. I don't want to be stranded out here if it really flares up.'

'Suit yourself.' Winnie looked around. 'You take care. They've got their blood up.'

Hazel began to walk away, then felt a hand on her shoulder. Ken's eyes shone with excitement. 'I'll see you home,' he said. He took out a handkerchief and wiped his forehead.

'Kensington, isn't it? We'll need a drink first, though.' He pointed to a pub on the opposite side of the road. 'My treat.'

Hazel was tempted to say yes. She was thirsty and she needed the lavatory, but when she looked up at Ken he winked and gave a sideways smile that was almost a leer.

'It's kind of you but I'll be fine. Plenty of police around.'

Ken looked towards the end of the street, still teeming as people streamed away, but there was no sign of any fighting. He shrugged, his face hardening at her refusal. 'I'd take that off if I were you.' He nodded down at her armband. It showed the new party emblem – the white lightning flash encircled in red – stark against her black sleeve.

'Yes. Yes, thank you.' She rolled the band down her arm and put it in her skirt pocket, then turned away from Ken and set off towards Stepney Green.

The sun was low and there was a chill in the autumn breeze. She shivered and hugged her arms around her chest, wondering where Lucia was now. She'd been in one of the marching columns at Royal Mint Street. If the march had been turned back as everyone said, Lucia would probably be at Westminster by now. She would be fuming.

'Mosley's whore.'

It was a woman's voice. Hazel jerked her head to look behind. There were three people, two men and a woman. Close behind. The woman took a large stride, moving to Hazel's side so that their shoulders clashed. Hazel looked again. She was a little older than her, twenty perhaps, tall and angular, wearing a thin sweater and a necklace of red paste beads. Hazel quickened her pace but they kept close, the woman next to her, the men behind. Was that a hand on her back, or the blade of a knife? When she reached a junction she stood on the kerb and looked around for a policeman or anyone who might help. 'Excuse me,' she blurted to a man wheeling a bicycle, but he looked at her, at her black shirt, and he shook his head and carried along the road.

The woman with the red beads stepped in front of Hazel and pushed her back from the kerb into a narrow shop doorway. 'Blackshirt bitch,' she said. 'You dare to come here?'

'We've a right to march,' said Hazel. 'It would have been a peaceful march.'

The woman stood on Hazel's toes and thrust her face forward so that it was less than an inch away. Hazel angled her head back against the cold glass of the shop door.

'Peace? You goad us, insult us—'

Hazel closed her eyes. A fleck of the woman's spit had landed on her lips. Her stomach heaved. She was about to be hit or stabbed, or sliced with a razor, and there was nothing she could do to protect herself. The other two had the doorway covered: escape was impossible.

'Leave her.'

Hazel opened her eyes. A fourth person had arrived. His cap was pulled low so that she couldn't see his face, but when he spoke again there was something familiar about the voice, the richness of it.

'Leave her. We're not thugs like them. Let her alone.'

'She's scum,' said the woman.

'She might be scum, but let her alone. Did you read the party guidelines? Non-violent protest, remember? We need to be bigger than them.'

'All right, comrade,' said the woman, her voice spiked with sarcasm. She rolled her eyes and stepped back. 'Come on,' she said to the others. They put their hands in their pockets and sauntered away.

Hazel slumped against the doorway, weak with fear and

hope. It was him, wasn't it? He had found her – found her and saved her.

'Tom?'

The man pushed up his cap brim, and now she could see his face clearly: small, wide-spaced eyes, grey hollows for cheeks. He was an older man, thirty-five at least. A stranger.

'You got me mistaken,' he frowned. 'And now I'd say it was high time you fucked off home.'

17

He'd been in the thick of it all afternoon. There were splinters and cuts in his hands where he'd helped haul pallets and old doors and rusting prams up to Cable Street, and a rat had bitten him on the ankle when he'd disturbed a nest in the dump behind Back Church Lane – but apart from that he was not injured. Bloody miracle, considering the way the police had charged at them, horses' hooves rearing and batons thwacking from all directions.

Now Tom walked down the Commercial Road, on his way to Bill Cork's place in Limehouse where Petra would be waiting for news. Tom had become separated from Bill at some point, hardly surprising in the chaos around the barricades. Perhaps Bill was home already, and by Christ they'd have some stories to share with Petra over lemon tea and slices of seed cake. He imagined Petra's face, her brown eyes aglow, her little gasps of alarm as they told her what had gone on.

At the junction of Commercial Road and Salmon Lane a huge crowd roiled around the pavements. Tom stopped, remembering that Mosley had planned to speak at Salmon Lane during the parade. It amused him to think of the blackshirts stuck waiting all that time, only to find that their dear leader hadn't managed a single step of his promised march through the East End. Those fascists would be looking for trouble now, Tom was sure of that. He could hear his lot chanting – 'They did not pass!' – the sound of drums and the blare of a loudhailer. It was tempting to join the celebrations. He stopped at the street corner, then thought again of Petra and her poppy-seed cake. He ought to get back to Bill's, no point taking risks. They might be worrying about him, and that couldn't be good for Petra in her condition.

Bill had a shiner swelling around his right eye. 'Walloped with a baton,' he said, flinching as Petra dabbed wet cotton wool on the bruise.

'Just a little witch hazel,' said Petra. 'You have any battle wounds, Tom?'

Tom held out his hands. Petra tutted and motioned for him to sit on the stool next to Bill. A cold draught snaked under the scullery door, but his chair was near the copper and the heat from the fire warmed his legs. Petra filled a bowl with hot water and told Tom to soak his hands. When they were clean, he held them out again for her to inspect. She patted them dry with a small towel, and smeared a yellow ointment into the cuts. '*Magia*,' she said. 'It will soon heal.' She paused and narrowed her eyes. 'What is this?' She traced a finger along the jagged scar on his left palm, the skin still raised and pink.

'I cut it at the beach last year. Down in Sussex.'

Bill looked over. 'That would have been in your fascist days, eh, Tommy? Mosley's seaside camp, was it?'

Tom tried to smile. He was used to the teasing, but after all these months it was beginning to irk. 'Something like that. It was just an accident, climbing a wall.'

'Looks like they branded you,' said Bill. He took hold of Tom's hand and angled it towards the window. 'It's the shape of a lightning bolt. Uncanny.'

'It was just an accident, I told you.' Tom pulled his hand away.

'Leave the boy alone,' said Petra. She ruffled Tom's hair. 'You know that's all in his past. He can't be helping what he was born to.' She sat down on Bill's lap and he put his arms around her pregnant belly.

Tom stood up and said in any case he ought to be getting home.

'Take care, Tommy,' called Petra, her soft voice following him as he slipped out into the darkening yard.

As he walked to the Tube, the scar began to itch. Tom tried to ignore it, kept his hands drilled into his pockets, but once he was on the train he opened his palm and scratched the skin hard. The cut had never completely healed; sometimes it woke him at night, hot and prickly, and he couldn't touch it without thinking of Hazel and what he had lost. Where was she now, he wondered? Still living in that big house by the sea? Perhaps she'd spent this summer enticing a whole procession of unsuspecting fellows over her garden wall. The thought sparked a needle of pain, and he scratched the scar harder. Then again she might have moved back to the Bloomsbury flat she'd mentioned, in which case she'd be living the high life, evenings spent up west with her rich friends. Whenever Tom went on a delivery near the British Museum he told himself to keep his head down, focus on the pavement and the job in hand. But still he found himself looking up into the windows of those red-brick mansion blocks, imagining Hazel behind the glass, gazing out with a cigarette in her hand. Perhaps even scanning the streets for a glimpse of him . . .

Well, there was no use imagining. Hazel had lied about loving him, and that was that. You were better off with a straightforward girl like Jillie Smith, someone from your own class who wouldn't let you down.

Lewisham already. He scrambled off the train and slammed shut the carriage door. It was dark now and a mist was lurking. He fancied a pint but first he'd put in an appearance at home. No doubt his mum would be going spare, wondering where on earth he'd got to.

18

'I thought I heard the door,' said Edith, hurrying into the hall. She looked at Hazel and attempted a smile. 'Thank heavens you're back. I've been listening to the wireless. Was it very frightening?'

The hallway was stuffy and still smelt of fresh paint. 'It wasn't the best afternoon,' said Hazel. 'Everything all right here?'

They walked through into the kitchen. Jasmin was sitting in her high chair, chewing on a crust of bread. She smiled and kicked her legs against the footrest. One knitted sock was on the floor; the other dangled from her pink toes.

'She's been a darling,' said Edith. 'I took her to Kensington Gardens, and after lunch she had a long nap. We've just finished tea. Poached egg on toast. I hope it was OK. I'm not much of a cook.'

Hazel lifted Jasmin from the seat. 'Thank you. It's so good of you.' She sat down with the baby on her lap, pressed her nose to Jasmin's soft hair and felt a wave of calm. 'Have you heard from Lucia?'

'She called in, then dashed out again. Everyone at HQ's trying to make the best of it. Mosley spoke in Westminster and there was a terrific crowd. She reckons this will do more good than harm.'

'Oh? The Reds seem cock-a-hoop.'

'They would, wouldn't they? But ordinary people will be outraged when they find out how the protestors behaved. Lashing out at the police like that to stop a perfectly peaceful march. Anyway, Lucia will tell you all about it. She'll be back any minute, I should think.' Edith picked up a bracelet from the kitchen windowsill and fastened the clasp. 'If you don't mind, I'd better go. Starting to get foggy out there.'

Jasmin began to cry immediately Edith left. It was always the same. At the nursery, Mrs Allen often said what a lovely baby Jasmin was, so bonny and placid. When Edith or Lucia looked after her, she was always a darling. Not that Lucia looked after her very often. Not once, in fact, these last few weeks.

Hazel carried Jasmin into the bathroom and lay her on a towel, then reached up to jiggle the washing line that hung from the ceiling. The sight of swaying laundry generally distracted Jasmin, but this evening she rolled onto her side and began to cry harder, trying to reach a rubber ball that was wedged under the cabinet. Hazel lit the geyser over the bath, then gave Jasmin the ball. Quickly she hurried out into the narrow WC next to the bathroom, almost weeping with relief because she'd been desperate for what seemed like hours. When she went back into the bathroom, she found that Jasmin had somehow crammed the ball in her mouth. Her lips were stretched back wide, and the ball glistened shiny black above her tongue.

'No, Jasmin. *No!*' Hazel snatched Jasmin from the floor, tilted her forwards and whacked her on the back. The ball flew out, bounced once and rolled away. Jasmin began to scream.

Hazel tried comforting her, but she only screamed harder. With a free arm, she twisted on the hot tap and Jasmin quietened for a while at the sound of running water. When Hazel lifted her into the bath she cheered up, smiling and babbling, splashing the water with flattened palms. She could almost sit on her own but Hazel kept a hand on her back, and with the other hand she washed Jasmin with a sponge, squeezing fat drips of water onto her skin. Would it always be this hard, she wondered? She was doing her best, but she was so very tired.

She imagined what it might be like for other mothers, mothers with nannies and doting grandparents. Mothers with husbands. And again she heard the voice in the shop doorway, remembered the rush of relief when she thought Tom had appeared to save her. Stupid, stupid. What if the man had been Tom? Tom wouldn't want her, even if she wanted him. Which she didn't. She didn't want any man. She knew about men now, knew about power, and she knew that Mr van de Velde was wrong. Equality between the sexes? What an impossible, ridiculous idea.

19

Francine did not usually take a newspaper, but this morning she walked to the newsagent's after breakfast to buy *The Times* and the *Guardian*, as well as the *Daily Mirror*, which she tucked inside the broadsheets. It really was an unpleasant shop – a wonder Mr Arnold managed to keep any custom. The acid tang of his sweat lingered on her cashmere scarf even as she walked home.

The blackshirt business still baffled Francine. This fanatic who'd befriended Hazel – Lucia – she must have mesmerized Hazel somehow, infected her with unsavoury views. She had exploited Hazel when she was vulnerable; lured her to London just when she, Francine, had found a way to resolve the difficulty. And now there had been this shocking melee in the East End, and for all Francine knew Hazel was injured or traumatized, but she had no way of contacting her.

Francine leafed through *The Times*, stopping to read the full report on page nine. Pictures of police officers wielding batons, crowds fleeing. She scanned the faces for a glimpse of Hazel, but it seemed that most of those under attack were counter-demonstrators, anti-fascists who'd built barricades to keep the blackshirts out.

Not to know where her own daughter was living – it was

preposterous. There had been just two postcards from Hazel in the three months since she went to London, both of them bland with assurances that she was safe and well. *When I feel ready for visitors*, she had written in the second, *I'll send you my address.* Visitors? Since when did one's mother count as a visitor?

On the day that Hazel disappeared, Francine had gone to the police station in Bognor, clutching the letter that had been left on the kitchen table. The sergeant listened sympathetically but he hadn't been any help. 'She's sure to come round soon,' he said. 'Seventeen, did you say? Perfectly old enough to travel to London and stay with a friend. Modern times, Mrs Alexander, like them or not. The fact is, no crime has been committed.' Francine hadn't mentioned anything to the sergeant about the child. Would that have made him more sympathetic, or less? He was an older man with Edwardian whiskers. If he knew there was a baby involved, he would probably lose interest completely; in fact he might even deliver a lecture on the loose morals of post-war society.

Francine still felt a glimmer of embarrassment when she remembered the manner of the revelation. It had been the end of December, and she was in the kitchen with Mrs Waite, finalizing the menu for the New Year's Eve party they had decided, on a whim, to throw. Paul was back from Paris, and they'd invited friends down from London, along with a few of the least boring couples from Aldwick Bay. Christmas with Paul had been a surprising success; Francine had begun to wonder whether the marriage – or some semblance of marriage – might bc salvaged after all.

The proposed menu was adventurous, given the limits of Mrs Waite's capabilities: anchovy eggs, smoked salmon canapés, cheese aigrettes and stuffed mushrooms. Afterwards there would be profiteroles and madeleines and coconut ice – a favourite of Hazel's.

Francine looked down at the list and shook her head. 'Perhaps we shouldn't have the coconut ice,' she said. 'Hazel will eat the lot and she really can't afford to put on any more weight. I wonder whether she ought to go on a diet. Could you bear that in mind, Mrs Waite? After the party, I mean.'

Mrs Waite pressed the pencil point hard into the notepad. She kept her eyes fixed on the list. 'Oh?' she said. Her cheeks flushed and she seemed unaccountably ill at ease.

'Nothing radical,' added Francine. 'But perhaps less pastry, fewer puddings? I believe there's a slimming section in one of my magazines. I'll cut out the recipes.'

Mrs Waite shifted in her seat and bit her lip. 'It might not be my cooking, Mrs Alexander,' she said. There was a grim edge to her voice.

'Yes, I know Hazel likes to buy sweets now and then.'

'Not the sweets.'

Francine stared, perplexed. 'You think she's ill?'

'Not ill exactly. In a . . . certain condition.'

There was a beat of silence, broken only by the call of a tawny owl in the trees outside. Francine put her hand to her mouth, then quickly removed it. She stood up, the chair legs rocking on the terracotta-tiled floor.

'She was mixing with some funny characters last summer, Mrs Alexander, if you don't mind me saying.' Mrs Waite didn't pause to establish whether or not Francine minded. She rushed on breathlessly, almost tripping over her words, as if the information had been festering inside her, clamouring to get out. 'My friend Ciss saw her at a blackshirt meeting at the theatre, last July I believe it was, when you were in London with Mr Lassiter. Knew it was her – recognized the ribbon on your white hat. And then I could have sworn I heard her speaking to someone, a young man's voice it was, late at night, after midnight, down at the bottom of the garden. Then there was the business of Bronwen . . .'

'Bronwen?'

'That same week Hazel said she was out with her, to the cinema, and another day for a picnic, but I bumped into the Vaughans' cook and she told me the whole family was away. Grandmother was ailing.'

'Why on earth didn't you tell me at the time?'

'I did think about it, Mrs Alexander. Tell you the truth I worried myself silly. But the girl was sixteen. I decided it was a bit of mischievousness that would blow over. I never dreamed . . . this!'

Mrs Waite's eyes filled with tears and Francine hadn't the heart to reprimand her. It wasn't the woman's fault in any case. She was a housekeeper, wasn't she? She'd never been hired as a nanny.

'Thank you, Mrs Waite,' said Francine. 'Please do not speak of this to anyone.' She paused. 'Especially not to Mr Alexander. I'd be most grateful.'

Mrs Waite nodded and blew her nose as Francine turned and left the kitchen. She stood in the winter-cool hallway and looped a hand around the banister, wondering how she could have been such an idiot, to have missed what was in front of her. Well, she wasn't the only dimwit. She was quite sure Paul had no idea either. He'd made a passing remark, *Isn't Hazel filling out?* – something along those lines – but there was no concern in his voice, only a sense of surprise at the change in his little girl.

Paul didn't know, and he mustn't know. She could only

imagine his disapproval and quite possibly his fury. And of course the blame would be laid at her door. He'd say she'd been a neglectful mother, disappearing to London to see her lover. Oh yes, it would be all Francine's fault, and then the rapprochement would disintegrate, and the word 'divorce' would be back on his lips.

Francine climbed the stairs and stood outside Hazel's bedroom door. She was playing music on the portable gramophone that Paul had given her for Christmas, but instead of the Bach and Schubert that had come with the gift, she'd taken his American records from downstairs. The mournful chords of 'Death Sting Me Blues' made Francine's heart sink.

She looked at her watch. Just after five. It wasn't too early for a drink, especially at this time of year when one could start before lunch and no one would pass comment. A small brandy, for the shock. She went downstairs again, passing the closed door of the study where Paul was checking through the accounts. In the dining room she opened the drinks cabinet and took out the Rémy Martin. She poured half a glass, sipping at first, then gulping the last mouthfuls.

The music had finished and Hazel's room was silent. Francine knocked lightly and opened the door. She still hadn't decided how she felt. She was surprised, yes, and she supposed she ought to be angry. She felt sorry for Hazel, too. And now, with the warming rush of the brandy, she couldn't deny that a small part of her was actually rather impressed.

Hazel was standing at the gramophone, winding the handle. Her blouse was loosely tucked and her skirt hung low on her hips, as if the top button was undone. Francine sat on the bed.

'What is it?' asked Hazel.

'Sit down.' She patted the eiderdown. 'I think we should have a talk.'

Hazel's face crumpled instantly. She pulled a handkerchief from her cardigan pocket and covered her eyes.

'You don't have to say anything,' said Francine. 'I've guessed.'

Hazel nodded and a sob heaved from her throat. She collapsed onto the bed, flopping sideways so that her head sank into the pillows.

Francine did her best to keep her voice gentle and delicate. 'And the father?' she asked.

Hazel cried harder and shook her head. Francine decided she wouldn't press for his name. They'd get to the truth. It couldn't really have happened last summer, could it, as Mrs Waite had suggested? She couldn't have been pregnant all this time, she wasn't nearly big enough. Francine thought of the Nielsen brothers who had both danced with Hazel at the harvest social. Guy Nielsen was the sort of young man who could charm a naive girl into bed. Yes, Guy Nielsen was the father, she felt absolutely convinced. Would he marry her? He worked at a solicitor's firm in Chichester. There could be worse fates for Hazel. Then again it would be a pity for her to marry so young, a provincial bride at seventeen. Everyone would guess the reason, and though Francine herself could shrug off the scandal, Hazel might find it trying. In which case . . . there might still be time to do something about this baby.

Francine reached across to the glass of water on Hazel's bedside table. 'Have a little sip, darling,' she said. 'We can't sort this out until you calm down.' She patted Hazel's back as she took the glass and began to drink. 'Good girl. Now, you should have waited, of course, but I'll spare you the lecture. We just have to set about solving the problem. When did it happen, do you know?'

Hazel blotted her eyes with the handkerchief and nodded. 'Summer. July.'

'Ah.'

Not the harvest dance, then. Was it safe to have an operation, five months along? One of Flick's friends had tried at around the same mark, and it hadn't ended well. Perhaps Charles's friend Veronica Cutler might be able to help? This was her field, after all.

'We'll find you a nice comfortable clinic,' said Francine decisively. 'The baby can be . . . dealt with, or adopted, and you can start afresh. If we're careful no one need know. You're only just showing now. It must be a small baby.'

'I can feel her kicking.'

'Feel "it", darling. You mustn't give in to sentiment.'

Hazel put her hands on her stomach and began to cry again. The bump was quite visible with Hazel's palms pressed to it like that. Tears dropped onto her pale young hands, sliding into the smooth dips between her knuckles, and Francine felt a sudden surge of abhorrence, to think that her daughter's hands had been wrapped around a man; hands that only a short while ago had been happy to build sandcastles or thread together a daisy chain. It was too soon. It made her feel sick and it made her feel old. Hell. She was going to be a grandmother.

No.

Francine stood, a quick flush spreading from her chest. Her thoughts whirled and she wanted only to get away from the room. But she must hold her nerve because there was more to discuss.

'I'm glad we've had this chat,' she said. 'At the moment the main thing is to keep it a secret. Your father mustn't know. He'll be safely back in Paris within the fortnight.' She bit her lip and walked towards the window, speaking to herself as much as to Hazel, working out how it would be. 'And if Paul wants to come home again soon, we'll send you away, tell him you're on a school trip. Oh, there are plenty of discreet hospitals for girls like you. July, you say, so if you were to have the baby it would be born –' she splayed her fingers on the windowsill and counted out the months – 'seven, eight, nine . . . April some time. A spring baby. Everything will be back to normal by summer next year. And you'll be almost eighteen with your whole life ahead of you – we need never speak of the trouble again. But the father . . . ?' She spun round from the window. 'Will the father make a scene, Hazel? Really, darling, you need to tell me who he is. I can't fully help unless I know what we're dealing with.'

'It's nobody you know.'

'Is it Guy Nielsen, darling? From the Fairway? Or his younger brother. I've seen you dancing—'

'No! It's someone from London. It was a mistake, in the summer. He was here on holiday.'

'A holiday romance? A fascist from London, was it?'

'What?' Hazel's face told Francine all she needed to know. 'How did you—?'

'People talk, darling. You were seen at a blackshirt meeting. Honestly, how on earth did you fall in with such an unsavoury crowd?'

'It doesn't matter. It was just a . . . fleeting friendship.'

There was something to be said for that, thought Francine. A summer passion, quickly spent. Boys like that were bound to disappear, *tout de suite*, once they'd had their fun.

He wouldn't come knocking on the door and, frankly, that was for the best.

'So you're no longer in touch?'

'No. I've never seen him again.' Hazel had stopped crying and her voice was flat and bitter. She bunched the eiderdown in her fists and her knuckles strained white. 'I'm never seeing any man again.'

'Now you're being overdramatic. We can find a bright side, darling. You were desperate to leave school anyway, weren't you? I'll tell Miss Lytton you've decided not to stay on. And to your friends we'll say you're unwell, tonsillitis – you've had it before, do you remember? – and perhaps you'll have the tonsils out, and you'll need some time to recuperate. A visit to your uncle Edward in Bristol. Don't worry –' Francine picked up a Christmas card from the sill and fanned her face – 'we'll solve this problem. I promise, darling.'

Francine sighed and pushed the newspapers away. She had done all she could to help Hazel overcome the hiccup – she'd worked out a perfectly good plan. Veronica Cutler could have taken care of everything, and when that failed there were the Misses Shaw. But no, Hazel had her own ridiculous ideas.

Yet she had seemed so compliant at the outset. When Francine suggested a shopping trip to London, a few days after the initial chat in the bedroom, Hazel had been keen, agreeing that she would need new clothes. Of course, Francine hoped there'd be no need for new clothes. She hadn't actually mentioned that their trip would include a visit to Dr Cutler; Hazel might only worry and become tearful again.

Paul waved them off from the front porch, and Francine felt curiously sentimental as she watched him through the taxi window, his smile broad and his eyes acorn-brown in the pale winter sunlight. She and Paul had been more than civil this holiday: they had actually enjoyed each other's company, and the New Year party had been a tremendous success. After the party they had shared a bed and made love in surprising ways. Evidently the spell in Paris had broadened Paul's mind, and there was no sign of the old trouble.

On the London train they settled in their compartment and Hazel took out her book. Francine remembered that she had brought the latest issue of *Theatre World*. Hazel was more keen on cinema than theatre, but Francine had imagined they might leaf through the pages together; Hazel might be tempted by one of the plays, and they might even plan another trip to London to see a matinee, once the trouble was over.

Strange, thought Francine, that this little crisis seemed to have united them as never before. It was their secret (not counting Mrs Waite, who had never again referred to Hazel's condition), and for once Francine knew exactly what to do and what to say to her daughter. For the first time, she was able to speak to Hazel as an *adult*. Perhaps this had been the problem: she simply wasn't cut out to mother a small child.

Pages and pages of *Theatre World* were devoted to pictures of Diana Wynyard and Emlyn Williams. 'Look at her divine shoes,' Francine said to Hazel, angling the page towards her. Hazel smiled and nodded, and said wasn't the dress perfect, but Emlyn Williams didn't look nearly as handsome with the moustache. Francine agreed and settled back into her seat. The train clattered along and she read the magazine to the very end, glancing finally at the restaurant directory and the miscellaneous advertisements for typewriters and clairvoyants and dry-cleaning services. One advertisement caught her eye:

> **RESIDENTIAL HOME** for Infants and Small Children. Long or short visits. Expert personal care for mothers in confinement. Special attention diet and health. The Misses Shaw, Harris Road, Selsey.

Selsey. If Dr Cutler couldn't solve the problem, the Misses Shaw might be ideal. Selsey was a little *too* close to home – gossiping distance – but it would make life so much easier in terms of visiting Hazel. And if a baby was born, the Misses Shaw could no doubt arrange for it to be taken care of. Yes, Selsey wasn't a bad idea at all. She folded the magazine and tucked it into her handbag.

The appointment in Torrington Square began well. Francine told Hazel it was a routine check-up, and everything did seem to be routine at first – blood pressure, temperature, measuring of the abdomen. It was only when Dr Cutler began to talk about *the procedure* that Hazel became difficult. There was quite a scene. A gown was flung across the room, a kidney dish tipped from its stand, sharpened instruments scattered across the floor. There was no option but to leave.

Afterwards Hazel was quite hysterical. They checked into their room at the Grosvenor, and when Hazel finally stopped crying, Francine suggested miniature golf on the roof garden at Selfridges. This set her howling again.

Later, once Hazel had had a sleep and a bath, and allowed Francine to disguise the puffiness of her face with a little make-up, they went out to Pagani's for dinner. 'All the best people come here,' Francine whispered to Hazel as the waiter showed them to their table. 'Musicians and singers and radio announcers. They troop in from the BBC.' Hazel gazed around, catching her reflection in the long mirrors that were painted with climbing flowers on gilt trellises. A man dining alone at a nearby table also saw Hazel's reflection, ogling for a little too long so that Francine had to fix him with a stare. He couldn't be blamed: Hazel did look lovely in the mauve dress, and the golden wallpaper and low lighting gave her face a gorgeous luminescent glow. Even Hazel's hair was behaving itself, now that Francine had taken her to the hairdresser for a proper wave. The man couldn't see Hazel's thickening waist, of course, because she was still clutching her coat across her middle.

They were finishing their soup when Francine spotted Charles at the door. Her heart leaped and she hated herself for it. Hadn't she and Paul just enjoyed a marvellous few days together? Still, she shouldn't be surprised to see Charles at Pagani's. It was his favourite restaurant, after all; she was quite aware of that when she asked the hotel to book the table.

Charles was chatting to the maître d', gesturing towards a table near the window. In came a much older, hunched man who walked with a stick. Charles and the old man made slow progress to the table. As Charles was about to sit, he noticed Francine and peered in surprise. He said something to his dinner companion and handed the waiter his coat. Oh Lord, now he was coming over.

Francine pretended not to have noticed him, so that when he arrived at their table she exclaimed in amazement,

'Charles! This *is* a surprise.' She looked pointedly at Hazel. 'Isn't it, darling?'

'Yes,' Hazel replied, grabbing up her napkin and pressing it to the corner of her mouth.

Charles looked down at Hazel. 'Wonderful to see you,' he said. He rested his hands on the tablecloth and lowered his voice. 'I would love to come and join you but it's my father's New Year outing. Trying to keep the old boy sweet.'

'Your father?' said Francine. She looked sideways towards the table, and then turned her head quickly back. 'I wouldn't have recognized him.'

Charles pulled a face. 'Shadow of a man,' he said. 'Come over and say hello?'

'Charles, I couldn't possibly . . .'

'No. No, of course. Look, telephone me once you're home. You can tell me how it went with Dr Cutler.' He slid his hand towards Francine's so that their fingers were touching.

Hazel coughed and her spoon dropped into the shallow bowl. There was a loud clang of silver against china and the diners at the neighbouring tables turned to stare at the young girl crying into her soup.

On the journey home the next day Hazel barely spoke. She was tired, she said, and she fell asleep soon after the train left Victoria. They had shopped for several hours – the new clothes would be needed after all – and the trail around Oxford Street had not been without tears. Francine looked through the train window at the electric lights already burning in the back rooms of dreary terraces. Her view was obscured by a small rectangular sign that read NON SMOKING on the outside of the glass, and NO SMOKING inside.

She wondered at the dull little railway committee agonizing over the wording, some self-satisfied pedant explaining the grammatical niceties. She lit a cigarette. If the guard came she would simply say she hadn't noticed the sign.

Francine's head buzzed. Seeing Charles last night had razored her nerves. She had been feeling so much more in control, so . . . *serene*, almost, to think that Paul might come back and she might have a second chance at being a wife and mother. She felt she was ready to play the part; might even attempt to become more domesticated, more like Bronwen's mother who baked cakes and telephoned through her own weekly orders, and managed with that funny little cook rather than a live-in help. Francine drew hard on her cigarette, tapped the ash on the floor and attempted to kick it under the seat opposite. Hell. Two minutes in the company of Charles had made the domestic life seem laughable again.

She pulled down the compartment window and tossed her cigarette end onto the track. A London-bound train whistled past, but the noise and the blast of dirty cold air did not wake Hazel.

'More coffee, Mrs Alexander?'

'What?' Francine hadn't heard Mrs Waite creep in. The woman was like a skinny old cat, slinking around. 'No, no, thank you.' Francine frowned at her ink-smudged hands. 'I'll go up for a bath, I think.' She had read enough about Cable Street. She looked out to the garden, where the leaves on the pear tree were already starting to mottle and fall. It would soon be winter. If Hazel refused to send her address, Francine would just have to find her. Next time she was in town she would go to the blackshirt headquarters and ask if they could put her in touch with Lucia. Surely that way it would be possible to get a letter through?

Of course there was another option – to give up on Hazel completely, to accept that she had ignored all sensible advice and gone her own way. But Paul was putting on pressure, accusing Francine of being an irresponsible mother, hinting that it would not look good in the divorce courts. So much for salvaging the marriage. Their union was sunk for ever, that was certain now. Francine preferred not to remember that Saturday in March when Paul had arrived home from Paris unannounced. She had tried to steer him into the study, but he had marched into the living room where he found Hazel, huge in a plaid smock dress, and Charles out on the terrace, drinking brandy from Paul's best crystal.

Mrs Waite fussed around, clearing away the figs, the toast rack. Francine stood up. 'I'll be leaving for town tomorrow, Mrs Waite.' She handed over her coffee cup. Yes, she'd go tomorrow. Charles could drive her to the blackshirt headquarters. The address was there in the news reports: Great Smith Street, Westminster. 'I'll be gone for a few days.'

'Is there any word of Hazel?'

'Not yet,' said Francine. She couldn't blame Mrs Waite for asking, but it was irritating all the same. 'Do listen out for the telephone while I'm gone, won't you?'

'And the doorbell. She might appear any day, tail between her legs.'

'Thank you, Mrs Waite.' Francine brushed past her into the hallway. How presumptuous of Mrs Waite to speak about Hazel like that. Francine imagined the chatter around the estate, the hushed conversations of domestics on their half-day outings. Let them gossip and judge; let them cast her as the faithless wife who couldn't keep her husband, and you can only imagine the effect it must have had on the poor daughter. Small wonder the girl had got into trouble and run away.

Francine told herself that the gossip didn't matter. What mattered was getting Hazel to see sense. By now she might have tired of motherhood. She might be exhausted by the reality of caring for a baby with no money and no one to support her but a crowd of ludicrous zealots.

Hazel might be ready to accept that Francine was right all along.

20

It was before six and Jasmin had started to snuffle and kick her legs. She was getting too big for the Moses basket. Lucia had promised to buy a cot, but Hazel didn't like to remind her because she had already been so generous, insisting on paying the rent, bringing home extravagant treats from Fortnum's food hall. Lucia had even offered to pay for a daily, but Hazel was firm about that. She didn't want a maid in the flat. It was a relief to be free of Mrs Waite – why risk another pair of disapproving eyes? Hazel could clean and shop; her wages covered the grocery bill at least – the everyday food that Lucia never thought to buy. It wasn't exactly an equal arrangement, but it was the best Hazel could offer.

She got up from her bed and began to potter around the room, folding clothes, pairing bootees. The noise seemed to soothe Jasmin, and she quietened back to sleep. Hazel looked through the window into the small patch of communal garden, the mansion block rising behind. How strange it still seemed to be in London, to call this city her home once more. She thought back to July, to the single staccato rap of the door knocker that had sounded her salvation. Mrs Waite had answered, and from the top of the stairs Hazel was astonished to hear Lucia's voice. She raced down to see Lucia on the doorstep, her shirt as black as the look on Mrs Waite's face.

Lucia lifted her sunglasses and smiled at Hazel. 'You're still alive, then.'

'Lucia! You're in Aldwick—'

'Another year, another jolly camp.' She fluttered her lashes, exaggerating the movement as if she were a doll blinking. 'Can you come out to play?'

Mrs Waite, who had not let go of the door, began to edge it shut. 'Hazel's been unwell,' she said through the gap. 'I'll have to ask her mother.'

'Mother is away for the weekend,' called Hazel, grabbing the door and shouldering past Mrs Waite. 'Yes, I'll come out. Shall we go into town?'

Walking the beach path into Bognor, Hazel felt almost breathless in the warmth of Lucia's friendship, the relief of conversation after so many months of secrecy and loneliness. She'd given up calling on Bronny. Mrs Vaughan would answer the door, her fixed smile polite but firm, and the script always prepared: No, Bronwen was busy with an essay. Sorry, Bronwen was horse riding with Patricia. Asleep in the garden. Now here was Lucia, glamorous in her dark glasses, saying how simply glorious it was to see her, and forgiving her absolutely for not replying to the letters.

'I'm sorry I lost touch,' said Hazel. 'I haven't been well – Mrs Waite was right about that.'

'Poor thing, you do seem rather low somehow. Here, shall I buy us an ice? You can tell me all about it.'

They sat under a beach shelter east of the pier. Hazel began hesitantly, skirting around the truth, muttering about missed monthlies. Lucia soon drew out the meat.

'You mean you fell pregnant?' she asked, in too loud a voice. 'Who's the beau?'

'There's no beau,' replied Hazel quietly. 'It was no one special. A mistake.' She remembered her mother's comment about the Nielsen brothers. 'A boy I met at a dance, we got carried away, and, well . . .' Hazel glanced at Lucia's wide-eyed stare. There was something admiring in her gaze, envious even, and Hazel had the horrible feeling that Lucia was going to start quizzing her on the particulars of the act. Sure enough, the question came.

'Do tell. What was it like?'

'I don't want to talk about that, if you don't mind,' Hazel said. 'I'm trying to forget it.' She told Lucia instead about the miserable Christmas, the visit to Dr Cutler, her banishment to the Misses Shaw.

'But where is the baby now?'

'She's still there! With the ghastly Shaw women. I'm allowed to visit once a week. And by the end of the month Jasmin will be gone. Adopted. I won't even know her new name.' She began to cry into her half-eaten cone.

Lucia put her arm around Hazel. 'Adopted against your will?'

'Oh, I'll have to sign the papers, but what else can I do? Mother won't have Jasmin in the house. Father's in Paris with his mistress. He can't even bring himself to speak to me. There's nowhere I can go, Lucia. I'd leave home, I'd sleep on the streets, in this shelter – under the pier, for heaven's sake! But how can I with a baby?'

'They'd take you into one of those homes for fallen girls,' said Lucia, flicking away some cone crumbs that had fallen in her lap. 'Or the poorhouse.'

Hazel cried harder, and Lucia's arm tightened around her shoulders.

'Don't be upset, dearest Hazel. I have an idea. Listen, I've been desperate to move out, find a flat, but Father won't let me leave unless I have a flatmate, and not one of my friends has the gumption. Edith's so *safe*, you know?'

Hazel's head lifted. Hope flared in her chest, though she tried to beat it down. 'But he won't let you move in with me, will he? A girl with a baby?'

'We won't mention that bit.'

'What if he visits?'

'Unlikely. Barely moves from his chair. But if he does turn up, we'll find some story. You might have a married sister, mightn't you, a little niece come to stay?'

Hazel nodded, unable to speak because she was too terrified the moment might somehow disappear, that Lucia would laugh and say it was a mad idea after all. But Lucia didn't laugh. She gave Hazel a tender pat on the shoulder, then stood up with a smile.

'Come back to camp with me now,' she said. 'We can chat it through while we're walking. And there's a meeting in the marquee at five. I'm one of the speakers, can you believe? Do come, Hazel. It might take your mind off everything. It'll be just the tonic you need.'

It was part of the bargain, Hazel realized, her contribution along with the housework. And she was happy enough to become a blackshirt; it seemed a natural thing to do. Lucia was right: when she was at meetings or drum practice, her thoughts never wandered to darker territory. Her mind was focused, organized, looking only to the future, the next beat in the bar. It was a relief to have something to believe in.

The first fortnight in the flat had been dream-like, settling in to her new room with Jasmin, the two of them together, properly, for the very first time. Lucia looked after Jasmin while Hazel went for job interviews, and when she was offered a post at Morris & Weaver, Lucia found the nursery for Jasmin. There'd been an article about it in the *Blackshirt* – a new crèche just half a mile from their flat, open from seven-thirty in the morning till six at night, founded in memory of Sir Oswald's late wife. 'Poor Cimmie loved children,' said Lucia. 'Such a tragedy she was taken so young.'

Early-morning shadows played on the ceiling. Jasmin began to whimper – a yell was imminent. Hazel tiptoed across the cold cork tiles into the kitchen. She lit the gas ring, poured milk into a small pan and placed the pan over the heat. Half-awake, she opened the cupboard for a bottle, and it was only then that she noticed the letter on the table. It was addressed to her, and there was a note from Lucia scrawled in pencil across the front of the envelope. *Your mother appeared at HQ*, Lucia's note read. *She left this letter. PS Back v late, please don't wake me in the morning.*

Hazel picked up the envelope and held it for a while. She put her finger into the top corner but could not bring herself to break the seal.

The milk puffed and sizzled and boiled over onto the stove.

She reached the crèche just after eight and rang the bell. Mrs Allen answered, a stout woman and a dedicated blackshirt. Jasmin put her arms out and Mrs Allen took her with a smile. 'Here's my pretty girl,' she said, trying not to wince as Jasmin tugged at an ivory clasp that fixed the bun in her thick greying hair. Mrs Allen produced something from her pinny pocket – a crudely jig-sawed animal that could have been a lion or a horse – and Jasmin's fist curled around it.

'She'll only try to eat it,' said Hazel.

Mrs Allen laughed, pushing the hair clasp back into place. 'I know, I know, everything in the mouth. She's teething, bless her. Look at her little face.'

Hazel looked. Jasmin's cheeks were bright red and her nose was running. What could that have to do with teeth?

'Does it hurt her?' asked Hazel. 'Only . . . well, she cries a lot at night.'

'Some of 'em breeze through it and others aren't so lucky. You'll find powders and potions at the chemist,' said Mrs Allen. 'And we all have our own pet remedies. My mum swore by an egg in a sock, hung above the cradle. Ask your mother, dear. She'll remember what worked for you. And your husband's mother, if you're close?'

Mrs Allen cast a sly glance downwards. Hazel put her hands into her pockets, cursing herself because in the daze of the morning she had forgotten to put on the wedding ring. The fiction had been Lucia's idea, to stall any gossip. Hazel had a husband, a ne'er-do-well who'd let her down. The word 'abandoned' was not to be mentioned, but that would be the unspoken truth, should anyone cast for details.

'Yes, good idea. I'll ask my mother.'

'Leave the pram there, dear. Poppy will put it under the awning later. Running a little late, are we?'

Hurrying to the bus stop, Hazel brushed herself down and checked for any signs: splodges of sicked-up milk on the shoulder of her coat, or a smear of Germolene on her wrist. Usually she would remove the wedding ring once she was safely on the bus. Morris & Weaver did not employ married women, still less an unmarried woman with a baby. This morning, at least, the ring was one less thing to remember.

Morris & Weaver sold high-class wallpaper and soft furnishings, with a shop in Tottenham Court Road and offices in Pimlico: a Regency house over three floors. There were two rooms on each floor, and Hazel worked in accounts, the top room at the back of the building, above the light-flooded studios where the designers sketched and coloured. From the window she could glimpse the pale brick of the Tate Gallery, and she was half tempted to visit in her lunch hour, but she never quite dared because there was a chance she might run into her mother or one of her friends, visiting the latest talked-about exhibition. Instead she wandered along Millbank and ate her sandwiches on a quiet bench. It was best not to take lunch with the other girls from the office. They tended to ask questions that Hazel did not want to answer. She kept her story simple: she was Miss Alexander, up from Sussex, studying accountancy in the evenings, which meant she was too busy to go out to concerts or dances after work. As a result the girls tended to leave her alone and the office manager, Mr Boyne, seemed grateful to have a junior who was so sensible and who didn't tip in with giggly tales about the previous evening's high jinks.

The chimes of Westminster struck the half-hour and Hazel quickened her step. She tried not to think of the letter from her mother which she'd stuffed unopened into the pocket of her dressing gown. Another image came to mind: an egg in a sock. She almost laughed, but then her throat began to tingle and when she breathed in, the air seemed sharp, as if it were stuck with pins. Not now, she thought. Please not now. She dodged into a narrow alley between two buildings and lit a cigarette. The smoke soothed her throat. She remembered the Irishman patting her between the shoulder blades, and fought back the echo of his words. *You've buried it deep.*

Hazel waited until that evening to read the letter. Jasmin was finally asleep and Lucia had gone to a meeting at HQ, emergency planning after the events of the weekend. Lucia was certainly in demand at head office. She said it was marvellous the way the movement promoted women – the blackshirts were far more modern than the Nazis on that point. Hitler would have all German women dressed in dirndls, their faces scrubbed of make-up, but Mosley liked his women to be strong and glamorous. Look at Diana Guinness. You couldn't imagine anyone *more* glamorous.

Hazel lit a cigarette at the table in the living room and sliced at the envelope with Lucia's silver letter opener. The letter was brief, all of three sentences. Francine wanted to meet. Sunday 11th – this Sunday – 3 p.m. on the steps of the Tate Gallery. The Tate, of all places. Had Francine discovered that she worked nearby, or was it simply chance? A coincidence, surely. It was the kind of place Francine would suggest.

Ash flakes dropped from Hazel's cigarette onto the letter, obscuring her mother's signature, the three lavish kisses inked below her name. Outside, the autumn night was drawing in and loneliness yawned in the dark space between the undrawn curtains. Hazel ran her finger along the sharp edge of the letter opener. She had been so grateful for Lucia's friendship, for her assurances that she would always be there to help. But Lucia was less and less interested in Jasmin – seemed jealous, almost, of the time Hazel had to spend with her daughter, and the nights when she went to bed at nine because she was simply too tired to stay up chatting or listening to the wireless.

Tears pressed at Hazel's eyes. She needed someone, something. What was it Mrs Allen had said? *Ask your mother, dear.* Perhaps it was time to forgive Francine.

They were back in the summer house and she could feel the weight of him, his breath sighing into her hair. She kissed his neck, tasted the salty sweetness of his skin. A piano was playing, Brahms's Lullaby floating through the black sky. Was that a gull she could hear, crying into the night? The noise grew more insistent, and Hazel woke suddenly to the sound of Jasmin wailing, her small body thrashing in the basket.

She sat on the end of the bed, lifted Jasmin and pressed her close, aware of their heartbeats, wild and unsynchronized. She rubbed Jasmin's back and began to sing under her breath. '*I had a little nut tree, nothing would it bear. But a silver nutmeg and a golden pear . . .*' She couldn't remember the end of the rhyme. There were nursery books in Aldwick, on her bedroom shelves. Her mother would know the words. Singing was something she'd been good at: she liked the sound of her own voice.

Jasmin only cried harder. She must be hungry. Hazel's breasts ached but any hope of feeding her baby had been long abandoned. The Misses Shaw insisted on bottles – it was more sensible in the long run, they said. Mothers were less emotional once their milk had dried up.

The night-time bottle was standing on the marble shelf in the larder cupboard. Hazel lay Jasmin on the bed and quickly went into the kitchen. As she closed the larder door she heard a dull thump. There followed a beat of silence, and then a scream. She flew to the bedroom. Jasmin was lying on her face where she had fallen onto the cold floor. Hazel picked her up and tried to soothe her, rubbing her back. *There, there. There, there.*

It took forever to calm her, but finally Jasmin took the bottle and Hazel could check her face in the lamplight. There was a small mark on her left cheekbone – a bruise would surely follow – but apart from that she seemed unharmed. As Jasmin guzzled the milk her little fist reached up and grabbed a curl of Hazel's hair. She twined her fingers into it and pulled hard, so that Hazel's head sank lower and lower until their cheeks clamped together, hot and tearful.

At last Jasmin slept but Hazel knew her night had ended; she would be awake now until it was time to get up for work. The dream had stayed with her – it was as if Tom was by her side, his breath trapped in the room. She thought of the last time they had been together, the storm baying outside. The promises they had made.

Perhaps she had been too quick to lose faith, to believe the other words, those words that came later in the dread quiet after the storm.

She would never trust a man again, that was the vow she had sworn. And yet the dream, the memory of that moment when she had believed love was possible: here it was, like a silken thread swaying, almost within her grasp.

On her dressing table was the reply she had written to her mother. She dropped it into the waste-paper basket, picked up a fresh sheet of notepaper and slowly began to write.

From the steps of St Paul's she could hear the organ playing: a fugue she didn't recognize. It was five past three and she resolved to wait ten more minutes. If he hadn't arrived by quarter past she would go back to the flat and burn the unanswered notes and the scrap of paper with his scrawled-on address, and she would never, ever think of him again.

The day had felt cool when she left Kensington, but now the sun was struggling through the clouds, warming the streets. She looked towards the statue of Queen Anne, the four carved figures at her feet. There was Britannia, naked to the waist, her small breasts exposed to the weak sunshine. Hazel flushed and bowed her head. To think that he had seen her undressed, pale as stone in the moonlight . . .

Still, what did it matter? He wasn't coming anyway. She sat on the granite steps, shielding her eyes from the sun.

The fugue ended and a stillness fell over the city. At the foot of the steps a huddle of tourists gazed up at the cathedral. They looked at Hazel, too, as if she were part of the tableau. She angled her body away from them, hugging her knees closer to her chest, trying to make herself smaller.

If Tom came, would he appear from the east or the west? She could see down Ludgate Hill well enough, but there was no sign of anyone who looked like Tom.

'Ah, you meant *these* steps.' Suddenly he was next to her, his hands in his pockets. He wore a white shirt, open at the neck, and his skin was tanned from the long summer. 'I was waiting round the other side.'

She rose quickly, smoothing the creases in her skirt. 'I didn't think you were coming.'

'I don't like to let people down.'

The barb hung in the air. They stood awkwardly, looking down the steps rather than at each other, and then they spoke at the same time, and stopped at the same time, and returned to silence for a pained second until Tom asked whether she might like to go for a walk or a cup of tea. She nodded, and they took the steps slowly, Hazel assessing each one, concentrating, because she felt certain the slightest distraction might cause her to trip and tumble, to knock herself out, and eventually she would wake and Tom would no longer be by her side.

They crossed the road and headed towards the river, past St Benet's Church and the wharves of Upper Thames Street. White Lion Wharf, Horseshoe Wharf, Puddle Dock. The weather was pleasant for October, they agreed. She asked if his parents were well and he said that they were.

'And yours?'

'Fine.'

She looked across the water to Bankside, to the jetties and the coal hoists, the dark buildings with their rows of black windows like unblinking eyes.

'You wanted to meet,' said Tom, slowing almost to a halt as they approached the path under Blackfriars Bridge. 'Was there any particular reason?'

She turned her head to him but his eyes remained fixed on the shadowed arch ahead. 'I wanted to apologize,' said Hazel.

'Oh?'

'I'm sorry I didn't see you again after that night, didn't write. Everything changed. My . . . circumstances changed,' she faltered.

A small child ran under the bridge towards them, stout pink legs and scabbed knees. He was chasing pigeons. His parents followed, a young couple, arm in arm. 'Slow down, sausage,' shouted the father. Tom seemed to be watching the little boy with a tenderness in his expression, the trace of a smile on his lips. And at that moment Hazel decided. She would tell him today. Yes, she would tell him everything.

They passed the couple and the man nodded an 'Afternoon.' Beyond the bridge was a refreshments kiosk. Hazel insisted she would buy the tea, and so Tom found an iron bench and sat down as she queued.

A hazy film of cloud hung low in the sky and there was barely any wind, not even this close to the river. They sat side by side on the bench, clutching their cups of tea, blowing the surface of the liquid, trying to coax away the heat. A jackdaw flew from a plane tree and landed on the low river wall. The Thames flowed smooth and fast and Hazel felt a rush of emotion towards Tom. Her love was an undercurrent, forever tugging. But she needed more than love; she needed belief, the certainty she'd held dear for that short precious time. She must try to recapture it, for Jasmin's sake. There would be no better time than this.

'What happened last summer—' she began.

'Don't worry,' he interrupted, holding up his hand as if to dismiss her apology. 'Your circumstances have changed, you said. Mine have changed too. My politics, well – I told you about that already. I've swapped sides. And I'm off to Spain soon.'

'Spain? But the war . . .'

'The war, exactly. I'm going to fight Franco.'

'Fighting?' She gripped the teacup but found no comfort in its warmth. 'What do your parents think?'

'Oh, I haven't told them yet. Mum's still a devoted Mosleyite.'

A bell began to ring at the fire station next to the bridge, and a volley of shrieks sounded inside her head. How could the conversation have turned to Mosley? To the war in

Spain? She breathed deeply, trying to dredge up a reasonable response. 'Lucia says the communists and fascists actually have a lot in common. We both want what's best for the working man.'

Tom tapped a foot on the pavement. 'Is that right? I think you'll find Franco has some strange ideas about the working man. He's a bloody murderer. And meanwhile Britain stands by and refuses to help.' He put down his cup, scratched the palm of his hand and flinched.

Hazel looked up at the dull sky and the grey cloud pressing down. How could she possibly tell him now? He was fixed on Spain, that was clear. Dear God, had she actually thought they might be together?

'When do you leave?'

'End of the month, if all goes to plan.'

She paused, dared herself to look directly into his eyes. 'Can I write to you while you're away?'

He returned her gaze and moved his arm as if to reach for her hand, but then pulled back and picked instead at a frayed thread in the seam of his trousers.

'I suppose you could . . .' He took a deep breath. 'And your boyfriend wouldn't mind?'

'Boyfriend?'

'Your circumstances. I assumed . . . a boyfriend or a fiancé or something.'

She shook her head. 'There's no boyfriend. I'm too busy for that. I have a job now, and there's the movement. I'm in the new drum corps, the women's section. Lucia roped me in but it's actually good fun.'

She stopped. Tom's face had hardened at the mention of the movement. How idiotic of her to gabble like that. He checked his watch, then stood up.

'Perhaps it's best if I write to you first, once I know where I'm based,' he said. 'Can you give me your address?'

She hesitated. Yes, it was the fairest way. If he had her address, he held the cards. It would be her turn to suffer and wait. Because there would be more suffering, she knew that now. She could burn anything she liked, but she could not simply forget him.

'I don't have a pencil, I'm afraid.'

'Just tell me. I'll remember.'

As he repeated the address, despair invaded her body like a terrible sickness. She realized she had been picturing a future with Tom – a quiet wedding in the register office, a modest little house in Lewisham – when of course all she could hope for was a room in Lucia's flat, a narrow single bed and the endless frightening nights waiting for the crying to begin . . .

'You're living with your mother?'

The question surprised her somehow. To think he knew so little. 'No, I'm sharing with Lucia. You remember her?'

'Oh, yes.' He gave a sarcastic laugh. 'It was Lucia on Aldwick beach, wasn't it, took all the credit when you saved that little lad from drowning?'

Hazel nodded. She had forgotten entirely about the boy, the way he had dragged her down, the horrible panic as the seawater closed over her head. She felt again the weight of the water, the sensation of being crushed. 'I believe Lucia was there that day, yes. She's been very good to me.' *Very generous*, she was going to add, but that might set Tom thinking, might make Hazel sound as if she was desperate or needy, and then he might start asking questions. No, she must attempt to be breezy. She stood up beside him and stuck out her right hand.

'Very best of luck in Spain,' she said. 'I'll wait for your letter.'

They shook hands, his fingers warm and firm around hers, and she felt the shock of contact as their eyes met again.

'I must be mad,' he said, and walked away.

21

Housework was her only release, and Bea embraced it with vengeful energy. She lifted a cushion from the fireside chair, plumped it with a punch and dropped it back on the seat. Kicking away the footstool, she rolled up the front-room rug, hung it outside over the washing line and walloped it with the carpet beater. Dust clouds billowed into the sky. She took a hankie from her housecoat pocket, sneezed and blew her nose. She thought she had finished crying, but the dust had set her off again.

She blamed herself. It was her fault because she had brought Tom up to be interested in politics, to stand up for what you believed in. Now – God knows how – he'd decided that he believed in Karl Marx and the communist claptrap. Months, this had been rumbling on, but when the trouble started in Spain he began bringing home the *Daily Worker*, and as they sat reading after tea he would hold the paper up to his face, muttering over Franco and the poor Republicans and what he called the scandal of non-intervention. He tried to start arguments about Spain, but she and Harold had agreed they wouldn't rise to it. She couldn't bear the house to become a battle zone. 'It's a hot-headed phase he's going through,' Harold said. 'Best thing is to humour him.'

But that was August and now it was October, and Tom's mind was made up. He was going.

He'd announced his intentions on Monday, after they'd finished their tea and Mr Frowse had gone out for his evening walk up to Blackheath. Tom insisted that no amount of pleading would prevent him; in fact it would only make him more determined. Bea wondered what she could have done to make him hate her so much that he would volunteer to fight for another country's war, when all she had wanted was to protect him from becoming a soldier.

'You're only eighteen,' she said. 'You're too young.'

He told them about a boy called Ronnie Burghes who was already out there, and he was only seventeen. Burghes's mother was a communist, he added, and *she* supported her son all the way.

Bea had cried then. What chance did she have in the face of such wickedness? Tom had crumpled a little, tried to comfort her. He'd held her hand and said he was truly sorry, but it was something he had to do. She couldn't bear him to be tender; that was worse. If he felt a scrap of genuine love or tenderness towards her, he wouldn't be going at all.

Bea left the rug airing on the line and went inside to reheat the mince. Harold would be home at any moment. She held the match to the gas and watched the flames leap into a ring of fire. It was too cruel, she thought. Just when Harold had a job back at the factory and life was looking up, Tom had ruined everything with his fixation on Spain.

She tasted the mince and added another spoonful of salt. Perhaps it was just talk and he wouldn't go after all. And how would it look at the branch? Her own flesh and blood fighting for the Reds? She'd keep it quiet for as long as she could, but it wouldn't be easy. *Please,* she prayed silently. *Please, God, let him change his mind.*

The back door opened and Harold came into the kitchen. He was carrying a large brown-paper bag.

'Thought these might cheer you up,' he said, putting the bag down on the table.

'Biscuits?'

'Bourbons included.'

She was holding a wooden spoon. She didn't know whether to take a swipe at Harold or to strike her own head with it. She took a deep, shuddering breath. Stirred the mince.

'Lovely day,' he said. 'Been busy, I see.' He nodded towards the garden where the beaten rug hung on the line.

Something bubbled and shrieked inside her. And when she spoke her voice was strangled, high-pitched. 'You think a bag of broken biscuits will cheer me up? Make things right?'

He looked down at the biscuits. 'I didn't mean it like that, Bea. I just thought . . .'

Tears sprang again to her eyes. Her head swam and the anger seemed to drain from her. She didn't have the strength for a fight. 'He's going, Harold. Our boy. He's going.' She let the spoon drop into the pot and sat down hard on the kitchen chair. 'Maybe there's still a way to stop him. Speak to him again, can't you?'

'I can give it another go, love. But it's like he said. The more we try to persuade him, the more determined he'll be. Give him a few weeks and he'll soon grow sick of it. He'll be home and we can get back to normal.' He chuckled. 'We might even find it funny in years to come—'

'What?' She raised her voice. 'Funny? You actually think

this could ever be—' She shook her head. 'I've heard it all now. You promised you'd love him the same, Harold. You promised. But you can't. How can you? Oh, I knew it would come home to roost in the end. This pain –' she slapped a hand to her heart – 'I swear it will kill me. And in you come with your bag of biscuits . . .'

She began to unbutton her housecoat, fingers clumsy, head shaking. She would go out this minute, take a walk around Manor Park, let Harold serve up his own dinner. Harold stepped forward and put his right hand on her shoulder. As her trembling fingers struggled with the last button, there was the sound of footsteps on the stairs. They turned in surprise.

'Mr Frowse?' asked Harold under his breath.

Bea shook her head. Mr Frowse always had a meal at his work canteen. He would have said if he was coming back for dinner.

The kitchen door opened. Tom stood with a bulky envelope in his hand. He looked pale as milk. 'Just some paperwork I needed,' he said, lifting the envelope. 'I forgot to take it this morning.'

Bea wiped her face but she knew it would be red and puffy and Tom would see that she had been crying. Had he heard their argument? She tried to recall exactly what had been said, but her brain felt flat and dead. She was so tired.

'Have some dinner, will you?' she said, taking three plates from the rack. 'I'm just serving up.'

'I can't. Sorry. Work's busy this afternoon.'

'Suit yourself.' She slid one plate back. It cracked against another and a flake of chipped china dropped onto the drainer.

'See you tonight then.' He nodded and disappeared.

Bea looked into the garden at the yellowing leaves drooping from the Bramley. What did it matter if she was outside at Manor Park or inside eating dinner with Harold? Tom would be going just the same. She took the cutlery from the drawer and laid up for two.

The morning after he left for Spain, Bea picked through the large cardboard box on the landing. Outside, a church bell was tolling a funeral, each low note measuring out another endless second. She wondered about the mourners inside the church and whether their grief could be as deep and as wretched as her own.

'I've sorted through my room,' he'd said. 'Some of the stuff might do for a bazaar. If not, put it out for the bins.'

She took each item from the box: comic books; a wooden boat without a mast; his old Boy Scout uniform. A bazaar? Unthinkable. She would keep the lot. There'd be room for another box under their bed, Tom's things pressed up against Jack's.

His room was cold with November air. She wiped a little condensation from inside the window, held damp fingers to her lips. Moisture from his own breath. What had he decided to keep, she wondered? His collection of birds' eggs was still on the shelf. She took down the wooden box and opened it. The eggs were nestled in their beds of cotton wool, and below each one Tom had recorded the name and the date and the place where the egg had been found. The last was a bullfinch egg. *Aldwick Bay, Sussex, July 1935.* Their summer holiday at the blackshirt camp. It was around that time he went on the turn. What had happened to change him so completely? She picked up the egg and held it in the palm of her hand, amazed at its weightlessness. As she replaced the egg she saw there was an envelope tucked into the side of the box, almost hidden by the fluffy white layers. She slid the envelope out. Blank. Opening the unsealed flap, she drew out a single sheet of white paper. It was dated last year, *September 18th*, and it began, *My only love Hazel.*

No, she mustn't read it.

Bea replaced the letter and put the box back on the shelf. She sat on the edge of Tom's bed. He had pulled over the bedspread but the linen was rumpled underneath. She ought to strip the sheets this morning. Give everything a thorough clean.

Anger rose, tight in her throat. It seemed to come in waves, back and forth like a tide. When the tide was out, she felt only emptiness and grief. When it rushed in, her body swirled with such fury she felt giddy. Bea twisted a strand of thread on the tasselled bedspread and looked up again at the box of birds' eggs. Why should she bother with niceties and respect when Tom had shown her neither? She would read the letter, yes, she'd read it now. She snatched the box down from the shelf and pulled out the envelope.

> *My only love Hazel,*
>
> *I've thought about nothing else. Why didn't you meet me that night? Did you get my notes, the letter? I've tried to work out how I might have given offence or whether I did or said something that changed your mind. If you would only explain, then at least I could understand. Until then, nothing can sway me. I think you are the most beautiful girl in Aldwick and the world, and I love you.*
>
> *Tom*

A girl in Aldwick? Who on earth could she be? There was no one called Hazel that she could remember at the camp.

Bea read the letter again. Well. If this Hazel wasn't at the camp, she must have been an outsider, a local from the village. Perhaps she was the one who put the communist ideas into Tom's head. It made sense, the timing was right. She was to blame! Bea wished there was an address on the envelope, because if there had been, she would take the train down to Sussex and have it out with Hazel and her family. No doubt Hazel was at the heart of the whole Spain calamity. He was trying to impress her, prove that he was true to her and true to the cause. Oh, it all made sense now. Bea sat on the bed and let the letter float down to the bedspread. A queer calm washed over her. If it was all for a girl, surely there was more chance he'd see sense, once he'd accepted that she didn't want him and no amount of bravado would win her over? Yes, that was it. He'd acted impulsively because he had a broken heart, and soon it would mend and he'd be home. Now she wished desperately that she had found the letter sooner: she could have talked it through with Tom, and that might have been enough to keep him in London. Then again . . . better this way. Let him come to the decision himself.

She tucked the letter back into its place and looked again at the untidy bedclothes. Poor boy. To think of him lying there, lovesick. When he came home she'd make more effort to understand him and in time they would become great friends again, just as they always had been.

22

He'd palled up with a chap called Jacob, a ruddy-faced clerk with a thespian bent who claimed to be bound for theatrical glory until the Spanish cause beckoned. Jacob was partial to poetry: he kept volumes by Charlotte Mew and Francis Thompson in his knapsack, and he often quoted lines from poetry or plays that Tom vaguely recognized from English lessons at school.

They'd met in a Newhaven cafe, sailed together on tourist tickets, then taken the train from Dieppe to Paris where French comrades were waiting. In Paris they were given their itinerary. They would journey into Spain with a band of fellow volunteers – Americans, Mexicans and Australians. *We few, we happy few*, said Jacob.

A small bus rattled them over the border into Spain. As Tom looked out of the grimy window at the snow-topped peaks of the Pyrenees, he thought how proud Bill and Petra would be to know he was finally here. Was that why he'd done it, to prove to Bill that he was a serious communist, that his blackshirt days were truly over? Bill had been doubtful when Tom first said he wanted to go to Spain. But once he was certain of Tom's commitment he'd helped him get the necessary papers – a backdated union membership card and a letter from a Communist Party stalwart to vouch for his trustworthiness and dedication to the cause. Dedication – yes, he was proving that all right! There could be no more ribbing about his fascist past after this. Tom remembered the trace of envy he had seen in Bill's eyes when he went up to Limehouse to say farewell. 'I'd be coming with you, comrade, if it wasn't for this.' Bill stretched out his hand and rested it on Petra's swollen belly. She'd smiled and clasped her husband's hand. 'Please be careful, Tommy,' she'd said, then stepped forward to kiss his cheek. Tom turned away so that they couldn't see the blush creeping up his neck.

The bus left them in a tumbledown village, where locals gave solemn clenched-fist salutes and girls handed out mugs of strange coffee and shrivelled oranges. A lorry drove them on to the barracks at Figueras. Uniforms, of sorts, were issued. The next morning they climbed back into the lorry and travelled south in convoy to the training camp at Albacete. They hadn't been at the camp long when the *¡Avión!* whistle sounded and they were shouted at by a furious Spanish corporal for failing to take cover. Tom pulled Jacob down, diving just as the planes appeared overhead. Daring to look up, one cheek planted into the cold wet earth beside a water trough, Tom saw that they were German aircraft, Junkers and Heinkels heading north. He thought of the girls with the oranges, the white terrier pup that had bounded by their sides.

The barracks were full, so they were to build their own makeshift shelters from pine branches. They worked together – Tom, Jacob and two miners from Derbyshire – and when it was finished their four-man shelter was surprisingly welcoming, the straw palliasses snug against each other, a space behind the head of each for their scant belongings.

'How long do you think we'll be here?' Tom asked one of the Derbyshire men.

'Fortnight at least.' He took a screw of tobacco from his breast pocket and began to roll a smoke.

Jacob whistled. 'We'd better make ourselves at home.' He paused, and Tom imagined that his comrade was searching for some apt line, but evidently none would come.

Tom was woken from a dead sleep by the call of a bugle. His eyes flew open and he was startled not to see the white canvas of a bell tent. The pine-branch roof sent his mind into a spin. Where was he? Where were Fred and Jim, where was that rough bastard Beggsy? He turned to one side and saw the back of Jacob's head, and a jolt of fury shot through him. For pity's sake. He'd trekked all those miles across Europe and still the blackshirts claimed him!

At the water trough he splashed his half-naked body, trying to cleanse the memories of Sussex that had plagued him afresh these past few weeks. It was Hazel's fault, asking to meet up at St Paul's that afternoon, looking so sad and beautiful as she offered her half-baked apology. Seeing her again had dragged everything up, and now the ache from last summer was as keen as it ever had been. How foolish to say he'd write! He'd honour his promise of course – he wouldn't be able to stop himself – but then he'd be the one waiting again. Waiting and waiting and never knowing.

'Oh, that this too, too sullied flesh . . .' said Jacob, rubbing his skin with a tatty flannel.

'Speak for yourself,' said Tom.

Jacob threw the flannel at him and they might have wrestled like schoolboys had not the squat *cabo* been standing on the other side of the trough, surveying his latest recruits with a weary frown. They fell silent, and Tom heard the drumming of a woodpecker in the pines just beyond the camp. He looked up to see another bird circling high in the cloudless sky; it was some kind of raptor, most likely an eagle. The *cabo* might know the name of the bird, but Tom wouldn't dare ask. For the first time he felt homesick: to be in a country where the birds were a mystery. His ignorance unsettled him more than he thought possible.

After breakfast a British commander appeared on the parade ground to brief the new arrivals. A fresh consignment of rifles was on its way, he said. Full training would be given – target practice, skirmishing, trench digging, grenade throwing. In rest periods there would be political lectures from the battalion commissar. All men were encouraged to write home. 'Not just to your loved ones but to your local parties, your MPs and your newspapers,' said the commander. 'We must keep the cause in the public eye.'

Tom listened carefully. He'd write home all right. But it wouldn't be simply a letter to the *News Chronicle*, it would be a full-blown report. Mr Crow knew he was out here, had even wished him luck on his last day. 'Keep in touch,' Crow had said, and Tom wouldn't let him down. He'd already been promoted from messenger to copyboy. If he could write some decent stuff out here, get a piece published, he might be given a chance as a reporter once he got back home.

'Make no mistake –' the commander's voice was grave now – 'this is a dangerous war, a lethal war, and many loyal comrades have already laid down their lives. But we have something that Franco's forces will never have. We have democracy and freedom, and above all, we have the will of the people on our side!'

The recruits cheered and raised their fists into the air.

'Written to your mother yet?' asked Jacob. They had finished another game of cards, and the Derbyshire boys had drifted off in search of more wine.

'Not yet. You?'

'She thinks I'm acting in Paris,' he laughed. 'Suppose I'll have to own up sooner or later. What did you tell your lot?'

'The truth.' It hadn't occurred to Tom to lie to his parents. But Jacob was an actor, so presumably he'd be good at spinning a line. 'Might have been kinder to lie, now I think of it,' added Tom. 'The old girl wasn't best pleased.'

'I'll bet. And what about sweethearts? Someone pining for you back in Lewisham?'

He thought of Jillie and her big pleading eyes, Jillie plucking at his shirt and begging him not to go to Spain.

'Her name's Hazel,' he said, closing his mouth in surprise.

'What's she like?'

Well, he'd said it now. And what a thrill it was to speak her name aloud! Hazel, Hazel.

'Ginger Rogers. But from Bognor.'

Jacob laughed. 'You're lucky then. I had a fiancée but . . . it wasn't to be. *For Fate with jealous eye does see Two perfect Loves, nor lets them close: Their union would her ruin be, And her tyrannic power depose.*' He pulled a piece of straw from his palliasse and put it between his teeth. 'Marvell.'

'Perhaps it's easier not to have anyone,' said Tom, though he realized as he spoke that he was wrong. Love was painful, but it was a pain you had to bear. It was a pain that meant you were alive.

The shelter felt colder that night and Tom found it difficult to sleep. His palliasse butted against the sloping timber wall, and a keen east wind blew in through the gaps. Tomorrow he'd stuff up the holes with twigs and pine leaves. He wished he'd drunk more wine; Jacob and the Derbyshire pair had downed flask after flask, and they seemed to have drifted off without any trouble. Queer the way they let you drink at the camp. It was the Spanish way, he supposed. Wine was like water.

He turned onto his back and looked at the starlight blinking through the shelter roof. Tom wondered whether it might get boring at the camp if they were stuck here for weeks. There was nothing much to do until the rifles arrived, and nothing much to write yet for the *Chronicle*. He decided that tomorrow he would write his letters home. One for Jillie – a brief note would do, she wasn't much of a reader – one for Hazel and one for his mum and dad.

Something was nagging at his brain but he couldn't pin it down. A scene at Boone Street, a conversation with his mother. No, not a conversation, an argument he'd overheard. He'd been creeping down the stairs with some papers that Bill was waiting for. His mum was agitated. *You promised you'd love him the same, Harold.* And then something about coming home to roost. What was coming home to roost? She was rambling, upset about Spain. In truth she'd become a little hysterical.

He pulled the thick blanket tighter around his body. He'd been so determined and bloody-minded before he left; there'd been no space in his mind for guilt. But now, when he thought of his mum, his conscience got the better of him. Still, there was nothing he could do about it while he was here. Best to put Boone Street out of his mind. Silently he began to list his egg collection in alphabetical order. He was asleep before he reached the jay.

23

How quiet the house was without Mrs Waite. Francine heard a *tap-tap* and listened – someone knocking at the door? – but it was only a hot-water pipe clicking in the bathroom. She sighed and drew a line of black kohl under her right eye. The skin puckered and dragged.

When her lips were done she picked up the postcard that was propped against her dressing-table mirror. It was a picture of the Grenadier Guards leaving Buckingham Palace. She turned over the card and read the message again. *Just another note to let you know we are well and happy and there is no need to worry. I will be in touch properly soon. Love, Hazel.* No mention of the letter Francine had sent, no apology for failing to meet her that Sunday at the Tate. Still, *Love* was an advance on the previous two *Regards*.

What on earth would she do with herself today? She lay the postcard down and reached into her jewellery box, tilting her head to clip on an earring. She combed her hair and arranged the curls to mask the grey strands that had begun to appear at her temples. A colour rinse would solve that: she reminded herself to speak to her hairdresser. There. At least she would be presentable if anyone should call.

Downstairs, she drifted into the kitchen. How she hated

these dark November mornings. There was a thin band of light to the east but it had a cruel edge to it, like the pale glint of marble in a cemetery.

Mrs Waite's parting gift two days earlier had been a pork casserole, *Best with mash*. There was a full sack of King Edward's in the garage, she'd added. The casserole remained untouched on the cool shelf; Francine had lifted the lid once, and the sight of the grey meat entombed in tomato-tinged fat had made her nauseous. Instead she had snacked on wrinkled apples and overripe Conference pears, thin slices of Cheddar layered on crackers. Well, she would be in London again at the weekend. Perhaps, once back with Charles, her appetite would improve.

Not that there would be a great deal of time for dining. So much to do! If Charles wasn't too busy with appointments he might come flat-hunting with her and with luck, she would be able to move by the end of the month. Francine tried to feel excited. After all, she would not be sorry to leave Aldwick; it was especially soulless during the winter, apart from the tolerable fortnight of gaiety over Christmas.

Christmas. What on earth would she do this year? Charles would be with Carolyn at their Gloucestershire house. Harriett and Jeremy would be in Highgate with their children. Happy families gathered together – she couldn't possibly impose. Paul with Adriana in Paris. She thought of Edward and immediately dismissed the idea; she would not be welcome. Her brother's life was a mystery to her. She had tried, over the years, to maintain a friendship with him. When she telephoned he would answer with a breezy 'Well, he*llo*!', delivered in high camp as if the caller might be some exotic thespian friend – Noël Coward himself, perhaps, ringing to suggest a weekend in Monte. And then she would say,

'Darling, it's Francine,' and the response would be a flat 'Oh.' His voice became dull and ordinary, and she was always sorry, because she didn't mind the camp, couldn't care two pins how he chose to live his life or whom he took as a lover. Why should it matter at all, especially now that their parents were dead? There was no family reputation to protect, no one who might disapprove.

Christmas on her own in a cheap London flat. It would be somewhere dismal, she supposed, like Shepherd's Bush or Hammersmith. East London was unthinkable and south . . . Unless she considered Barnes or Wimbledon, but really one might as well be living in the suburbs. If Paul could only get the tenants out of the Bloomsbury flat, but even when that happened he insisted the place must be sold. She'd have her share in the end, he promised, and she trusted his assurances. But right now everything was horribly uncertain.

She pictured the type of place she could afford: a cramped third-floor flat in a Georgian terrace, a shilling-in-the-slot meter and a communal hallway. Christmas Day alone with a plate of cold ham and a bottle of cheap wine chilled on a window ledge.

From the fruit bowl she took a small pear and placed it on the chopping board. Why should she spend Christmas Day alone? She had a daughter, for heaven's sake, and she would find her and they would enjoy Christmas together. She sliced into the pear and cut it into quarters, licking the sweet juices from her fingers. Yes, she would write again, and this time her letter would be more conciliatory. Of course she'd have to back down over the baby, accept that Hazel would not take the obvious route, the sensible route, and that she was determined to shackle herself to a fatherless child and end her life before it had even begun. Somehow

– she did not know how – Francine would have to swallow that and pretend in her letter to be happy for Hazel.

The next day she began to sort through the packing cases in the attic. Edward had wanted nothing to do with their dead parents' belongings. Knick-knacks, he called them. They both knew that anything of real value was long gone – sold to pay off her father's City debts. For three years Francine had tried to ignore the cases sitting up here in the box room, but now the job simply had to be done.

In one corner Francine made a pile of the few things she thought might interest the antiques dealer: a collection of paperweights; two crystal ashtrays and a bronze *pétanque* set. There was a hideous green vase that her mother had always loved – Chinese, probably – but it had been chipped years ago and the restorer had botched the repair.

The final chest contained books – a set of Shakespeare plays and various volumes of Victorian poetry. Francine decided she would keep these for the new flat: books always helped to warm a room. The chest was almost empty now. Delving between the screwed-up pages of newspaper, she pulled out a foolscap box, something she'd used to store sketches and letters when she was a girl. It had been hidden at the back of a drawer in her childhood bedroom; she must have left it behind when she went to Paris. Francine unwound the string fastener and opened the lid. There was a watercolour of the bridge at Lostwithiel and a pencil drawing of a cat. More sketches, some postcards, a programme for *A Midsummer Night's Dream*. As she leafed through the programme a small blue envelope slid out.

She unfolded the two sheets of notepaper. It was not so much a letter as a short essay, dated *August 6th 1910*. Underneath the date was an underlined title: *A Confession*. Then: *Ever since your visit last summer I have been in a kind of agony. Have you guessed?*

Had she guessed? She had suspected – hoped – but she had not been sure.

When they'd arrived that summer Charles had been his usual unwelcoming self, slouching in the hall against the yellow-striped wallpaper, scowling at his baby brother Lawrie when he toddled in tooting his little wooden whistle.

That night she had been sitting at the dressing table staring at her reflection when she saw the blue envelope slide underneath her door. She smiled as she read it, and afterwards she lay on her bed, inhaling the scent of Mrs Lassiter's roses which drifted in from the open window.

By morning she was breathless, too nervous, almost, to go down to breakfast. When she took her seat and Charles passed her the sugar caddy, her nerves stirred into a fury of excitement. As their parents discussed the news of the day – the latest on the Crippen case, the launch of the battleship *Orion* – Charles touched her thigh under the table. He let his hand rest for a moment, and she crossed her legs, trapping his fingers. Mrs Lassiter pronounced on Crippen's lover. 'She dressed as a boy, they say, but not a soul was fooled. Still, it's hard to feel sorry for any of them. The murdered wife had taken up with a lodger . . .'

'Most unsavoury,' said Francine's father, coughing into his teacup.

Lawrie dropped his bread and began to cry.

Charles smiled as Francine uncrossed her legs.

Would he be amused to see the letter, after so many years? No. It belonged to another time, a summer turned black, a tragedy they had tried so hard to forget. She refolded the paper and slipped it back inside the programme. Lostwithiel was not to be mentioned. Charles lived in the present, and she must strive always to do the same.

24

'Darling, what a beautiful coat.'

Hazel turned and saw her mother. She seemed thinner; her shoulders were swamped by a black fur stole, and her hair had been coloured. The shade was redder than her natural auburn, and it looked peculiarly harsh in the winter sunlight, set off by a mink pillbox hat to which Francine had attached a small spotted feather. She was like a creature in the zoo, an exotic animal that had somehow fetched up in the shadow of Marble Arch.

'Your hair,' said Hazel. 'It's—'

'Just a little tint.' Francine patted the waves around her ear with a gloved hand. 'Do you like it? Anyway, come here. How wonderful to see you at last. And in such a lovely ensemble.'

Hazel accepted her mother's kiss but kept her fingers tight around the handle of the pram. 'Lucia gave me the coat. She says green doesn't suit her.'

'It certainly suits you.' Francine took a slight step back and her face became very serious. 'How are you, darling?'

If she cried she would be furious with herself. She swallowed and looked away for a moment, focusing on a paper bag scudding along the gutter, and opening her eyes wide so that the cold wind could bite. 'I'm very well. I'm enjoying being back in London.'

'I'm sure. And Jasmin?' Francine looked into the pram for the first time. The baby was fast asleep with her plump chin tucked into her neck. 'Oh, that little bonnet!' said Francine. 'Adorable. My goodness, she's grown.'

'Eight months old now.'

'And is she a good baby?'

An impossible question. Jasmin cried at night because she was teething. Did that mean she wasn't good – that she was *bad*?

'Of course. She's absolutely perfect. Fast asleep as you can see – this cold air has knocked her out.'

'Jolly good,' said Francine, then added hurriedly: 'But she'll wake soon? I simply can't wait for a cuddle. Aren't you excited, her first Christmas coming up?'

Hazel thought how painful this must be for Francine, all this pretend cooing, the talk of cuddles and Christmas. She would see what it was her mother wanted and then get back to the flat.

'Let's walk into the park,' Francine suggested. 'Have you travelled far, darling? I still don't know where you're living. You *have* been a dark horse.'

Hazel relaxed her grip on the pram handle as they crossed into Hyde Park. Her mother seemed so harmless: diminished, somehow, with her garish hair and winter-pale cheeks.

'It's a garden flat in Kensington. Just off the High Street.'

'The chances!' said Francine. Her voice was shrill and an elderly woman walking ahead turned to look.

'Chances of what?' Hazel stopped, a ripple of alarm spreading through her body.

'We're almost neighbours. My new flat. It's in Earls Court

– the Kensington side. It must be only a short walk from you. *Quelle coincidence*. To think we came all the way to Marble Arch!'

Hazel couldn't look at her mother. Instead she stared into the pram and saw that Jasmin's eyes had flicked open. Francine's shriek had probably woken her, and now her nose was screwing up and she was about to cry.

'I didn't know you were moving.'

'Your father insists the Aldwick house must be rented. Holidaymakers, seaside breaks, you know? So I found a little flat, for the winter months at least. I picked up the keys just yesterday. There's an awful lot of building work going on at the exhibition hall but I'm told that will finish soon.' She nodded towards Jasmin. 'Oh, the sweetheart. Has something upset her? Look at that, she has your colouring. Pale one minute, puce the next.'

They walked quickly towards a bench under a willow tree. Hazel lifted Jasmin from the pram and her cry quietened as she blinked into the sunlight, reaching a tiny hand towards the swaying canopy of thin branches.

'Did you want to hold her?'

Francine sat down and tossed one end of the stole over her shoulder. 'Of course,' she said, patting her lap. 'Pop her here.'

Wind rushed through the branches, and for a moment Hazel hesitated. She watched a dead leaf spin down from the willow. Francine had done everything she could to obliterate Jasmin from their lives. The appointment in Tavistock Square, the hideous Dr Cutler with her white coat and her weasel words, telling her it would be the work of a moment and no one would feel a thing . . . And later, when Hazel was with Jasmin at the Misses Shaw, Francine had made a point of ignoring her granddaughter. She would bring a green apple and a magazine for Hazel, and disappear after twenty minutes with the excuse of a headache, or a haberdashery order that needed urgent collection, or a train she simply couldn't miss.

Jasmin's breath was warm on her neck. Months had passed since that time – it was possible that her mother had had a genuine change of heart. What was the point in agreeing to the meeting if she wasn't willing to give her a chance? Hazel bent down and put Jasmin on Francine's lap. Jasmin squirmed, turning and reaching up towards the black stole. She grabbed a handful of fur and tugged.

'She's strong,' said Francine. Jasmin smiled and babbled, 'Mamama.' 'And she's speaking already?'

'Not really.'

'But almost. You were a very early talker, darling. *Duck*, at seven months old. Nanny Felix was ever so impressed. You had a duck in the bath every night, you see, painted white with a yellow beak. A present from your uncle Edward. Probably the only present he ever sent . . .' Francine lifted Jasmin upright so that their faces were level and Jasmin's legs bounced down on her grandmother's thighs. Jasmin smiled again, her bottom lip glossed with dribble. 'Two teeth! I expect the nights are hellish?'

'I bought some teething powders.'

'Nanny Felix was all for a tot of brandy but your father wouldn't have it. He was ever so good with you, pacing up and down when Nanny needed a rest. I just didn't seem to have the knack. Does Lucia help out, darling, when the nights are bad?'

'She's marvellous.'

'It's very good of her, I must say. And you plan to stay with Lucia?'

'Of course.'

'Well, now we're neighbours I shall be able to give you a little break every so often. Yes, I shall, shan't I?' She addressed this last sentence to Jasmin, speaking in a girlish baby voice and planting a kiss on her cheek.

Hazel began to cough. She took a packet of cigarettes from her bag.

Francine raised her eyebrows. 'A smoker, now?' She laughed and shrugged her shoulders. 'Perhaps you wouldn't mind sharing? I left my cigarette case at Charles's.' She stood up and settled Jasmin back into the pram, tucking the crocheted blanket around her. Jasmin grabbed at the blanket, poking her fingers through the holes. 'What a sight we shall be, smoking together on a park bench like navvies!'

Hazel lit her mother's cigarette, then her own. Smoke mingled with the icy air, sharp at the back of her throat. Charles was still around, then. She would not have her mother turning up at the flat, calling in whenever she felt like it. Her mother and Charles. There would need to be some kind of arrangement. A regular date. Francine wouldn't like that, she'd say it was a bore, she liked spontaneity, not timetables. But that was too bad. If she wanted to make amends it would have to be on Hazel's terms.

Jasmin began to cry again, arching her back and kicking off the blanket. She would be getting hungry. Hazel looked in the bottom of the pram for the rusks and the cup of milk, but the bag wasn't there. She must have left it on the kitchen table in her hurry to leave the flat.

Francine took a drag from her cigarette and then balanced it on the arm of the bench. 'I almost forgot,' she said, blowing the smoke in a thin plume as she reached into her handbag. She pulled out a tarnished silver rattle and jangled it. 'Sorry it's not polished,' she said. 'I had to let Mrs Waite go, you see. I searched everywhere for the silver cloth but . . . anyway, I thought baby might like this.' Francine leaned across to the pram, shaking the rattle, and Jasmin quietened at the sound of the tiny bell. 'I finally unpacked the cases from your grandparents. I believe this belonged to my mother, and then to me. An heirloom!'

Jasmin reached out and drew the rattle towards her mouth, grazing it with her two bottom teeth. Francine smiled and let go of the handle.

'The tarnish,' said Hazel. Jasmin was gnawing at the rattle as if it were an apple. 'It might make her ill.'

'Oh, you mustn't fuss about that. You'll turn into one of those over-protective mothers. I gather that's all the rage, nowadays. Too much attention is not good for children.'

Hazel dropped the cigarette and stepped on the end with the sole of her boot. So her mother was an expert on babies now? She took a deep breath and stifled a cough. 'It's time I left,' she said. 'Jasmin will want her lunch soon.'

'You're walking back to Kensington?'

Hazel nodded.

'I'd go with you but I promised to meet Charles at Pagani's. Unless you'd like to join us, of course, but I'm not sure –' she waved in the direction of the pram – 'whether they welcome babies.'

There was a pause, a chill between them. A black Labrador bounded up to the willow and began to bark at a squirrel.

'And what about you?' asked Hazel. 'What's your view on babies now?'

'Please, Hazel. Don't use that abrasive tone. We had enough of that—'

'I'm curious, that's all. Why the change of heart?'

'Darling, I just want us to be friends. It's not been easy for me. Have you stopped to think how I've felt, not knowing where you were or what you were doing? Running away like that with Jasmin. The Shaw women were frantic, and as for the poor couple, I'm told it was a terrible shock for them.'

'Doubtless they've found another baby to adopt. An unwanted baby.' Hazel kicked the brake off the pram wheels. It had been a mistake to come. She had been weak and stupid to answer her mother's letter.

'Darling, please wait.' Francine rushed towards her and held on to the pram hood so that Hazel had no choice but to stop. 'I'm so sorry, I didn't mean to upset you. You did what you had to do, I understand that. At least, I'm trying to understand, I really am. And now I've seen Jasmin again, well, she really is marvellous. I'm proud of you, Hazel, truly. I'm proud of you and I'm proud of my . . . my granddaughter.'

Hazel tried to speak, but a sob rose in her chest with such force that she could not hold it down. Francine embraced her, and Hazel cried into her mother's shoulder until the fur stole was spiked wet with tears.

Jasmin shook the rattle. The wind had dropped away, and the silver bell chimed in the wintry air.

'It's definitely true,' said Lucia. 'He married her in Germany. In Herr Goebbels's drawing room. And it was weeks ago. Just after the Cable Street fiasco.'

Lucia flopped onto the sofa, disconsolate. They had all heard the whispers, but Hazel still wasn't sure whether to believe the story. It didn't matter to her in any case. Lucia was the one who had harboured dreams of being seduced by Sir Oswald and becoming the next Lady Mosley. He was an incorrigible philanderer, everyone knew that, so it wasn't too far-fetched to imagine his eye might fall on a loyal blackshirt girl who was devoting her life to the cause.

'Of course Diana Guinness is terrifically rich, and well connected in Germany,' Lucia sighed.

'Not forgetting her intelligence and dazzling beauty,' said Hazel.

Lucia turned her head sharply. 'Meaning?'

'Meaning nothing.' Hazel tried to laugh but she could see that Lucia had somehow taken offence.

'Philip is forever telling me how beautiful I am,' she said, tipping up her chin with her forefinger. 'And I like to think I have a reasonable intellect.'

Hazel had not yet met Lucia's lover. Philip was a married economist who was an adviser at HQ; he had taken Lucia to nightclubs in Soho which Sir Oswald frequented, and Lucia freely admitted that she spent those evenings trying to catch O.M.'s eye. Once, he had asked her to dance, and pronounced her a 'handsome filly' as she rejoined Philip at his table.

'Of course you are . . . and you do. You're as good as Diana Guinness any day. But if it's true, why are they being so secretive?'

'He doesn't want the press finding out. Diana is very private. If I married Sir Oswald I'd be yelling from the rooftops. Just imagine.' She pushed off her heels and lay back on the sofa. There was still an edge to her voice: it would probably last for the whole evening. 'Get me a cup of tea, would you? I'm shattered. Any thoughts about dinner?'

'You're in tonight?'

She nodded. 'Philip's back in Surrey with the family.'

'There's ham. I could make omelettes, once Jasmin is in bed.'

'Omelettes, yes.' Lucia turned to look at the baby. She was sitting on the rug in front of the fire, playing with the rattle. 'That's a very tinkly toy,' she said. 'It's going right through me. I barely slept last night.'

'It was a gift from my mother.'

'You've seen your mother?' Lucia propped herself on an elbow and frowned. 'You didn't say.'

'I wasn't sure I would be seeing her. I dithered until the last minute.'

'And?'

'We had a walk around Hyde Park. It was bearable. Civilized.'

Lucia was silent for a moment, then her voice softened. 'Please don't tell me you're going back to Sussex? I couldn't possibly live here without you.'

'Of course not. Mother has left Sussex, in any case. She's back in London. Earls Court.'

'So close?' Lucia rolled her eyes. 'She won't interfere, will she, Hazel? I'm surprised you'll have anything to do with her. You said she was demented.'

Had she said that? Yes, she remembered telling Lucia about the scene in the clinic, Francine's refusal to accept that Hazel could possibly want to keep her baby. 'I think she's calmed down. Got used to the idea, I suppose.'

'So long as you're not planning to desert me.' Lucia twisted the ring on her finger. 'We're a good team, aren't we? I couldn't manage without you.'

'I'm not deserting you, Lucia. Where on earth would I go?'

'Quite.' She shivered and rubbed her eyes, child-like, with

the heels of her hands. 'Now be an angel and turn up the fire.'

The kettle took an age to boil. When Hazel carried the tea tray through to the sitting room, Jasmin had crawled closer to the electric fire. Her cheeks were flaming pink and her arm was stretched out towards the metal casing, almost touching the bars. Hazel dropped the tray onto the table, the cups skidding off their saucers as she grabbed Jasmin clear.

Lucia's eyes flew open and she put her hand to her forehead.

'Goodness,' she said. 'I must have dozed off.'

The Saturday post brought a third letter from Tom. The previous two had been short and factual; friendly but not familiar. He made life in Spain sound like an enjoyable adventure, describing the everyday things – the food and the friendships, the strange birds and the scenery. He was still at a training camp, learning drills and tactics. Hazel had responded with similarly light-hearted replies, trying to make something interesting of her life so that he would not be bored. She told him amusing stories about uptight Mr Boyne the office manager, whose right ear turned scarlet when his in-tray filled up, or the girls at work, pretending she had been out to the cinema or to dances with them. Some nights she dreamed she *was* that unfettered person, and when she woke to Jasmin's crying, the familiar dread dropped like a stone in her stomach.

Hazel stood in the cold hallway holding Tom's letter, aware of its weight in her hand. It felt different from the other letters. Heavier. Carefully she opened the envelope. There were three sheets of notepaper; his handwriting wasn't neat and stilted as it had been before, but slanted across the page in hurried rows. She drifted into the kitchen and began to read.

Dearest Hazel,

Your letter was wonderful but it made me melancholy. Perhaps I will regret replying in haste, but you would be surprised how little there is to do out here, and that is why I have time to think and write. Truth is, I think about you more than I should, Hazel. I picture you at the cinema with your friends, or at the Saturday dance, and I'm ashamed to say I feel envious to imagine those men lucky enough to be close to you, to hold you in their arms as I once did. I know I shouldn't press you, Hazel, but I cannot rest until I know your thoughts. This politeness is all well and good but how do you feel about our – what to call it – our courtship? Were we too young, too rash, is that why you chose not to keep in touch? Yet you wrote again after a year, but when we met at St Paul's you seemed ill at ease. Tell me, did I do something wrong? If it's some silly thing, easily mended, please, please let me know and I can put it right.

Maybe this life in Spain is getting to me. I told you about Jacob, didn't I? Chap loves to spout poetry, he must be turning me into a romantic. Not that I need much prompting when it comes to you, Hazel. I only have to think of that first time I saw you – <u>half</u> saw you. But even in the dark I knew you were knockout. It still amazes me, how brave you were to talk to the stranger crouching on your garden wall in his pyjamas. I must have looked a prize idiot, but what a sight for sore eyes you were, standing there, smoking *your cigarette! I'm getting back into the habit over here, by the way. Not that there's much tobacco about, but what we do have we roll into twig-thin smokes and we count ourselves lucky.*

More than anything, I want to see you. I'd come home to London if I could but it's impossible. Deserters are liable to be shot and in any case, I've no intention of deserting. Things might be quiet right now but battle plans are being drawn up. There's talk of something big. We hear such stories about the fascists, pure evil. I believe I should be here, I believe it with every bone in my body . . . but now I'm on to politics and that won't do. It's an odd thing between us, isn't it? But we mustn't let politics divide us. I want to know what's in your heart.

I suppose I should tear up this letter and throw it onto the fire that I'm huddled around. It's getting very cold here now. This morning we woke to a fall of snow.

No, I won't tear anything up. I'll seal this and give it to the clerk. Because really I have nothing to lose. I love you.

Tom

She dragged her eyes from the last page and stared beyond the kitchen window. The rowan tree was rimed with frost, berries red as blood. Tom's words sang in her mind, lifted her heart, and yet her heart could not stay lifted: there was always the answering plunge of despair. How much could she tell him, truly? She wanted to be honest, but to be too honest was to risk losing him completely.

'Is there tea?'

She hadn't heard Lucia come in. Clumsily she folded the letter and shoved it in her skirt pocket. 'I'll make a fresh pot.'

'Heavens, that must have been exciting post. You're bright red!'

'What? Oh, nothing that interesting.'

Lucia sidled up, took her hand from her dressing-gown pocket and tugged one of Hazel's curls, teasing it straight. 'Come on, tell all.'

For once Hazel was happy to hear Jasmin's yell. She jumped up from the chair. 'Honestly, it's just a letter from a cousin. Boring. Sorry, you'll have to make your own tea.'

25

Bea preferred not to go into town when the weather was so wicked, but she couldn't let her branch down. The Christmas bazaar depended on the goodwill of women from the districts, and Lewisham had been tasked with providing items for the knitwear stall. She had been knitting circle-and-flash tea cosies for weeks.

The rain was icy, and the fierce wind meant there was absolutely no point battling with an umbrella. By the time she arrived at Great Smith Street her coat was soaked through and the damp had seeped into her shoes and stockings.

A haughty girl brandishing a clipboard let her in – Bea recognized her from the summer camp and from HQ meetings where she sometimes gave an address. She stared at Bea as if to say, *Look what the cat dragged in*, then took her name and directed her to the cloakroom where she could hang her coat. 'Try not to drip on the parquet,' said the girl. 'We wouldn't want the wood to warp.'

The knitwear stall turned out to be over-staffed, and Bea was asked to help in the kitchen because the leader in charge of refreshments had been taken ill. Bea would have preferred to stay in the main hall, amongst the hubbub of the stalls, but there it was, she couldn't very well refuse.

The haughty girl introduced her to the other kitchen helpers. 'Eleanor, Alexia – this is Mrs Smart. Oh, let's not be so formal. What's your Christian name, Mrs Smart?'

Bea bridled, but tried not to show it; she could be modern, if pushed. 'Beatrice. Bea.'

'Bea. You'll be handy with a dishcloth, won't you, Bea?'

'I've had plenty of experience if that's what you mean.'

'Wonderful. Here's Hazel now.' A blonde girl came out of a storeroom carrying a large pat of butter. 'Hazel, this is Bea.'

Bea looked at the young girls – not one of them more than twenty years old. They seemed the types who'd never washed up a breakfast bowl in their lives, let alone laid on teas for a Christmas bazaar. It was just as well she'd been drafted in.

The clipboard girl – Lucia, she was called – strode off and the one with the butter went back into the storeroom to find a spare apron. Bea realized she'd forgotten their names already. Lucia had thrown her with the Christian-name carry-on.

'You'll have to remind me of your name again,' she said to the blonde girl as she came out of the storeroom.

'Hazel,' she said, handing over the apron.

Hazel. It struck her, then. Hazel wasn't a common name. Bea tied the apron strings and tried not to stare.

By six the bazaar was closed and they had almost finished clearing away. Bea was terribly tired but her heart felt glad as she swept the kitchen floor. Hazel was the girl from Tom's unsent letter, she was sure of it. She was a pretty young thing, and although her face was pale she had a lovely smile. Best of all she'd turned out to be a good little worker, unlike Alexia who'd twice pleaded stomach pains and had disappeared into the cloakrooms just as the queue was at its peak.

Yes, this must be the Hazel that Tom had fallen for. *The most beautiful girl in Aldwick.* Bea found it funny to think she'd had her down as a communist, a communist who'd lured Tom away from the blackshirts, when all along she was one of the party faithful. A member of the women's drum corps, no less.

They'd had a very nice chat at the sink earlier on. Bea washed, Hazel dried. It was an easy way to talk – eyes on the job, a steady rhythm between them as they ploughed through the piles of dull green crockery.

'You're from London?' asked Bea.

'Originally, but we moved to Sussex. And now I'm back in London again.'

At this Bea felt a twist of excitement. She *was* from Sussex, then.

'I was down in Sussex the summer of last year,' Bea said. 'For the blackshirt camp. Near Bognor?'

Hazel paused for a moment, her tea towel wedged into a cup. 'Aldwick Bay. I used to live there.'

'Smashing spot. Perhaps it was your family that came up with the idea, invited Sir Oswald down?'

Hazel gave a short laugh. 'Oh, no. My family aren't supporters. I went to Sir Oswald's talk at the theatre, sort of by accident, and that's how I met Lucia.'

Bea was tempted to mention Tom. She could simply say that her son had talked of a girl called Hazel, and might she by any chance know him? But something had gone on between Hazel and Tom – that was clear from his letter. She'd let him down in some way, for whatever reason, and it might embarrass Hazel if she brought his name into the conversation. Better to keep quiet for now, she sensed, and wait for the right moment.

'So your family has moved back to London?'

Again Hazel hesitated. For all her pleasantness, there was something guarded about her manner. 'I share a flat with Lucia,' she said.

Ah. Bea couldn't help feeling surprised. Hazel was young to be living away from home, sharing a flat with another girl. Perhaps she'd fallen out with her family – they may have disagreed over her politics. There were plenty of families split in that way. Mrs Beggs's brother, a diehard trade-union man, hadn't spoken to his sister in over two years.

'That must be great fun,' said Bea, dunking a sticky plate in the water.

'Yes,' said Hazel quietly.

'And I expect you have a sweetheart?'

'No . . . not at present.'

Hazel pulled a plate from the draining rack and Bea turned to look sideways at the girl. It was unmistakable. There were tears in her eyes, and she was blinking them back as fast as she could, but it was no use because a great fat one had already dropped onto her cheek.

She was a lost soul, poor thing. Bea wished she could do something to help. But it was unlikely they'd meet again soon, not unless Bea joined the drum corps or started coming up to HQ more often. Neither option appealed. But she knew she must somehow stay in touch with Hazel. It was clear to her now that there had been a mix-up or a misunderstanding between Hazel and Tom. She seemed too sweet and sincere to have let him down purposely. Perhaps she, Bea, could set things right between them. It was just a case of treading gently. Smoothing the way, without interfering. What had he written? *If you would only explain, then at least*

I could understand. She could try to understand on his behalf. And then, tactfully, she could let Tom know.

Bea put the broom back into the store cupboard and untied her apron. Now that the idea had taken root, she felt happier than she had since October when Tom announced he was leaving. Surely he'd come back from Spain if he thought Hazel was waiting for him? The winter was getting cold out there, and although she tried to avoid all news of Spain, it seemed the Republicans were struggling. He stayed cheery in his letters, of course, just as Jack had when he wrote from Flanders.

In the kitchen Lucia was holding court, her posh voice echoing off the scrubbed white tiles.

'Takings for the refreshments are good,' she said, clanking coins in a canvas money bag. 'Up on last year. Bric-a-brac is down. Overall a success, but did you see those women haggling over the prices?' She sighed and wrinkled her nose.

'Did somebody let the Semites in?' said Eleanor.

Alexia snorted. 'I thought there was a strange smell at one point. Blasted cheek, coming here.'

Bea flinched. She thought of Mr Perlman and the two frightened children, great-nieces of his late wife, who had arrived from Germany the previous weekend.

'Quite,' said Lucia. 'But apart from that unpleasantness, it was an excellent afternoon. Well done, ladies.' Lucia leaned towards the girls. 'See you on Wednesday evening for envelope duty?'

'Envelope duty?' asked Bea.

'Oh, just a little gathering at my flat,' she said with an airy wave of her hand that made it clear Bea was not included. 'Stacks of members' Christmas cards to address.'

'I'm happy to help,' said Bea.

'You?' Lucia looked at her as if she doubted her ability to write.

Hazel broke the silence. Her cheeks had pinked – at least she had the decency to feel embarrassed, thought Bea. 'That's very kind, don't you think, Lucia?' said Hazel. 'Many hands and all that.'

'Yes, I suppose an extra pair of hands . . . It's Kensington, though. You're from the districts, I gather?'

'I can find my way around town, dear.'

'Of course. We'll look forward to seeing you.'

It was a pig of a journey but she arrived in good time. The flat was on the ground floor of a mansion block, just off High Street Ken, a nice part of town. Bea rang the polished brass bell for Flat 1, and stood waiting on the chilly doorstep for half a minute. She was about to ring again when the door was opened by Hazel, dressed in a velvet evening gown with a green silk corsage pinned to the collar. One half of her hair was styled and curled, the other half frizzed in all directions. A cigarette dangled from her left hand.

'Bea,' she said. 'Please come on through. I'm sorry I look such a sight.'

'Not at all. That's a lovely dress.'

She wondered why Hazel was dolled up, and why her nerves seemed jangly, but there was no need to ask because Hazel began to gabble, all the while standing at the hall mirror fiddling with the corsage between puffs of her cigarette.

'I got completely muddled with my dates,' said Hazel. 'My mother's coming in half an hour. She's taking me to dinner, so I can't help with the envelopes after all. Thank goodness you volunteered. I don't have to feel so guilty.'

Oh, glory, thought Bea. The whole point of the exercise was to get to know Hazel better. Now she was going to be stuck for the evening with Lucia and the other two.

'Not to worry,' she said. 'I suppose you can't let your mother down.'

Hazel smiled and showed Bea into the living room. The girls were sitting at a table where cards and envelopes were stacked in a dozen or more piles. 'Here's Bea, good as her word,' said Hazel. 'Got the hair irons on in the bedroom. Must go.'

Bea took off her headscarf and unbuttoned her coat. No one offered to take her things, and so she laid them on the arm of a settee. She noticed something silver wedged under a cushion. A baby's rattle? Queer.

With her stockinged foot, Lucia nudged out a chair from under the table. 'Do take a seat,' she said. 'We're drawing up a system. You can be R to Z.'

Bea felt in her bag for her fountain pen, marvelling at the manners of these supposedly well-bred girls. She hadn't even been offered a cup of tea. Still, she was here now, and she'd have to get on with the job in hand. At least it was warm in the room, with the heavy brocade curtains drawn and all the bars glowing on the electric fire. Unscrewing her pen lid, she took her section of the list and began to copy out the first address. She was proud of her handwriting – it was better than Alexia's untidy scribble – but then a loud bell sounded and her pen jumped with the surprise, splodging a blob of ink directly on the H of Hillingdon. She reached for the blotting paper.

'The door again!' said Lucia. 'Hazel's mother must be early. Alexia, can you let the witch in?'

Bea's back was to the living-room door. She twisted around

in her seat, ready to smile at the woman as she walked into the room. *The witch.* There was a man beside her. The ceiling light was bright, and the table lamp was burning. There could be no mistaking this couple. Immediately she turned away, staring back down at the envelope, pressing the blotting paper onto the smudge of black ink and praying that Lucia would not suddenly remember her manners and introduce Bea to the visitors.

'Mrs Alexander, how lovely to meet you,' said Lucia. 'Hazel won't be a moment.'

'You must be Lucia?' said the witch. She pronounced it *Looseeya.*

'It's Lucia, actually,' she said. '*Ch.* Italian.'

'Very well.' She sniffed. 'Please don't let us interrupt anything. Just that I thought if I were a little early I might see Jasmin.'

Bea's cheeks blazed. Jasmin? Who might Jasmin be? She wanted to look around the room again – had she missed someone? – but she kept her eyes fixed downwards, her fingers firm on the blotting paper.

'She's fast asleep,' said Lucia. 'I doubt Hazel will want to wake her. Oh, here she is now. Your mother's arrived, with—'

'Charles. Charles Lassiter,' said the man. His heels clicked on the floor as he stepped forward. 'Charmed to meet you, the mysterious Lucia.'

Bea's spine stiffened. She realized she was holding her breath and she exhaled, quietly, quietly, praying again that no one would notice her. This prayer, at least, was answered.

Sleep was impossible. Harold was dozing, sick with a winter bug, a fever that wouldn't go away. He slept on his side without his pyjama top, the skin loose and wrinkled on his back, and she could feel the heat from him creeping along the sheets. In the early hours she slipped out of bed and wandered onto the landing. There was no sound but the slow whirr of the meter wheel in the cupboard. She wished for something shocking and sharp: spears of rain attacking the windowpane; a cat fight; even a dog whining to show that she was not the only creature awake and suffering. It was a cold night but her skin was burning hot. Perhaps she was catching Harold's bug. She would get into Tom's bed. The linen was freshly made up; the sheets would be cool.

There was a time when the memory of Charles was something to savour, a treat Bea might allow herself on those long afternoons when Tom was at school and Harold was working at the factory.

To see Charles again, to be in that warm room with him – it was too much to take in. He looked a little older, of course – the fair hair had darkened, and his skin was weathered – but in essence he was unchanged. Had he noticed her, sitting at the table, gripping her fountain pen so hard that her thumbnail scored the barrel? No, he wouldn't have noticed her, same as he hadn't noticed her in the Aldwick pub, and even if he had he wouldn't recognize her because she looked decades older – transformed into a dumpy sack of a woman whose long shiny hair had become an unkempt bob flecked with suet-grey strands.

Tom's sheets were too hot now. Hot and damp and heavy. She tiptoed downstairs and into the front room. On the mantelshelf was the photograph from Margate – Tom in the middle holding their hands, the wind blowing his fringe across his eyes.

Next to Margate was the snap taken by a street photographer in Greenwich: Harold with his arm draped around her shoulder, a few months after he'd been sent home from the war. They were standing near the river, a barge drifting behind them. They looked happy, and she supposed they were, in a cautious kind of way. Harold's injury was a terrible pity but they were making the best of it. Bea felt she could manage without the act itself, and in any case they could still be close: a kiss and a cuddle and other things she'd never known about in their newly-wed days.

What she couldn't manage was the thought that she'd never be a mother, and it was worse to bear because she'd once come so close, the summer of 1914. Perhaps it was the shock of the war being declared, the worry that Harold or her brother might have to fight, that led to the disaster. The poor scrap was born four months early. She'd caught a glimpse of its tiny body as the doctor wrapped it in muslin and hurried out of the bedroom door. 'A boy or a girl?' she asked the doctor when he came back into the room empty-handed. 'Best not to ask,' he answered. 'Least said soonest mended.' Oh, how she wished that were true.

Later, when Harold was called up, they convinced themselves that losing the baby was a blessing in disguise. All those mothers around the world, driven half-mad trying to cope single-handed. It was hard on the kiddies without their dads around. No, there was plenty of time to start their family after the war. It would happen eventually.

Harold never saw the front line because of his poor eyesight. They had him working as an orderly at a military hospital near Rouen. He wrote letters from his dorm in an old chateau. There were some terrible goings-on, he said, but weren't they lucky that he was safe here, miles behind the line, though often you'd feel the ground shake with the shelling.

Meanwhile Jack was in the thick of it, a gunner in the Royal West Kents. From his postcards you'd think he was on a jolly to Brighton. Bea knew the forced cheeriness meant things were really bad, because Jack was a serious boy in truth. He wasn't given to daft jokes.

Their parents were both dead and Jack wasn't married, so Bea was down as next of kin for her brother as well as for Harold. That meant double dread when she heard next door's terrier barking: the signal that the postman was on his way.

The first letter was typewritten and signed by Jack's C.O. *It is with the deepest regret that I have to inform you . . .* Poor, poor Jack – the sweetest baby brother. Eyes the colour of lightest amber, dimples to melt your heart. She felt the grief might end her. There was only one way of coping, she discovered, and that was to pretend it wasn't true. She collected Jack's things from his Catford lodging house and stored them under the spare bed, ready for the revelation – the stories weren't unknown – that the C.O. had got it wrong, mixed up the identity discs in the chaos of battle.

And then came the telegram. Harold had been injured and he was on his way to a hospital in England. Bea sat on the bottom stair and cried. The injury was grave, they said, but his life was not in danger.

It was not until he came home, just before Christmas 1916, that Harold was able to explain. A patient in the hospital, a young Frenchman, had taken against Harold, something to do with a sleeping draught and Harold not fetching a nurse quick enough, and the patient had somehow hidden a knife beneath his sheets. When Harold came up to his bed to take away a screen, the Frenchman attacked him with the knife, plunged it right into Harold's groin and another cut down his thigh. The patient stabbed himself next, straight through the heart, which finished the job at least, said Harold, because if he hadn't done himself in, it would have been the firing squad.

Bea replaced the Greenwich photograph and went into the kitchen to drink a glass of milk. Moonlight fell through the window onto the table. There was her purse, the coins for the milkman stacked neatly beside it. The old magazine advertisement was still hidden inside, behind a sewn-up tear in the purse lining. *Wives of Wounded Soldiers: Discreet Fertility Service Offered.* She had cut the advert out with kitchen scissors and kept it under the cutlery tray for weeks. Eventually she found the courage to show Harold. He scanned the clipping, then handed it back in silence. 'Is it worth writing off?' she asked. He said he wouldn't object, if it was what she wanted. And so it began.

'Charles Lassiter' was the name he'd given to Lucia. Bea had known him only as Charles. She'd asked the woman who ran the clinic, Dr Cutler, whether it would be possible to arrange a prior meeting, just so that she might have some knowledge of the man before the meeting proper. Dr Cutler said it wasn't usual, and frankly it was inadvisable, but not to worry because she had no doubt that Mrs Smart would find Charles charming, courteous and utterly alive to the sensitive nature of the situation.

They arranged to rendezvous outside a small hotel in Bloomsbury, a short walk from Russell Square station. He would be wearing a red-and-white polka-dot handkerchief in his jacket pocket, Dr Cutler said, and a homburg hat. Bea's heart reared up when she turned the corner into Bedford

Place and saw a young man in a homburg leaning against the hotel's iron railings. It had to be him. He turned to look at her, tipped his hat, and then it was too late to change her mind.

They shook hands and she smelt a drift of citrus-scented cologne. 'Charmed to meet you, Mrs Smart,' he said, as the concierge held open the door into the lobby. They went into the bar, and to her surprise no one took any notice of them. She thought she would be shown up in her home-sewn evening dress, but it wasn't such a flashy place after all, and of course the war had kept everyone to a certain level. She had her mother's necklace, at least, and the moonstone earrings that Harold had brought back from France, wrapped in a twist of soot-blackened newspaper. Her long hair was piled into a bun, and her dress was laced at the back, pulled tight against her curves. Perhaps it was even possible that Charles found her attractive.

A port and lemon was what she'd normally have, but when he suggested gin and vermouth, she nodded and said that would be lovely. He chatted about his travels in Europe, and the war, and how it might be over soon, now the Americans were in. His manner was gentlemanly, almost condescending, yet she was certain he was younger than her, twenty-six or twenty-seven, perhaps. Bea wondered why he wasn't fighting and Charles must have read her thoughts, because he briefly mentioned something about war work – an administrative role, he said. Rather confidential. Never once did he ask a question about her own life. That was part of the understanding, and she was glad of it.

The room was on the second floor. She was breathless when they reached the top of the stairs, her blood rushing with the gin and the strangeness of the evening. He unlocked the door and pushed it wide. When Bea hesitated he smiled: a kind, encouraging smile. She met his eyes and stepped over the threshold.

Quickly she glanced around, taking in the large bed with its cream embroidered linen, the vase of long-stemmed lilies in front of the fireplace, the silver ice bucket in which stood a bottle of uncorked wine.

'I took the liberty,' said Charles. 'Trebbiano?'

She felt tipsy already yet she nodded, hopeful that one more drink would offer the courage she needed. He poured two glasses and handed one to her. Bea stepped towards the window. He followed and stood at her side, parting the delicate lace curtains to reveal a tall chestnut tree that filled the hotel garden. The branches were so close to the window, it was almost possible to reach out and touch the May blossom. Bea's eyes were drawn to the pink flush at the base of the ivory petals. Such pretty flowers; she had never noticed their beauty before.

She took a sip of wine. 'Spring is my favourite season,' she said.

Charles made no reply, and she knew that the time for talking was over.

Afterwards, they had lain in the bed for almost an hour. Charles put two pillows under her thighs. 'Tried and tested,' he explained, 'Helps the fellows on their journey.' She blushed at the reminder that this was something Charles had done goodness knows how many times before. It hadn't felt like that, earlier. It had felt as though they were truly intimate. The way he had touched and kissed her . . . it had been all she could manage not to cry out. If this was an act he was a terrific actor, and she did not regret one penny of the ten pounds she had paid to Dr Cutler.

She sat up and drank the last of her wine. Charles reached out and touched the lobe of her ear. 'Beautiful earrings,' he said. 'French?'

Bea nodded. 'My husband brought them back—' She blushed again and bit her lip. It seemed wrong to have mentioned Harold, yet after all he was the reason they were here. She pictured him for a moment, sitting at home with a glass of Watney's and the evening paper, trying to ignore the ticking of the clock.

'Well, your husband is a lucky man,' said Charles. 'And I have no doubt that you would make the most wonderful mother. Here's hoping, eh?'

She nodded, and felt her throat swell with emotion. A baby. Please God, a baby. It was likely, surely, after all Dr Cutler's talk of dates and optimum times, her temperatures and her charts. Everything had been so precise.

Bea tore open the purse lining and took the advert from its hiding place. She'd kept it all these years, just in case, but in the event she'd never dared to suggest a second visit; a brother or a sister for Tom. Standing over the sink, she lit a match and touched the flame to the corner. The paper burned yellow, a sudden star tilting at the moonlight, fading quickly and fluttering to ash.

It was too awful to contemplate, the thought of Tom getting involved with Hazel's family and finding himself in a room with Charles. Lucia had gossiped that Mrs Alexander was going through divorce proceedings. Charles was the woman's beau. It wasn't fanciful to imagine he might become Hazel's stepfather.

In the morning she would write to Tom. She'd mention in passing the bazaar, and the envelope night, how she'd got to know a few of the blackshirt girls, and that all those rumours of loose morals amongst the young women at HQ were certainly true. She composed the sentences in her head: *A girl called Hazel Alexander is the most notorious. She's carrying on with a district commander (married), and by all accounts there are two other poor unfortunates dancing to her tune . . .*

That should do it. Any fond thoughts he might still have of Hazel would be well and truly squashed. It was harsh but it was necessary. Especially if, as she suspected, the girl had a baby and goodness only knew about the parentage.

She was sorry for Hazel, really she was. But as she rinsed the ashes down the plughole, she whispered, 'It must not happen.' Tom and Charles must never meet.

If that meant leaving the movement, well, she would leave.

Whatever it took to protect her boy, that is what she would do.

26

'Take cover!'

Armistead's shout echoed in Tom's ears as he flung his body flat to the hillside. Take cover – what a bloody joke that was. How was a scraggy olive tree going to protect him from Franco's machine-gun fire? Their own machine guns were useless – he cursed again to think of whoever it was who'd loaded the cartridge belts with the wrong ammunition. Six hours they'd been on this ridge, attempting an advance. Every time they moved a few yards down into the valley, they lost another ten or twelve men. Three men for every yard, he reckoned. He'd tried to help his comrades, dragged one lad behind a blackened bush and gave him water, but the blood pooled in a red halo, and his eyes closed before he could even swallow. There was no saving him.

Yet Tom had survived this far. Jacob too, and now night was falling and Armistead told the company to dig in. It was February and the ground was hard, but they made a foxhole of sorts and collapsed, back to back, hugging their legs, resting their foreheads on their knees.

Jacob's voice had dulled. There was no longer any humour in it, no lines of poetry. 'Wrong bloody bullets,' said Jacob.

Tom could feel the back of Jacob's head, slowly shaking from side to side. 'Wrong bullets.'

'We'll be all right,' said Tom. 'New ammunition's on its way. Reinforcements.'

''S'good . . .' His voice tailed into sleep.

The valley was almost silent, just the occasional sniper shot into the darkness and the faint sound of the Jarama river rushing below. Tom screwed his eyelids shut. This was what he'd wanted, wasn't it? Proper action, a real show? He'd been desperate to get out of the training camp. They'd spent too long there, long enough for those letters to arrive. Long enough for Hazel to make a fool of him once more.

He should never have written that daft declaration of love. Oh, she'd replied quicker than he could have hoped, and she swore she loved him too. There were complications, she said, but she would explain everything once he was home. Complications? Wasn't everything that was worth fighting for bound to be complicated? They could overcome any obstacles, he was certain of that. For a fortnight he treasured her letter, hurled himself back into love with a kind of violence that gave him strength. Hazel's love was something to fight for, and when he sang the 'Internationale' after morning drill he felt boundless as the eagle which circled above, sovereign of the skies.

Christmas at Albacete had been almost enjoyable. There was a barrel of brandy, chicken stew, chocolate bars and almonds. Tom had a good feeling about the coming year. Battles would be won in 1937. The *Chronicle* would publish his eyewitness reports. He would return home and Hazel would be waiting. His mum and dad . . . well, they would forgive him.

The letter from his mum came on the last day of the year.

Jacob tossed it to him as he crouched in the shelter, polishing his disassembled rifle. He put the rifle back together before opening the envelope. The usual small talk, and then the bullet. *A girl called Hazel Alexander is the most notorious.* He tried not to believe it at first, but it was no use. What reason had he to doubt his own mother? She had no grounds to invent such a story. Of course it was true! He knew for a fact that Hazel was easy – hadn't she given herself in the summer house that stormy night? Kissing him, unbuckling his belt, letting him take her without so much as a murmur of protest. At the time he'd convinced himself it was something more than sex; it was an act of love between them, beautiful and unstoppable – sacred – but now he saw it was nothing of the sort. Not for her, anyway. *By all accounts there are two other unfortunates dancing to her tune.* What an idiot he'd been! At least now he understood the 'complications' she'd mentioned. The complication was that she was a faithless tart.

'Tom!' Jacob was shaking him, kicking him in the back. 'Jesus Christ, Tom, wake up!'

He blinked and scrambled to his feet. The drone of engines from the west was unmistakable. Heinkels, flying low. Where was their air cover, the Russian fighters? The machine guns were no use – they'd have to defend with their rifles. It would be funny if it wasn't so deadly, so pathetically serious. Around him he could see the shadows of men taking up their positions. He could weep at their bravery. Giants, these men, every one. Whatever happened, he would never regret coming here. He would be a communist till he died, a defender of the people . . .

Bombs dropped on the neighbouring hill. The air seemed

to scream before the dull burst of the explosion. Now the planes were overhead, the German gunners strafing. Tom turned as he heard Jacob's cry, saw his body thrown into the air. He crawled, cursing, on his stomach towards the spot where his friend had landed. Jacob's guts were open to the sky, wet and pulsing, coiled like a thrown-down skipping rope. Pages of poetry flapped and scudded over the hard earth and Tom scrabbled to retrieve them, trying to keep the pages flat, the verses true. And then the gunners fired again and there was nothing but darkness.

27

August 1937

At last Jasmin had started to sleep through the night. She was walking now, toddling around the flat at astonishing speed. Mrs Allen at the nursery said she kept them all on their toes. 'Fanny Fanackapan', was Mrs Allen's nickname for Jasmin, spoken with a half-smile that seemed to mask a grimace.

Edith rarely called at the flat. She was engaged to a banker named Martin and spent all her time on long walks and picnics and boating on the Serpentine. Edith barely gave two hours a week to the movement. If she wasn't careful she'd get her service badge taken away, said Lucia, and then it would be the uniform – not that their uniforms counted for much now they'd been banned in public – and then Lucia would begin a rant about government crooks and the outrageous attacks on civil liberties.

It was a shame about Edith. Hazel had never much liked her, but she'd always been willing to mind Jasmin on drumming nights. Fortunately, the porter's wife from along the road had stepped in. She loved babies, she said, which was lucky because Lucia never seemed able to help out. She'd screwed a bolt to the inside of her bedroom door so that Jasmin couldn't toddle in. Sometimes Hazel wondered whether Lucia would ask them to leave the flat, but there had never yet been any hint. Hazel made sure she was useful: if it wasn't for her, the place would be an awful tip and there'd never be any proper food or a clean pair of drawers.

'Good-ger,' Jasmin babbled, placing another wooden brick atop a wobbly tower.

'Good girl,' said Hazel, looking up from the ironing board. 'Good girl!'

Jasmin laughed and clapped her hands, but her fingers brushed against the tower and the bricks crashed down. She began to wail.

'Shhh, shhh. We mustn't wake Lucia.' Hazel unplugged the iron and lifted Jasmin from the high chair, putting her hand over her mouth to stifle the yell. It wasn't nine yet but perhaps they could have an early walk. Jasmin liked to watch the squirrels in Kensington Gardens, and by mid-morning the older children would begin to arrive at the pond with their little sailing boats.

She opened the larder cupboard to check there was enough milk and bread for Lucia's breakfast, and found a biscuit to keep Jasmin quiet while she tidied the kitchen, emptying the leaves from the teapot and rinsing out her cup. Sometimes Philip stayed on a Friday night, but she was certain that Lucia had come home alone last night. She laid out breakfast things for one.

There was a letter face down on the doormat in the hall, a small creamy-coloured envelope of the kind Tom had used. She snatched it up, but the letter was addressed to Lucia. The postmark was from Germany – it would be from one of the fascists she'd palled up with on her trip to Berlin.

She let the envelope drop back to the floor. Idiot. Tom had not written since December – not for eight whole months – so why would he suddenly write now? It was a good thing, she reminded herself, that the letters had stopped. He must have regretted his outburst of affection, felt overwhelmed, perhaps, by her gushing reply. In any case, the correspondence had been a deception, at least on her part. If he ever came back from Spain, she would have to carry on the lie, the pretence that Jasmin didn't exist, or else she could tell the truth, with every chance then that he would disappear for good. He didn't want to be tied down with a child. Hadn't he told her that when they were first together? He'd shuddered to imagine being stuck in a room with a screaming baby. Perhaps, somehow, he'd got wind of the truth, and that was why the letters had stopped.

Every day she bought a paper and scanned the pages for news of the Spanish war. It was not going well for the Republicans. British casualties were published regularly in the *News Chronicle*, and to date his name hadn't appeared. She even went to King Street once, to the communists' head-quarters, thinking she would go inside and ask if there was any news of Thomas Smart. But she lost her nerve – a black-shirt at Red HQ! – and left Covent Garden with a pound of apples and a bunch of spring violets. On the bus home, she reassured herself that if anything had happened to Tom, there was certain to be gossip at party meetings. A turncoat blackshirt, killed fighting the fascists in Spain? People would crow and say it was just deserts. No, Tom was all right. He might even be back home, in love with some other girl.

It didn't matter. She and Jasmin would manage, because Hazel had a plan. Each week she saved a little money. She'd even stopped smoking, adding the extra pennies to her tin.

Her throat felt better for it, too; she hadn't had a coughing attack in weeks. In two years or so she would have enough money to rent a flat, or a decent-sized room, just her and Jasmin. Pimlico was the plan, somewhere close to work, which meant she would save money on buses and Tubes, and Jasmin could go to the infant school which was close to her office. Two years seemed a horribly long time, but Hazel liked having the goal; it buoyed her on the darkest nights, gave her a focus when she lay in bed trying not to listen to Lucia in the bedroom with Philip, the cries that might have been pain or pleasure and seemed, in some strange way, designed to mock Hazel as she attempted to sleep, alone in her small bed.

It was cloudy but the air was warm. She walked quickly along the High Street towards the Gardens, ignoring Jasmin's pleas to be let down from the pram. 'Down, down!' she cried, kicking out her legs and twisting against the harness. Passers-by smiled sympathetically at Hazel, and as she waited to cross the road, a tall thin woman struck up conversation. 'Little one looks determined,' she said, dipping her head towards the pram. Jasmin quietened at the sight of the woman's old-fashioned hat with its bunches of waxed fruit, the little fake bird stuck with dull black feathers.

'She's desperate to see the squirrels,' said Hazel.

The woman shifted her gaze to the pram handle – to the fingers of Hazel's left hand.

'Your little sister, is it?' she asked.

Dear Christ, thought Hazel, I'm sick of this. To her work colleagues she was a single girl. To the blackshirts she was an abandoned wife and mother. Always playing a part, just to make other people feel better. She was eighteen now, old enough to be her own person, to stand her ground. What would happen if, for once, she played herself?

'My daughter.' Hazel caught the gleam of judgement in the woman's eye and felt a snip of sudden rage. 'If it's my wedding ring you're wondering about, I'm not married.'

The woman jerked her head back as if to deny that she had been ogling Hazel's naked finger, and her eyes darted across the road and up towards Kensington Church Street where a soldier stood sentry outside the army barracks.

'And this is what our laddies fought the war for, is it?' she said. Her soft voice became coarse and loud. 'So that hussies like you could swan about with their –' she hesitated, her lips forming the B and then pulling back to show a ragged line of teeth with sharp brown canines – 'with their *offspring*, and not even an ounce of shame does she show.' The woman was addressing the wider street now, shaking her head so that the bird on her hat seemed to peck and scold in time with her wagging finger.

Hazel stood paralysed for a moment. What had she been thinking, goading the woman like that? She could not muster a response; she wanted only to disappear. Spinning the pram on its back wheels, she began to run, turning right onto Palace Gate and then down Gloucester Road. She almost tripped over a man sweeping litter from the doorway of a pub. 'Mind yourself, darling,' he called. Jasmin thought it was a great adventure and she clapped her hands, screeching 'Mumumumum!' as they raced along the pavement. At the bottom of the road there was a newsagent's shop. Hazel left the pram outside, ignoring Jasmin's shouts. In the shop she bought a packet of Pall Malls, a box of matches and a bar of Fry's.

She gave Jasmin the chocolate and lit a cigarette. She

would smoke it here, on the street corner, in this seedy neighbourhood, because that was where she belonged. The sole of her shoe stuck to the pavement – there was a broken bottle, a dried-up puddle of orangeade, insects crawling at the edges. An ant ventured onto her shoe, her stocking, but she didn't bother to brush it off. She remembered what Charles had told her. She was a slut, a whore.

The air here stank of motor fumes and morning-after booze. She smelt the whisky on Charles's breath, felt his hand gripping the top of her arm, pushing her back into the dark summer house. His clothes were wet from the storm. Soaked through.

He had been spying. Had he seen everything?

She was nothing but a whore, he slurred, and she deserved all she got. If she ever played around with that young lad again he would have him in court for rape. And then he stared at her, silently put a hand to her cheek.

'What about you?' Hazel had asked afterwards. 'What if I told the police about you?'

Charles was quiet for a second and Hazel wondered whether he might have sobered up, whether he might feel any remorse for what he had just done. But then he ruffled her hair and laughed. 'Oh, I don't think the police would believe a silly sixteen-year-old with a crush on her mother's lover. Do you?' His laughter died away and he shook his head in mock-seriousness. 'Imagine the humiliation. You'd be the talk of the town.'

'But—'

'Don't bother denying it. I've seen you looking at me. I know what you've been reading this summer.'

He picked up the book from the floor and placed it on the tea chest.

Hazel wanted to rip the book to pieces. How foolish she had been, to believe van de Velde's words. Charles had revealed the truth to her. Sex wasn't about love and equality. It was about humiliation and pain.

She lit another cigarette and stared down at her daughter. The yellow cardigan was covered in dribbles of chocolate. 'Good girl,' said Hazel, turning her head to blow a stream of smoke up towards the sunless sky.

Ridiculous to think she could ever get a flat on her own, to imagine that she could exist without lies. No respectable landlord would rent a flat to an unmarried mother. She supposed that Charles was right: she was no better than a whore. She needed Lucia. She needed the movement. This was her family and she must be grateful for it.

28

'Tonight?'

'It can't be helped, Frangie. I'd rather spend the evening with you, naturally, but Veronica says this client is absolutely desperate.'

'Aren't they all?'

Charles sighed and reached for Francine's hand across the narrow kitchen table. He had called round to Earls Court unexpectedly, and she was still in her nightgown, uncomfortably aware that yesterday's eye make-up would be smeared into the creases around her eyes.

'Timing is everything. You know how precise Veronica likes to be.'

She sniffed and told herself that she must try to smile, try to be gracious.

'It's no fun for me,' he continued. 'She's another of Veronica's social cases. I have to get them to bathe first.'

'Don't!' said Francine, pulling her hand from his grasp. 'It's too squalid.'

'But Frangie, you've always been so understanding. Open-minded. I rely on you—'

'You say Veronica screens them, but how do I know?

Sooner or later you'll pick up some vile disease from these slum women.'

'Not exactly slum women, darling. The fee is still considerable. Vee's not running a charity.'

'You just said yourself they're filthy! They need to bathe before you'll bed them.' She stood up and walked to the kitchen window. Labourers were dismantling the scaffolding from the roof of the exhibition centre: the building work was finally coming to an end. She thought of the day ahead – stuck in the flat with the scaffolding clank-clanking; workmen yelling and catcalling whenever a woman passed; the man in the flat above practising on his wretched oboe – and now not even the prospect of dinner with Charles to look forward to. She felt a twist of anger as she turned back to look at him. He was fiddling with a cufflink, and there was a look of weariness – or was it boredom? – upon his face.

'You don't care where these women are from, do you?' she hissed. 'You don't care what they look like or smell like. You fuck them for money and you love every single minute of it. All those babies, those children running around London. You must have hundreds of them now.'

'Two hundred and eighty-two,' he said in a faraway voice.

'What?'

'Two hundred and eighty-two, since 1916. One child a month, near as dammit. At least, those are the successes we know of. Not every woman keeps her follow-up appointment.'

He smiled and her rage flared brighter.

'This is a joke to you?'

'Frangie, really,' he said, rising from the table. 'If you're having a bad day I think it's better I leave. Though I must confess I had hoped—' He reached out and pulled at the silk cord of her dressing gown. The bow slowly unlooped.

She looked down at his hand, felt the light pressure of the cord against her waist. He smiled again and stepped towards her. She caught the scent of his cologne.

'Had hoped?' she asked.

The cord slid to the floor and he stroked a finger along her bare collarbone.

'I might fuck them for money. But I fuck you for love, my darling.'

When he kissed her she felt the rage melt away. It would be all right. He still wanted her. The other women meant nothing. They were simply . . . business.

There was no food in the flat, so she walked to the Italian delicatessen on the Cromwell Road. The grey skies had lightened and the temperature was rising. Perhaps it would be a sunny day after all. In the delicatessen Francine bought bread and tomatoes for lunch. She hesitated over a tray of pastries decorated with glazed apricots and strawberries.

'*Tre . . . grazie*,' she said, pointing to the pastries. Jasmin had a sweet tooth, just like Hazel, of course. She'd pop by and surprise them. The delicatessen sold wine, too. Hazel wasn't keen on wine, or any alcohol, it seemed, but it would be a shame to arrive without a respectable offering. She bought a bottle of Chianti, and the shopkeeper parcelled everything up in brown paper.

The walk took twenty minutes, and she wished she'd worn different shoes, or hailed a cab, but the wine would have to serve as her extravagance for the day. How tiresome this money situation was. The Aldwick house had not been let as frequently as expected, and the last guests had refused to pay the balance because the water heater had broken down on the third day.

She passed a solicitor's office, its brass plaque glaring in the sudden dazzle of sunshine. She had not yet heard from Paul's solicitor. Paul was chasing recompense for a cancelled contract; it seemed he couldn't afford the time or the money to invest in a divorce. Everything hinged on selling the Bloomsbury flat, but that was far from straightforward. Property in town was hardly the most desirable, with all this tiresome talk of war.

Hazel looked unwell, thought Francine. When she answered the door her face dropped, and she gave a guarded glance over Francine's shoulder, asking whether Charles was on his way.

'Charles is busy today. I'm feeling a little lonely, as a matter of fact. I've brought us some treats. Have you had lunch?'

She held up the paper parcel and Hazel opened the door a little wider.

'Not yet . . . We've been out. Come in.'

Jasmin's face broke into a wide grin when she saw Francine. She was wearing a knitted yellow cardigan that looked as if it was covered in mud or chocolate, and her face was just as grimy. 'Nee-nee,' she called, clapping her hands. 'Nee-nee.'

How sweet, thought Francine. Jasmin seems to have decided on her own name for me. Nee-nee. Yes, that was much better than Grandma or Granny. Clever little girl. She bent down and stroked Jasmin's head.

'It's Nee-Nee come to visit, that's right. Haven't you grown?'

'You haven't seen her for a while.'

'Isn't it silly, darling? I honestly have no idea where the time goes. Of course there was the fortnight in Biarritz – it was so kind of Deborah to invite me. Dreadfully hot out there, though. As much as one could manage to take a dip in the pool.' She looked down again at the parcel and handed it to Hazel. 'Just a few luncheon things. And a bottle of *vin*. I'm ever so thirsty.'

Hazel mumbled a thank-you and disappeared into the kitchen. Francine sat on the edge of the sofa, surveying the room. It was an odd set-up. Rather bare and unfeminine, considering the occupants were two young women. A dining table was pushed against the back wall, and on it were several foolscap files, piles of papers and a coffee-stained cup and saucer. In the corner next to the table was a standard pole with a huge flag wound around it. Francine didn't have to unfurl the flag to know it would be emblazoned with some ghastly fascist emblem. She had given up trying to fathom why Hazel found the Mosley party so attractive. The way the man preened and strutted; he was plainly ridiculous.

Next to her on the sofa was a copy of the *Blackshirt*. She glanced down at a cartoon on the front page that showed a group of Jewish bankers, stunted and grotesque. The image made her feel queasy. Was it possible that Hazel found this loathsome Jew-baiting amusing? Francine knew it was the kind of thing her dead father would have admired, anti-Semite that he was. She'd managed to hide Paul's ancestry from him, but there'd been a suspicion from the start. 'Always imagined you with a taller fellow,' he'd sniffed. 'Rather exotic isn't he? Interesting face . . .'

Francine folded the paper and slid it underneath the sofa, out of sight.

'Nee-Nee.'

Jasmin had pulled herself up and now she was toddling over to Francine, her chubby button toes splaying on the rug with each wobbly step.

'Clever girl!' said Francine, holding out her hands. 'Clever girl has learned to walk! Come to Nee-Nee, that's it.' Jasmin lunged towards her, almost overbalancing, but Francine clasped her under the arms and lifted her onto her lap. 'We'll have a little song, shall we, Jasmin? Now let's see . . .' She began to sing: '*Daffydowndilly has come to town, sweet and fresh as a country breeze. In a yellow petticoat and a green gown, daffydowndilly has come to town.*' At the end of the song she blew into Jasmin's hair, and her wispy curls lifted in the stale air.

''Gain,' laughed Jasmin. ''Gain!'

'Again? How about Nee-Nee's favourite? Mummy used to like this one, too.' Francine began to rock Jasmin. '*Bye baby bunting, Daddy's gone a-hunting, to fetch a little rabbit skin, to wrap his baby bunting in.*'

Jasmin's warm body melted into hers; she lay in Francine's arms staring up with devoted eyes.

'That's meant as a dig, is it?'

Hazel was standing in the doorway holding a glass of wine, her face pinched and angry.

'A dig?'

'Daddy's gone a-hunting.' She slammed the glass down on the table so that the wine sloshed over the edge.

'I honestly didn't give it a second thought, darling. It's just a nursery rhyme. You're being ridiculous. Oversensitive.'

'If you're so desperate to know who the father is, I'll give you a clue,' said Hazel.

She strode across the room, lifted Jasmin from Francine's lap and held her against her hip.

'There are two possibilities,' said Hazel. 'And one of them is Charles.'

Francine sat motionless, allowing the seconds to pass until Jasmin began to cry and squirm in Hazel's arms. She stood and staggered towards the table, picked up the glass and gulped down the wine. Without a word she walked towards the door.

''Gain!' shouted Jasmin. 'Nee-Nee 'gain!'

Jean stood with her arms crossed, the hem of her drab petticoat flapping below her skirt. 'Mr Lassiter didn't say to expect you.'

'Didn't he? Oh, it's all arranged. I know he won't be back until later but I found myself at a loose end.'

Francine's legs were trembling, but Jean didn't seem to notice. Grudgingly, she let Francine through the front door and showed her to the sitting room. 'I'm in the scullery,' she said, 'in case you need anything.'

'Actually, I might go up for a lie-down,' said Francine, putting her hand to her forehead. 'I've this headache. It's rather close, suddenly, don't you think?'

'Heatwave coming,' sniffed Jean. 'The ants are getting ready to swarm.'

'The ants. Yes, quite.'

Upstairs, she sat on the bed and tried to summon a sliver of calm.

There are two possibilities.

What did she hope to find in his bedroom? A journal, perhaps. A list of his conquests. Letters. Proof. She began to open the chest drawers, quietly in case Jean was loitering, running her fingers through the layers of socks and underpants, shirt collars and braces. She searched through his bedside cabinet, under the mattress, under the bed. Nothing. Finally, she opened the drawer at the bottom of the wardrobe. There were some tennis whites there, and an old scuffed cricket bat. She was about to close the drawer when she saw a cigar box pushed towards the back. Inside were a few photographs – Charles as a baby in a Victorian studio, trussed up in his christening gown; a photograph of herself with Charles and Miss Heath, taken on the banks of the Fowey. On the back was an inscription in careful handwriting: *Me with Francine, Summer 1909.* It was the first summer that Edward had not come to Lostwithiel, the summer before—

She dropped the picture face down in the cigar box, and now there was just one photograph in her hand. It had been taken a year later, the summer when—

Francine gazed at the picture: a shot of Charles with his brother Lawrence at twenty months old, little Lawrie dressed in a blue linen romper, holding the red-painted toy train that Francine's mother had brought as a gift when they arrived for the August holiday.

Francine felt an icy sweat break on her forehead. Here he was – Lawrie, smiling for the photographer who'd come to the house that rainy morning. She remembered how the flashbulbs had excited Lawrie and made him giddy so that he'd refused to have a nap after lunch. The weather cleared in the afternoon and the two families went into the garden to enjoy the sunshine. Lawrie cried for his mother to put him in the hammock, and then cried for her to get him down again, and the rigmarole repeated itself until Mrs Lassiter sighed and said nannies really oughtn't to be allowed half-days. Finally, exhausted, and with the bribe of his green bedtime blanket, Lawrie settled in the hammock and fell asleep.

As the early-evening sun filtered through the oak leaves the parents went into the house to dress for dinner. 'Keep an eye on the baby, won't you, children?' said Mrs Lassiter. 'Call me when he wakes.'

They both nodded and smiled. When Mrs Lassiter disappeared Charles gave a bitter laugh.

'Children? I'm almost eighteen.'

'Wouldn't you rather they think of us as children?' asked Francine. She sat straight-backed on the rug, her legs folded sideways beneath her. 'If they had any idea, we'd never be left alone.'

He stared at her body and smiled. One hand reached out and stroked the underside of her calf. She put down her magazine.

'Not here,' she said. 'Come tonight.'

'I can't wait until then. I've been in torment all day, Francine. Agony. Just a short walk down to the field.'

'We can't leave Lawrie . . .'

They looked into the hammock. Lawrie's thumb was planted in his mouth, his blanket snuggled to his cheek. 'He's fast asleep,' said Charles. 'A kiss, that's all. You wouldn't deny me that?'

Francine slipped her shoes back on and stood up. 'I'll go first,' she said. 'Come and find me.'

The field at the end of the garden was edged with a row of sprawling beeches. She stood with her back against a beech trunk, watching a flock of half-grown lambs grazing in the distance. A tiny fly landed on her forehead and she flicked it away. When she heard his footsteps shushing through last autumn's fallen leaves she stepped on a twig to make it snap. The footsteps stalled for a second: Charles had heard. Now he was before her, his eyes locked on hers, his face grave with love.

How long were they gone – ten minutes? Twenty? Afterwards Francine went ahead, Charles promising to follow at a respectable distance. Reaching the garden, she knew before she peered into the hammock that Lawrie was no longer sleeping inside. The fabric was light and empty, the fringed calico swaying unburdened in the breeze.

Scanning the lawn, Francine quickened her pace towards the house. By the steps to the veranda she saw a flash of green – Lawrie's blanket, snagged on the wooden post. He had toddled into the house then; that was good. She would follow him inside and with luck, no one would ever know that they'd left him alone.

At the top of the veranda steps she heard Charles running up the lawn. A clot of colour hit her eyes as she turned her head. The toy train.

It was floating blood-red in the barrel that collected rainwater for Mrs Lassiter's roses. Below the train was a small pale hand, fingers reaching up like fragments of lifeless coral.

Francine and her parents had boarded the first train back to London the following morning. They sat stiffly in the carriage, white-faced with shock. A tragic accident, the police inspector had pronounced, but Mrs Lassiter had made it clear she blamed Francine for Lawrie's drowning. Charles did his best to defend her – the walk down to the field was his idea, he told his mother – but Mrs Lassiter took little notice. Charles was a boy; boys were liable to be distracted. Francine was a young woman; she would be a mother herself one day. She should have known better than to abandon a sleeping baby.

They never returned to Lostwithiel. Francine's father would bring home the occasional snippet of information, gleaned on the golf course or at bank dinners. Charles Lassiter had suffered some kind of breakdown, it was reported, and when war came he was registered unfit and shoved into a clerking role for a merchant-shipping firm. 'I'd like to know how much Lassiter paid for the psychiatrist's report,' sniffed her father.

It was Harriett who had reintroduced Francine to Charles, unwittingly, at the opening of a Sickert exhibition one summer in the late twenties. 'Have you met Charles Lassiter?' Harriett said to Paul and Francine as they stood in the gallery sipping white wine. 'Charles, this is Paul Alexander and his wife, my friend Francine.'

Lassiter. Francine looked at the blithe blue eyes and the combed hair and could see little trace of the young man she'd once known. But there was his straight sharp nose, the full lips now upturned in an easy smile.

'Charles?'

He took her hand. 'Francine. How delightful to see you after all this time.' He kissed her hand, and then both her cheeks, and she found it impossible to hide her astonishment. Even when they moved apart she was acutely aware of him: the way his face crinkled with each laugh; the sun-weathered hands which pushed through his hair; the adolescent intensity replaced with such effortless charm.

Harry thought it was marvellous that two childhood friends had been reunited, and she threw a drinks party so that Charles and Francine could reminisce at leisure. There were more drinks parties. Luncheons. Dinners. Francine tried to resist Charles's overtures, but after Paul's infidelity she saw no reason why she shouldn't indulge. And God, what a joy it had been. Just the memory of that first night together was enough to make her pulse quicken.

They had endured so much. They were bonded, even when they were apart, when she was with Paul or he was with Carolyn or his clients or any number of lovers he had enjoyed over the years. Nothing had been able to break the bond. But Hazel?

Francine lay on the bed until she heard Charles's car pull up outside, the click of his heels on the pavement and his key in the door. She hurried down the stairs into the hall and almost collided with Jean. The two women spoke at the same time.

'Mrs Alexander said you was expecting her—'

'Charles, I won't be staying—'

Charles dropped his keys next to the telephone and tossed his hat onto the stand.

'Yes, thank you, Jean,' he said, taking Francine by the elbow. 'How lovely to see you, Frangie.'

He steered her into the sitting room and closed the door behind them. 'Is everything all right?' he asked. 'You look rather wild.'

PART THREE

29

London, May 1940

'Do you like butter, Mummy?'

Jasmin had found a clump of buttercups in the churchyard near the nursery. Hazel crouched beside a gravestone and tilted her head back a fraction.

'You do!' said Jasmin, holding the flower under her mother's chin so that the yellow light reflected on Hazel's pale neck. Jasmin's eyes became earnest: this was a serious experiment. 'You *love* butter, Mummy.' She skipped ahead on the church path, twirling the buttercup stalk between her thumb and forefinger. The small brown box bumped against her hip. Jasmin had named her gas mask Angie, after a friend from nursery who had been evacuated to Scotland. The mask should have a pretty name, she'd announced, to stop it from being so ugly. 'Angie's like angels. Angels are always there, even when you can't see them, aren't they, Mummy?'

'Wait at the gate,' Hazel called. She preferred to walk as slowly as possible through the churchyard, and as she walked she tried to imagine that they were in the countryside rather than the centre of London. She wanted to delay the moment when they would arrive at the nursery, when Jasmin would be out of her sight, out of her reach, for another endless day. Every single air raid in the months since the war began had been a false alarm. People were calling it a twilight war, but no one believed it could last. Hazel hated the raids when she and Jasmin were apart, each in their own subterranean gloom. Mrs Allen had strung a line of bunting across the steel roof of the nursery's Anderson shelter, as if a row of cambric triangles cut out with pinking shears might ward off a high-explosive bomb.

The office was eerily hushed. Mr Weaver had been recalled to his old regiment. Ancient Mr Morris sat in his office drinking Darjeeling, speculating as to when the firm's moth-balled commissions might reasonably be revived. The girls all agreed that he was going doolally-tat: what person in their right mind would kit out a house in luxury wallpaper and velvet curtains when Jerry was about to come calling? They – the girls – might as well join the WAAF or the WAAC or move out to the country to help on a farm. Bridget had already gone. Anne had handed Bridget's latest postcard round that morning: *I'm up to my ankles in cow shit and it's glorious.*

Hazel kept quiet about her own plans.

In her lunch hour she bought a copy of the *News Chronicle*. It was a while now since she'd last seen his name, but that was no reason to stop looking. He'd been doing well – a reporter at last – and until a month ago there had been quite a few news stories written by Thomas Smart. They tended to be the less consequential stories towards the back of the newspaper – thunderstorm damage to barrage balloons, a goods train derailed – but she cut out every one and kept the collection in a Manila envelope, hidden under the seat cushion of her bedroom chair.

It was warm enough for short sleeves, and the breeze blowing off the river held the promise of summer; there was a ripe saltiness to the air, and from a distant jetty came the screech of gulls. If she closed her eyes, she could almost be in Aldwick.

The bench where Hazel usually sat was taken by two men in uniform, so she walked a little further along Millbank, ignoring the whistle from one of the men as she passed. She brushed a sprinkling of white blossom from the bench and sat down, opening the paper and scanning through the pages. Nothing. Of course there was a chance that Tom might have moved to another newspaper, but she could hardly buy each paper every single day and anyway, the most likely explanation was that he had joined up. Why wouldn't he? He'd been quick enough to fight the fascists in Spain. The only surprise was that he hadn't gone sooner.

She read through the paper again, slowly this time. There was a story about fundraising for Jewish refugees, a photograph of children who'd arrived on the *Kindertransport*. Hazel had seen the pictures many times now, girls of Jasmin's age and younger, wide-eyed and afraid, clutching their pathetic possessions. It was too awful. Hazel had tried to speak to Lucia about the Jews, of the persecution in Germany, but Lucia seemed incapable of sensible discussion. She parroted phrases from the *Blackshirt* – 'Oh, to hell with the refu*jews* and their sob-stuff, charity begins at home!' – or she repeated lines from Sir Oswald's speeches, learned from the recordings she'd played over and over on the gramophone. Hazel always backed down, let her rant on. It was easier that way because she still needed Lucia – for now, at least.

She folded the paper into her bag and wandered back along the riverside. It was low tide and the wind had dropped; the water looked calm, benign. Hard to believe that the Thames could be the Nazis' secret weapon. *London will always be betrayed by the river. At night, from the air, it reflects the moon or the sky.* Tom had written that in one of his reports on air-raid precautions. The words stuck in her head like lines of poetry.

After work she called in to Derry & Toms and took the lift up to the luggage department. The woman on the counter was pushy and tried to sell her a set of three leather cases – 'Outstanding value,' she gushed – but Hazel would not be persuaded. She chose a small blue valise for Jasmin, fitted with tiny brass clasps, and a large board-backed case for herself.

Kensington High Street seemed deserted as she walked back to the flat, an empty case in each hand. She remembered that summer Saturday, cold and wet, when she boarded the train at Chichester clutching Jasmin in one arm and a rain-soaked hessian bag in the other. She had left the Misses Shaw's pram outside Selsey bus station with a note giving the return address. She would not be accused of stealing anything, least of all her own baby. At Victoria station, Hazel had searched the crowds, fear thumping behind her eyes. But there was Lucia, next to the telegraph office as promised, forearms resting on the handle of a brand-new pram. They queued for a taxicab, Lucia giggling as they tried to lift the bassinet from the chassis, to fold down the shining frame.

The pram had been sold now, and Lucia donated the proceeds towards the latest fundraising drive at HQ. In the bottom of Hazel's wardrobe, the hessian bag still lay folded. Their possessions were few: it would not take long to pack.

'You're leaving? I don't quite – *tomorrow*, did you say?' Lucia put down her pen and stared at Hazel in disbelief. The sitting room was dark and chill despite the sunny evening outside.

'Tomorrow morning. We're going to Devon. Winnie's family have taken a pub. They've invited me and Jasmin.'

Lucia scrambled up from the table, knocking her chair hard against the back wall. 'How terribly generous of Winnie. You've had enough of my charity, then?'

'I'll work to earn our keep. It will be safer for Jasmin to leave London.'

'For heaven's sake. This obsession, this *paranoia* about the Luftwaffe—' Lucia paced across the room, stood at the window and looked out onto the street, tapping her fingernails on the wide sill. Outside, a torn-eared cat stalked across a wall, stopped on a brick pier and arched its back.

'I am grateful to you, Lucia.' She got up from the sofa and stood beside her at the window, ventured a hand on her shoulder. 'You know I am. I couldn't have . . . well, I would have lost Jasmin if it hadn't been for you. But everything has changed now. The war, the movement—' The movement has failed, Hazel wanted to say. All those meetings and rallies, the canvassing for peace. None of it had made any difference.

'So it's all about you and the shop girl now,' said Lucia, shrugging off Hazel's hand. 'I take it you and Winnie aren't inviting me along to Devon. Happy for me to take my chances here?'

Hazel hesitated. She'd assumed that Lucia would never

leave London, because London meant Philip and her work – such as it was now – at HQ. She wouldn't leave, would she? She had to be bluffing.

'I'm sure Winnie would be happy to invite you.' Hazel did her best to sound enthusiastic, cheery. 'They might be grateful for an extra pair of hands.'

Lucia whirled around from the window. 'I'd rather die here.' Her dark eyes narrowed and her lips peeled back to show her teeth. The expression was somehow familiar to Hazel – yes, it was the expression of the communist girl who'd cornered her in the shop doorway. There was the same wild loathing in Lucia's eyes, the same flash of danger.

'Don't say that—'

'Or perhaps I'll leave London altogether. I'll go back to Berlin.' Lucia's face softened and broke into a distant smile. 'He'd welcome me, you know, Karl. Our correspondence—' She stopped abruptly and walked back towards the table.

Correspondence? She must mean the Nazi commander she'd struck up with on her last trip to Berlin. A man who, Lucia claimed, worked closely with the Führer.

'Germany? You wouldn't. How would you get there, and how on earth would you get back?'

'Don't pretend to care!' Lucia's voice rose to a shriek and she lunged towards Hazel, grabbing her by the arms and digging her fingernails through the thin fabric of her blouse. 'Don't you dare pretend to care for me now, don't you dare!'

'Lucia! Of course I care.'

'Liar. I've been useful, that's all. You've used me. You don't truly believe in the movement – do you think I hadn't noticed? All this time you've used me as a cover for your sordid little secret.'

Hazel tried to shake herself free. *Sordid little secret.* Did she mean Jasmin? 'Please,' she said. 'Please don't shout. You'll wake Jasmin.'

'Jasmin, Jasmin, Jasmin.' Lucia dug her nails harder into Hazel's flesh. 'Jasmin, Winnie, the girls at work. Thomas treacherous Smart – don't think I don't know! Loyal as a pup to everyone but me.'

'Tom? How do you know—'

'It's my flat, isn't it?'

'You've been in my room, read my letters?'

'He let you down, though, didn't he? Cut you off!'

Hazel swallowed down her fury. Just for one more night, she told herself. One more night. 'I do care for you, Lucia. I owe you everything. I'll never forget what you did for me. But I have to take Jasmin away from London. I have to put her first. Surely you can see?'

Lucia released her grip and turned away with a heave of disgust. She sank onto the sofa and put her head into her hands. Her shoulders began to quiver and Hazel realized that she was crying.

'Do you remember when we met?' asked Lucia, her voice trembling.

'Of course I remember.' Hazel knew she ought to sit next to her, to comfort her, but her feet remained planted under the window. 'The rally at the theatre.'

'No. The very first time. You were watching the parade.' She looked up, wet lashes glistening. 'I'll never forget that day. I thought you were the most perfect girl I'd ever seen. I wanted us to be friends, true friends.'

'And we have been. We are. I'm so grateful.'

Lucia gave a curt laugh. 'I don't want you to be *grateful*, Hazel. I want you to love me back. The same. Instead you're betraying me. Ambushing me with your news. You must have been plotting for weeks.'

Hazel struggled to reply. It was true: she and Winnie had been discussing the move since Easter. So why hadn't she told Lucia? Because she *didn't* love her, that was why. Lucia was right. In fact, for a long time now, Hazel hadn't even liked her.

'I didn't think you'd mind so much, Lucia,' she said, forcing a note of nonchalance. 'Thought you might even be pleased. You'll have more time alone with Philip. And if you want another flatmate you'll find one soon enough. A girl with no ties, more fun than I'll ever be.'

'I don't want anyone else,' said Lucia, her voice steady now, steel-edged and low. 'I only want you.'

Winnie and her brother had promised to come at ten. They were bringing a van, and from Kensington they would all drive straight to Devon. 'We'll arrive in time for tea,' said Winnie. 'Scones and jam. Butter not marg!'

Everything had been packed, filling the two suitcases and the hessian bag, along with three apple crates from the greengrocer. That their lives could be parcelled up so simply saddened Hazel, and she wondered whether it would always be like this; whether she would ever manage to find a proper home for Jasmin – their own home with a cluttered dresser and a toy chest filled to overflowing.

'Bored,' said Jasmin. She picked flakes from a wax crayon. 'Why can't we go to the pond?'

'Sorry, poppet. We can't go out because Auntie Winnie is coming and we're going on a long drive. A holiday, do you remember? And we'll be staying in a lovely village with a great big pond with baby moorhens and coots and ducklings. Do you remember Auntie Winnie told you all about it?'

Jasmin's face brightened. 'Baby moorhens like blobs of soot?'

'That's it,' smiled Hazel. 'Scraps of soot, aren't they? All black and fuzzy.' She picked up a teddy and nuzzled it into Jasmin's neck.

'Is the holiday coming soon?'

Hazel looked at her watch. It was just after nine. 'Quite soon. Less than an hour.'

'Is Nee-Nee coming?'

'No. Nee-Nee prefers to stay in London.' Hazel picked up a blanket and refolded it so that the corners were tight. 'Now, see if you can draw me another picture. How about a lion, like we saw at the zoo?'

She drank two more cups of tea. Lucia was still in bed. Hazel didn't want to wake her, but she knew she could not leave without saying goodbye. Last night, when Lucia had finished crying, they had become oddly polite and formal. They switched on the wireless at nine and listened to the news without commenting. When Billy Cotton and his band came on, Hazel lit a cigarette, and Lucia didn't sigh or complain as she generally did.

Ten minutes to ten. Hazel hovered outside Lucia's door and raised her arm, but as she was about to knock there was a loud creak of bedsprings and an exaggerated yawn. The door opened. Lucia was wearing men's pyjamas, the pair that Philip kept for his overnight stays.

'Is it really so late?' she said. 'I'm due at a meeting. And I suppose you're— It's any minute, isn't it? Winnie and the van?'

Hazel opened her mouth to reply just at the moment the doorbell rang. Lucia raised her eyebrows. 'Right on cue,' she said. Her eyes were puffy and her lips looked dry and chapped. 'You'd better answer it.'

Jasmin had already run ahead to the front door. Hazel followed her down the dark hall passage, watching as she stretched up on tiptoes to turn the latch and pull the door wide. On the doorstep stood two men in cheap grey suits.

Jasmin shrank back and buried her head in Hazel's skirt. 'Not Auntie Winnie,' she whined.

The taller man asked Hazel if she was Miss Lucia Knight. Hazel said she was not, and she asked who might be calling. He held up a piece of paper and said, 'Police. We have a warrant to search the premises.' He spoke loudly, but Hazel wasn't sure whether Lucia could hear. She had gone into the kitchen, and the kettle was beginning to whistle on the stove.

The men strode into the living room as Hazel shepherded Jasmin into the bedroom. 'Stay in here and draw me one more picture,' she said. 'A really good one for Mummy.' She rushed into the kitchen. 'The police are here,' she whispered to Lucia.

Lucia's eyes widened. She leaned against the sink, gripping the edge.

'They asked for you.'

She half-shrugged her shoulders as if to make light of what Hazel had just told her, to pretend she hardly cared. She drew herself up and tilted her chin outwards.

'Typical of this small-minded little government,' she said. 'All the Germans and Italians have been rounded up. Now it's our turn. Fascists are patriots to the core and yet they'll accuse us of being fifth columnists.'

'Not us, surely? We're no danger—'

Lucia cut in. 'They're at the door?'

'No, they're in the flat. The living room. Apparently they have a warrant to search—'

'What?' The colour drained from Lucia's face. 'My papers!' She pushed past Hazel and ran into the living room. Hazel twisted off the gas under the kettle and followed her.

In the living room the taller policeman – the one who seemed to be in charge – was sitting calmly at the dining table, picking through the notebooks and correspondence that were stacked in messy piles.

Lucia stood in the doorway, Hazel close behind.

'Members' address list,' said the man, holding up an opened ledger. 'Damned considerate of you to leave that out.'

Lucia flew towards the table and thrust out her hand for the ledger. 'Those are my private papers,' she said. The policeman laughed, snapped the ledger shut and held it close to his chest. Behind him the other officer was unfurling the flag that leaned against the wall in the corner of the room. He whistled as he stared down at the circle-and-flash emblem. 'Christ,' he said, turning his head to look around the room. 'What sort of a place is this? A veritable fascists' coven, I'd say.'

'Now then –' the officer at the table slapped the ledger down – 'I don't believe we've been properly introduced. I'm Superintendent Farr. This is Inspector Travers. Miss Knight, I understand you're an active member of the British Union.'

'I am,' said Lucia. She straightened her spine as if on parade, unabashed by the fact she was wearing pyjamas.

'And this is . . . ?' Superintendent Farr nodded towards Hazel.

Hazel knew she was expected to give him her name, but she found herself unable to speak. She coughed, and felt her breath light and jagged in the back of her throat. Perhaps she could invent a name. Her thoughts scrambled and the only one which came to mind was Bronwen. Could she lie? It might buy her time, just until Winnie arrived. She opened her mouth, but now Lucia was talking.

'This is my flatmate, Hazel Alexander,' said Lucia. 'Also an active member.'

A shiver coursed through Hazel's body. Had Lucia really said that? Did she hate her so much? And it wasn't even true – she wasn't an active member, not any more. She and Winnie had agreed; they'd sent their letters of resignation to Mrs Dunn, enclosing their drum corps badges.

'In actual fact I'm no longer a member,' said Hazel. She croaked out the words, doing her best to battle the cough. 'I've resigned,' she said. 'I'm about to leave London.'

'I bet you are,' said Inspector Travers. 'Fortunate we came when we did.'

'No! I have a daughter, you see. We're going to the countryside. To safety.'

'And your husband?'

Hazel looked down. There was a smear of dried mud on the sole of the inspector's shoe. He would consider her to be less than the mud. He would squash her and she had no power to fight back.

'I'm not married.'

Her eyes were on the floor but she could sense the men raising their eyebrows, exchanging a glance.

'Indeed?' said Superintendent Farr. 'You're not married. And you claim *not* to be involved in the British Union. Yet Miss Knight here says you are an active member.'

'Hazel is one of the faithful – a valued member of the women's drum corps,' said Lucia. 'Along with Winifred Harris who, I believe, will be arriving here at any moment.'

Flashes of white smudged Hazel's vision. She sank to the arm of the sofa and doubled over, trying to catch her breath. 'I need a drink of water,' she gasped. 'Please?'

The superintendent nodded, and Hazel walked slowly to the kitchen. Running the tap, she did her best to conjure reassuring thoughts. These policemen are simply throwing their weight around, she told herself. They're just trying to give us a scare.

'Finished!' It was Jasmin, calling from the bedroom. Hazel gulped down the water then hurried in.

'Do you like it?' Jasmin held up a piece of scrap paper decorated with green scribbles above a wonky brown rectangle.

'A tree? It's lovely. Clever girl.' Hazel looked down at the scattered crayons and picked up a black one. 'Now listen carefully, Jasmin. I'm going to write a special message on this picture, and when you hear the doorbell ring, I want you to rush out and answer the door. It's sure to be Auntie Winnie this time and you must give her this picture right away. And then come back inside.'

Jasmin nodded solemnly. Hazel's hands shook as she wrote the message: POLICE ARE HERE. LEAVE NOW.

She folded the picture and gave it to Jasmin. 'Can you be a grown-up girl and remember what I said?'

Jasmin nodded again. 'Give the picture to Auntie Winnie when the bell rings.'

'That's right.' She turned away, tears in her eyes. 'Just wait nicely in here until you hear that noisy old bell. She'll be along any minute now.'

'Where are you going?'

'Mummy needs to talk to the visitors. It shouldn't take too long.'

They were told to sit on the sofa, to wait quietly while the documents were gathered and itemized. When the doorbell rang, Jasmin's little footsteps scampered down the hall. Hazel heard Winnie's cheery, 'Hello, love!' and then there was silence, before the front door quietly closed.

Inspector Travers went into the hall but already the van engine was revving. He came back into the room with Jasmin by his side. 'Did it, Mummy,' she smiled.

The superintendent looked perplexed.

'Did what?' asked Inspector Travers.

'Oh, she means . . . her business,' said Hazel. Her pulse hammered but somehow she kept her nerve. 'Come with me, Jasmin.' She held out her hand. 'We'll check you left the lavatory clean.'

'If that was the Harris girl she didn't hang around,' said the inspector.

'Pity,' sighed Superintendent Farr. 'But I think we have enough to keep us busy here.'

While Travers carried the boxes to the police car, another officer arrived. This one was in uniform, a tall unsmiling woman who stood with arms folded in front of the fireplace as if she were guarding the mantel clock.

Hazel sat on the sofa with Jasmin on her lap, reading a story. Lucia got up and stood at the window, tapping her foot and staring onto the street.

'Again, Mummy.'

Hazel flicked back to the beginning of the book for a third time. Slowly she read the story and turned the pages, reciting the words without registering any meaning. Her thoughts raced. She hoped that Winnie had gone on to Devon regardless. Soon the police would be finished here and she could join Winnie later, take a train instead. They'd have to leave the crates behind but that was all right, they would manage with the minimum. There would be shops in Devon. She had her savings. '*And Mr Drake Puddle-Duck, and Jemima and Rebeccah, have been looking for them ever since*,' she read. It was the end of the book again. She became aware that everyone was looking at her. Superintendent Farr was speaking, nodding in her direction.

'When it comes to the child,' he said, 'you are permitted to take her with you, although I would advise against.'

'Take her?' said Hazel. 'To Devon, you mean?'

'Miss Alexander, you are not going to Devon.'

'Where then? Where are we going?'

'Holloway Prison. We're detaining you. I'm sorry, you clearly don't understand at all, do you? Let me spell it out. Miss Hazel Alexander and Miss Lucia Knight, you are to be detained until further notice under the Defence Regulation Act, Clause 18B.'

'Until further notice?' cried Lucia.

'You might have heard of the new amendment to the law?'

'Swine!' screamed Lucia. 'We've done nothing but honour our king and country.'

'You can make your case in due course,' said the superintendent, holding up his hand. 'Now –' he turned to Hazel – 'if you don't wish the child to accompany you, I suggest you make other arrangements. WPC Gallagher here can escort you to a telephone box if necessary.'

*

The strangest thing was that the operator sounded bored. Hazel was seized by a savage twist of envy: how odd that her own life had become something surreal, something beyond a nightmare, yet this telephonist could sit on her stool and speak as if she were staring at her fingernails and wondering what shoes to wear for the weekend dance.

'Connecting.'

The line rang three times, and Hazel willed her mother to answer. It was almost midday; she might have gone on a shopping trip or a lunch date with one of her friends.

Finally, there was the click of a lifted receiver, a sleepy hello.

'Mother?'

'Hazel? Are you in Devon already?'

'No, I'm in a phone box near the flat. Can you come round, please? As soon as possible? There's a . . . problem, with the police.'

'What on earth has happened, darling? Is it a burglary?'

'Nothing like that.' Hazel looked through the glass pane of the telephone kiosk and met the eyes of WPC Gallagher. She would not cry. All that mattered was Jasmin. She had to make sure Jasmin was safe, had to be brave. Her fingers tingled and the telephone felt strange; weightless and heavy at the same time. 'Mother, they're going to detain me. Me and Lucia. They're taking us to Holloway. Jasmin is allowed to come, apparently, but I couldn't possibly – she mustn't know I'm in a prison. I need you to look after her, Mother. Can you do that?'

Silence, then the faint rasp of a cigarette lighter. Francine spoke again, her voice husky with smoke. 'I think you might have to say that again, darling. I must have misheard.'

30

Francine replaced the receiver and slumped back against the pillow. One thought dominated all others: thank God she'd stopped him from answering. He had leaned across her in the bed, and his hand had been hovering over the telephone, but she'd batted him away, assuming the caller would be Paul, and heaven knows with the divorce negotiations so fraught, she didn't need to offer Paul any more ammunition.

But it had been Hazel, not Paul. Francine closed her eyes, hoping again that she had somehow misunderstood. That this was in fact a bizarre hallucination.

Charles patted the bedcovers above her thigh. 'Well, Frangie?' he said. 'Whatever it was, it sounded weighty.'

'It was Hazel. She's . . . she's been arrested. They're taking her and Lucia to Holloway prison. Hazel wants me to look after Jasmin.' She threw back the covers and swung her legs over the side of the bed. 'I have to get to their flat right now.'

'Damnedest thing. Arresting her for what?'

'For her politics, of course. She's a fascist, isn't she? An enemy. The *silly* girl.' Her thumbnail snagged on her stocking and she cursed.

'I'll drive you.'

'You can't possibly.'

'I'll drop you at the next street. She'll think you caught a cab.'

Francine hesitated as she zipped up her dress. 'All right. But not the next street. Two streets away. If she knows I've been with you there'll be the most almighty scene.'

Cromwell Road was busy, so Charles decided to take the backstreets, the engine straining as he careered past grand terraces and mansion blocks. Neither of them spoke. Francine stared out of the window at the black railings flicking past, blinking at the flashes of sunlight that dazzled through the gaps between buildings. She wondered whether she might be able to reason with these police officers who wanted to take Hazel away, to separate a mother from her daughter. Two mothers from two daughters. Francine thought she might just hold some sway if she smiled pleasantly enough and apologized and explained that Hazel was simply an impetuous young girl. As for Lucia, well – she wouldn't speak up for her.

But what if pleasant smiles weren't enough? If Hazel was taken regardless, and she, Francine, was left to care for the child? On the telephone, she'd tried to get some idea as to how long this detention might last, but Hazel hadn't been able to say. Just a night or two, perhaps. They'd question the girls, and surely when they discovered that there was nothing dangerous or traitorous about Hazel, she would be released. But in the meantime, where would Jasmin sleep? The flat had only one bedroom. The sofa would be comfortable enough, she decided; it was small, but it should be a perfect fit for a four-year-old. And what on earth would she give her to eat? Francine tended to eat dinner in a restaurant, or not at all. Well, there was always cheese on toast. Porridge.

Marco at the deli would see that Jasmin had a treat now and again.

The car passed a man in a cravat with a newspaper under his arm. Francine thought she recognized him. He was an actor, she remembered, someone she'd met at one of Harriett's parties. She thought of the play at the Adelphi next Saturday. She would have to find someone to look after Jasmin that evening, or perhaps she wouldn't be able to go at all. She sighed, her heart heavy. There wasn't a great deal of gaiety to life these days, but what little interludes she enjoyed would now be snatched away.

'Blasted nags.' Charles swerved around a rag-man's pony, the Brough almost clipping the side of the cart. Jasmin would enjoy a ride in the Brough, but that was out of the question, decided Francine. She was such a bright little thing, chattering away like a child twice her age. She'd remember his face, and his name, and then she'd tell Hazel all about Charles once the pair of them were reunited.

It pained Francine to deceive Hazel. Deception was not in her nature. And after all, she *had* tried to break it off with Charles, hadn't seen him for three whole months after Hazel's revelation. She had lived like a nun until that Sunday evening in November when he had arrived at the flat with a bottle of chilled white wine. Perhaps it was because it was her birthday, and she was feeling particularly alone, horribly sober, in fact, after a dry birthday lunch with Hazel, that she invited him in. This time she listened. Gave him a proper chance to explain.

He said he loved her, he had always loved her. Everything that had happened, happened because of his love for her.

'Can't you see, Frangie?' he pleaded.

They were sitting opposite each other in the dull lamplight of the sitting room. Raindrops slunk down the windowpane. It was cold but she had not bothered to switch on the fire.

'Lawrie's death . . .'

Francine almost gasped, to hear Charles mention his brother's name.

'It was my fault,' Charles went on. 'I abandoned Lawrie because I loved you. I wanted you. I've tried somehow to make amends, all those extra babies, the new little boys . . .'

She couldn't bear it. Couldn't bear to hear this – what? – confession? It was the first time Charles had ever spoken of Lawrie since the accident. But why mention him now? Her thoughts hardened. This wasn't about Lawrence: it was about Hazel.

'And sleeping with my daughter? That was because of your love for me?'

Charles flinched and cast his eyes down. 'No. That was a terrible – an unfor*givable* mistake. I was drunk, Frangie. Very drunk. I don't know if you remember but you had gone to bed early that night – a rotten headache, wasn't it? I tried to sleep but couldn't, and so I went downstairs for a nightcap, sat in the living room for a while in the dark, drinking. I heard Hazel go out into the garden. I wanted to know what the girl was playing at, thought it would be a help to you, I suppose. So I followed her, saw what she was up to in the summer house with the boy.'

'Why didn't you stop them? Chase him off?'

'I kept on drinking, straight from the bottle, like an idiot in a trance. Just wasn't thinking straight, Frangie. When the boy left, scrambled back over the wall, I thought, Here's my chance to confront her. Warn her to be careful. But she wouldn't listen.' He paused, sighed. 'And the way she smiled, well, it was as if you were there in front of me, Frangie, you at sixteen, beautiful and alive, and all the desire I had felt for you earlier in the evening, somehow it overwhelmed me. I'm not proud of what I did.' He looked up, thumped his fist on the arm of the sofa. 'The fact is, I've never been more ashamed. It happened just that once. I swear to you.'

'She says you forced yourself on her.'

'Really? There was no force that I recall. But, the whisky . . . perhaps my memory . . .'

She stared down at the rug, trying to absorb his words. *All the desire I had felt for you earlier in the evening, somehow it overwhelmed me.* What did that mean?

'You're trying to say it was my fault, for having a headache that night?' she said. 'If I'd gone to bed with you it would never have happened.'

'Of course I'm not. The evening could have passed quite differently, it's true –' He looked up, and she met his gaze with a warning stare. 'But no, the responsibility is all mine. I accept that.'

'And what about Jasmin? Is she your responsibility? Hazel says you could be the father.'

'No. I don't think so.'

'Why?'

'Let's just say it wasn't my finest hour. Rather too much whisky.'

'Please.' The detail – the image – was too much.

'Jasmin is a little like you.'

'Hardly. She's fair – so is Hazel.'

Francine wished she knew what the boy had looked like. Charles had seen him, of course, but she preferred not to think of what he had seen through the windows of the summer house. She poured another glass of wine.

He sighed and reached in his pocket. 'Please forgive me, Francine. I lost you once. I can't bear to lose you again.' He held out a small box wrapped with a red velvet bow.

She took the box and opened it. Inside was a gold ring, a night-blue stone encircled by white diamonds. Francine shook her head. He couldn't possibly mean . . .

'It's a blue diamond,' he said. 'Terribly rare. Look, I can't divorce Carolyn yet. These cursed loans. But when my father finally bows out, well, the inheritance will change everything. I do want to marry you, Frangie. It's all I've ever wanted.'

Her hand flew to her mouth. 'But it's too beautiful!'

'Let me see if it fits.'

He stood and took the ring from the box, then knelt beside her. She could smell him now, feel his hands on hers, the band of warm gold slipping onto her finger. It was too much.

After that night, the ring had stayed in her jewellery box. She couldn't marry Charles, could she? Yet the promise was enough. They had made a vow.

A policewoman answered the door to Hazel's flat. 'The mother?' she asked, in a granite voice that was more statement than question. Francine nodded and the policewoman motioned for her to step inside.

In the living room, Francine's attempts to reason with the superintendent had no effect. She tried pleading and dabbing the corners of her eyes with a handkerchief, explaining that Jasmin was unusually close to her mother, that it would be utterly cruel to separate them.

'18Bs can take one child with them,' said the superintendent. 'They're entitled to certain privileges.'

'You'd put a child in prison, too?'

'Shhh,' said Hazel. 'She'll hear.' Jasmin was in the kitchen with a biscuit and a glass of milk. 'Jasmin mustn't know. And Mother –' she paused, trying to steady her voice – 'I want you to take her to Aldwick.'

'Aldwick? But your father's in the house now! Your father and Adriana. For heaven's sake, I can't possibly—'

'It's not safe in London. I've made up my mind to get her out. The Aldwick house is big enough for all of you. Please. It might not be for very long. I can't bear to think of her at Earls Court. Traipsing down all those stairs to the shelter.'

Francine nodded. Now was not the time to argue.

'Please. I need you to promise.'

Hell. She could raise it with Paul, at least. These *were* exceptional circumstances. And it was about time he met his granddaughter.

'I promise to ask your father. I'll do my absolute best. And try not to worry. Jasmin will be quite safe with me.'

There was a snort from the far side of the room. Francine turned to look at Lucia. She was standing at the window, biting a fingernail, manically tapping the sole of a black patent shoe. It was all Lucia's fault, thought Francine, whichever way one looked at it. Oh, if only the blackshirts hadn't come to Sussex that summer. Why couldn't they have chosen Kent or Dorset for their wretched camp?

Jasmin appeared, half a biscuit in one hand and a small blue case in the other. She offered the biscuit to Francine. 'Want some, Nee-Nee?'

'Nee-Nee's not hungry, darling. You finish it, there's a good girl.'

'Not hungry neither. I want to go on the holiday now.' She placed the case on the floor and sat on it.

Hazel crouched in front of Jasmin and grasped both her hands.

'I'm afraid we can't go on the holiday with Winnie today.' Hazel's eyes were wet but somehow she was smiling. 'Mummy has been asked to do some special war work. It shouldn't take very long, and until I get back Nee-Nee is going to look after you. Won't that be exciting?'

Jasmin nodded, but she looked uncertain. 'Can I see the lions with Nee-Nee?'

Francine put her hand on Jasmin's head. 'We'll have all manner of adventures, darling. It will be great fun, just you see.'

The inspector coughed. Hazel put her arms around Jasmin and hugged her. 'Bye, sweet girl.' She kissed her daughter's cheek, then disappeared into the hall where the policewoman was waiting.

31

A wasp had landed near the ashtray on Tom's desk. He finished the water in his tumbler, shook the drips onto the floor and turned the glass upside down to trap it. Once this story was written, he'd open the window and set the wasp free.

'Smart!'

When the news editor yelled the whole office jumped. Tom grabbed up his notebook and pencil and strode across to the newsdesk.

'More 18Bs. Fascists, in the main. Five pars should do it.' Crow thrust the wire into his hand without looking at him. His face was set in its usual grimace, the pinched and yellowed skin stretched across his cheekbones.

'Yes, Mr Crow. And the scrap-metal story?'

'Why are you still here? File the fascists first, for fuck's sake.'

Tom hurried back to his desk. It was a hot day and the sun beat in through the fourth-floor windows. It was a terrible thing to be out of Crow's favour. All because of a tiny mistake in a story about a train derailment. Did anyone really give two hoots which class of engine had left the tracks?

He told himself to focus on the 18Bs story, to ignore the fine sweat which had broken out on his forehead. Bill Cork had never let on about Tom's past, thank Christ; if Crow found out he used to be in the British Union he'd be ripped to shreds, never mind that he'd left four years ago and that he'd only ever been dragged into it by his mother.

Amazing to think that the British fascists were all but finished now. At first there were just a handful of arrests, Mosley and other high-ups, speakers whose names he recognized from meetings and rallies. But this past week they seemed to be going for anyone who'd ever delivered a leaflet or sold the *Blackshirt* on a street corner. He thought of his mum in Boone Street, her old uniform still hanging in the under-stairs cupboard along with the winter coats. She'd be all right, wouldn't she? Surely the police had better things to do than to come after her?

He wiped his forehead with his shirtsleeve, then began to read the Press Association report. *The following members of the British Union were this morning arrested and detained under the Defence Regulations 18B* . . . He scanned the list of names. Closed his eyes as a pulse hammered below his brow.

Gerald stopped battering his typewriter keys and stared across from his seat opposite. 'All right, my man?' he said. 'You look rather rattled.'

Tom realized he was holding his breath. 'Just a bit warm in here,' he said, pulling his shirt collar away from his neck. He fanned himself with the wire, then angled it towards Gerald. 'More blackshirts banged up.'

'Good show.'

Tom swiped the saucepans story from his typewriter, wound in a fresh sheet of paper and began to type. He ignored the wasp's buzzing, the angry *tap-tap* of its body as it threw itself against the sides of the glass.

*

Gerald and the others were going to the pub at the end of the shift, but Tom didn't fancy joining them. They were decent enough but they were older men, ex-public school mostly, drinkers with dicky hearts, Great War veterans. The young and the fit had already gone.

Instead he went down to the composing room to see if Bill was around. 'Day off,' shouted old Charlie, hunched over his stone. Tom wiped his brow: even hotter down here with the heat from the machines. Each clank of a mallet was like a direct hit on his skull.

'Not to worry. I'll catch him next week.'

'You'll have to be quick. Call-up's come.'

Did he hear Charlie right over the din? Of course he did. The only surprise was that Bill hadn't got his papers sooner. Petra would be beside herself. He made up his mind to visit Bill and Petra at the weekend, use his coupon to buy the children some sweets.

In the pub opposite Lewisham station he ordered a pint, careful to keep his left hand in his pocket so as not to attract the stares of the girls who were looking across at him from the table in the window. He recognized one of them – Elsie Warlock, whose parents owned the fried-fish shop on Lee High Road. Elsie knew Jillie, didn't she? Well, he couldn't be bothered to go over, to grin through the congratulations and all that gushy stuff.

Fixing his eyes on the evening paper, he tried to read the front page but found it impossible to concentrate. His mind kept returning to the PA wire, the alphabetical list of names. She'd been there, right at the top. *Hazel Alexander.* The thing that really pained him was that when he'd read her name, he'd felt a punch of relief. She's not married then, was the thought that flew into his mind, and now he loathed himself for it. What could it possibly matter to him whether or not she was married? Hazel was in prison and it served her bloody right. She ought to be locked up along with the other fascists, separated from her lover, or lovers – those men his mother had mentioned in her letter. To think he'd been taken in by Hazel a second time, had even confessed his love in that ridiculous letter from Albacete. When he found out the truth, the life she was really living, he'd longed for revenge and now, in a sense, he had it. It was just a pity he couldn't seem to summon any pleasure.

He ordered a second pint and lit a cigarette. There'd been another name he recognized on the list: Lucia Knight. Lucia, the snooty one who liked the sound of her own voice. Tom had always thought she was dangerous. And wasn't that the point of these 18B detentions, to imprison people who might be dangerous to the State? Strange to imagine all those posh girls slumming it inside, though. Not that the 18Bs had it too bad. All sorts of privileges, apparently. Mosley had denied the reports about champagne and red wine but if Tom had learned one thing in Fleet Street, it was that these stories were never a complete fiction . . .

'Tommy Smart!' It was Elsie, tottering up to the bar, all heels and lipstick. 'You're a dark horse, all right.'

'Evening, Elsie.'

'When's the party then?'

Tom raised his eyebrows and Elsie elbowed him, catching his left arm. He tried not to wince. 'Party?'

'Engagement party. You and Jillie! She came in the shop, showed us the ring.'

'We thought we'd keep things low-key. Jillie doesn't like a fuss.'

'That what she told you, is it?' Elsie winked and took a ten-bob note from her purse. 'You'd better start saving, I'd say.'

Tom screwed his cigarette end into the ashtray. 'Love to stay and chat but the old girl's expecting me.' He smiled and tipped his trilby, then strode four steps to the pub door. He used the remains of his left hand to pull the door open, and he could feel the girls' eyes on him. Why not let them get a good look after all? They were just the type to enjoy a freak show.

At home, his mum started up the minute he walked in the door. She still had on her best blouse because she'd been to see the Quaker minister, the Friend-in-Chief or whatever he was called.

'Ever such a simple ceremony,' she wittered. 'No pomp or fuss, and you get a lovely certificate that we all sign. The whole congregation!' She put her hand to her heart as if a signed certificate was akin to a divine blessing. 'What do you think? A Quaker wedding, will it be?'

Tom loosened his tie and draped his jacket over the stair-post. 'I don't mind, Mum. If Jillie's happy with it—'

'But I want you *both* to be happy with it. As for timings, it's whenever you're ready. Next month if that suits.'

'You know that's too soon.' He went into the kitchen and his mum followed. 'We'll need savings.'

'There's soup. Or shall I fry you egg and chips?'

'Soup's fine,' he said, reaching for the matchbox to light the ring. He tried to grip the box with the mangled stumps of fingers but it slid out of his grasp and matches scattered across the floor.

'Let me do it, love.' She'd already bent down to start picking up the mess. Christ, he hated it when she treated him like an invalid, when she clucked with sympathy. And it was a dishonest kind of sympathy, because he knew that she was absolutely bloody delighted he'd had half his hand shot off at Jarama. 'Escaped with a Blighty,' he'd overheard her telling one of the new Quaker friends, barely disguising the glee in her voice. To think how upset she'd been about him going, yet the fascists in Spain had been able to achieve what Mosley never could. They'd got him sent home and would keep him home for good. No army would want him now.

He crouched and picked up the last few matches, dropped them into the box which she held open. She was on about the wedding again.

'Maybe not next month, love, but the autumn, perhaps? September's good for a wedding. *Married in September's golden glow, smooth and serene your life will go.*' She lit the gas ring and took a bowl from the rack.

Tom sat down heavily at the table. 'Next year, more like. There's no rush, is there?'

She sighed. 'I'm looking forward to it, that's all. To having Jillie here, and God willing, you'll want to start a family. It's awfully quiet since Mr Frowse went. Can't believe I'm saying it but I miss the racket from his wireless, I really do.'

'We won't be living here permanent, you know that, Mum.'

'But a year or two, while you're saving up? And think what a help I could be to Jillie. She's a smashing girl but she won't know much about homemaking, if the mother is anything to go by. We'll be a marvellous team, I know it.'

'She's very fond of you.'

Bea smiled. 'You couldn't have chosen better.'

32

The minute he came in from work she could tell Tom was in a strange mood: jittery with the matches, snappy about the wedding. And now he'd disappeared to bed for an early night. She could hear him moving around in the front bedroom. It was a nice-sized room, there'd be plenty of space for Jillie too, and of course the box room next door would be perfect for a new arrival.

It was nine-thirty, a warm evening, and she hadn't yet drawn the blackout blinds: there was still enough light to knit by. She had almost finished another blanket for the refugee children. Poor little mites with their twiggy legs and shadows under their eyes. What a crime it was, she thought, to have bags under your eyes at the age of seven.

She'd washed the jumpers before she unpicked them but Harold's presence was there somehow, the inky smell of him mixed up with the scent of soap flakes. Even before the funeral there were mutters about clearing his clothes – Mary next door had been fixated on it, seemed to think Bea would never stop grieving until all traces of Harold had been removed from the house. But Bea had held firm and now she was glad. Harold would be pleased to think of his old pullovers helping out those unfortunate children. 'Isn't that right, love?' she said to him under her breath.

Upstairs, there was a creak as Tom climbed into bed. He'd filled out over the past couple of years. Thank heavens, because when he came back from Spain he was a pitiful sight, thin and grubby, his poor arm strapped up against a too-big white shirt donated by the Red Cross. There were tears in Harold's eyes, the day Tom arrived home. Later, in bed, Harold sobbed with relief to have him back, and Bea felt guilty for ever doubting his love for their son. Harold was very ill. The winter fever had turned out to be something much worse: a 'mass' was what the doctor called it, a mass in his lungs that would only grow bigger. They'd known nothing but fear since the diagnosis, but when Harold stopped crying that night Bea sensed a new peace in his soul. With Tom home, Harold gave himself permission to die. It was as if he had found his Inward Light, just as the Quakers described it.

Bea looked up and realized she was sitting in near-darkness. She drew the blinds, switched on the lamp and fiddled with the wireless dial. When the knock came on the door it was very quiet at first, and she dismissed the tapping as drumbeats on the music programme. But no, there was the knock again, in the silent seconds before the dance band began the next number. She lifted the edge of the blind and peered through the side pane of the bay window, onto the path. The person on the doorstep was standing close to the front door. All she could see was the sleeve of a dark-coloured jacket.

The argument had blown up over a pair of tweezers, of all things. The mother had lost the tweezers and accused Jillie of taking them, and Jillie knew she hadn't but her mother flew into a rage, lobbed a high-heeled shoe from the top of the stairs right down to the bottom where Jillie was standing in the hallway. She hadn't dodged quick enough and there was a lump on the back of her head where the heel had hit.

'Sorry to turn up so late,' sobbed Jillie. She was on the settee between Tom and Bea. 'I can't go back there. Not tonight. She's cracked.'

Tom looked at Bea over Jillie's bowed head. 'I'll walk you back home if you like,' he said. 'See if she's calmed down.'

'Nonsense, Tom,' dismissed Bea. 'You can't go out like that.' She flapped her hand in his direction, frowning at his pyjamas. 'Stay here, Jillie. I'll make up the spare room.'

Jillie blew her nose and gazed at Bea. 'Would you? Oh, Mrs Smart, I'd be ever so grateful.'

'Won't your mum worry?' asked Tom.

'I told her I was coming here. Anyway, it serves her right.' She sniffed triumphantly and circled her shoulders, stretched a hand out – her fingernails were painted cherry red, Bea noticed – and rested it on Tom's knee.

Next morning Bea watched Tom saying goodbye to Jillie on the front path. She had tipped her little face up to him, and both arms were flung around his neck. He patted her in a way that was kind but not tender. Perhaps it gave him discomfort to be embraced so fiercely; his poor arm had never completely healed, and his hand often flared up around the scars. Eventually she peeled off him, and then he pecked her on the cheek and rushed off towards the station. Jillie had to get to her job, too, but she didn't seem in much of a hurry. She checked her face in a pocket mirror, patted some powder over the spots and then sauntered towards the park.

Bea went into the box room and saw that Jillie hadn't pulled the sheets back for airing. Hadn't even drawn the curtains. The girl was under a lot of strain, bless her. She'd find no arguments once she was living here, thought Bea. No tweezers or flying shoes.

The billboard headline leaped out as she passed the newsagent's *en route* to the library: MORE FASCISTS DETAINED. Her breath quickened a little, to think what might have been if she'd stayed in the movement. Fortunate to have got out when she did, to have broken all ties. It had been difficult at the time, quite a wrench. But once she was out she'd begun to feel a giddying sense of relief. She could go to Mr Perlman's with a clear conscience. She no longer had to puzzle over the rights and wrongs of this policy or that. Harold had been pleased, too. 'Never quite trusted Mosley,' he'd muttered. And of course if she hadn't left the blackshirts, she would never have found the Quakers. Odd how things turned out.

She wasn't one for mysticism, for souls and spirituality. But the Friends talked about the spirit in a matter-of-fact, gentle fashion – nothing hellfire or hocus-pocus about it. They left you alone to find peace in your own way. *Shine a light into the dark corners of your mind* – that's what you had to do. And you could do it just by sitting quietly and thinking peaceful thoughts. It was a kind of deliverance.

On the way home from the library, her basket weighed down with a fresh set of books, she took a detour into Manor Park. It was warm and the young squirrels played among the branches. The avenue of horse chestnuts was in full bloom, magnificent white spikes that took your breath away. For the first time in months she thought of Charles – the chestnut in flower outside the hotel window, the lilies in the vase – and she allowed her mind to drift and sway around the memory.

A memory. That's all it could ever be. She would never see him again now, she'd made sure of that. Sometimes Bea remembered Hazel, swallowed down a surge of guilt at the letter she had sent Tom, but it didn't take much to reassure herself. The means had justified the ends. As a mother, you had to do what was right, even when the right thing seemed awfully close to the wrong.

33

Jasmin had decided that she didn't like the beach. 'Too hurty,' she said, when the pebbles dug into her feet as she struggled towards the patch of sand beyond the shingle. Francine had some sympathy – she herself had always found the shingle an abomination – but she would have to jolly Jasmin along, otherwise they would be stuck in the house all afternoon and the prospect of that was enough to make Francine weep.

'We'll buy you some beach shoes for next time, darling,' called Francine. She watched Jasmin lunge forward, her tangled hair lifting in the breeze, bucket wobbling in her hand. 'There, you've made it now. Build a sandcastle. Good girl.' Francine huffed warm breath onto the lenses of her sunglasses, polished them with the hem of her dress and put them on. She would keep her eyes straight ahead, out towards the horizon, and try to believe that the world was normal. The barbed wire hadn't quite reached this stretch of beach yet. Bognor seafront looked a fright, and Mrs Waite had told her that the foreshore would soon be mined. Gun emplacements, scaffolding – Sussex was ready for the Hun.

The evacuation from France had begun at the end of May, the rag-tag fleet sailing across the Channel while at home anyone with a traitorous whiff was rounded up and detained. Infuriating that Hazel should be among them, but Francine could understand the government's paranoia. And now the troops, what was left of them, were home. France had fallen, and nothing but the sea and this *hurty* beach stood between England and the enemy. God, the irony was almost amusing. All those children evacuated from London to the south coast, yet now their parents were demanding their safe return to the capital. Perhaps, when she visited Holloway next week, she could explain to Hazel that Sussex was no longer a haven, that they'd actually be better off in Earls Court. If the Nazis stepped onto the beach at Aldwick, where on earth would they hide? In London there would be options.

Separation had been the tactic thus far – separate mealtimes, separate outings, separate rooms. Paul and Adriana had, grudgingly, conceded the master bedroom to Francine, decamping to the guest room, while Jasmin was in Hazel's old room, delighted with the teddy bears and the music box and the patchwork eiderdown sewn by Nanny Felix all those years ago. There were occasional conversations in the hallway or the drawing room, polite words masking a thousand resentments. The formality couldn't last. One more week – one more day – and the pretence would be blown apart.

She yearned for Charles. The ring was still in its box, and she took it out every night and wore it for a minute or two, flashing her hand in front of the dressing-room mirror. Marriage seemed more of an impossibility than ever, and the war was just another complication. Still, there was Tuesday to look forward to. After Holloway, she would take a cab straight to Bruton Street.

Closing her eyes, she listened to the swish of the incoming tide. It wouldn't be long before the sand was swallowed. And then it would be shingle or nothing, and Jasmin would whine to go back to the house, and Mrs Waite would pounce, fretting about what to cook for dinner and whom to serve, when and where.

'Nee-Nee, look!'

Jasmin had fished something out of the large rock pool at the base of a breakwater, and now she was waving it in the air. It looked like a tin hat, seaweed dripping from the strap.

'Put that down, darling.'

But it was too late. Jasmin had tipped it onto her head. The hat covered her eyes and rested on the pink bridge of her nose.

'Please take it off!' Francine called. 'We don't know where it's been.'

Jasmin giggled and marched unseeing towards the shingle with her arms outstretched, as if she were playing a game of blind man's buff. Her right foot stubbed up against a rock and she fell sideways, screeching as her head hit the sand.

'*Silly* girl!' Francine said under her breath. She sighed and stood up from the beach chair. Its wooden frame creaked – the old thing was on the verge of collapse. She didn't want to step onto the wet sand in her white leather shoes, but really there was no choice. Jasmin didn't seem to be getting up; she was howling, the hat still over her eyes. Gulls wheeled and screamed as Francine picked her way across the pebbles.

'Sit up, darling. Come on.' Francine crouched over her granddaughter, grasped her shoulders and pulled her up to sitting. It was only then that she noticed the holes on one side of the hat, the side where Jasmin had fallen. Like bullet holes, she thought, and then with a twist of fear she realized that in all likelihood they *were* bullet holes, and for all she knew the hat might have company; there could be a dead soldier or a mash of brains or any monstrous sight washed up by the hideous tide.

Carefully she tried to lift the hat but it was strangely resistant. One of the holes was almost triangular, folded inwards. Francine edged the hat to one side and felt a lurch of nausea as she realized the bent metal was wedged into Jasmin's scalp. Gently she pulled, and as the hat finally came free there was a sickening slicing sound. Blood spilt from the deep wound, darkening Jasmin's blonde tangles. Francine let the hat drop, heard it thump to the sand. A hush fell over the beach – the waves, the gulls, Jasmin's cries; all were silent – and Francine looked around in bewilderment at the sudden, terrible peace.

34

It was like living inside Schoenberg's head. Mornings were the noisiest. Metal doors clanked, keys jangled, Blakeys on boot heels struck like tolling bells on iron spiral staircases. The clash of chords would echo in her ears even after the morning had quietened.

Hazel looked down at the mug of weak cocoa. A layer of grease floated on the top. Soon, when she could summon the strength, she would take her spoon and skim off the grease, clasp the handleless mug, like a child, and gulp down the lukewarm liquid, trying not to taste or to smell. Trying not to gag. Then she would chew the bread – ignoring the flecks of unidentifiable grey – and wait to be let out for the half-hour's exercise. In the yard she would walk slowly with her eyes raised to the sky. She would not look at Lucia, she would not look at the Holloway ground. Only the sky above gave her comfort. It was not part of this place; it was free and belonged to her as much as it belonged to Jasmin. A brief moment of sharing.

Sixteen days. Sixteen days she had been imprisoned and still no date for her appeal to be heard. She hadn't been charged, had barely been questioned. It didn't matter how much she pleaded, the wardresses just stared stone-faced, parroting the same lines about 18Bs and the Advisory Committee and backlogs and *patience*.

F-wing's cells had been recently whitewashed. She was lucky, one inmate had told her, to have escaped the filth of other wings, where mushrooms and rats were liable to spawn overnight. But the whitewash masked nothing. Already it was flaking, wet with damp, impervious to the hot June sun and the tantalizing summer breezes that swooped into the exercise yard.

She had dreamed, once, that this cell was the summer house – its size was similar, she supposed – and she was with Tom, could feel him inside her, his skin welded to hers, their bodies moving like a tide, and the moment was coming, that indescribable moment, when their love would be equal and pure. She felt the truth even for a fraction of a second after the air-raid siren wailed and she woke to see the dim blue landing light seeping beneath the cell door.

Warnings were frequent; some nights she could hear aircraft overhead. But still no bombs.

'Hazel, please.'

Lucia had fallen into step beside her and she was trying – again – to strike up conversation. Hazel dug her fingernails into the palms of her hands, kept her focus on a faraway cirrus cloud, ignoring the crunch of pain in the muscles at the base of her neck. Never again would she speak to Lucia. She would not speak to any of the fascist women, the believers, the defiant inmates who clustered in the yard and around the trestle tables at mealtimes, humming fascist anthems when they thought the wardresses weren't listening. They feigned cheerfulness, affected a kind of camaraderie. Mrs Dunn had appeared for the first time a few days previously and there was a round of quiet applause as she took her seat on the bench, her right arm lifted in a coded half-salute.

'All right, you won't speak to me,' said Lucia. 'But that doesn't mean I can't speak to you.'

Hazel watched the cloud drift southwards. It was shaped like a swallow on the wing. Its shape would change, it might divide into two, or three, but later Jasmin might look up and her eyes might fix on the same patch of moisture and air.

'I should have covered for you when they came to the flat. Hazel? I know I shouldn't have mentioned the drum corps. But they probably would have taken you anyway, don't you see? Forgive me? I can't bear to see you punishing yourself like this.' She reached out her hand and touched Hazel's elbow.

Hazel stood still in the yard and screamed.

It was Tuesday and her mother was visiting later in the morning. The wardresses listened in on conversations, made it clear that they would be writing reports. Hazel saw this as a good thing: they could listen and report as much as they liked, because then they would learn that she should not be here, that she had only become a blackshirt because she needed a home for her daughter. What a cruel bargain that had turned out to be.

Lying on the rough-woven blanket, she began the ritual mental torture, the game of *if onlys*. If only Winnie had arrived fifteen minutes earlier. They would all be in Devon by now; the police wouldn't have bothered coming after her there, would they? If only they'd gone the week before, the date Winnie had first mentioned, and that Hazel hadn't said she'd need a little more time to tie up her work in the office, because it wouldn't be fair to leave Mr Boyne high and dry.

If only Lucia had been a true friend. Hazel understood her now. Lucia wanted someone she could possess, a kind of pet, dutiful and loyal. Yet she had chosen badly – first Hazel, and then Philip, each with ties beyond Lucia's control: a daughter, a wife. No wonder she was bitter.

With a blunt fingernail Hazel picked at a flake of white paint on the wall, exposing the murky red brick beneath. No. The *if onlys* were an indulgence, an attempt to mask her own culpability. No one had forced her to join the movement, had they? She had been intrigued by it, flattered by Lucia's friendship that summer when she was sixteen and hopelessly bored. And the following summer, when she was so desperate to keep Jasmin, sharing a flat with Lucia had seemed like the perfect solution, a wonderful blessing. Blackshirt meetings were a distraction; she had looked forward to drum practice with Winnie, the weekend parades, the escape from her relentless routine. She had learned to salute along with the rest of them, found herself swept up in the speeches and the singing. Oh, she had never swallowed the rhetoric, had never shared the obsession with the Jews, but she had gone along with it, and perhaps that made her worse than the others. She had marched and cheered, but she had never truly believed.

Would she have joined the movement if it hadn't been for Jasmin? She turned away from the brick wall and faced the crooked chair in the corner of her cell. It was a hard question, but she was getting closer to the heart. And in the heart, that black heart, lay Charles. It was Charles who had changed everything, twisted her mind, turned her against the truth. Against Tom.

If only she had never known Charles.

'Alexander!' The wardress threw the door wide and stood back. 'Visitor waiting.'

Her mother looked surprisingly undecorative. She wore a mustard-coloured sundress with a plain silk scarf and no jewellery. She had taken off her hat, revealing grey roots around her temples.

As Hazel approached the table, Francine stood up. There was a pained expression on her mother's face. No doubt Francine was shocked to see how thin Hazel had become over the last fortnight, how lank and untidy her hair had grown.

'Darling,' said Francine. There was a handkerchief in her hand. Hazel felt dazzled by the whiteness of the cotton, its purity against the grime of this low-ceilinged room. The handkerchief was wet, she registered. Her mother had been crying. It was not like Francine to cry.

'What is it?' asked Hazel, leaning across the table to grasp her mother's arm. 'What is it? Not Jasmin?' The pitch of her voice rose and heads turned towards them. 'Jasmin?'

A voice called out from behind her. 'The prisoner must sit!'

Hazel dropped into her seat. Hysteria bubbled in her chest and her breath came in gasps. Nothing had been said yet. Nothing. She was being ridiculous.

Francine dabbed at her eyes with the handkerchief. 'I'm afraid there's been an accident,' she said.

Flashes of sun-white light pulsed across the room. Hazel heard her mother's words as if through a distant gramophone. The skin on the back of her neck tightened and froze.

'Jasmin is in the hospital. She's going to be all right, we . . . we think. The doctors are very positive. It's a cut to her head, a piece of metal on the beach, silly accident, happened in a heartbeat, there was nothing I could have done. One of those silly, silly things.'

'A cut?'

'Well, it's rather deep, they worry about infection. But darling, honestly, she's in the right place. Your father is with her today.'

'She needs me.'

'In an ideal world, of course, but –' She twisted one corner of the handkerchief and wound it around her forefinger.

Hazel clutched at the table, fixing her eyes on a cigarette scorch in the wood, willing the prison walls to crumble into dust. She would go insane if she could not be with Jasmin. She wanted to run to the wardress, to shake her and demand to be released that very second. 'They have to listen,' she said, her voice rising again. 'There must be a way . . . some compassion. Please!' She scraped back the chair, stepped across the floor to face the wardress. She was a middle-aged woman with a crescent of small moles on one cheek, not so hard-faced as some of the others.

'Let me see the committee. Please.' Hazel laced her fingers together, prayer hands pleading. 'I must see the committee.'

The duty doctor gave her a sleeping draught but it did nothing to still her mind. Back in her cell, Hazel stared at the 25-watt bulb burning in its metal cage. Twenty minutes till lights out. A letter, that was her only hope. There was time to write a letter, if she was quick. Tom worked on a newspaper, didn't he? He would have connections. They would vet the letter but it would get through, so long as she kept it superficial, said nothing about the prison or the conditions.

Gripping the pencil, her hand began to tremble, and as she wrote, a dreadful weariness trickled and dripped through her limbs.

35

'Post for you,' his mum said, nodding towards the rack on the wall where they kept the keys and the letters.

It had been a difficult day at work. Crow on the rampage again – no one was safe from his curses. All Tom wanted was to unlace his shoes and stretch out on his bed, drift off to nothingness. But no, here was a letter and his mum was clearly curious. He took the envelope from the rack. You couldn't blame her for hovering. The writing wasn't familiar and the postmark was faint, impossible to distinguish in the gloom of the hall passage. He balanced the envelope on his knee and tore it open with his good hand. Shaking out the letter, he scanned down to the name at the bottom.

'Not bad news, I hope?'

'What?' He fought to unscramble his brain, to counteract the shock. 'No . . . a comrade from Spain. He might be passing through London.' Tom refolded the letter and stuffed it into his jacket pocket, searching for the right words, the small talk to stall her interest. 'Warm again, eh?' he said. 'I'll have some lemonade if there's any left?'

'Just about,' she said, disappearing into the kitchen. 'Last of the lemons, though.'

He went into the front room and sat on the settee next to

a stack of neatly folded blankets. Strange to see his father's pullovers reconfigured: those familiar earthy colours – brown, beige, moss green. He chewed his lip as he pictured the grave, new grass grown over the mound, lush and thick. He walked across to the window. Quickly he took out the letter again and read through the short paragraph. She wanted him to visit her in Holloway. *An urgent family crisis. Please believe I do not ask this lightly.* And then that strange phrase, the writing growing fainter, weakening. *It is of your intimate concern.*

The nerve of her! He ought to rip the letter to pieces, pretend it had never arrived. It would be easy enough to ignore, no harm done. For all she knew he no longer lived at Boone Street. Yet she had remembered the address, must have kept the notes that he'd stuffed under the summer-house door. It had been – what? – over three years since they were in touch.

Bea took a coaster from the mantelpiece and set the glass down on the side table. 'Seeing Jillie tonight, love?'

Jillie. What had they arranged? 'She's coming over, I think.'

'Off out?'

'We'll stay in with the wireless, Mum. Keep you company.'

'You'd better have a shave. She won't think much of you looking like that.'

In the bathroom, he lathered his face with shaving soap. His left hand ached; there was a pain in his missing fingers, and the scar on his palm itched. It had been joined by other scars, a criss-cross of shrapnel wounds working their way up his arm, yet this one was still distinct, still had the power to set his teeth on edge. Her phrases dangled and looped. *It is of your intimate concern.* What the hell was she talking about? He drew the razor across his skin. Through the open window, he heard a woman laugh. Water splashing onto a parched flowerbed. He rinsed the blade in the sink, turned his face to shave the other side. Perhaps he *would* visit her, and he'd do it soon. Yes, he'd see if he could get a visiting order. After all, there might be a story in it, he might be able to stand up those tales of luxury living for the 18Bs. God knows he could do with getting into Crow's good books.

The order was granted, no questions asked. All right, he wasn't a famous reporter, hardly a household name, but he'd thought someone in the prison might run a check, discover that he was a journalist for the *Chronicle*. But no, here he was on the number 29 bus, the visiting pass folded inside his shirt pocket. He could feel the friction of the paper, the heat of it. It might be dangerous, he knew that. It might as well be ticking.

The bus passed St Pancras, close to the tenement block where Jacob had lived. Tom had visited once, when he was just home from Spain. On the hillside at Jarama, he'd pieced back together the Charlotte Mew, and now he felt that Jacob's family would like to have the book, with all its scribbles and underlinings, the jottings of Jacob's own poetry in the blank pages at the back. There were photographs to pass on too, and an old pocket watch that had somehow survived the attack.

Arriving at the flat, Tom had seen that the blinds were still drawn. Inside, Jacob's mother greeted him with an embrace. A young woman, the ex-fiancée, was there too. 'He often spoke of you,' Tom said to the girl, and she had pawed at her heart as if it would break.

Holloway loomed, ugly and ornate, its Victorian turrets and crenellated walls deep red against the morning sky. He'd never been inside a prison before, assumed it would be nothing like he'd imagined, but in fact it was exactly as he'd imagined: bunches of keys hanging from the belts of unsmiling guards; gloom and damp; a stink of boiled cabbage and disinfectant. He was patted down and shown into the visiting room with the others who were waiting. They were women in the main, some higher class, others down-at-heel in threadbare cardies hugged to their skinny bodies. It was cold in here, despite the June sun blazing outside.

He took his seat on one side of a wooden table and waited. His tactic, he'd decided, would be to say very little. To let her speak and see what came out. Then, once the ice was broken, he'd steer her in the direction of his hoped-for story. *So, how are they treating you? Plenty to eat?*

The prisoners began to file in. A scrawny girl with dark hair scraped into a bun drew out the chair opposite him. He rose, meaning to tell her she'd made a mistake, that he was waiting for someone else, but then the girl's mouth opened in a half-smile and he saw the chip on her tooth.

'Hazel?'

Her smile disappeared as she sat in the chair. She looked a decade older, her face too thin and her forehead screwed into a frown.

'Your hand?' she said.

Damn. He'd meant to keep it on his lap under the table. But of course he'd stood up and now the mangled lump was on display.

'Wounded in Spain.'

'I had no idea. When your letters stopped. Well –' she took a deep breath – 'now I can see why.'

'Oh, I'm not left-handed. I can still write.'

There was a pause, a spike of silence between them.

'But you chose not to.'

'I'm surprised you noticed,' said Tom. 'I heard you were rather busy entertaining at home.' Christ, so much for his tactic, for laying low, letting her speak. Turned out he couldn't keep his bloody mouth shut.

'Entertaining? You mean – what do you mean?' Her eyes seemed to ignite, a flash of understanding. 'Entertaining lovers?'

'Apparently so.'

She swallowed and looked over to the clock on the far wall. 'There isn't time to go into much detail, Tom. I have no idea what you've been told, or by whom.' She gave a bitter laugh. 'There haven't been any lovers. What I'm going to tell you now is the truth. I swear it on my daughter's life.' She put one hand to her heart and sobbed.

Tom reeled back in his chair. A daughter? So she *had* been about! Why, she even had a bastard to show for her efforts.

But he was here now, so he would have to listen. He folded his arms, right over left, so that she would not stare or be tempted to show him any pity.

Light a cigarette and keep walking. Turn south down York Way towards King's Cross. He recited instructions as he walked. If he were a machine, it would be easier; moving parts and cogs that didn't have to think. But his legs only grew more unsteady and his heart roared louder than the stoked furnaces in the engines beyond the high station wall.

Turning into a side street, he saw a pub with its doors just opening for the lunch-time trade. He ordered a brandy and downed it at the bar, almost choking as the heat flared in his throat. Next he ordered a pint, and took it to a tucked-away table near an open door which led onto the yard. A dog was tied up, asleep in the shade of an old advertising hoarding. MY GOODNESS MY GUINNESS.

It was the detail of Hazel's story that made him dizzy. Only a lunatic could have made all that up. She was frantic, that was clear. Beside herself with anxiety. Not a lunatic, though. It was hard to believe she was mad.

Impossible to stop his thoughts racing. Charles. The mother's lover. The swine had forced himself on her, threatened to have him – Tom – arrested for rape. Told her she was a whore. It was no wonder he'd never heard from her again that summer. Girl must have been terrified. He'd thought it was the start of something wonderful, turned against her when the promised letter never arrived. He should have tried harder to get to the truth, should have persisted, shouldn't have been so proud. And then when they *did* meet, when she was all set to tell him about the daughter as they sat drinking tea by the Thames, he'd boasted about Spain, took pleasure in surprising her with the news. He'd relished the opportunity to let *her* down, to get his own back.

Oh, he'd softened soon enough, treasured her letters when they began to arrive. But when his mum's letter came, pride kicked back in. He never seriously questioned the truth of Bea's gossip.

He swigged the pint and felt his shoulders begin to loosen. Of course he'd believed his mum. There was no reason not to: she had never lied to him before. And what if Hazel was lying again today? She was desperate, wasn't she?

Prison could do strange things to your head. There were comrades who'd been in Franco's camps, still struggling to recover. Focus on the facts: he knew for a fact that Hazel was easy, she'd proved as much in the summer house. Slept with him – when? It was only the fourth time they'd met. There'd been no persuasion on his part, no weasel words. The sex had happened, natural as breathing. At the time he'd thought it was something beautiful and magical between them, a pact of love. Now here she was, saying he'd been right all along. It *had* been extraordinary, she had felt the same. She had never loved anyone else.

The child. Jasmin. He tested the name, repeating it under his breath. She was four years old, born April '36. He counted back again. The dates were right. 'She has blonde hair and a dimple,' Hazel had said, and Tom had put his hand to his own face. 'I believe, I hope, that Jasmin is your daughter . . . but I can't be sure. So I kept it a secret. I was ashamed. And you didn't want children. You'd said that.' She stared down at her fingernails.

'Why are you telling me this now?' asked Tom.

'Jasmin is very ill in hospital. An accident, some kind of infection. I have to get out of here. Tom, please, if there's anything you can do . . . Any influence you might have. I thought – with your job on the newspaper?'

The wardress had coughed and tapped her foot on the oilcloth floor.

That was the reason she'd summoned him, then. The daughter was ill. She believed he might be of some use.

He went out into the pub yard and found the privy, knees almost buckling as he took a piss, the last remnants of energy draining from him. If Hazel's story was true, then he should try to help her. He could speak to Gerald. Gerald was well-connected. Old school tie and all that, played golf with a cousin of Churchill's. But did he want to confide in Gerald? Christ. It was tempting just to stay here, to keep drinking until his brain was flat. But he had to get back to Lewisham. There were a few questions he needed to ask his mother.

At Charing Cross the trains were delayed; a signalling problem outside Peckham. He stood against a pillar near the tobacconist's stand, keeping his head down because the last thing he needed was to see anyone from work. He'd swapped his day off with Gerald, said it was to take his mum to a hospital appointment.

An older man in a tan jacket ambled up to the stand, bought twenty Viceroy and walked off in the direction of Villiers Street. The man was about his dad's age, fifty-odd. He wore the same kind of boots, dark brown and polished to such a shine you could see the girders of the station roof reflected in the leather. Grief dropped an iron weight on his chest. His dad had been dead three years, and some days Tom found it easy to forget. Not on a day like this, though. A day when he discovered that he might be a father, that his dad might have died without ever knowing he had a granddaughter, a little fair-haired girl with a dimple in her chin.

He waited until after tea, when they were settled in the front room. 'I've been looking through my old letters,' he said. 'The ones you wrote to me in Spain.'

'Best forgotten, I would have thought.' Bea shook her head. 'Dreadful days.'

'Worse to come.'

'Not for you, God willing.'

'Do you remember writing to me about the blackshirt girls?'

'Not especially.' The click of her knitting needles slowed. The question had unnerved her, he could sense that.

'You mentioned a girl called Hazel Alexander. You said she was notorious, men dancing to her tune.'

Bea replied that she couldn't possibly remember. It was years ago, a different time. But her cheeks had coloured, there was a hesitancy in her voice, and in that moment Tom felt certain that his mother was lying. She had lied about Hazel going with other men. Why? Had she got wind of his correspondence with Hazel, tried to sabotage their love? My God. She was jealous! Jealous of his relationship with a better class of girl. Did she think she'd be left behind?

Tom stood up and turned off the wireless; Elgar crackled and died. 'Tell me why you lied about Hazel.'

'For goodness' sake, Tom! I've no idea what you're talking about.' She leaned over and dropped her knitting on the lid of the sewing basket. 'You've spent too many hours up the Gaumont, gawping at films. All this melodrama –' she folded her arms against her bosom – 'my own son calling me a liar!'

He crouched at her feet and put one hand on her knee, speaking in a low voice and in a tone that seemed to come from a dark place that neither of them knew existed. 'Mum. If you can't give me a good explanation, I swear I'll never forgive you. You can't know how important this is. It's the most important—' His voice cracked and he stood up quickly. 'I'll move away, I swear. Don't expect to come to the wedding.'

Her face paled. She was silent for a moment and her lips moved soundlessly, as if she was trying to remember something, and then she cleared her throat and began to speak in a jumble of words. 'Hazel, you say? No, no, thinking back I must have made a mistake, got my names muddled. So many of them at HQ, it was a Christmas bazaar, I think, when we met. Perhaps Hazel might have been the wrong name – it was the friend who was a strumpet. Fancy name. Lucia, was it?'

'Oh Christ, Mum.' Tom groaned and paced over to the window, balled his hand into a fist and held it against the glass. 'Mum, what have you done?'

'What on earth does it matter?' She raised her voice, trying to keep it strong, to mask the tremble. 'Those girls are nothing to you. You have Jillie!'

The air-raid siren answered, a wail that claimed Jillie's name and seemed to twist and toy with it as they made their way wordlessly to the Anderson shelter in the back garden. Tom fumbled with the matches and managed to light a candle, then wedged the door shut with sandbags. He glanced at Bea's face in the candlelight, caught the look of alarm in her eyes. It didn't make sense. His mum was good with names, always had been. Now she was staring at the photograph hanging on the shelter wall – the family snapshot taken at Margate; Tom in the middle, his mum and dad either side.

'You did it deliberately,' he said. 'Why? Why did you lie about Hazel?'

The siren stopped but the silence was more threatening. Tom waited for his mum to answer the question. 'I didn't see it as a lie,' said Bea, finally. 'A white lie, maybe. I was trying to protect you.'

She perched on the edge of the straight-backed chair, her eyes still focused on the shadowy photograph. Her hands were slotted under her thighs and she rocked a little, forwards and back, forwards and back. Tom stood, his heart knocking in his throat, swallowing down his rage.

'Go on,' he said.

'I found a letter you'd written to Hazel in your bedroom, tucked in a box of birds' eggs. So I knew there was something between the two of you. And then I met her at the bazaar, and I saw the set she mixed with, and, well, I took against them. I'm not ashamed!' she burst out. 'They're ill-mannered, for all their money, and Lucia was the worst of them, gadding about with married men. Hazel was Lucia's friend so it stood to reason . . . I didn't want you to get hurt.'

'It was none of your business,' said Tom. 'You should never have interfered.'

'I'm sorry. I didn't see it would harm, honestly I didn't.'

'You don't see much, do you?'

Bea started at the crump of a direct hit, a few streets away to the west. The glass shook in the Margate photograph. Tom knew he couldn't stay here, no matter that there were bombs dropping outside. He had to get out, get away from his mother and the oppressive shelter walls. He kicked aside the sandbags, wrenched open the door and banged it shut behind him, ignoring Bea's cries as she pleaded with him not to leave.

The house seemed sticky in the honeyed twilight. A trap. In the front room he lifted one of the folded blankets from the settee and held it to his nose, inhaling the faintest scent of his father. He ought to go back to Bea, ought to watch over her, but the betrayal was too great. He couldn't forgive what she'd done. She deserved to be punished.

Outside, the street was empty: good citizens, hiding, all. Tom strode away from the house thinking he would go to Jillie's, but instead he started walking north, up Mounts Pond

Road, across the Heath and down into Greenwich. Aircraft whined overhead. There was the sound of machine-gun fire, shrapnel rattling off roof tiles, and his thoughts turned to Spain, to Jacob and his poems. *For Fate with jealous eye does see two perfect Loves.* Fate! His mum fancied herself as fate all right; sticking her oar in, trying to control his life.

A warden yelled at him to take cover, and he was forced to clatter down the steps of a basement shelter. When the all-clear sounded he was first out, on towards the river, pushing through the crowds spilling free from the foot tunnel under the Thames. On the Isle of Dogs he stayed close to the dock walls, kept heading north, guided by the reddening clouds to the west.

Finally, he reached Limehouse and turned in to Bill's narrow street. He tapped on the front window of the end terrace and waited until he saw Petra's face peeping from behind the blind. She squinted and he called softly: 'It's Tom.'

The front door opened and she bustled him in, kissing him on both cheeks. 'You're not well?' she said. 'Come and sit. Bill is on his late shift. His last shift too, you know?'

'I heard. I'm sorry. I shouldn't have come today.' Christ. What a shameful thing. He'd been so wrapped up in himself that he'd forgotten Bill's papers had come. He ought to leave now, couldn't possibly burden Petra with all his troubles.

'No, no. I'm pleased. The children are asleep and it's lonely. Just my stories –' She gestured at a book that lay face-down on the armchair. It would be a book by some Russian writer, ever so highbrow. The kind of book he'd like to read one day.

'Schnapps?'

He nodded. A strong drink was what he needed, the stronger the better.

She poured the clear liquid into two small gold-rimmed glasses and handed one to him. He took a sip and swallowed, enjoying the burn on the back of his throat. Petra picked up the book and sat down in the armchair. How beautiful she looked under the pink-shaded lamp. 'I think you have a story of your own?' she said, leaning down to place the book on the floor. Tom nodded and took another sip. Why not tell her everything?

Petra listened quietly, her face impassive even when he reached the most sordid part of the story. When he had finished speaking she put a hand out and touched the side of his arm.

'Do you believe Hazel now, about her love for you – that she was always faithful?'

He bowed his head and screwed his eyes shut. Yes, the truth was that he did believe Hazel. He believed every word. He looked up at Petra and nodded.

'And do you love her?'

'Yes.' He tightened his grip around the glass. 'But it can't work, can it? Not when it's such a mess. And the child. This man who forced himself upon her – the mother's lover. He could be the little girl's father.'

'Naturally it can work, if you have enough love. Look at me. My family said they would never speak to me again if I married a *goy*. They love Bill now as their own son. What is the little girl's name?'

'Jasmin.'

Petra repeated the name and smiled. 'I hope that you can see her. That she gets well.'

'I hope so too. Really.' He sighed and pushed back the hair that had fallen across his eyes. 'I don't know whether I can forgive my mother. The way she interfered, slandered Hazel . . . Yet I still don't think she's telling the truth. I feel there's more to it.'

'Don't seek out trouble, Tommy. Your mother has apologized. Perhaps that can be enough?'

Tom bit his lip. 'Hazel reminds me of you,' he said. Petra shifted in her seat and he realized, too late, that he had embarrassed her. 'No, I didn't mean like that. Not in looks. I mean – her spirit reminds me of you. She's different. Interesting.'

Petra nodded. 'Different to Jillie?'

'Oh, God.' He almost laughed. 'Yes, different to Jillie.'

At home he found his mother still awake, sitting at the kitchen table. Her face was blotchy and her dressing gown was buttoned up all wrong.

'I'm back, Mum.' He lingered at the threshold, watching her veined hands as she stacked and re-stacked a small pile of coins. A sudden lurch of affection propelled him forward. 'It's all right,' he said. 'Don't cry.'

She stood to embrace him, her downy cheek soft against the stubble of his chin.

'You're safe.' Her shoulders began to shake. 'The fright you gave me, disappearing like that. Oh, Tom!' she sobbed. 'I was wrong. I should never have written that letter. I can't imagine what I was thinking. Half-crazed, I was, with you in Spain—'

Her tears were wet on his skin as he drew back. 'I can't marry Jillie,' he said.

'I know, love,' she replied. 'I know.'

36

How Tom's face had changed in the years since they'd met. Bones sharper, eyes less trusting, a shallow crease between his brows. He had seemed taller than Hazel remembered. The injured arm – terrible to think of his suffering. Yet he was making a career for himself, a reporter, just as he'd dreamed. Hazel experienced a sudden glow of pride, then shook her head. What did Tom's bravery and resilience have to do with her?

He had listened to her story without making any promises, without any sign, in fact, that he believed a single word. Leaving the visiting room, he'd walked in an exaggerated straight line as if following an invisible yardstick, his spine stiff and unyielding. She'd dragged herself back to the cell with little hope, but greater understanding. One puzzle, at least, had been solved.

How did she do it? She must have found his address when she was snooping through the letters, then written to Tom pretending to be . . . goodness knows who. No, an anonymous letter – that would be it, purporting to be from a well-wisher, poisoning Hazel's reputation with malicious talk of 'entertaining'. Cowardly, devil of a woman. Astonishing, really. Hazel hadn't thought it was possible to hate Lucia any more than she already did.

Footsteps stopped outside her cell door. It would be the doctor, she imagined, with his leather bag of pills and potions. He was early, but that was good. After Tom's visit, she needed something to make her numb.

The door swung slowly open and a wardress stood, key in hand. She jerked her head to one side. 'You're to come to the front office.'

The committee had reviewed her recent letter, and they were satisfied that she did not pose any danger to the British state. Hazel listened in disbelief. She looked at the man – the governor's clerk or whoever he was – but his words swirled, as if she was underwater and he was speaking to her from a boat bobbing on the waves. She was to reside at a fixed abode, he said, and report to the nearest police station every Monday morning at nine a.m. She was not permitted to own a camera or a motor car.

'And your address?' The clerk looked up, raising his eyebrows when she failed to respond. What was her address? Not the Kensington flat. No, she needed to get to Sussex. She gave the Aldwick address and asked when she would be free to leave.

'You may leave now.'

It took a moment for his reply to register. 'Now?' she repeated. She looked around, expecting to hear sniggers, fingers pointing and the wardress laughing because she had fallen for the trick. But there was no laughter. From the road beyond the prison, motor engines chugged and a tram bell sounded. Her pulse began to race. She was free. Almost free. 'My things. My purse?'

'The wardress will fetch your belongings. Good day.'

Hazel waited behind the counter of a locker room until the wardress reappeared with a jute sack tied with a name tag and number. 'Here you are, Miss Alexander.' She handed over the sack and smiled. 'Good luck,' she said. 'I've a niece the same age.' She smiled again, and Hazel looked at her more closely. It was the wardress with the moon-shaped moles, the one who'd been supervising – listening in – when Francine had visited earlier in the week with the news about Jasmin.

'The committee, was it you . . . ?'

The wardress straightened her back and her smile disappeared. 'The committee is obliged to examine every case on its relative merits,' she said. But there was something about her manner, a hint of conspiracy.

'Of course.' Hazel wanted to take the woman's hands, to kiss them, but it would not do, she knew. It was important to keep her guard. 'Thank you,' she said, lifting the sack and clutching it to her chest. 'Thank you with all my heart.'

Outside the prison gates, Hazel fumbled inside the sack and found her handbag and purse. The money was still there, the five-pound note and the half-crowns she had saved for Devon. It was late afternoon. She would take the Tube to Victoria. And from there a train to Chichester, to the hospital where Jasmin was waiting.

Visiting hours were over, but Hazel pleaded with the auxiliary until she gave way and went off to fetch the ward sister.

'You've been away on war work, I hear,' said the sister. She looked Hazel up and down in the corridor wondering, no doubt, why she wasn't in uniform, why she looked dirty and unwashed and smelt of sour sweat. 'I'm afraid your daughter is gravely ill. The wound is infected. Sepsis.'

Sepsis. That was blood poisoning, wasn't it? A cousin of Bronny's had sepsis after a ruptured appendix. He'd died on his tenth birthday. But Jasmin would not die. Hazel would not let her die. She felt a rush of strength through her fear.

'I must see her.'

'It's a question of *infection*, Mrs Alexander. You may wish to . . . smarten up?'

'Please. Is there a bathroom here? I have clean clothes.' She had tried to hide the jute bag by dangling it over her back, but now she let it drop in front of her. The name and number on the tag glared up, stark under the fluorescent light.

'It's out of the question,' said the sister, frowning down at the bag. She looked up and met Hazel's eye. 'Mrs Alexander, it's highly irregular for you to be here at all after visiting hours. However –' she checked the time on her fob watch – 'the patient has been calling for you. A visit may result in a more restful night. If you can return within the hour I will allow you to see her briefly. Any later than ten p.m. and you must wait until tomorrow.'

Hazel turned and ran from the hospital, down the long drive, past the lawn with its towering cedars. Ahead rose the spire of the cathedral, bone pale in the fading light. An hour was not enough time to get from Chichester to Aldwick and back. Night was falling and the streets were unlit, cars crawling along Broyle Road with their headlamps dimmed. On the right of the road was a pub. She could just make out the name on the pub sign, the small board underneath pronouncing ROOMS. She would try the Bell, and if they didn't have any vacancies, the landlord might know of a guest house nearby.

'If you don't mind the attic,' said the landlady through cigarette-clenched lips.

'Is there a bath?' asked Hazel.

'Lavatory on the downstairs landing but there's a sink in the room. You can top and tail at least.'

Hazel nodded her thanks as the landlady handed over a small towel and a sliver of soap. She was so grateful she couldn't speak. If she tried to speak she would cry.

The attic was stifling hot and spiders scurried around the eaves, but after the dank of Holloway, the room seemed close to heaven.

Hazel arrived back at the hospital with fifteen minutes to spare. The sister gave a brisk nod and asked a nurse to take Mrs Alexander to Ward 3.

'Ten minutes, no more,' she said.

Night had fallen and the ward was dark, pungent with the hot sweet smell of sickness. Blackout blinds were fixed to the windows. It couldn't be right, thought Hazel, for ill children to be entombed like this, in a room with no air. The nurse switched on a dim torch and led Hazel to a bed under the farthest window.

Jasmin's head was bandaged, and she lay sleeping on her back. Even in this feeble light, Hazel could see the high colour on her cheeks, the clammy sheen above her brow.

She reached over to stroke her daughter's cheek but the nurse stepped forward, palm raised.

'Please don't wake her,' she whispered. 'Finally dropped

off twenty minutes ago and she's a devil to get back to sleep. I'll find you a chair.'

Hazel sat on the chair beside the bed and fixed her eyes on Jasmin. Her small hands lay on the blanket, fingers curling lightly upwards. She was wearing a nightie that Hazel didn't recognize, the neckline crudely stitched. Tears welled in Hazel's eyes and she was unable to stop them. This was a new kind of torture. To be so close, yet unable to touch, to embrace, to speak. But she was here. And she would be here again tomorrow, and the next day. Every day until Jasmin was better.

The minutes ticked past. Hazel shifted in her seat and the chair moved, metal legs scraping on the floor. The sound was enough. Jasmin's eyes flickered open.

'Mummy?'

Hazel put a finger to her lips, then blew her a kiss. 'Yes, it's Mummy, and I'm here for you now,' she whispered. 'Go back to sleep. You'll have a lovely sleep and I'll see you in the morning.' Jasmin smiled and closed her eyes.

Now the nurse was marching down the ward, signalling that her time was up. Hazel followed the nurse into the corridor. The floor began to vibrate beneath her feet: a fleet of aircraft passing overhead. It couldn't be the enemy or the siren would have sounded. Furies or Spitfires, scrambled from Tangmere?

'What do you do in an air raid?' asked Hazel.

'We pray.'

All night Hazel sweated and coughed in the hot attic room. She couldn't sleep but she didn't mind, didn't need the oblivion of the prison doctor's potions. By five the sun had risen and she climbed from bed. She lit a cigarette – the landlady had sold her five Black Cats from a jar behind the bar – pulled back the lace curtain and stood at the open sash window. Birdsong filled the glittering dawn. Every note imaginable, an explosion of joy. Her cough eased as she inhaled the cigarette smoke, listened to the birds – a robin's rich trill, the *peep-peep* of blue tits – then a low rumble. The sound was coming from inside the room, she realized. Her own body. When did she last eat? Well, there would be time enough for breakfast: visiting at the hospital was not until eleven. She doused the cigarette end with a trickle of water from the tap, then climbed back into bed. Finally, she fell into a deep sleep. At eight she was woken by the landlady knocking on her door, asking if toast and marmalade would be sufficient because they were completely out of bacon.

After breakfast she walked to the telephone box at the top of North Street. Her father answered after just two rings, and she felt comforted by the surprise in his voice. He sounded pleased – delighted, even – when she told him she'd been released.

'You're out? Oh, that's marvellous.' He must have muted the receiver with his hand, because his voice became muffled. 'Hazel. Released,' he called to someone – Francine? – and then he was back. 'You're in London?'

'Chichester. I caught the train yesterday evening, went straight to the hospital. I found a room for the night.'

'You should have called sooner. But how is Jasmin? Is she any better?'

'She was asleep. The nurse didn't say much. I'm visiting again at eleven. Is Mother there?'

'I thought she was at the hospital. You saw her?'

Hazel paused. 'I must have missed her somehow.'

'All-night vigil, she said.'

'We'll cross paths this morning, I expect.'

'And afterwards you must come back to Aldwick.'

'Yes. Yes, I'll see you later.'

'Shall I collect you?'

'Could you?'

The pips went and she garbled a goodbye, replaced the receiver. Her father seemed to want to see her. He had asked after Jasmin, had appeared concerned. It sounded for all the world as if he had forgiven her. That was what came of a crisis, she supposed.

There were still some coppers in her purse. The operator would be able to put her through to the *Chronicle*. She pictured Tom's face across the prison table yesterday, when she'd told him about Jasmin. The disbelief, the mistrust. Yet there was no malice. A part of him had believed her, surely?

She began to dial the operator, but her hands started to shake and in a panic she replaced the receiver. It would be better to ring Tom after the morning visit. She would have more information then. Might feel more composed.

As she walked up the hospital drive a car swept by and pulled in at the main entrance. The passenger leaned across and kissed the driver, and he put his hand up to her face, caressed her cheek.

Hazel was closer now, and as the woman climbed from the car she recognized the white sandals, the flower-shaped buckle at the ankle. The engine revved and the car spun around in a U-turn. Hazel kept her head down as the Brough passed. Now Francine was just a few paces ahead; she was climbing the stone steps up to the hospital entrance, adjusting her hat to the required angle. Why wait and let her go in first? Better to meet now than inside the hospital where people would be watching, listening.

'Mother!' Hazel called.

There was no response. Francine lifted her hand towards the brass door plate.

'Francine!'

She turned around this time, narrowed her eyes and then gasped. 'It's Hazel! Darling, how . . . ?' She flew down the steps and kissed Hazel's cheek. 'Well, this is wonderful. Have they let you out at last?'

'So it would seem.'

Francine took Hazel's hand. 'I'm so, so pleased. It will be a huge comfort to Jasmin. Now, darling, I must warn you, she doesn't look at all well.' She glanced down at her wristwatch. 'We're a few minutes early, and they're terrible sticklers. Shall we take a wander around the lawn?'

Hazel nodded. 'I saw Jasmin last night,' she said. 'I came to the hospital. Father thought you'd be here, keeping vigil.'

'Did he? I *was* here. Until tea-time.'

'And then you were with Charles.'

'Ah.'

There was no sound but the whisper of wind in the cedar branches. They walked slowly beside the flowerbeds, and when they reached a sprawling hydrangea, Francine plucked at a pink petal and began to speak.

'I've been wanting to talk to you about Charles, for a long time after your –' Francine hesitated – 'your accusation. I confronted him, you know. I told him I knew what he'd done and I was appalled, wanted never to see him again. And I didn't see him for months, many months, but he came to the flat pleading forgiveness.' She let the petal drop and fingered the chain around her neck. 'He'd been very drunk that night, he said, and he was possessed by a sort of madness. Oh, it's a poor excuse, I know. I've felt so torn, Hazel, you must know that. It's been agony. But he does love me.'

'I don't want to see him, ever. I don't want him near Jasmin.'

'I can understand that, darling. Truly. Though you mustn't worry about him being Jasmin's father. He says he can't possibly be.'

Hazel stopped. Charles couldn't be Jasmin's father? How had he convinced Francine of that? Her mother began to speak again. 'He was rather blotto, you see—' but Hazel thrust out her hand, hissing at her mother to be quiet, and Francine closed her mouth with an indignant pout.

It was too hateful to speak of. She would not discuss it, because in that moment it did not matter, could not have mattered less. All that mattered was the certain fact that she, Hazel, was Jasmin's mother, and she was free, and she must see her baby and make her well.

It was visiting time at last. Hazel turned away from Francine, towards the hospital and the narrow bed where her daughter lay waiting.

37

When Tom arrived at the office, Gerald was already on the telephone, scribbling as he spoke.

'Thomas, my man!' he said as he put the receiver down. He stood up and took his jacket from the coat-stand. 'Hello and goodbye.'

'Going out?'

'Interesting tip-off.' He tapped the side of his nose in an imitation of Crow. 'Need-to-know-basis.'

Tom smiled. He wouldn't put it past Gerald to have invented the tip-off; he had a mistress in Holland Park, and would often return from a hush-hush interview smelling of French scent.

'You'll be back this afternoon?'

'Doubtful. Off to the Home Counties.'

'Ah.'

'Everything A1? You're looking rather bewildered this morning, old chap.'

Tom shut his mouth and sat down at his desk. Gerald was in a hurry, and he needed time to explain about Hazel. He'd have to wait until this evening or tomorrow: whenever he could get Gerald on his own.

'Everything's fine, thanks. Just a bit weary. Wretched siren.'

All morning his thoughts crashed and collided. He tried to summon a fraction of Petra's calm from the previous night, her wisdom, but calm was impossible. Should he visit Jasmin? He was a stranger to her. What comfort could he offer, in the unlikely event they let him in to the hospital? The infection was serious, Hazel had said. If it killed her . . . no, he couldn't, couldn't begin to think.

He would write to the prison governor, at least. A letter might help Hazel's case in some small way. He wound a fresh sheet of paper into the typewriter but before he had struck the first key, the telephone on his desk rang.

The line was crackly but her voice was unmistakable. Surprising that the prison should let her use a telephone, thought Tom. But then he began to absorb what she was saying. She was ringing from Chichester. She had been released yesterday evening, just a few hours after he'd visited the prison. 'Thank you', she said. 'If you played a part – thank you.'

'I'm afraid there's nothing to thank me for.' He took a shallow breath. 'I was just writing a letter now. Nothing's been sent.'

'Oh.' There was a pause for a moment, and then she garbled something about a wardress. 'It must have been her. Must have.'

'You've seen Jasmin?' asked Tom.

Hazel began to cough. When she spoke, her voice was tight. 'The fever is still very high.'

'I want to visit. Can I see you, Hazel? See Jasmin?'

*

It was Friday, and the three o'clock train was crowded. Sunlight angled in through the compartment window. A young boy with a crooked fringe sat opposite, crunching noisily on a carrot as he stared at Tom's left hand. Tom tried to smile but the boy shrank away, cuddled closer to his mother's side. Tom tucked the hand in his trouser pocket, though the heat made his scars throb.

At Chichester he saw her before the train had come to a halt. She was standing on the platform in a yellow dress, her hair loose around her neck. Now he was opening the compartment door, and he was on the platform, and he saw that she was crying. As they clung together he could not stop his own tears. She kissed him then, and took his arm. They walked through the city, along the time-worn pavements, past the cathedral and on towards the hospital.

Tom took a sip from his pint. She'd agreed to join him in the Bell after the hospital visit. They were on to their second drink and their conversation, stilted and emotion-choked at first, had finally begun to soften. It was the right time, he decided, to explain to her about the letter; the reason he'd stopped writing to her from Spain.

'A letter came from home, you see, just after Christmas in Albacete. When I read the gossip about you – you and . . . other men – I suppose I just gave up. I was weak. Too proud.'

'I can never forgive her for telling those lies,' said Hazel. She circled a finger around the rim of her port glass. 'I can see it clearly now. She's twisted, jealous.'

Tom drew in a sharp breath. Hazel couldn't be blamed for her reaction – yes, the letter had been wrong, it had been hurtful and destructive – yet it pained him to hear his mother described in such terms when she had simply been over-protective. She wasn't twisted or malicious. She *was* jealous, that was true, but jealous only of his well-being and his happiness.

'There were reasons behind it –' he began to say, but Hazel wasn't listening. She was talking about Lucia, how possessive she could be, sulky if she didn't get her own way.

'Lucia must have been desperate to separate us,' said Hazel. 'And you fighting for the communists, too. Did she sign with a false name? Or anonymously?'

The realization hit. Tom opened his mouth to speak and then took a gulp of beer. Hazel thought that Lucia had sent the letter to Albacete. She'd taken 'home' to mean London, England, not Boone Street, Lewisham.

He should interrupt now, set the record straight.

Yet what did he owe to Lucia? Lucia, who had ratted on her supposed friend when the police came calling. Lucia, who had claimed credit when Hazel saved the drowning boy. Lucia, whom Hazel already hated. Why bring his mother into it, when Hazel had satisfied herself with a perfectly feasible explanation?

Tom reached out and took Hazel's hand across the table. 'We needn't ever speak of it again. I should have been more trusting. It's my fault. I should have believed in you, not some daft letter.'

She sighed and raised the port glass to her mouth. Tom watched as she swallowed. When she set the glass back on the table her lips glistened deep red.

'It doesn't matter anyway,' said Hazel. 'All that matters is Jasmin.'

'Of course.' His mind returned to the darkened ward, the still body in the hospital bed. 'Jasmin.'

Hazel's fingers tightened around his, and he closed his eyes, wishing with all his being that there might be a God to hear his prayer.

38

On the day of the wedding they drive into Soho, to Baudin's where the wine cellar is still stocked with champagne and the kitchen serves an excellent steak tartare. They park on Romilly Street. A working girl stares from a high window as they step from the Brough onto the pavement: Charles in his white tails and Francine in a black Schiaparelli embroidered with large white lilies.

Inside the club, no heads turn. To be overdressed on a Saturday afternoon? There are stranger sights in this louche basement: a stocky man in a sequinned leotard, a woman with one breast spilling from a too-tight bustier.

The champagne is poured by the sommelier himself, his small hand firm against the ice-wet bottle. Charles raises his glass, meets Francine's mid-air.

'To the Uninvited,' he says.

'The Uninvited.'

Their glasses chink. The band strikes up a rhumba.

They dance and they dance, fuelled by the champagne and the perfect steak and the lines of white powder that Charles has secured in the velvet-draped side room. As the afternoon slips into evening, Francine thinks she has never been happier. She was made to choose and she has chosen correctly.

Oh, it would have been nice to see Jasmin in her flower-girl frock, but what does Jasmin care for her, Francine, now that the Smart woman has appeared on the scene? 'Nanny,' Jasmin calls the woman, tugging at her skirt and smothering her drab face in kisses, while the blackshirt boy smiles on, his ugly hand around Hazel's waist.

They can all go to hell.

At ten the warning comes but nobody cares. They are in the right place, aren't they, safe below stairs? When the ceiling plaster begins to crack and crumble, they dance on.

'Just like confetti!' giggles Francine, and she lifts her face to the ceiling, licking away the flakes of musty white paint.

Wall lights fizz and spark. Dancers falter, caught out of time. Dark shapes hurry across the floor.

Charles laughs, takes Francine's hand and leads her towards the wine cellar. But the wine cellar is already full, painted faces smiling up, glasses held aloft, cocktail cherries trembling.

They stumble towards the cloakroom, but rubble has blocked the stairway to the street. In the darkness they kiss. Strings from an abandoned violin vibrate as a high-explosive bomb slams through the Soho sky.

'I've always loved you,' Charles says. 'Only you,' and Francine smiles as a white light screams through the black.

39

August 1941

The sweet peas in the garden had almost gone to seed, but on this sunlit evening the perfume of the last few blooms hung heavy in the warm air. Bea picked the flowers and held them to her nose. She closed her eyes against the sun and opened her mind to the Inward Light.

Allow the light to shine into all the dark corners of the mind.

There was a time when shadows were stubborn, but now the light came easily. She had only to think of her granddaughter and her mind became a dazzle of possibility and hope. When Jasmin smiled it was almost like having Jack back: the light in those amber eyes, the tilt of her dimpled chin. She pictured Jasmin's face as they'd leafed through the photograph album that morning. *Yes, that's right, love. It's your daddy when* he *was five years old. And there's your granddad Harold. You never met him but he was a very good man.*

Bea walked down the steps into the Anderson and pulled open the door. She blinked into the darkness until her eyes grew accustomed and she could see the enamel jug on top of the narrow cabinet. She arranged the sweet peas in the jug; they wouldn't last more than a day or two, but how pretty they looked, such delicate colours. If there was a raid tonight, Jasmin would be cheered to see fresh flowers in the shelter. She noticed little things like that. You might even say she was a touch too curious – it was one question after another! After elevenses today, Jasmin had somehow spotted the torn-up letter in the kitchen bin, though Bea had covered it with a flattened box of Lux flakes. 'Why's this letter all ripped, Nanny?' she'd asked, clutching a shilling-sized scrap of notepaper that was scrawled with black ink. Bea looked up from her ironing and of course it had to be the fragment where the Knight girl had signed her name.

'Put that back in the bin and go and wash your hands,' Bea had said, unable to keep the sharpness from her voice.

'But—'

'No buts. Curiosity killed the cat.'

Jasmin had looked alarmed at that, and she spent the next hour in the garden fussing over next door's puss.

It was odd about the letters, though. Why Lucia persisted in writing when no one ever replied, Bea couldn't say. Anyone would think she was lovesick.

This summer heat was so tiring. As Bea sat down on the chair in the corner of the shelter she heard the distant swish of the bead curtain at the back door, the heavy tread of brogues down the path.

'So this is where you're hiding,' said Tom. He came in and sat on the wooden bunk that ran along one side of the shelter.

'Where's Jasmin?' he asked.

'They've gone for an ice. Mr Boyne let Hazel off early. Should be back shortly.'

Tom nodded and reached out to rest a hand on her shoulder. They sat for a while longer as the setting sun beamed a shaft of gold through the open shelter door. Bea wondered whether to tell Tom about today's letter. No; that would only cast a shadow. Hazel had made it clear – ignore any post from Lucia. Put the letters, unopened, into the bin. Lucia would give up eventually, of that Bea had no doubt.

From the house came the sound of the front door banging, the clank of faltering piano keys, 'London Bridge' again. Tom chuckled to himself.

'Jasmin's determined, I'll give her that,' he said, standing up from the bunk. 'Better go and say hello.'

Bea watched him stroll down the path as Hazel appeared on the patch of lawn holding the small watering can in one hand and a cigarette in the other. She kissed Tom's cheek and he put an arm around her waist, said something that Bea couldn't hear. Hazel smiled and stretched up to kiss him again. Wisps of smoke curled above their heads, and the hem of Hazel's dress shifted in the breeze.

'They're home, Harold,' Bea murmured. 'All of them. Home.'

The sweet peas glowed in the sunlight, and it seemed to Bea for that brief silent moment as if the whole world was at peace.

Author's Note

Many books and sources helped to inspire *The Faithful*. The following were especially useful:

Booker, J. A., *Blackshirts-on-Sea: A pictorial history of the Mosley Summer Camps 1933– 1938* (Brockingday Publications, 1999).

de Courcy, Anne, *Diana Mosley* (Chatto & Windus, 2003).

Durham, Martin, *Women and Fascism* (Routledge, 1998).

Gottlieb, Julie V., *Feminine Fascism: Women in Britain's Fascist Movement* (I. B. Taurus, 2000).

Griffin, Frank, *October Day* (Secker and Warburg, 1939).

Harris, Carol, *Blitz Diary: Life Under Fire in World War II* (The History Press, 2010).

Jump, Jim ed., *Poems from Spain: British and Irish International Brigaders on the Spanish Civil War* (Lawrence & Wishart, 2006).

MacDougall, Philip, *If War Should Come: Defence Preparations on the South Coast 1935–1939* (The History Press, 2011).

Pugh, Martin, *Hurrah for the Blackshirts: Fascists and Fascism in Britain Between the Wars* (Jonathan Cape, 2005).

Rosenberg, David, *Battle for the East End: Jewish responses to fascism in the 1930s* (Five Leaves Publications, 2011).

Sweet, Matthew, *The West End Front: The Wartime Secrets of London's Grand Hotels* (Faber and Faber, 2011).
Wheeler, George, *To Make the People Smile Again: A memoir of the Spanish Civil War* (Zymurgy Publishing, 2003).

While some of the events described in *The Faithful* are factual – such as the blackshirts' seaside camps and the wartime detention of Mosley's fascists – this novel is a work of fiction. The lead characters – Hazel, Tom, Lucia, Francine and Bea – are entirely imagined.

Acknowledgements

Heartfelt thanks to Sophie Orme for helping to shape this novel, and to Sam Humphreys, Associate Publisher at Mantle. It's been a privilege to work with two such wonderful editors. I am indebted also to Maria Rejt, Mantle Publisher, and the excellent team at Pan Macmillan including Josie Humber, Laura Carr and Jess Duffy.

Thanks to my agent Hellie Ogden for her advice and positivity, and to all at Janklow & Nesbit including Jessie Botterill, Kirsty Gordon, Rebecca Folland and Rachel Balcombe.

For valued comments on various drafts, I'm hugely grateful to Isabel Ashdown, Torben and Victoria Betts, Alex Bristow, Alison Laurie, Jane Osis, Angela West and Steve Wilson.

Many people have helped with research queries, but particular thanks are due to staff at the Imperial War Museum, the Screen Archive South East at Brighton University, the British Library and Bognor Regis library, as well as Dr Julie Gottlieb of the University of Sheffield and Val Bentley at the Sussex Ornithological Society. Any inaccuracies are my own.

Thanks to Joan Barker, Stuart Coupe, Elayne DeLaurian, Louise Gilchrist, Joan Goddard, Sam Kendall, Mary Laven, Ron MacKenzie, Sandra Walsh, Roger West, Gill and Jim Wilson, friends at The Prime Writers and Horsham Writers' Circle.

Most of all, my thanks and love to Steve, Izzy, Jessie and James.

Reading Group Guide

1. Why do you think Hazel was drawn to Tom, and Tom to Hazel?
2. *'Political cranks,' Francine had said, hurrying past with a look of distaste. 'Don't flatter them with your attention.'* What do you think initially attracted Hazel to the blackshirts?
3. Francine and Bea are two women with very different attitudes towards motherhood. Which family would you rather have grown up in? Who was the 'best' mother?
4. Blackshirt seaside camps were held regularly on the south coast during the 1930s. Do you feel this real-life setting worked well as a backdrop for the novel?
5. Did your attitude towards Hazel change after she joined the blackshirts?
6. Charles is based on a real-life character. Do you think that Charles's line of work was immoral, or was he simply offering a service?
7. Was Hazel right to keep her secrets from Tom for such a long time?
8. Were you surprised to learn that women, including former suffragettes, supported British fascism in the 1930s? What do you think motivated 'ordinary' women like Bea to join?
9. *'I've been useful, that's all.'* Was Lucia right to accuse Hazel of using her? How do you view their relationship?
10. Discuss the ending of the novel.